1, 2 Peter

THE CROSSWAY CLASSIC COMMENTARIES

1, 2 Peter

by

Robert Leighton

and

Griffith Thomas

Series Editors

Alister McGrath and J. I. Packer

CROSSWAY BOOKS

A PUBLISHING MINISTRY OF GOOD NEWS PUBLISHERS

WHEATON, ILLINOIS • NOTTINGHAM, ENGLAND

1, 2 Peter

Copyright © 1999 by Watermark

Published by Crossway Books
        a publishing ministry of Good News Publishers
        1300 Crescent Street
        Wheaton, Illinois 60187

Scripture taken from *The Holy Bible: New International Version*®. Copyright © 1973, 1978, 1984 by International Bible Society. Used by permission of Zondervan Publishing House. All rights reserved.

The "NIV" and "New International Version" trademarks are registered in the United States Patent and Trademark Office by International Bible Society. Use of either trademark requires the permission of International Bible Society.

First printing, 1999

Printed in the United States of America

Library of Congress Cataloging-in-Publication Data
Leighton, Robert, 1611–1684.
   1, 2 Peter / by Robert Leighton and Griffith Thomas.
      p.   cm. — (The Crossway classic commentaries)
   ISBN 13: 978-1-58134-064-8
   ISBN 10: 1-58134-064-8 (pbk. : alk. paper)
   1. Bible. N.T. Peter—Commentaries.   I. Thomas, Griffith,
1861–1924. II. Title. III. Title: First, Second Peter. IV. Series.
BS2795.3.L45 1999   99-11104
227'.92077—dc21

VP		16	15	14	13	12	11	10	09	08	07	06
15	14	13	12	11	10	9	8	7	6	5	4	3	2

First British edition 1999

Production and Printing in the United States of America for
CROSSWAY BOOKS
Norton Street, Nottingham, England NG7 3HR

ISBN 1-85684-188-X

Contents

Series Preface

The purpose of the Crossway Classic Commentaries is to make some of the most valuable commentaries on the books of the Bible, by some of the greatest Bible teachers and theologians in the last 500 years, available to a new generation. These books will help today's readers learn truth, wisdom, and devotion from such authors as J. C. Ryle, Martin Luther, John Calvin, J. B. Lightfoot, John Owen, Charles Spurgeon, Charles Hodge, and Matthew Henry.

We do not apologize for the age of some of the items chosen. In the realm of practical exposition promoting godliness, the old is often better than the new. Spiritual vision and authority, based on an accurate handling of the biblical text, are the qualities that have been primarily sought in deciding what to include.

So far as is possible, everything is tailored to the needs and enrichment of thoughtful readers—lay Christians, students, and those in the ministry. The originals, some of which were written at a high technical level, have been abridged as needed, simplified stylistically, and unburdened of foreign words. However, the intention of this series is never to change any thoughts of the original authors, but to faithfully convey them in an understandable fashion.

The publishers are grateful to Dr. Alister McGrath of Wycliffe Hall, Oxford, Dr. J. I. Packer of Regent College, Vancouver, and Watermark of Norfolk, England, for the work of selecting and editing that now brings this project to fruition.

THE PUBLISHERS
Crossway Books
Wheaton, Illinois

Introduction

This volume brings together two Britons of similar outlook. Both were learned Celts, one Scottish, one Welsh; both were Episcopalians; and both gave top priority to advancing the life of God in human souls through applicatory Bible teaching. Though separated by two and a half centuries, Robert Leighton's exposition of 1 Peter and Griffith Thomas's outlines of 2 Peter will be found to form a happy and harmonious pair.

The modern stereotype of a Puritan is of an anti-Anglican, so that "Puritan Archbishop" sounds like a contradiction in terms. But historic Puritanism was a reforming movement within the Anglican church that produced several bishops and at least two archbishops—James Usher, Archbishop of Armagh in Ireland and Robert Leighton, Archbishop of Glasgow in Scotland. Ironically, Leighton (1611-1684), a moderate Episcopalian of Erastian leanings, was the son of the fierce presbyterian Alexander Leighton, who for flaying the Laudians in *Zion's Plea Against Prelacy* (1630) was sentenced by the royal kangaroo Court of Star Chamber to be publicly whipped and pilloried and to have his nose slit, his ears cut off, and his cheeks branded, after which he was to be imprisoned for life. When made a bishop in 1662, as part of the Restoration plan to impose episcopacy on the Church of Scotland, Leighton spent a decade trying to persuade Scotsmen to take bishops into their presbyterian system before resigning in despair in 1672 to live in retirement with members of his family in Sussex, England, for the rest of his life.

His exposition of 1 Peter, posthumously published, is one of the finest works of its kind in the whole Puritan legacy. Philip Doddridge, Congregationalist pioneer, leader, educator, hymnologist, and latter-day Puritan, as his *Rise and Progress of Religion in the Soul* shows, edited Leighton's literary leavings in 1748. He spoke glowingly of "this wonderful man," "this great adept in true Christianity," and of the "wonderful energy of his discourses." He quoted with approval the verdict: "There is a spirit in Archbishop Leighton I never met with in any human writings;

nor can I read many lines . . . without being moved." And he added that he himself had never spent "a quarter of an hour" with Leighton without receiving "some impressions which I could wish always to retain." "The reader will, I think," he declares, "find great light poured on many very difficult passages . . . in the First Epistle of Peter, in a very masterly manner, and often by a few weighty words. But these hints are generally very short; for the good Author appears to have lopped off every thing as superfluous, which did not immediately tend to make his readers better." In other words, Leighton's inner identity as an "affectionate practical" Puritan teacher shines throughout. Readers will find that Doddridge is right. Persons wishing to be made better, therefore, are the ones who should read what Leighton has written.

Griffith Thomas (1861-1924), who labored as pastor, scholar, teacher of preachers, and conference minister in England, Canada, and the USA, "excelled in spiritual depth, practicality, and a simplicity of expression that made the most profound truths come alive with excitement" (Warren W. Wiersbe). The businesslike punchiness and concentrated elegance of his analyses made his material an ideal source for both personal learning and public teaching—as indeed it still is if you can get hold of it (most of it is currently out of print). Second Peter, like 2 Timothy, is a last letter from an apostle facing death and has special solemnity as such; its weight is well captured in Thomas's succinct, searching summaries. I can imagine Leighton and Thomas enjoying each other in heaven, and I am sure that Christians who work through their material in this book will enjoy them both here on earth.

J. I. PACKER

1 Peter

By Robert Leighton,
Minister of Newbattle in Mid Lothian

———

1 Peter
Chapter 1

Verse 1

Peter, an apostle of Jesus Christ, to God's elect, strangers in the world, scattered throughout Pontus, Galatia, Cappadocia, Asia and Bithynia.

The grace of God in the heart of man is a tender plant in a strange, unkindly soil. Therefore, it cannot grow unless great care is taken by a skillful hand that cherishes it. To this end God has given the constant ministry of the Word to his church, not only for the first work of conversion, but also for increasing his grace in the hearts of his children.

The extraordinary ministers of the Gospel, the apostles, had principally the former for their charge—the converting of unbelievers, Jews and Gentiles, and so the planting of churches, which were to be looked after and watered by others, as the apostle intimates in 1 Corinthians 3:6. However, they did not neglect the other work of strengthening God's grace in the new converts by visiting them and personally exhorting them, and through writing to them when absent from them. Through God's providence God's church in succeeding generations benefits from this.

This excellent letter of 1 Peter, full of evangelical teaching and apostolic authority, is a brief and yet very clear summary both of the consolations and of the instructions needed to encourage and direct Christians in their journey to heaven, elevating their thoughts and desires to a higher happiness and strengthening them against all opposition from corruption from within and from temptations and afflictions from without.

The main doctrines in it are many, but the three dominant ones are faith, obedience, and patience, in order to establish them in believing, to direct them in doing, and to comfort them in suffering. Because faith is the basis for the other two, the first chapter is taken up with persuading the addressees of the truth of the mystery they had received and believed—that is, their redemption and salvation through Christ Jesus, the inheritance of immortality bought for them by his blood, and the evidence and stability of their right and title to it.

Then he uses this belief, this assurance of the glory to come, as a spur to holy obedience and constant patience, since nothing can be too much to give up or go through in order to attain this blessed state. With this aim in mind, in this first chapter he encourages patience and holiness, and in the following chapters the special duties Christians have who are enduring suffering. He often sets before them the matchless example of the Lord Jesus and their need to follow him.

In the first two verses of this chapter, we have the inscription and greeting, in the usual style of the apostolic letters.

The inscription has the author and the readers—from whom and to whom. The author of this letter is named as **Peter**, and his calling is that of **an apostle.** This name was given by Christ, as the evangelists teach us (Matthew 16:18; John 1:42). From what is said about Peter in various passages in the Gospels, he was very remarkable among the apostles, both for his grace and for his failings. He was eminent in zeal and courage, and yet often stumbled, and once fell very badly. These are recorded in Scripture by God's providence and check the excess of Rome's conceit about this apostle. Their extolling and exalting him above the rest is not for his sake; much less is it for the honor of his Lord and Master, Jesus Christ, for he is dishonored by it. It is to suit their own wishes. Instead of the cross of affliction, they make the crown or miter the badge of their church and will have it known by prosperity and outward pomp.

An apostle. We see here St. Peter's office or title—**an apostle**, not "chief bishop." He is not "prince of the apostles" but **an apostle**, restored after his fall, through repentance, by Christ himself after his own death and resurrection (see John 21). Thus we have in our apostle a special instance of human frailty on the one hand, and the sweetness of divine grace on the other. Free and rich grace it is indeed that forgives and swallows up multitudes of sins, even the greatest sins, not only sins before conversion, as in the case of St. Paul, but foul offenses committed after conversion, as in the case of David, and in the case of this apostle. By God's grace Peter becomes God's messenger.

Of Jesus Christ. Peter is called and chosen by **Jesus Christ** to preach about him and the salvation that he brought.

An apostle of Jesus Christ. Peter was sent by **Jesus Christ**, and his message was none other than **Jesus Christ**. The ministry of the Word today involves being an ambassador for the greatest of kings (see 2 Corinthians 5:20).

To God's elect. This letter is written to **God's elect.** They are described here by their temporal and by their spiritual conditions. If we look at the order of the words, their temporal condition is only an interjection. For it

14

is said, **to God's elect** first, and then, to those **scattered throughout Pontus** . . . Peter wants this, as it were, drowned in the other: **who have been chosen according to the foreknowledge of God the Father** (verse 2).

Strangers in the world, scattered throughout Pontus, Galatia, Cappadocia, Asia and Bithynia. From James 1:1, where the same term **scattered** is used, it appears that these **scattered** strangers were Jews: "To the twelve tribes scattered among the nations" (James 1:1). Peter in Galatians 2 is called an apostle of the circumcision since he exercised his apostleship among them, and some parts of this letter are especially directed to believing Jews (see 2:9-10).

Some people argue from the term **strangers** that Gentiles are meant here, but this does not seem to be the case. Proselyte Gentiles were indeed called strangers in Jerusalem by Jews, but were not the Jews strangers in such places as **Pontus, Galatia, Cappadocia, Asia and Bithynia?** The places mentioned here, to which they were scattered, are all in the province of Asia. It should be noted that some of those who heard Peter in Acts 2:9 were from these regions. Although they were scattered in different countries, they were gathered together in God's election, for they were chosen or picked out. They were strangers to the people among whom they lived but were known **according to the foreknowledge of God** (verse 2).

To God's elect. The apostle here calls all the Christians he writes to true believers, calling them **elect** and sanctified (verse 2). The apostle Paul writes in the same style in his letters to the churches. Not everyone in these churches was indeed redeemed, but because they professed to be such, they were called by the name Christian. The question about the necessary qualifications of all members of the true visible church cannot be determined from the inscriptions of the letters. But they are definitely useful in teaching Christians and Christian churches what they should be and what their holy profession requires of them, and in sharply reproving them when they act in a way that is not consistent with being Christians.

Because of the difference between today's churches and those of the apostle's days, we may be rebuked to think that if the apostle were to send us a letter today, he might write, "To the ignorant, profane, malicious, etc." Like the man who, when he heard the Gospel being read, said afterwards, "Either this is not the Gospel or we are not Christians" [Dr. Whitaker, Master of St. John's College, Cambridge, who died in 1595]. In the same way, either the characteristics given in the inscription of these letters are not true characteristics or we are not true Christians.

Verse 2

Who have been chosen according to the foreknowledge of God the Father, through the sanctifying work of the Spirit, for obedience to

Jesus Christ and sprinkling by his blood: Grace and peace be yours in abundance.

In this verse we have their condition and the reasons for it. Their condition is that they were sanctified and justified—the former expressed by **obedience**, the latter by **sprinkling** by the **blood** of Christ. The reasons for this are, first, eternal election, and, second, the execution of that decree—that is, their effectual calling, which, I believe, is what is meant here by election (**God's elect**, verse 1). They are selected out of the world and joined to the fellowship of God's children (see John 15:19). The former, election, is particularly ascribed to **God the Father**, the latter to the Holy Spirit (**through the sanctifying work of the Spirit**) and the **sprinkling** of Christ's **blood**. So the Son of God is here assigned as the cause of their justification; and so the whole Trinity concurs and dignifies them with their spiritual and happy state.

First I shall look at these separately and then together.

The State or Condition of God's Children

1. Their justification: To God's elect . . . (verse 1)—**sprinkling by his blood** (verse 2). The sprinkling of blood in Old Testament times foreshadowed the true ransom of souls. The purpose of sprinkling was purification and expiation, because sin merited death, and the pollutions of human nature came through sin. Such is the pollution that it can only be removed by blood (see Hebrews 9:22). There is no blood able to purge sin except the most precious blood of Jesus Christ.

Filthiness needs sprinkling; guilt, which deserves death, needs the sprinkling of blood. Everything that the apostle says applies to justification. First, Christ, the Mediator between God and man, is God and man. Second, he is not only an interceding Mediator but also a satisfying Mediator (see Ephesians 2:16). Third, this satisfaction does not reconcile us unless it is applied. Therefore **blood** is not mentioned by itself, but **sprinkling by his blood.** The Spirit, through faith, sprinkles the soul, like hyssop. The prophet Isaiah refers to this when he writes, "so will he sprinkle many nations" (Isaiah 52:15). Hebrews prefers this sprinkling to all legal sprinklings (Hebrews 9:12-14).

2. Their sanctification: **Through the sanctifying work of the Spirit, for obedience.** It is easy to see who must be obeyed. When submission to God is expressed by the simple absolute name of obedience, it teaches us that to him alone belongs absolute and unlimited obedience, all obedience by all creatures. Here **obedience** signifies what Paul in Romans 1:5 calls "the obedience that comes from faith." Christ is received, and so the believing soul is united to Christ, who sprinkles us with his blood for the remission of sins. This is the root of all future obedience in the Christian life.

By **obedience**, sanctification is also meant here. This signifies both habitual obedience, renewal of heart, and conformity to the divine will.

The mind is illumined by the Holy Spirit, so it can know and believe the divine will. This faith is the main part of obedience (see Romans 1:8).

The Causes for This Condition

According to the foreknowledge of God the Father. The apostle tells his readers that they are sanctified and justified because of Jesus Christ. He is to them both righteousness and sanctification. The **sprinkling by his blood** purifies them from guilt and gives them life so they can obey. We now consider how this is applied. It is achieved by the holy, and holy-making or sanctifying, Spirit, the author of their selection from the world and their effectual calling to grace. The source of this is **God the Father.**

By the sanctifying work. See 1 Corinthians 1:26, 28. This is the first act of the decree of election, which separates people from the profane world and consecrates them to God. So in relation to election and to its own nature it is appropriately called **sanctifying work** (see John 15:19; Acts 2:47; 13:48; Romans 8:28, 30).

Sanctification in a narrower sense, when distinguished from justification, signifies the inherent holiness of a Christian, or his being inclined and enabled to perform the **obedience** mentioned in this verse. But here it means renewal—people being dedicated to God by his Holy Spirit drawing them to him. So it embraces justification and the start of faith, through which the soul is justified by the application of the righteousness of Jesus Christ.

Of the Spirit. The Word calls people externally and through that external calling prevails with many to an external receiving and professing of religion. But if it is left like that, it proceeds no further. It is indeed the means of sanctification and effectual calling (see John 17:17). But it does this when the Spirit, who speaks through the Word, works in the heart and causes it to hear and obey. A person's spirit or soul is the chief and first subject of this work, and it is but a slight work if it does not start there.

The Spirit, in this verse, is the Spirit of God, not the spirit of man, who is the subject of sanctification. Therefore our Saviour prayed to the Father that he would sanctify his own through the truth of the Word (see John 17:17). He does this by the concurrence of his Spirit with that Word of truth that gives life, making it become the power of God for salvation for all who believe (see Romans 1:16). It is a suitable means in itself, but it is a prevailing means only when the Spirit of God brings it into the heart. It is a sword. "The word of God is living and active. Sharper than any double-edged sword, it penetrates even to dividing soul and spirit, joints and marrow; it judges the thoughts and attitudes of the heart" (Hebrews 4:12). But the Word does not do this unless it is in the hands of the Spirit and he is penetrating and dividing. The Word calls, but the Spirit draws—not severed from the Word, but working in it and by it.

We must endeavor to have this sanctifying Spirit in ourselves and pray much for it, for his promise to give the Holy Spirit to those who ask (see Luke 11:13) applies to us. Shall we be so foolish as to lack this because we do not ask? When we find our souls weighed down, then let us pray, "Draw me."

According to the foreknowledge of God the Father. God sees everything from the beginning of time to the end of time. But the **foreknowledge** here relates peculiarly to the elect (see Psalm 1:6; Amos 3:2; Romans 8:29; 9:15). This foreknowledge is his eternal and unchanging love. That he chooses some and rejects others demonstrates his mercy and justice. He appointed one person to be chosen and rejected another. He made Peter receive mercy but Judas wrath. If this seems to be harsh, it is what the apostle taught.

The Connection Between the Two

The effectual calling is inseparably tied to this eternal foreknowledge or election on the one side and to salvation on the other. These two links of the chain are up in heaven in God's own hand. But the middle one is let down to earth, into the heart of God's children; and by taking hold of it they have a firm grip on the other two links, for no power can separate them.

The believer should derive much joy from this. This link is indissoluble, just as the agents are—the Father, the Son, and the Spirit. In the same way election and vocation (and sanctification and justification) and glory cannot be separated. Therefore, believers may, from a sense of the working of the Spirit in them, look back to that election and forward to that salvation, while those who remain unholy and disobedient have as yet no evidence of this love. If election and calling, sanctification and justification, are inseparably linked together, then through any one of them a person may lay hold of the rest and may know that his hold is sure. In this way we may attain, and ought to seek, that comforting assurance of God's love. The person who loves God may be certain that God loved him first. The person who chooses God to delight in may conclude confidently that God has chosen him to be one of those who will be happy in him forever. Discover within yourself sanctification through the Spirit, and this will demonstrate both justification through the Son and election by God the Father. He called those he elected, and he elected those he called.

Grace and peace be yours in abundance. It has always been customary for people to send good wishes to each other in their communications. The apostles did this in their letters in a spiritual way. It is fitting that messengers of **grace and peace** should send such greetings to each other. We have the Hebrew word for greeting here—**peace**; and we have the word that the Greeks greeted each other with—**grace.** Let us consider, first, what the apostle desired for his readers—**grace and peace**, and, second, how much of this he desired—**in abundance.**

Grace. Saving grace is understood as follows: First, grace in the fountain, that is, the special love and favor of God. Second, grace in the streams, the fruits of God's love; that is, all the graces and spiritual blessings of God bestowed on those whom he has freely chosen. The love of God can neither diminish nor increase, but it is multiplied and abounds in the manifestation and effects of it. So to desire that grace might be theirs in abundance is to wish them the living spring of grace. This is the first and last of Christian desires. Resolve to seek a share in this grace, the free love of God and the sure evidence of it within you, the fruit of holiness and the graces of his Spirit. Most of us are preoccupied with other things. As long as we neglect our noblest method of growing rich in grace, we act like fools.

Peace. For the Jews, when they wished peace on someone, it included every kind of good, welfare, and prosperity. So we may take it to mean here all kinds of peace, but especially the spiritual peace that is the appropriate fruit of grace and flows from it. We may and should wish that God's church is blessed, especially with outer peace, as one of the greatest and most valuable favors of God. The psalmist prayed: "May there be peace within your walls and security within your citadels" (Psalm 122:7; see also Acts 9:31).

We should also wish for ecclesiastical peace for the church, that she may be free from dissensions and divisions. To the Corinthians Paul wrote, "I appeal to you, brothers, in the name of our Lord Jesus Christ, that all of you agree with one another so that there may be no divisions among you and that you may be perfectly united in mind and thought" (1 Corinthians 1:10). Ungodly people not only stumble but fall and break their necks on these divisions.

As peace is a choice blessing, so it is the choicest peace when peace and grace are combined, as they are in this verse. The flower of peace grows on the root of grace. This spiritual peace consists of two things. First, reconciliation with God, and second, tranquillity of spirit.

In abundance. Consider the measure of the apostle's desire for his scattered brethren, that this **grace and peace** should be theirs **in abundance.** This the apostle wishes for them, knowing the imperfection of the graces and peace of the saints while they are here below; and this they themselves, under a sense of that imperfection, ardently desire. Those who have tasted the sweetness of this **grace and peace** constantly ask for more. This strong hunger for spiritual things is a virtue, and one that our Saviour called "blessed" because it brings fullness and satisfaction. "Blessed are those who hunger and thirst for righteousness, for they will be filled" (Matthew 5:6).

Verses 3-4

Praise be to the God and Father of our Lord Jesus Christ! In his great mercy he has given us new birth into a living hope through the resur-

rection of Jesus Christ from the dead, and into an inheritance that can never perish, spoil or fade—kept in heaven for you.

It is a cold and lifeless thing to speak of spiritual things secondhand. But those who speak about them from personal experience do so from hearts full of happiness and praise. The main subject of these verses is that which brings comfort and support to the godly in all circumstances.

1. Their **inheritance** (verse 4).
2. Their assured **hope** of it (verse 3).
3. The immediate reason for both of these things: **Jesus Christ** (verse 3).
4. All this comes from the **great mercy** of God (verse 3).

Consider, first, their title to this inheritance: **he has given us new birth;** second, their assurance of it: **a living hope.**

The title that the saints have to their rich **inheritance** is of the most unquestionable kind: that is, by birth. Not through their first natural birth, for by natural birth we are all children of wrath (see Ephesians 2:3). But we have a new and supernatural birth. That is why it is called a **new birth.** God, the Father of our Lord Jesus Christ, has given us this **new birth.** So we are regenerate children of an immortal Father and as such are entitled to an **inheritance** of immortality (see Romans 8:17). We are adopted children, and Jesus Christ is the one and only Son of God.

Nature cannot imagine any birth except what is within its own sphere. Only those who take part in this spiritual birth understand what it means. To others it remains a riddle. Nature cannot aspire to this **new birth.** It is not a superficial change but a new life and being. A moral man, in his changes and reformations of himself, remains the same man. The natural man turns from one thing to another but remains the same person. But the Christian, by virtue of this **new birth,** can say, "I am not the same man I was. I am a son of the King of kings." "To all who received him, to those who believed in his name, he gave the right to become children of God" (John 1:12).

Into a living hope. "Now we are children of God, and what we will be has not yet been made known" (1 John 3:2). These children are heirs and take part in this new birth and are given the assurance of this **living hope.** In the eyes of the world hope refers to something that is uncertain. But the hope of the children of the living God is a living hope and is definite. It is a fearful thing when a man and all his hopes die together (see Proverbs 11:7; 14:32). For those with Christian hope, death is a messenger sent to bring them home to possess their inheritance.

Through the resurrection of Jesus Christ from the dead. This refers again to being born again through Christ's resurrection, through which we have this **living hope.**

God's image is renewed in us by our union with him who is "the exact representation of [God's] being" (Hebrews 1:3). The conception of this new birth is expressed in Galatians 4:19: "Christ is formed in you." Christ's resurrection is especially assigned as the cause of our new life, and this new birth is called our resurrection, and his resurrection is called a birth. He is "the firstborn from the dead" (Revelation 1:5; Acts 13:33; compare Psalm 2:7).

In a similar way Christ's resurrection is the cause of our **living hope**, for it inspires and keeps life in that hope. Because Christ has conquered death and has risen from the dead, he is sitting at God's right hand and so has entered into this inheritance. This gives us **a living hope** that, according to his own wish, we will be where he is. So this hope is supported on one side by Christ's resurrection, and on the other by the abundant mercy of God the Father. Our hope does not depend on our own strength or wisdom or anything within us, but on Christ's resurrection, on Christ who will never die again (see Romans 6:9-10). This makes our hope as firm as an anchor and not like worldly hope.

In his great mercy. Mercy is the spring of all this; yes, **great** mercy. As St. Bernard says, "Great sins and great miseries need great mercy, and many sins and miseries need many mercies." And is it not a great mercy that the children of Satan become children of the Most High God? No wonder the apostle John wrote: "How great is the love the Father has lavished on us, that we should be called children of God" (1 John 3:1). The world does not acknowledge us because it did not acknowledge Christ. But no matter what their opinion is, we can say, "How great is the love the Father has lavished on us."

Praise be to the God and Father of our Lord Jesus Christ! Here we see that it stirs up the apostle to praise the God and Father of our Lord Jesus Christ. This is the style of the Gospel. Under the law praise went to the God of Abraham, Isaac, and Jacob, the God who had brought them out of the land of Egypt. Under the covenant of grace, Christ is now the Head, and we are in him. So in our consideration of God's mercies, we should think of Christ, for it is in him that they are conveyed to us (see Ephesians 1:3).

Praise. God blesses us, and we bless God by acknowledging his goodness. We ought to do this all the time (see Psalm 34:1). What are our lame praises when compared with God's love? They are nothing. They are less than nothing. But love will stammer rather than be dumb.

Into an inheritance that can never perish. A man who is weighed down with inner heaviness becomes more depressed if he is surrounded with worldly happiness, but spiritual joy applies to all situations. So Peter, as he writes to the scattered, afflicted brethren, begins his letter with this song of praise: **Praise be to the God and Father of our Lord Jesus**

21

Christ! The reason for this joy stems from remembering the happiness that is **kept** for them, their **inheritance**. This **inheritance** is described as having special qualities. These comprise, first, its excellent nature, and, second, the certainty attending it. The former is conveyed in three ways: **never perish, spoil or fade.** The latter comes in the last words of this verse: **kept in heaven for you.**

That can never perish. Although this seems similar to the third quality, **never fade**, I think there is a difference; there are progressive degrees in these three qualities. What does not **perish** cannot come to nothing. What will not **spoil** will not be stained with the smallest spot. This signifies purity and perfection. What does not **fade** stays the same and is immutable. Since our inheritance will **never perish**, it makes all earthly possessions and inheritances pale into insignificance. Everything that we see, including the heavens, will one day disappear (see Psalm 102:26; Hebrews 1:10-12; 2 Peter 3:11).

Never . . . spoil. All possessions on earth are defiled and stained with many defects and faults. All possessions are stained with sin, either in our acquiring them or in our using them. Jerome said, "A rich man is either a rogue himself, or the heir of one." Foul hands pollute all they touch. Our sin defiles what we possess. Sin burdens the whole creation so that it groans (see Romans 8:22). Our leprosy defiles our homes, the very walls and floors, our food and drink and everything we touch. Since earthly inheritances are stained with sin, why should we work hard to obtain and retain them? The greatest empires and kingdoms in the world have had their foundations laid in blood. Are not these defiled inheritances?

Never . . . fade. There is no trace of sin or sorrow in our spiritual **inheritance.** All pollution is wiped away, and all tears have disappeared. There is no envy or strife. This **inheritance** is often called a kingdom and a crown of glory. This word **fade** may allude to the garlands the ancients wore (see 5:4). In contrast with this, our **inheritance** knows nothing about change. Its joys will never fade.

Our **inheritance** is certain—it is **kept in heaven for you.** This will be dealt with when verse 5 is considered.

What does all this mean for us? If these things were believed, they would be enough in themselves to persuade us. Do we have anything surer and better here on earth (see 2 Corinthians 5:1)? Happy are those whose hearts God's Spirit fixes on this inheritance.

Verses 4b-5

Kept in heaven for you, who through faith are shielded by God's power until the coming of the salvation that is ready to be revealed in the last time.

It is undoubtedly a great comfort for God's children to hear about the excellencies of the life to come. It is a subject they do not tire of. Yet there is one doubt that, if it is not removed, may dampen their delight in hearing and considering this. The richer the estate is, the more their enemies will seek to deprive them of it and to keep them from possessing it. Against this fear the apostle comforts the heirs of salvation, assuring them that as the estate they seek is excellent, so it is certain and safe, laid up out of the reach of all adverse powers, **kept in heaven for you.** Besides that, this is a further evidence of the worth and excellence of this inheritance, and it makes it certain. It must have the greatest value if it is kept in the best and highest place possible, namely, **in heaven.** Nothing that is impure can enter there, let alone be allowed to stay.

In addition to this, as the country where it is kept is rich and pleasant, it also has the privilege of being the only land that enjoys rest and peace and is free from all possibility of invasion. It is not subject to decay and is in no danger from violent attack. Our Saviour speaks of this same happiness in a similar way in Matthew 6:20, and what is here called an **inheritance** is there called a "treasure." Christ expresses its permanency in two ways: it will not decay because of moths or rust, and thieves will not be able to steal it. Our **inheritance** is free from all danger. It is safe in God's hands, for it is **kept in heaven.**

For you. This **inheritance** is for us to enjoy. It is ours. When we hear about this glorious **inheritance**, this treasure, this kingdom that is pure and rich and lasting, we may add, "It is mine, it is reserved in heaven, reserved for me. I have received the evidences and guarantee of it, and it is kept safe for me. So I shall, in a similar way, be preserved for it" (see Ephesians 1:14).

The **salvation** that Christ has bought is indeed laid up in heaven, but we who seek after it are on earth, surrounded with dangers and temptations. What advantage is it to us since our **salvation** is in heaven? It is in a place of safety and quietness, while we are being tossed about by stormy seas in this world, in danger from being shipwrecked on rocks at any time. Our **inheritance** is indeed in safe hands, and our enemies are unable to hurt it. But our enemies may destroy us whenever they wish, for we are in the middle of them. We might think and grumble in this way and so lose our sweet thoughts about heaven, if there were not as firm a promise for our safety in the middle of our dangers as there is for the safety of our **inheritance** that is out of danger.

The assurance of this is certain. It is **kept** in heaven for us, and we are kept on earth for it. As it is reserved for us, we are no less certainly preserved for it. There is here, first, the estate itself, **salvation**; second, the preservation or securing of those who accept it, **kept**; and, third, the time of complete possession, **in the last time.**

1. The estate: **salvation.** Previously it was called an **inheritance.** Here we see that more particularly what is meant is **salvation.** The first part of our **salvation** is to be freed from those miseries to which we are subject through our guilt. We are set free: a. From the curse of the law and the wrath of God, from everlasting death. b. From all kinds of mortality and decaying. c. From all the power and stain of sin. d. From all temptation. e. From all the griefs and afflictions of this life.

The second part of our **salvation** is to have the perfection of grace in being full of holiness and the perfection of bliss—fullness of joy in the constant vision of God. How little we know of this. Our apostle teaches us here that it is veiled from us. Only a certain amount shines through to us here. It is **to be revealed at the last time.**

2. Their preservation, with the causes of it: **kept in heaven for you ... by God's power.** The **inheritance** is kept not only in safety but in quietness. God's children, for whom it is **kept,** while they are here, are kept safe, though not unmolested and unassaulted. They have enemies, cunning and powerful opponents. But in the middle of them they are guarded and defended. They do not perish, according to the prayer our Saviour poured out for them in John 17:15.

They have the prince of the power of the air and all his armies, all the forces he can muster, against them. Though his power is only gained through usurping others, yet because they were once under his control, he stirs himself to pursue them when they are led out from their captivity, just as Pharaoh, with all his chariots and horses and horsemen, chased after the Israelites going out of Egypt.

The Greek word for **kept** is a military one, used for those who are kept in a fort or in a town under siege. In the same way Satan is still attacking cities, trying every way he knows to capture them. In addition to all this, he has secret information from a party within us, ready to betray us to him. So it would be impossible for us to hold out were it not for a guard other than ourselves, and for other walls besides those our own powers can raise in our defense. In this, then, is our safety: there is a power above our own, above all our enemies, that guards us. **Salvation** itself forms our walls and defense. "We have a strong city; God makes salvation its walls and ramparts" (Isaiah 26:1). We should be watchful, but we should do so in obedience to our commander, the Captain of our salvation. He does not sleep or slumber, and he preserves us (see Psalm 126:1; Isaiah 27:3). Therefore, we are commanded to do two things at the same time: to "watch and to pray so you will not fall into temptation" (Matthew 26:41). "Watch" refers to the necessity of diligence. "Pray" shows us by whose power we are effectually preserved, and the power that keeps us safe. How can we be better protected than by **salvation**

24

itself? "The name of the LORD is a strong tower; the righteous run to it and are safe" (Proverbs 18:10).

There are two reasons for our preservation. First, and most importantly, the power of God; and, second, and less importantly, faith. Our stability and preservation rest on the supreme power of God. When we consider how weak we are in ourselves, even the strongest among us, and how much under attack we are, we rightly wonder that anyone can continue for a single day in a state of grace. But when we look at the strength that guards us, the power of God, then we understand why we remain stable to the end. For our omnipotent God supports us, and his everlasting arms are under us.

Faith is the second reason for our preservation, since it relates to the first reason, God's power. Our faith takes hold of his power, and his power strengthens our faith, and so we are preserved. Faith puts us within his walls and sets the soul within the guard of the power of God. The soul that relies on self-confidence and vain presumption in its own strength is exposed to all kinds of danger. Faith is a humble, self-denying grace; it makes the Christian nothing in himself, and it makes God everything.

The weakest people who are inside a strong place, even women and children, while they may not be able to resist the enemy on their own, will be safe so long as the place they are in has sufficient strength to hold out. Thus the weakest believer is safe because, through believing, he is within the strongest of all defenses. Faith is the victory, and Christ sets his strength against Satan's strength. When the Christian is hard-pressed with some temptation that is too strong for him, he looks up to him who is the great conqueror of the powers of darkness and calls to him, "O Lord, assist your servant in this encounter with your strength, so that the glory will be yours." Thus faith draws the power of God and of his Son Jesus into the difficulties we experience.

It is the characteristic of a good Christian to magnify the power of God and to have high thoughts about it, and therefore it is his privilege to find safety in that power. David is not content with one or two expressions about this but delights himself in having many such expressions: "The LORD is my rock, my fortress and my deliverer; my God is my rock, in whom I take refuge. He is my shield and the horn of my salvation, my stronghold" (Psalm 18:2). Faith looks above everything, including both what the soul possesses and what the soul seeks, and answers all doubts and fears with the almighty power on which it rests.

3. The time of full possession: **ready to be revealed in the last time.** This salvation is the great work in which God intended to show the glory of his grace, planned before time began, to be completed at the end of time. The souls of the faithful possess this when they leave their houses of clay. Yet their happiness is not complete until the great day of the appearing of

Jesus Christ. They are naturally imperfect until their bodies are raised and united to their souls, to take part together in their bliss. They are also mystically imperfect until all the other members of Jesus Christ are united with them.

But their joy will be complete when both their own bodies and the mystical body of Christ is glorified, when all the children of that glorious family will meet and sit down at the great marriage supper at their Father's table. The music of a new song will be complete when all those who have been appointed are present to sing it in eternity. In that day our Lord Jesus will be glorified in his saints and seen in all those who believe (see 2 Thessalonians 1:10).

You see what the Gospel offers you, and you may gather how great both your folly and your guilt will be if you neglect and slight so great salvation when it is brought to you and you are asked to receive it. This is all that the preaching of the Word aims to do, and yet who listens to it? How few take hold of this eternal life, this **inheritance**, this crown that is offered to all who hear about it.

Oh, that you could be persuaded to be saved, that you would be willing to embrace salvation. Consider what you are doing, how you misplace your diligence on ephemeral things. You must learn to use what you have here as travelers, and let your home, your inheritance, your treasure, be on high, which is by far the richest and safest place.

Verse 6

In this you greatly rejoice, though now for a little while you may have had to suffer grief in all kinds of trials.

The same motives cannot give birth to contrary passions in the soul. But the apostle shows that the combination of sorrow and rejoicing is normal in the heart of a Christian. His aim is to stir up and strengthen spiritual joy in his afflicted brothers. Having set this matter before them in the preceding verses, he now applies it to their situation.

We will consider these bitter and sweet waters, sorrow and joy, first, in their springs and, second, in their streams.

First, we consider the bitter waters of sorrow. The characteristics of divine supernatural grace are not acquired through study or hard work or exercise. They are directly infused from heaven. Yet they are infused so they may act and exercise themselves in the different conditions of Christians' lives, so they can grow stronger. Whatever opposition or difficulties grace meets with, we put them under the heading of temptations. By this word we mean the things through which people are tempted, especially God's saints (see James 1:2). God delights to call his champions to face great temptations and to make them bear especially heavy crosses.

God's grace is revealed to the world as Christians under strong attack triumph because they are relying on God's powerful grace.

In all kinds of trials. This covers many different difficulties, too divergent to mention. It is not hard to have an occasional trial, with plenty of respite between attacks. But to be faced with one attack after another, to have them crowding in after each other, is often the experience of people who are especially loved by God. See Psalm 42:7.

Though now for a little while you may have had to suffer grief. Grace does not destroy nature but adds a more excellent life to it. Grace does not only permit but requires us to feel afflictions. Some people are so proud in their spirits that they try not to feel any afflictions at all. Such people need to remember that we are not meant to despise the discipline of the Lord (see Hebrews 12:5). Where there is no feeling at all, there can be no patience in enduring trials. Think of it as God's hand, and then tell your soul to submit to it (see Psalm 39:9). But this heaviness is mitigated and set, as it were, within its banks, between two considerations—first, its utility or profitableness, and second, its brevity or shortness.

1. The usefulness of affliction. To a worldly person, great gain sweetens the hardest labor. To a Christian, spiritual advantage may do a great deal to move him to take those afflictions well that are otherwise very unpleasant. "No discipline seems pleasant at the time, but painful. Later on, however, it produces a harvest of righteousness and peace for those who have been trained by it" (Hebrews 12:11).

It is not easy to be drawn away from the love of this world, and this is what God particularly requires of his children, that they are not in love with the world or the things of this world. For this is contrary to the love of God. If in the middle of trials people are sometimes subject to this disease, how would they ever grow up if they only experienced ease and prosperity? So it is clear that there is need, great need, for trials, for many trials. Then the saints can be disciplined so they will not be condemned with the world (see 1 Corinthians 11:32).

There are many ways to illustrate this truth from nature and art, but they are unnecessary. The experience of Christians tells them how easily they become proud and secure and worldly and at ease when outward things go smoothly with them. Therefore, what unhappiness it was for them to be very happy in that way!

Let us learn, then, that with respect to our present frailty, trials are necessary, so we will not set our hearts on being exempt from them, no matter how calm our seas may be at present. Their number, frequency, and strength we totally commit into the hands of our wise Father, who knows perfectly our makeup and our illnesses, and what kind and quantity of discipline is necessary for us to be cured.

2. The other consideration that moderates these trials is their shortness.

Because we willingly forget eternity, the moment looms large in our eyes. But if we could look at it correctly, how little we would be concerned about our present condition on earth. If it were as prosperous as we could wish or imagine, it is but for a short time. The rich man in the Gospel talked about "many years," but "God said to him, 'You fool! This very night your life will be demanded from you'" (Luke 12:19-20). Well may Augustine say, "Use me here as pleases you, so that hereafter it may be well with me."

In this you greatly rejoice. We now consider the sweet waters of joy. The Christian rises above all that is liable to change and casts his anchor within the Most Holy Place. He rejoices in what remains immovable and unalterable. Even if his own personal circumstances and the whole world were turned upside down, he would not change. As the psalmist said, "Therefore we will not fear, though the earth give way and the mountains fall into the heart of the sea, though its waters roar and foam and the mountains quake with their surging" (46:2). When we receive that rich, pure, and abiding **inheritance,** the **salvation** that is **to be revealed in the last time,** when time itself will cease to be, there will be no more calculating our joys by days and hours, but they will all be seen in the light of eternity. Then all our love, which is scattered and spent on the vanities among which we live here on earth, will be united and fixed on God, and our soul will be filled with the delight of his presence.

The sorrow was limited by the considerations we mentioned. But this joy, this exultation and leaping for joy, is unlimited. Its extent knows no bounds. The trials, the burden of heaviness, are only passing touches of pain. But this joy is built on permanent, boundless, infinite delight that is beyond all hyperbole. We do not have the words to express it. It is beyond everything that we can say. "For our light and momentary troubles are achieving for us an eternal glory that far outweighs them all" (2 Corinthians 4:17). Even in the middle of the struggle itself, this joy is not overwhelmed by deep sorrow. This oil of gladness rises to the surface and cannot be drowned by all the floods of affliction. Indeed, it is often most sweet in the middle of the greatest disaster. The soul relishes spiritual joy best when it is not cluttered up with worldly delights but finds them turned into bitterness.

This is the way this should be applied to us. Insofar as we profess to be Christians, we all say we are children of God, and so heirs of this glory. If each person were asked about this, he would say he hoped to attain this. But were there nothing else, we might think we were being deceived, for only a few of us really find this height of joy, gladness, and exultation in our thinking about our heavenly **inheritance.** How many of us daily delight ourselves with the thought of what is kept for us above more than we think about our enjoyments here below?

Consider how the news of some trivial outward pleasure that we are about to enjoy makes our hearts leap within us. And yet this news of the kingdom prepared for us, if we are indeed believers, does not stir us. Our hearts are left unaffected as if it had nothing to do with us at all.

People who concentrate on worthless things are in a fool's paradise. How often people go over in their minds all the things they are about to enjoy. But we who say we have hopes of the glory to come can spend many days without taking one hour to rejoice in our thoughts and future. If any one poor person became very rich and was greatly honored within the space of a week, enjoying all the health and pleasure imaginable, think how much time he would think about all those welcome changes. There is no comparison between that and everything we can imagine about the hopes we speak of, and yet how infrequent are our thoughts on these things, and how feebly we rejoice over them. Are we able to deny that this is caused by our unbelief in these things? This is the reason for our neglecting them. The words of men and angels cannot bring about belief in future happiness. Only the One who gives us faith enables us to understand it and take hold of it and, as we believe, fill us with its joy and hope.

Verse 7

These have come so that your faith—of greater worth than gold, which perishes even though refined by fire—may be proved genuine and may result in praise, glory and honor when Jesus Christ is revealed.

"The path of the righteous is like the first gleam of dawn, shining ever brighter till the full light of day," says Solomon (Proverbs 4:18). Still making progress and moving toward perfection, they are traveling as fast when they are surrounded with trials as at any other time. In fact, everything that seems to work against them helps them on their journey. Those graces that would possibly become heavy and unwieldy if we had too much ease become stronger through conflict. Divine grace, in the heart of weak and sinful people, is an invincible thing. Drown it in the waters of adversity, and it rises in a more beautiful way, as if it had not been drowned but only washed. Throw it into the furnace of fiery trials, and it is purified and loses nothing except the dross that makes it impure. Due to our trials we will appear in greater brightness at the revelation of Jesus Christ.

The special treasure of a Christian is the grace that he receives from heaven, and particularly the sovereign grace of faith. Through this **faith** he can be assured he will not only be able to endure trials more patiently, but will gladly welcome them. "We also rejoice in our sufferings, because we know that suffering produces perseverance" (Romans 5:3). Therefore the apostle sets this out before his brothers in the words of this verse. Here we see, first, the value and excellency of **faith** and, second, the usefulness of temptations in relation to **faith.**

1. The value and excellency of faith. The trial of faith is said to be **of greater worth than gold** because **faith** itself is more useful than **gold.** The apostle chooses this comparison because it suits his purpose for illustrating both **faith** and the usefulness of trials, since the first is represented by gold and the second by the purification of gold in fire.

Gold is valuable, first, because it is the purest and most precious of all metals, since it has many excellent properties that other metals do not possess. Second, gold is valuable because people hold it in such esteem. Note how they travel by land and sea in order to buy it. People are respected depending on how much gold they possess.

The Holy Scriptures, descending to our understanding, speak about the riches of the new Jerusalem in terms of gold (see Revelation 21). Here in 1 Peter our **faith** is **of greater worth than gold.**

I do not insist on the comparison of faith with gold just because of the qualities gold possesses, that it is pure and solid and malleable in ways that other metals are not. However, faith does genuinely enrich the soul and gives the soul propriety in all the rich consolations of the Gospel, in all the promises of life and salvation, in all necessary blessings. It draws virtue from Christ to strengthen itself.

Thus it is not only precious like gold, but it is **of greater worth**, more precious, yes, much more precious than gold, in the following ways. First, gold has to be dug out of the earth, but faith comes from heaven. Second, the nature of faith reflects its origin and shows it is immaterial, spiritual, and pure. We refine gold and make it purer, but when we receive faith it is pure in itself, though we make it impure through the alloy of our own unbelief. Third, faith is superior to gold in its endurance, for it does not perish. Gold perishes, and a particular owner of gold finds that he is often deprived of it during his lifetime.

All graces are tested in the same furnace, but faith is the root of all the others. Severe afflictions test a Christian's love for God. The grace of patience is especially tested during afflictions. But patience stems from faith, as does love. God has said that he will not fail us (see Joshua 1:5) and that we will not be tempted beyond what we can bear (see 1 Corinthians 10:13). Belief in such things brings patience. "The testing of your faith develops perseverance" (James 1:3). So the Christian is content to be tested, knowing that the length and intensity of the trial is in God's control, in the hands of his loving heavenly Father. So the test of these other graces is really the test of our faith.

2. The usefulness of temptation in relation to our faith. This trial, like that of the purification of gold, may be viewed in two ways. First, for the

demonstration of the truth and the pureness of a Christian's faith. Second, to refine a Christian's faith further and make it even purer.

First, the furnace of affliction reveals pure, upright faith to be what it is, for it stays the same in the fire. It is undiminished, like gold that loses nothing when it is put in the furnace. Doubtless many are deceived during times of ease and prosperity, having imaginary faith and strength. So while a man is surrounded by outward assistance from friends and riches, he may lean on them rather than on God, who is an invisible support and stronger than all visible supports and is the special stay of faith in all circumstances. But when all these outward props are removed from that person, it will be seen if there is something else that holds him up or not. If there is nothing else, he falls. But if his mind remains firm and unmoved as before, then it is evident that he did not place his weight on those things that surrounded him but on a foundation that, though impossible to see, was alone able to support him even though he was surrounded by many other supports and was attacked by many afflictions. As our Saviour says, "that house . . . did not fall, because it had its foundation on the rock" (Matthew 7:25).

Such a time tested the genuineness of David's faith, and he found that he was trusting God when there was nothing else he could do. If he had not believed in God, he would have fainted (see Psalm 27:13, KJV). "David was greatly distressed because the men were talking of stoning him; each one was bitter in spirit because of his sons and daughters. But David found strength in the LORD his God" (1 Samuel 30:6). David also said, "My flesh and my heart may fail, but God is the strength of my heart and my portion forever" (Psalm 73:26). The heart's natural strength of spirit and resolution may bear up under outward weakness or when the flesh fails, but when the heart itself fails, which is the strength of the flesh, what will then strengthen it? Nothing except for "God [who] is the strength of my heart and my portion forever." Thus faith alone works, as is seen in the case of the prophet Habakkuk:

> *Though the fig tree does not bud and there are no grapes on the vines, though the olive crop fails and the fields produce no food, though there are no sheep in the pen and no cattle in the stalls, yet I will rejoice in the LORD, I will be joyful in God my Savior.*
> —Habakkuk 3:17-18

In spiritual trials, the severest kind of trial, when the fire of divine discipline is within a man, when God not only shuts up his loving-kindness from his mind and soul, but seems to shut it up in great displeasure, when God writes bitter things against him, even then he must depend on God and wait for his deliverance. The more he is struck by God, the closer he clings to God. This is not only a genuine way to be refined, but a most effective one. Well might Job say, "Though he slay me, yet will I hope in him" (Job 13:15), and "but he knows the way that I take; when he has tested me, I will come forth as gold" (Job 23:10).

Second, as the furnace shows faith to be what it is, it also improves it and makes it more valuable and purer than it had been previously. The graces of the Spirit, as they come from God's hand, are nothing but pureness. But as they are placed in a heart where sin lives (which while the body remains cannot be totally purged away), faith is combined with corruption and dross. In particular faith mixes with unbelief, the love for earthly things, and a reliance on the creature—if not more than God, then together with God. The furnace is necessary to deal with this, so that the soul may be purified from its dross and made more spiritual in believing. It is a hard task to teach the heart to grasp loosely the things of the world. "Though your riches increase, do not set your heart on them" (Psalm 62:10). St. Paul calls riches "uncertain": "Command those who are rich in this present world not to be arrogant nor to put their hope in wealth, which is so uncertain, but to put their hope in God, who richly provides us with everything for our enjoyment" (1 Timothy 6:17).

So God is pleased to choose the more effective way to teach his people the right and pure exercise of faith, whether by withholding or withdrawing those things from them. He makes them relish the sweetness of spiritual comfort by depriving them of those outward comforts in which they were in most danger as they relied on them and so forgot God. When they are trained to let go of anything earthly and entrust themselves completely to the Rock, their faith is refined through those losses and afflictions they have to endure. People who take physical exercise, such as fencing, are not taught by sitting still and listening to rules or seeing others practice; they learn by exercising themselves. The way to benefit in the art of believing, the spiritual activity of faith, is to exercise frequently in a tough way and to make up all lacks and losses in God and to sweeten the bitterest griefs with his loving-kindness.

May result in praise, glory and honor. This is the purpose of all these fierce trials, and this will definitely be obtained from all their severe testings. Faith will win through them all and will **result in praise, glory and honor**. A casual observer may think it strange to see gold thrown into the fire and left there for some time. But the person who put it there would be reluctant to lose it. His aim is to make some expensive piece of work with it. Believers gives themselves to Christ, and Christ undertakes to present them blameless to the Father. None of them will be lost. That faith that is in the furnace in this life will then be made into a crown of pure gold. It will **result in praise, glory and honor**.

Praise, glory and honor may refer either to the believers themselves, as St. Paul uses this expression in Romans 2:7 ("To those who by persistence in doing good seek glory, honor and immortality, he will give eternal life"), or it may refer to Christ who appears. But both agree that it will be to believers' praise and to the praise of Christ, for it is certain that all their praise and glory will end in the glory of their Head, Christ, who is God and is to be blessed forever. Believers all have their crowns, but their honor will be to throw them all down before Christ's throne "on the day he comes to be glorified in his holy people and to be marveled at among all those who have believed" (2 Thessalonians 1:10). They will be glorious in him, and therefore in all their glory he will be glorified. They have derived their glory from him, but it will all be given back to Christ.

When Jesus Christ is revealed. This denotes the time when this will happen. Christ who is faithful and true has promised to come again and to judge the world in righteousness, and he will come and will not be slow. He will judge righteously on that day, even though he himself was judged unrighteously here on earth. This is called the "revelation." All other things will be revealed on that day; the most hidden things, good and evil, will be unveiled. But it will be eminently the day **when Jesus Christ is revealed.** Through his light and the brightness of his coming, all things will be revealed. But he himself will be the most worthy of all to view. All eyes will be on him. He will then gloriously appear before all men and angels and will by all be acknowledged to be the Son of God and the Judge of the world. Some people will know him with joy and will acknowledge him for who he is; others will be horrified and amazed when they see Christ. How beautiful will Christ be to those who love him, when he as the glorious Head will appear and his whole mystical body with him.

On that day the glory and praise with which all the saints will be honored will fully compensate for all the opposition and hardship they have endured on earth. And they will shine the brighter because of their trials. If only we thought more about this solemn day, how little we would bother about the opinions of men or be troubled by outward trials that come our way. How easily would we make light of dishonor here and cheerfully pass through it, provided that we may then be found in Christ, so as to take part **in praise, glory and honor when Jesus Christ is revealed.**

Verses 8-9

Though you have not seen him, you love him; and even though you do not see him now, you believe in him and are filled with an inexpressible and glorious joy, for you are receiving the goal of your faith, the salvation of your souls.

For the world it is a paradox when the apostle asserts that **joy** is found in the midst of sorrow. Therefore he insists on emphasizing this. He says that the saints do not only have some measure of **joy** in the griefs that surround them, but that this is an unimaginable and **glorious joy.**

To support this, and to support his brothers' experience of this, he gives details about the reasons for their **joy.** These are, first, the object or matter of it, and, second, the apprehension and appropriation of that object. These two combined are the complete reason for all rejoicing.

1. The object is Jesus Christ. **Though you have not seen him, you love him; and even though you do not see him now, you believe in him.** The **salvation** purchased by him is spoken of in verse 9: **you are receiving the goal of your faith, the salvation of your souls.** These two cannot be separated, and these two verses that speak about them ought to be thought of together.

2. The apprehension of these is set out, first, negatively (not by physical sight) and, second, positively. Whereas it might seem to dampen the liveliness of their rejoicing that it is about things they had not seen and still cannot see, this is abundantly made up for by three things, each of which is more exciting than the mere physical sight of Christ in the body, which many had but did not benefit from. These three things are three prime Christian graces: faith, love, and hope. **Faith** and **love** come in verse 8, and hope comes in verse 9. Faith in Christ gives birth to love for him, and both give the assured hope of salvation through him, making it as definite for them as if they already possessed it in their hands.

This is that one thing that concerns us so much. Therefore, we make a very big mistake and we ignore our best interests when we either speak of or listen to this casually and do not apply it to our hearts. What are all our thoughts and efforts aiming for? We may take several false paths toward it, and we often seek after it by our own efforts, but it still remains something that refreshes us and something we rejoice over when we attain it. It is in Christ, and it is useless to seek it elsewhere. It is offered to you, and it can be yours if you will receive it. You will then know that this is true, that in Jesus Christ is laid up true consolation and rejoicing, and that in him is this treasure. You will also know how to bring him into your hearts to live there and so have the spring of joy within yourself.

That which gives complete joy to the soul must be something that is higher and better than itself. In a word, he who made the soul can alone bring it **inexpressible and glorious joy.** But the soul, while it stays guilty in its rebellion against Christ and is unreconciled to him, can only see him as an enemy. Any belief that it can have concerning him while it is in this position cannot instill love and hope and joy. Rather, it produces the faith of the devils—terror and trembling. But the light of his presence shining in the face of his Son and our Mediator rejoices the heart. It is looking at him that enables the soul to believe and to experience love and hope and so rejoice. The apostle Paul, in his description of the state the Gentiles were in before they had Christ preached to them, links these things together: "remember that at that time you were separate from Christ, excluded from citizenship in Israel and foreigners to the covenants of the promise, without hope and without God in the world" (Ephesians 2:12). The apostle Peter, in the verses before us, says that Christ is the reason for our **joy** because our **faith, love,** and hope of **salvation** center on him.

The apostle Peter, writing to the scattered Jews, many of whom had not known or seen Christ in the flesh, commends their love and faith because it did not depend on physical sight, but was pure and spiritual and made them one with those whom our Saviour pronounced blessed, even though they had not seen him. "Blessed are those who have not seen and yet have believed" (John 20:29). You did not see Christ when he lived among people and walked about, preaching and performing miracles. Many of those who did hear and see Christ then did not believe in him. Indeed, they scoffed and hated him and persecuted him, and in the end they crucified him. You have not seen any of those things, but you have heard the Gospel that speaks about him, and **you believe in him.** So note carefully that faith does not depend on human ministry and gifts, for what greater difference can there be than between the Master and the servants, between the great Prophet himself and his weak, sinful messengers? And yet many of those who saw and heard Christ in person were not converted and did not believe in him. But thousands who never saw Christ were converted through his apostles, including some who were partly responsible for his death. (See Acts 2.)

Learn, then, to look beyond the outward ministry, and remember that if Jesus Christ himself were on earth and preached among us today, his incomparable words would be of no use to us if they did not meet with faith in those who listened. But where there is faith, then the worst delivery of the message will be greatly blessed.

Though you have not seen him. Faith elevates the soul not only above sense and things that can be experienced, but above reason itself. As reason corrects the errors of thinking, so supernatural faith corrects the errors of natural reason.

The sun appears smaller than the wheel of a chariot, but reason teaches the philosopher that it is much bigger than the whole earth, and that it appears to be so small because it is so far away. The naturally wise man is as much deceived by his earthly reason in his judgment about Jesus Christ, the Sun of Righteousness. The reason for this is the same—because he is so distant from him. As the psalmist says, "He ["the wicked man," verse 1] is haughty and your laws are far from him" (Psalm 10:5). The man who trusts in his own wisdom thinks Christ and his glory to be of little worth in comparison with gaining his own honor, pleasure, and prosperity. The latter are close at hand, and he thinks they are more valuable than everything else. But the apostle Paul and all who are enlightened by the same Spirit know through faith, which is divine reason, that the excellency of Jesus Christ surpasses all earthly things. "But whatever was to my profit I now consider loss for the sake of Christ. What is more, I consider everything a loss compared to the surpassing greatness of knowing Christ Jesus my Lord, for whose sake I have lost all things. I consider them rubbish, that I may gain Christ" (Philippians 3:7-8).

To give correct assent to Christ's Gospel is impossible unless the soul is infused with divine, saving faith. To believe that the eternal Son of God clothed himself with human flesh and lived among human beings in a tent like theirs and suffered death in the flesh, that he who was Lord of life has freed us from the sentence of eternal death, that he broke the chains of death and rose again, that he went up into heaven and there at the Father's right hand sits in our flesh and is glorified above the angels—this is "the mystery of godliness" (1 Timothy 3:16). Part of this mystery is that Christ is believed on in the world: "Beyond all question, the mystery of godliness is great: He appeared in a body, was vindicated by the Spirit, was seen by angels, was preached among the nations, was believed on in the world, was taken up in glory." Natural people may talk about this very knowledgeably and say that it may be historically true. But firmly to believe that there is divine truth in all these things and to be persuaded of it above everything else we see with our eyes—such an assent is the special work of God's Spirit and is certainly saving faith.

The soul who believes this cannot but choose **love**. It is generally true that the eye is the normal door through which love enters the soul, and it is true of this **love** also. Even though the physical eye has not seen Christ, the eye of faith has. **Though you have not seen him, you love him; and even though you do not see him now, you believe in him.** This is to view Christ spiritually. Faith, indeed, is distinguished from that vision that will be seen in glory. But it is the vision of the kingdom of grace; it is the eye of the new creature, that quick-sighted eye that pierces all the visible heavens and sees beyond them and looks to things that are not seen and to him who is invisible (see 2 Corinthians 4:18 and Hebrews 11:1).

It is possible that one may be much loved on account of reports and pictures. But when the person is seen, love is raised to a higher level. We have the report of the perfect deeds of Christ in the Gospels. In fact, we have such a clear description of him that it gives a picture of him that, along with the sacraments, is the only lawful and the only living picture of our Saviour. "Before your very eyes Jesus Christ was clearly portrayed as crucified" (Galatians 3:1). Faith believes this report and looks at this picture and so lets Christ's love into the soul. But in addition to this, it gives a special knowledge of Christ and acquaintance with him. It allows the soul to find all that is spoken about him in the Word, all his beauty represented there, to be abundantly true. It makes the soul really taste his sweetness and, through that, possesses the heart more strongly with his love, convincing it of the truth of those things, not through rational arguments, but through an inexpressible kind of evidence that only those who have it know about. Faith persuades a Christian of two things that are the reasons for all love, beauty, and propriety—the loveliness of Christ in himself, and our interest in him.

You love him. If this **love** is to be genuine, it needs three qualities: goodwill, delight, and desire.

1. Goodwill. Goodwill is earnest wishing, promoting God's glory, and stirring up others to do so. Those who are more concerned about their own welfare than Christ's, more about their own glory than Christ's, are strangers to this divine love. This bitter root of self-love is the hardest thing to remove. A strong and sweet love for Christ alone does this, though it does so gradually.

2. Delight. In true love there is a delight in God, a conformity to his will, a loving what he loves. Such a love will be careful to do his will, always seeking to know more clearly what it is that pleases him most. It often contemplates God and looks on his beauty. As the soul lets in this affection, so it serves it constantly. Thus the soul that is possessed by the love of Jesus Christ, that has its eye on him frequently, often thinks about his former sufferings and his present glory. The more it looks on Christ, the more it loves him. And the more it loves Christ, the more it delights to look on him.

3. Desire. The soul has but a small taste of Christ and his goodness here and therefore is looking and longing for the marriage day. The time while we are detained on earth is sad and tiring and seems much longer than it is. St. Paul says, "I desire to depart and be with Christ, which is better by far" (Philippians 1:23).

God is the sum of all things lovely. Gregory Nazianzen put it well when he said, "If I have any possessions, health, credit, learning, this is all the contentment I have of them, that I have something I may despise for Christ who is wholly desirable." This **love** is the sum of all he requires from us. It is what makes our feeblest service for him acceptable, and without it, everything we offer Christ is distasteful. God deserves our love not only because of his unequaled excellency and beauty, but because of his unequaled love for us. As the apostle Paul said, "[he] loved me" (Galatians 2:20). How did Christ love us? By nothing less than giving himself for us: "The life I live in the body, I live by faith in the Son of God, who loved me and gave himself for me" (Galatians 2:20). Clearly then, the way we must love is to give ourselves to Christ, who loved us and gave himself for us.

Grace does not pluck up by the roots and wholly destroy the natural passions of the mind that are polluted by sin. It does not dry up this stream but purifies it from the mud. The Holy Spirit turns the love of the soul toward God in Christ, for this is the only way we can understand Christ's love. Jesus Christ is the first object of the divine love. He is the One through whom God conveys the sense of his love to the soul and receives in return love to himself.

Many ways to increase this love for Christ have been offered. But the following one incorporates most of them, if not all of them: believe and you will love; believe a great deal, and you will love a great deal. Work for strong and deep conviction of these glorious things that Christ speaks about, and this will bring love. Seeking to believe how excellent Christ is in himself, and seeing his love for us and our interest in him, will kindle a fire in the heart that will culminate in a sacrifice of love for Christ.

The signs of this **love** are many and varied. But the most important sign is when the soul tries to keep Jesus' commands out of love, for whatever we do that is not from love is valueless. See 1 Corinthians 13.

This is the message of the Gospel. Therefore, ministers should be suitors, not for themselves, but for Christ, to bring souls to him, and to bring many hearts to love him.

During times of suffering, love will make the soul not only bear the suffering, but welcome the bitterest afflictions of life and the worst kinds of death for Christ's sake. In a word, there is in love a sweet constraint, a tying of the heart to all obedience and duty.

The love of God is required in ministers as they preach the Word. Our Saviour said to St. Peter, "Simon son of John, do you truly love me?" (John 21:16). It is necessary for people to receive the truth in love (see 2 Thessalonians 2:10; Ephesians 4:15-16). When Christ is preached, the soul must embrace him through faith and love.

You who have chosen Christ for your love, do not let your hearts fall, so that they become reacquainted with sin. This will only bring new bitterness to your souls, for some time at least; it will deprive you of the sense of the favor of your beloved Jesus. Delight always in God, and give him your whole heart, for he deserves it all. The largest heart of all is too small to receive all the consolations Christ brings with him. Seek to increase in this love. Even though it may be weak to start with, work to make it daily grow stronger and stronger, and to burn hotter and clearer, that it might consume the dross of earthly desires.

Receiving the goal of your faith (verse 9). Although the soul that believes and loves is in God's present possession, as far as it is possible to be during our earthly life, it still desires a complete enjoyment that it cannot experience without leaving this earth. As the apostle Paul says, "As long as we are at home in the body we are away from the Lord" (2 Corinthians 5:6). And because they are assured of that happy exchange, that prospect of being united and freed from this body, they know they will be present with the Lord; they have his own word that he goes to "prepare a place" for them (John 14:3). This brings an assured hope—**receiving the goal of your faith.**

This **receiving** also flows from **faith.** Faith apprehends the present truth of the divine promises and so makes future things present. Hope looks to their complete fulfillment; and if the promises are true, as faith declares, then hope has good reason for its expectation. This desire and hope are the wheels that carry the soul forward, and faith is the common basis on which they rest.

In these words we see two things. First, the good hoped for in Christ, who is so believed on and loved, and, second, the certainty of the hope itself. It is as certain as if it had already happened.

The Good Hoped For

Consider its nature (**the salvation of your souls**) and its associated characteristic (**the goal of your faith**).

1. Its nature is **the salvation of your souls.** It brings with it complete deliverance from all kinds of misery, and also the safe possession of perfect happiness when the soul will be out of reach of all of its enemies and adverse accidents. It will no longer be subject to evils such as being aware of sin, the fear of God's wrath, and outward afflictions like persecution, poverty, and disease.

Its being called the **salvation of your souls** does not exclude the body from that glory, for it will be raised and reunited to the soul. But because the soul is itself immortal and is the nobler part of man and the main recipient of grace and glory, and because it first enjoys that blessedness and for a time leaves the body in the dust, it alone is mentioned here. But Jesus is the Saviour of the body too, and he will, at his coming, "transform our lowly bodies so that they will be like his glorious body" (Philippians 3:21).

2. We see also the characteristics associated with this hope: **the goal of your faith.** Here we note that **faith** is both **the goal** and the reward. It is the **goal** at which **faith** aims, and it is the reward, not because of their deeds, nor because of their faith as a deed that deserves to be rewarded, but as the condition of the new covenant. This salvation is the proper reward of faith, which believes in the unseen Christ and so receives that happy sight. As Augustine has said, "It is the proper work of faith to believe what you do not see, and the reward of faith to see what you have believed."

The Certainty of Their Hope

It is as if they had already received what they had hoped for. If God's promise and Christ's merit are to hold good, then those who believe in him and love him must be made certain of their salvation. "For the Son of God, Jesus Christ, who was preached among you by me and Silas and Timothy, was not 'Yes' and 'No,' but in him it has always been 'Yes.' For no matter how many promises God has made, they are 'Yes' in Christ" (2 Corinthians 1:19-20). Rivers are more likely to run backwards and the orbits of the heavens change than that any soul who is united to Christ Jesus through faith and love will be separated from him and so fall short of the salvation hoped for in him. And this is the reason for their rejoicing.

Filled with an inexpressible and glorious joy (verse 8). The apostle Paul says, "The man without the Spirit does not accept the things that come from the Spirit of God, for they are foolishness to him, and he cannot understand them, because they are spiritually discerned" (1 Corinthians 2:14). If you speak to the man without the Spirit about spiritual mourning or a sense of guilt or feeling God's displeasure or the hiding of his favor and light from the soul, these things will not move him, for he does not understand what you are talking about. If you speak to him about a quiet conscience, a sense of God's love, or the joy that comes from this, he will also not understand you. As our Saviour said, "We played the flute for you, and you did not dance; we sang a dirge, and you did not mourn" (Matthew 11:17). But there is wisdom in these things, even though they appear to be foolish in the eyes of the world, for "wisdom is proved right by her actions" (Matthew 11:19).

The apostle has already said something about the reasons for spiritual joy, and he now mentions two more things about joy: first, how joy comes from these reasons, and, second, the excellency of this joy as it is here expressed.

We see here solid grounds for the heart being certain about this joy. It possesses it in part now and has complete trust that it will receive all later. What more can be required to make it joyful? Jesus Christ is the treasure of all blessings, received and united to the soul by faith and love and hope.

Is not Christ the Light and Joy of the nations? From the distance of many generations, over more than 2,000 years, Abraham saw such a light through faith, and seeing, he rejoiced. In Scripture light often represents joy. Christ, who is this light, brings salvation with him. He is the "sun of righteousness," and he "will rise with healing in [his] wings" (Malachi 4:2). "I bring you," said the angel, "good news of great joy that will be for all the people," and the angels' song has the theme of that joy in it: "Glory to God in the highest, and on earth peace to men on whom his favor rests" (Luke 2:10, 14).

To rejoice in Christ, we must believe him to be ours. Otherwise, the more excellent he is, the more reason our heart has to be sad without him. "My soul praises the Lord," said the blessed Virgin, "and my spirit rejoices in God my Savior" (Luke 1:47).

Thus, having spoken about our communion with Christ, the apostle John adds, "We write this to make our joy complete" (1 John 1:4). Faith produces this joy by uniting the soul to Christ and applying his merits, and from that application arises the pardon of sin. And so the burden of misery, which caused the sorrow, is removed. And as soon as the soul finds itself without the burden that was plunging it into hell, it cannot but leap for joy in the ease and refreshment it finds. Therefore that Psalm that David starts with the doctrine of the pardon of sin ends with an exhortation to rejoice: "Blessed is he whose transgressions are forgiven, whose sins are covered. . . . Rejoice in the LORD and be glad, you righteous; sing, all you who are upright in heart" (Psalm 32:1, 11). St. Peter speaks to his hearers about the remission of sins: "Repent and be baptized, every one of you, in the name of Jesus Christ so that your sins may be forgiven" (Acts 2:38), and they received his words "gladly" (Acts 2:41, KJV). Our Saviour links these two together by saying, "Take heart, daughter, your faith has healed you" (Matthew 9:22).

The prophet Isaiah spoke about the good news that proclaims freedom for the captives and said that those who mourned would have the oil of gladness and "a garment of praise instead of a spirit of despair" (Isaiah 61:3). Think how gladly the debtor who has been in prison for a long time receives with utter joy the news that he has been granted freedom and all his debts are paid. Think how a condemned man feels when he unexpectedly hears he has received a pardon. Such examples fall far short of the joy that faith brings through bringing Christ to the soul, and forgiveness of sins in Christ.

But that is not all. This believing soul is not only a debtor acquitted and set free but is also enriched with a new and great estate. He is not only a pardoned murderer, but he has a position of honor lavished on him through the promises, the "unsearchable riches of Christ" (Ephesians 3:8), is received into favor with God, and has the dignity of being a child of God. "He raises the poor from the dust and lifts the needy from the ash heap; he seats them with princes, with the princes of their people" (Psalm 113:7-8).

As there is **joy** because of **faith**, so there is also **joy** because of **love**. Though love is in itself the most sweet and delightful passion of the soul, yet when we foolishly misplace it, it often proves to be full of bitterness. But once it is set on Jesus Christ, the only right and worthy object, it causes **inexpressible** delight and rejoicing.

First, it is a matter of joy to have this love bestowed on us, as we are so unworthy to receive it. Though sometimes our Saviour seems to withdraw himself and sometimes saddens the soul that loves him with absences, even in those sad times the soul delights to love him. There is pleasure in the very pains within which it has been seeking Christ. And it knows that Christ's mercies are everlasting and that he will not be distant for long but will return and speak words of comfort.

Second, our love of Christ assures us that we will not be frustrated or disappointed in the end. It assures us that his love for us preceded any love we had for him. He has loved us and "freed us from our sins" (Revelation 1:5). He will not forget us in the midst of our conflicts, even though he himself is in glory. He prays for us there and will bring us there. What can happen to us that would stop us from rejoicing? For we will definitely arrive at that complete salvation that Christ has bought for us.

There is a third reason for our rejoicing, namely, our hope. "We have this hope as an anchor for the soul, firm and secure. It enters the inner sanctuary behind the curtain, where Jesus, who went before us, has entered on our behalf" (Hebrews 6:19-20). This anchor stays with us in all the storms that beat on the turbulent seas of our life. The soul that firmly believes and loves him may confidently hope to see what it believes and to enjoy what it loves, and in that it may rejoice. It may say, "Whatever the hazards, whether inward or outward, whatever the afflictions and trials I have to endure, yet this one thing keeps me safe, and in that I will rejoice, that the salvation of my soul does not depend on my own strength but is in my Saviour's hand." "Your life is now hidden with Christ in God. When Christ, who is your life, appears, then you also will appear with him in glory" (Colossians 3:3-4).

This empty world is full of shadows and running after we know not what. But the believer can say, "I know whom I have believed, and am convinced that he is able to guard what I have entrusted to him for that day" (2 Timothy 1:12). Now we not only have a right to these things, but they bring us joy. The soul should often think about them and so rejoice. "May my meditation be pleasing to him, as I rejoice in the LORD" (Psalm 104:34). The godly, when they fail to do this, deprive themselves of much of the joy that they might have.

The apostle speaks about this **joy** with the two words **inexpressible** and **glorious**. That it is an **inexpressible** joy is of little wonder since it is so inconceivable. It is an infinite good. God reconciled us to himself in Jesus Christ, testifying and sealing his love to our souls and giving us assured hope of that blessed vision of eternity. What could be more **inexpressible** than this? In the same way it is **glorious**, for it derives its excellency from the highest and most glorious person.

Inexpressible. The best worldly joys are easy to talk about, but they rarely live up to the opinion and expectation that people give them. But this spiritual joy is beyond any report that can be given of it.

Again, earthly joys are not glorious. In fact, people are ashamed of many of them. But the joys that arise from union with Christ bring complete satisfaction. This is their glory and the reason why we may glory in them. As David said, "My soul will boast in the LORD" (Psalm 34:2).

Here is the application of all this: if these things were believed, we would no longer listen to the foolish prejudices that the world has against religion.

Consider, first, that true religion does not prohibit any lawful delights but teaches that they should be used in a moderate and regular way, which is far more enjoyable. For those things that are lawful in themselves are sinful when used in excess, and so prove to be bitter in the end. Though lawful enjoyment may be given us for God and his glory, it is sometimes more delightful to deny them than to enjoy them.

Second, the delights and pleasures of sin are forbidden by religion. But they are exchanged for this **inexpressible . . . joy**, which is beyond them. It calls people from sordid and base delights to those that are pure delights indeed. It tells people, "Drink no longer from this puddle; here are the crystal streams of a living fountain to drink from." There is a delight in the despising of impure delights. As Augustine exclaims, "How pleasant it is to lack these pleasures!" We have the prospect of spiritual joy, but amazingly we do not all choose it, because we do not believe it.

Third, it is true that the godly are subject to great distresses and afflictions, but their joy is not killed off by them or diminished by them, but is often increased. When they have the least amount of this world's joy, they abound most in spiritual consolations and then delight in them most of all. They find them sweetest when their taste is not polluted by earthly enjoyments.

Fourth, spiritual grief, which appears to be the opposite of this spiritual joy, is not harmful to this joy. For there is a secret delight and sweetness in the tears of repentance, and a balm in them that refreshes the soul. And even in the saddest kind of mourning, such as the dark times of desertion, the soul knows joy because of the presence of its Beloved. Then all these spiritual sorrows, of whatever nature they are, are turned into spiritual joy.

Fifth, the person who does not have the Spirit has doubts about this joy we are speaking about. He sees and hears so little about it from those who profess to have it. We are told by the apostle Peter that this joy is **inexpressible**. And yet it would be a poor thing if he who possessed it was not able to speak about it. It is the same with joys as it is with cares. The deepest waters run most still. True joy lives more in the heart than in the countenance. But false joys are only superficial and skin-deep. They are all on the surface.

Do not think that the godly, as the prophet says of the wicked, have no peace. "'There is no peace,' says the LORD, 'for the wicked'" (Isaiah 48:22). The Septuagint reads, "There is no joy" for the wicked, and this is certainly true. The wicked experience no true joy. They may revel and make a great noise, but they do not rejoice. "Like the crackling of thorns under the pot, so is the laughter of fools" (Ecclesiastes 7:6). There is much noise but little heat, and it soon ends. There is no continuing feast except for a good conscience. Wickedness and real joy cannot live together, as the moralist Seneca often said. But the person who can say, "The righteousness of Jesus Christ is mine, and in him God's favor and the hope of eternal happiness" has a light that can shine in the darkest dungeon, even in the dark valley of the shadow of death. So do not say, "If I start on the way of holiness, I must say good-bye to happiness." On the contrary, you will never have a truly joyful day until then. You will have had no days at all, just night, as far as the soul is concerned, until you welcome Jesus Christ and his kingdom, which consists of righteousness, peace, and joy in the Holy Spirit. You must not sacrifice Isaac, which means "laughter," but a ram. It is not your joy but your filthy, sinful delights that end in sorrow.

Seek to know in your own experience what the promised joys mean, though no matter how much they are described and commended to you, you will not fully understand them. "Taste and see that the LORD is good" (Psalm 34:8). As Augustine says, "Praise the sweetness of honey to the utmost, he who has never tasted it cannot understand it." You cannot know and see this goodness except by tasting it. Once you have tasted it, all those joys you had previously thought to be sweet you will find bitter and distasteful.

You who know Christ is yours through believing, know your happiness, and rejoice, and glory in it. Whatever your outward condition may be, "Rejoice in the Lord always. I will say it again: Rejoice!" (Philippians 4:4). "Light is shed upon the righteous and joy on the upright in heart" (Psalm 97:11).

Verses 10-12

Concerning this salvation, the prophets, who spoke of the grace that was to come to you, searched intently and with the greatest care, trying to find out the time and circumstances to which the Spirit of Christ in them was pointing when he predicted the sufferings of Christ and the glories that would follow. It was revealed to them that they were not serving themselves but you, when they spoke of the things that have now been told you by those who have preached the gospel to you by the Holy Spirit sent from heaven. Even angels long to look into these things.

It is the ignorance, or at least the lack of consideration, of divine things that makes earthly things, whether they are good or evil, appear great in our eyes. Therefore the apostle's great aim is to show the certainty and excellency of the belief and hope of Christians to his persecuted brothers, in order to strengthen their minds against all discouragements and opposition. Then they would see that nothing was too hard to do or suffer for so lofty a cause and so happy an end. It is the shallow and mean thoughts and the feeble conviction we have of spiritual things that cause all our remissness and coldness regarding them. The doctrine of **salvation**, mentioned in the previous verse as the goal of our Christian faith, is illustrated here from its antiquity, dignity, and infallible truth.

The Gospel is no modern invention, for **the prophets** inquired into it and foretold it in former ages. Thus prejudice against it for being new is removed. It is no mean thing that such men were without question wise and holy. They studied much and were careful to publish their discoveries for their own times as well as for posterity. Their writings were not their own private thoughts, but they were guided by God's Spirit. This is what sets the truth about their testimony above all doubt and uncertainty.

In taking these three verses together we see three things that testify to the excellency of the Gospel. First, its main author. Second, the subject of these verses. Third, the value of those who are affected by its message. The best of men, the prophets and apostles, administered it, and the best of all creatures, the angels, admired it.

The Prime Author of the Gospel

The prime author is the Spirit of God through the prophets (verse 11) and the apostles (verse 12). **The Spirit of Christ** (verse 11) is the same **Holy Spirit** mentioned in verse 12 who was **sent from heaven** to come upon Christ's disciples after he had ascended to glory. He is also the one who spoke through the prophets before Christ descended to earth.

The Holy Spirit is in himself holiness and also the source of holiness. He is the author of this holy doctrine that breathes nothing but holiness and urges it most strongly on all who receive it.

Concerning the mysteries of salvation, it is the very life of divine faith to firmly believe the prophets' revelation through the Spirit of God. The Word testifies to this and carries the living stamp of divine inspiration, though there must be a spiritual eye to discern it. A blind person only knows the sun is shining at noon if he is told about it by other people. But those who are most sure about the sun's shining have seen it and know for certain because of its light. To ask someone who is a true believer, "How do you know that the Scriptures are divine?" is the same question as, "How do you know that light is light?"

The soul is nothing but darkness and blindness within until that Spirit who shines outside in the Word shines in the same way inside and brings in the light. Once this has happened, the Word is read and understood with the assistance of the same Spirit through whom it was written, and the soul knows that the Word is divine. God's Spirit within makes himself discernible in the Word. All arguments, all books and study, cannot bring this about. It is a gift for those who believe. "It has been granted to you . . ." (Philippians 1:29).

"No one knows the thoughts of God except the Spirit of God" (1

Corinthians 2:11). How does that apply here? If a person speaks out about the things that are in his spirit, others will know about them. But the apostle's aim here is to conclude that the things of God, even those revealed in his Word, could not be known except through his own Spirit. So although they are revealed, they remain unrevealed until the Spirit teaches us from within as well as from outside. So learn to distrust your own selves and to discover your own unbelief, that you may desire this Spirit to teach you inwardly those great mysteries that he outwardly reveals and teaches through his Word. Make use of the promise, and press the Lord with it, "All your sons will be taught by the LORD" (Isaiah 54:13; see also John 6:45).

The Subject of the Gospel

The subject of this teaching is seen in three different expressions. First, its goal: **concerning this salvation** (verse 10); second, the means: **the sufferings of Christ**; and, third, the doctrine of grace, from which both salvation and Christ's sufferings spring.

1. The Gospel is the doctrine of **salvation**, the only true teaching of true happiness, which the wisest of natural men have groped and sought after with much earnestness, but with no success. They had nothing other than the dark moonlight of nature, and that is not sufficient. Only the sun of righteousness shining in the sphere of the Gospel helps here, for it "brought life and immortality to light through the gospel" (2 Timothy 1:10). It is little wonder that natural wisdom, even at its most profound, is far from finding out about the true cure, since it cannot find out what the disease is that affects miserable mankind—that is, the sinful condition of nature resulting from the very first disobedience.

Salvation not only expresses what is negative (what we are saved from), but also positive (perfect happiness). So in Scripture forgiveness of sins often stands for the whole nature of justification. It is easier to say what this inexpressible happiness is not than what it is. It includes a future complete and final freedom from all enemies or afflictions. All tears will then be wiped away, and their fountain dried up. All dread, of even the least danger or evil, all fear of either sin or punishment, is then banished forever. There will in that day be no invasions, no robberies, no destroying in all the holy mountain. On this earth the best we have alternates between mornings of joy and evenings of crying, but in heaven there will be no light or any need for the sun or the moon. "The city does not need the sun or the moon to shine on it, for the glory of God gives it light, and the Lamb is its lamp" (Revelation 21:23). Well may the apostle, as he does throughout this chapter, present this salvation as a counterbalance to all sorrows and persecutions. The soul that is persuaded of this can enjoy calm, even in the midst of storms. The believer can grow richer through all losses and through death will come into immortal life.

2. The Gospel is represented as the doctrine of **the sufferings of Christ and the glories that would follow** (verse 11), the means of salvation. The person who brings about this salvation, whom the prophets and apostles make the sum of all their teaching, is Jesus Christ, in his humiliation and in his exaltation. This serves as an encouragement to Christians in their sufferings, for this is the way through which their Lord went to his glory. Because the sufferings and glory of our Redeemer are the main subject of the Gospel, they should be in our thinking much more than they are. Each day we should consider the bitterness of the cup Christ drank for us. We speak about these things now and again, but do they sink deep into our minds? Are we possessed with love for him? Oh, that these things were engraved on our hearts and that sin was crucified in us. "May I never boast except in the cross of our Lord Jesus Christ, through which the world has been crucified to me, and I to the world" (Galatians 6:14). We should train our eyes to be fixed on the place where Christ is. We need to see his glory and desire to be glorified with him. "Since, then, you have been raised with Christ, set your hearts on things above, where Christ is seated at the right hand of God. Set your minds on things above, not on earthly things" (Colossians 3:1-2).

3. The third expression here about the Gospel is that it is the doctrine of grace. The work of redemption itself and its different parts, and the teaching revealing it, all have the name of grace, because they all flow from the free, undeserved kindness of God. Grace is the spring and first cause of salvation.

This is why the doctrine of salvation is so comforting—it is free. "For it is by grace you have been saved" (Ephesians 2:8). This wonderful grace brings salvation as soon as we believe. Believe in Jesus for salvation, and live accordingly, and it is done. There is nothing more required for your pardon, but only that you receive it by faith. Truly nature cannot do this. It is just as impossible for us by ourselves to believe as it is impossible for us to achieve salvation by ourselves. This, then, makes it all grace from start to finish. God not only saves us once we believe, but he gives belief itself as a gift. Christ is not only called the "author and perfecter" of our salvation but "of our faith" (Hebrews 12:2).

Free grace, once correctly accepted, supports the heart in all circumstances and keeps us from fainting, even at the saddest of times. I do not look for comfort from myself, but from my God and his free grace. In him is enough comfort for every moment. When all seems to be going well, I should not, I dare not, rely on myself. When things are at their worst, I can and should rely on Christ and his grace, which is always enough. Even if I am the vilest sinner who ever came to him, I know that he is more gracious than I am sinful. The greater my sin is, the more glory it will bring him for his grace to pardon it. God's grace will be seen in an even brighter light.

David argues: "For the sake of your name, O LORD, forgive my iniquity, though it is great" (Psalm 25:11). But it is fruitless to consider grace in a general way. We must view grace as personally applying to us. It is not enough just to listen to it being spoken about. We must embrace it for ourselves.

Consider whether you have welcomed this grace or not, whether it has come to you and into you or not. As our Saviour says, "The kingdom of God is within you" (Luke 17:21). It is a terrible thing to be not far from the kingdom of heaven and yet to fall short and miss it. The grace of God revealed in the Gospel is entreating you daily to receive it, and it will become yours if you do not reject it. Were your eyes open to see the beauty and excellency of God's grace, you would not deliberate about making the decision. May you desire your eyes to be opened and enlightened from above, that you may know grace and have your hearts opened, that you may be happy by receiving it.

An apostle, speaking about Jesus Christ as the foundation of our faith, calls him "the same yesterday and today and forever" (Hebrews 13:8). "Yesterday," under the law; "today," in those times closest to his incarnation; and "forever," in all succeeding ages. Here we see that the things the prophets foretold and the things the apostles reported were the same, for they came from the same Spirit. Both cited **the sufferings of Christ and the glories that would follow** (verse 11). In this is our salvation by free grace.

The Ministers of Salvation

We have already spoken about the Author and the subject of this salvation. Now we will say something of those who are used to administer it. These are **the prophets**, the apostles, and the **angels**. The first foretold what was to come, the second preached them when they happened, and the third viewed these things with delight.

Concerning **the prophets** we note three things: first, their diligence; second, the success of the work; and third, the extent of its usefulness.

1. The diligence of the prophets takes nothing away from their extraordinary visions and revelations, or the Spirit of Christ who was in them when they foretold what would happen. It was their constant duty to search into divine mysteries through meditation and prayer and through reading holy writers who already existed. Daniel did this: "In the first year of his [Darius'] reign, I, Daniel, understood from the Scriptures, according to the word of the LORD given to Jeremiah the prophet, that the desolation of Jerusalem would last seventy years" (Daniel 9:2). "Prophecy only comes to a man who is great in wisdom and virtue, whose affections are not given over to worldly things, since through his knowledge he always overcomes his desires. On such a holy man the Holy Spirit comes down, and his soul is associated with angels, and he is changed into another man"

(Maimonides). The Holy Spirit brings light, and the holy prophets are inspired with it. So they knew their duty was to search the mysteries about salvation, which they were inspired to foretell. So they prayed, searched, waited for answers, studied, and opened up passages, as it were, upon which the beams of divine revelations could come. "I will listen to what God the LORD will say" (Psalm 85:8). "I will look to see what he will say to me" (Habakkuk 2:1).

The prophets who had God's Spirit in a special way were not exempt from the hard work of study and inquiry. Thus, how out of place are slothfulness and idleness in us. Some may say this only concerns those who follow on in the work of the prophets and apostles, that is, the ministers of the Gospel. And it is indeed necessary for them to act in this way. They should be diligent, as the apostle Paul exhorted Timothy: "Devote yourself to the public reading of Scripture" (1 Timothy 4:13). Above everything, ministers should study and have a personal knowledge of God and his Son Jesus Christ; and to achieve this, to free themselves, as much as possible from lower things, they must search into the heavenly mysteries. As ministers are called "angels" (see Revelation 2:1), this is what they should be, messengers who are in constant close contact with God.

"The LORD confides in those who fear him" (Psalm 25:14). The Lord will reveal himself and his saving truths to those who humbly seek him. So none of us should stop ourselves from searching and studying, as the prophets did. Our Saviour says, ". . . diligently study the Scriptures" (John 5:39). The reason for this is because "by them you possess eternal life." Eternal life is indeed to be found there. Christ, of whom the Scriptures speak, is our salvation and eternal life. Christ himself adds, "These are the Scriptures that testify about me" (verse 39). These are the gold mines where alone the abiding treasures of eternity are found and therefore are worthy of all the digging and trouble we can take with them.

In addition to the industrious way the prophets searched and studied, their strong affection and longings are seen. They desired and longed to see the day of Christ. "Your father Abraham rejoiced at the thought of seeing my day; he saw it and was glad" (John 8:56).

2. The success of their search is shown. Through the Spirit they prophesied about salvation and grace, when it would happen and what would happen. They **spoke of the grace that was to come to you** (verse 10). They were **trying to find out the time and circumstances to which the Spirit of Christ in them was pointing when he predicted the sufferings of Christ and the glories that would follow** (verse 11). They indeed prophesied very clearly about Christ's sufferings and **the glories that would follow** (see Psalm 22 and Isaiah 53). Our Saviour himself made use of their testimony in both matters: "'How foolish you are, and how slow of heart to believe all that the prophets have spoken! Did not the Christ

have to suffer these things and then enter his glory?' And beginning with Moses and all the Prophets, he explained to them what was said in all the Scriptures concerning himself" (Luke 24:25-27).

3. Their search is seen in the extent of its beneficial results. **It was revealed to them that they were not serving themselves but you, when they spoke of the things that have now been told you by those who have preached the gospel to you by the Holy Spirit sent from heaven. Even angels long to look into these things** (verse 12). This benefited the believers in the times of the apostles and the Christian church in the succeeding days and benefits us today. But in some special way the prophets ministered to the people in those times when Christ suffered and entered into his glory, for they were the first to enjoy the fulfillment of these prophecies.

The prophets were fully aware that the things they prophesied would not be fulfilled in their own times, and so **they were not serving themselves but you.** All the gifts of the Holy Spirit, the calling of the prophets, apostles, and evangelists, and the ordinary ministry of the Gospel through pastors and teachers accomplish God's great plan to build up his church. "It was he who gave some to be apostles, some to be prophets, some to be evangelists, and some to be pastors and teachers, to prepare God's people for works of service, so that the body of Christ may be built up until we all reach unity in the faith and in the knowledge of the Son of God and become mature, attaining to the whole measure of the fullness of Christ" (Ephesians 4:11-13).

Now we consider the **angels**, who not only administer this salvation but also take delight in it. The cherubim wonder how guilty people escape their flaming swords and come back into paradise. The angels see that their companions who fell from grace are not restored and yet behold heaven filled with the spirits of the just. **Even angels long to look into these things** (verse 12). This is added in verse 12 to show how wonderful the Gospel is. The angels look with delight on what they have already seen fulfilled. They do not just glance at this, but they fix their gaze on it. This "mystery of godliness," the apostle Paul says, "was seen by angels" (1 Timothy 3:16). The Word made flesh draws the eyes of those glorious spirits, and they wonder to see the Almighty Godhead joined with the weakness of a man—indeed, of an infant. He who laid out the heavens was bound up in swaddling clothes. It is no wonder that the angels admire these things and delight to look on them. They look at them steadfastly, and yet men neglect them. We either do not think about them at all, or we just give them a cursory glance. We see here excellent company and the examples of not only the best of men, but lessons that the angels teach us. All souls should delight themselves in Jesus Christ and in the redemption he has brought us.

Verse 13

Therefore, prepare your minds for action; be self-controlled; set your hope fully on the grace to be given you when Jesus Christ is revealed.

The great error of the human mind and the reason for all our mistakes in life comes when the soul moves away from God and turns to inferior comforts. This wrong choice is the root of all our miseries. So the main purpose of the holy Word of God is to disentangle people's hearts from the world and turn them to God as their only rest and lasting comfort. This is the subject of this verse and the goal of the preceding verses. It all meets in the exhortation, **prepare your minds for action.**

There are three things to note in this verse. First, the great comfort provided for the soul, which the apostle repeats and presents to his persecuted brethren; second, the apostle's exhortation to understand this correctly and to confidently expect it; and, third, the inference of that exhortation.

Comfort for the Soul

The great subject of their comfort is **the grace to be given you when Jesus Christ is revealed.** This may refer to the doctrine of grace in the Gospel, in which Jesus Christ is revealed, and the grace in him. It may also refer to the grace of salvation that is to be completed at the last and clearest revelation of Jesus Christ, which is not given the name "merit" despite all the obedience and sufferings the saints have gone through. Even the salvation to be **revealed** to them is called grace. The grace through which anyone serves and obeys God is also a gift from God. "Everything comes from you, and we have given you only what comes from your hand" (1 Chronicles 29:14). Both the ability to give and the desire to give are from God. God's initial grace is freely given, and so is his successive grace.

When Jesus Christ is revealed. This is repeated from verse 7. In Romans 2:5 this is said to be "the day of God's wrath, when his righteous judgment will be revealed." All this is the revelation of Jesus Christ. Therefore it is a day of grace, and all light and blessedness to those who are in Christ, because they will appear with him. If Christ is glorious, they will not be without honor and ashamed. If we were then to be confronted by our secret sins and have them exposed to the view of everyone, who could look forward to that day? This is how all unbelieving people view that day, and so they find it most frightening. But those who are in the shadow of the robe of righteous Jesus and who are made one with him will take part in his glory when he appears. This is the most comforting thought our souls can entertain as we remember the glorious revelation of our Redeemer.

As this is the day of Christ's revelation, it is also the revelation of the adopted children of God, who are all in Christ. They are thought of as rubbish in the eyes of the world and are exposed to all kinds of contempt.

But at Christ's revelation his beams of glory will make them beautiful, and they will be known as his. "Dear friends, now we are children of God, and what we will be has not yet been made known. But we know that when he appears, we shall be like him, for we shall see him as he is" (1 John 3:2). "When Christ, who is your life, appears, then you also will appear with him in glory" (Colossians 3:4).

The Exhortation Itself

Next comes the exhortation itself, through which the apostle stirs them up to rightly appreciate and be confident about this grace: **set your hope.** The difference between the two graces of faith and hope is so small that the one is often taken for the other in Scripture. Each is but a different aspect of the same confidence. Faith understands the infallible truth of those divine promises of which hope does definitely expect the accomplishment. Faith establishes the heart on Jesus Christ, and hope lifts it above the head of all dangers, crosses, and temptations and sees the glory and happiness that come after them.

Fully. "To the end" (KJV). This word literally means "perfectly." Christians seek most earnestly and wait most patiently. "My soul waits for the LORD more than watchmen wait for the morning, more than watchmen wait for the morning" (Psalm 130:6). Worldly hopes are by their very nature imperfect. They imply doubt and wavering because they are built on inconsistencies, doubts, and uncertainties and because they are full of deceit and disappointments. How can that kind of hope be immovable since it is built on moving sands? What is itself not secure cannot give stability to anything resting on it.

But because the truth and goodness of the immutable God are the foundation of spiritual hope, that hope is assured and cannot be moved. "Those who trust in the LORD are like Mount Zion, which cannot be shaken but endures forever" (Psalm 125:1). Now the apostle exhorts his brothers to have their hearts full of **hope.** Since this **hope** is in itself perfect and firm, Peter wants them to aspire to it. When this **hope** is acted on, it becomes stronger.

Prepare your minds for action; be self-controlled. These words of exhortation are stated to make this **hope** more complete and secure. A similar exhortation is given by our Saviour about waiting for his coming: "Be dressed ready for service and keep your lamps burning" (Luke 12:35). The Israelites were to eat the Passover in a similar state of readiness, as they were expecting their deliverance: "This is how you are to eat it: with your cloak tucked into your belt, your sandals on your feet and your staff in your hand. Eat it in haste; it is the LORD's Passover" (Exodus 12:11). We are expecting our complete and final freedom.

If you want to enjoy this **hope** fully, cut off your affections for other things. The same eye cannot look up to heaven and down to earth at the same time. The more your affections are disentangled from the world, the more they can be actively engaged in this **hope**. The more sober they are, the less they will fill themselves with the coarse delights of earth, and the more room they will have to be filled with this **hope**. "Do not get drunk on wine, which leads to debauchery. Instead, be filled with the Spirit" (Ephesians 5:18).

Be self-controlled, or "watch." The same word means both, and for a very good reason, for you know that a drunkard cannot keep watch. The apostle Paul says, "Everyone who competes in the games goes into strict training" (1 Corinthians 9:25). Take to heart our Saviour's exhortation: "Therefore keep watch, because you do not know the day or the hour" (Matthew 25:13).

The opposite of this is described elsewhere. "He is a double-minded man, unstable in all he does," says St. James (James 1:8). Although the word translated "unstable" usually means deceitfulness, here I think it has a different meaning that fits in with what the apostle is saying. It implies doubt and an unsettled wavering mind. In religion the main thing is to have the heart fixed in the belief and hope of the great things we look for. This will strengthen our resolve and make us stronger to face suffering.

Prepare your minds for action. "Gird up the loins" (KJV). The custom in those countries was to wear long garments that were tucked in for work or for a journey. Chastity is indeed a Christian grace and a great part of the soul's freedom and spiritualness and fits it for divine things, but I do not think that is what this expression means, as St. Jerome and others have said. For while the girding of the "loins" seems to favor that sense, it is only an allusion to a way of tucking in clothes. And besides that, the apostle makes it clear that he means something else, for he says, **your minds** are to be prepared or girded up. "Gather up your affections so they do not hang down to hamper you in your race and your hopes of winning. Do not just gather them up, but tie them up, so they will not fall down again. Be ready like people who are about to set off on a journey." Our home is not on this earth; so our affections must not keep dragging us down.

People who are completely earthly and profane are so far from preparing their **minds for action** that they set themselves totally on this earth. The highest part of their soul is glued to the earth, and they take part in the serpent's curse each day as they go around on their stomachs eating the dust. "Their destiny is destruction, their god is their stomach, and their glory is in their shame. Their mind is on earthly things" (Philippians 3:19). This disposition is inconsistent with grace. To travel through this sinful world in a godly way we must gird up our affections completely.

The Inference

The apostle's exhortation is followed by the inference that he draws from all the doctrine of his preceding discourse. **Set your hope fully on the**

grace to be given you. This perfect **hope** is strengthened by his whole argument, for we may fix our hope on that happiness to which we are appointed in God's eternal election (verse 2), and to which we are born through our new birth (verses 3-4) and for which we are preserved by his almighty power (verse 5). We cannot be deprived of our joy and comfort in the assurance of this hope (verses 6-9). And we are taught the greatness of that blessed salvation by the doctrine of the prophets and apostles and the admiration of angels, and all these combine to confirm our hope, to make it perfect and help us persevere to the end.

We also learn from the previous teaching that this earth is the place of our trial and conflict, and the place of our rest is above. We must here have our minds ready for action, but when we come there, we may wear our long, white robes at their full length, for there is nothing there except peace. There is no danger of defilement, for there are no unclean things there. Indeed, the streets of the new Jerusalem are paved with gold. To Christ, then, who has prepared that city for us, let us always give praise.

Verses 14-16

As obedient children, do not conform to the evil desires you had when you lived in ignorance. But just as he who called you is holy, so be holy in all you do; for it is written: "Be holy, because I am holy."

"Your word is a lamp to my feet and a light for my path," says David (Psalm 119:105). The light does not just comfort the eyes—it is a guide for the feet. Thus here the apostle does not just furnish consolation against distress but exhorts and directs his brothers to walk in the way of holiness, without which the understanding and feeling of those comforts cannot subsist. This is none other than a clearer and fuller expression and further argument for the seriousness and spiritual mind and life that he exhorted in verse 13. "If you wish to enjoy this hope, do not be conformed to the desires of your previous ignorance, but **be holy.**"

There is no doctrine in the world that is either so pleasant or so pure as Christianity. It is matchless, both in its sweetness and its holiness. The faith and hope of a Christian have in them an abiding precious balm of comfort. But this is never to be wasted and poured into the puddle of an impure conscience. "Everyone who has this hope in him purifies himself, just as he is pure" (1 John 3:3). Here in 1 Peter the believers are commanded to **"Be holy, because I am holy."** Faith starts by purifying the heart (see Acts 15:9) as it empties itself of the love for sin and then fills it with the consolation of Christ and the hope of glory.

It is a foolish, groundless fear to imagine that the assured hope of salvation will bring unholiness and presumptuous boldness in sin, and that therefore the doctrine of that assurance is a doctrine of licentiousness. Our apostle, we see, does not take assured hope and holiness as enemies but links them as the closest of friends. They mutually strengthen each other. The more there is assurance about salvation, the more holiness and delight in it and study of it there is.

The apostle issues his exhortation negatively (**do not conform to the evil desires you had**) and positively (**be holy**).

1. The negative part of the exhortation. The apostle wants us to separate from **evil desires.** This is the normal name given in Scripture to all the irregular and sinful desires of the heart. This includes the polluted habits of the heart, both from within and also as they reveal themselves outwardly in the lives of men. The apostle John calls it "the world and its desires" (1 John 2:17) and says, "Do not love the world or anything in the world" (verse 15). Then the apostle John says this has three branches, a base anti-trinity that the world worships: "the cravings of sinful man, the lust of his eyes and the boasting of what he has and does" (verse 16).

The soul of an unconverted person is nothing other than a den of impure desires, where pride, uncleanness, avarice, and malice live. It is like Babylon: "With her the kings of the earth committed adultery and the inhabitants of the earth were intoxicated with the wine of her adulteries" (Revelation 17:2). "Desert creatures will lie there, jackals will fill her houses; there the owls will dwell, and there the wild goats will leap about" (Isaiah 13:21). If people had their eyes opened, they would find their position as abhorrent as living in a house full of snakes and serpents, as Augustine has said. The first part of conversion is to rid the soul of these dreadful inhabitants, for no one at all is naturally free from them. Thus the apostle here says to the believers he is writing to that these **evil desires** were theirs when they **lived in ignorance.** There is a deep truth implied here. All sins come from some kind of **ignorance**, or at least from turning the mind away from the light. Thus the results of sin are all called "the works of darkness," for if sin was seen in full light, undressed and unpainted, it would be impossible for any soul to be in love with it. Rather, we would run away from such a hideous abomination.

But because the soul is not renewed and is in complete darkness, it has **evil desires** and a love for sin. There is no order there because there is no light there. It is like the beginning of the world, when confusion and darkness were together, and "darkness was over the surface of the deep" (Genesis 1:2). It is the same with the soul. The more ignorance there is, the more evil desires reside there.

The light that frees the soul and rescues it from the kingdom of darkness must be beyond what can be attained by nature. All the light of philosophy, natural and moral, is not sufficient. Indeed, even knowledge of God's law, apart from Christ, does not enlighten and renew the soul from the darkness and **ignorance** spoken of here. For our apostle writes to Jews who knew the law and who were taught in it before their conversion, and yet he calls those times when Christ was not known to them a time when they **lived in ignorance**. Even when the stars shine most brightly and there is a full moon, that does not make it daytime. It is night until the sun appears. Therefore, the Hebrew commentators said of Solomon's words, "Vanity of vanities, all is vanity": "Vain even the law, until Messiah come." Therefore, about the Messiah Zechariah says, ". . . because of the tender mercy of our God, by which the rising sun will come to us from heaven to shine on those living in darkness and in the shadow of death, to guide our feet into the path of peace" (Luke 1:78-79).

A person without the Spirit may acquire a great deal of knowledge about the teaching of Christ and talk about it very confidently, and yet his soul may still be in the chains of darkness, locked in by the **ignorance** mentioned here, so that he still has **evil desires**. The saving light of faith is a beam from the Sun of Righteousness himself. Christ sends this into the soul, and through it he makes the soul discern his incomparable beauties and through that sight alienates it from all those sinful desires, which then are seen for what they are. Their vileness and filthiness is shown so that the soul wonders how it ever loved such base rubbish for so long and resolves now to choose Jesus Christ. "You are the most excellent of men and your lips have been anointed with grace, since God has blessed you forever" (Psalm 45:2). "The Son is the radiance of God's glory and the exact representation of his being" (Hebrews 1:3).

Once the soul is acquainted with Christ, the person disdains and turns away from all sins and orders them to leave. He can now tell them, after his view of Christ, that they no longer have any hold on his heart.

The apostle emphasizes this exhortation in this way: "It is true that the **evil desires** and vanities that are in the world were with you, but that was when you were blind. They were the **evil desires** of your **ignorance**. But now you know how inappropriate they are in the light of the Gospel that you now profess and that inner light of faith that is in the souls of those who really believe. Therefore, since you have renounced them, keep them away from you. Never allow them to live with you again." As St. Paul says, "Have nothing to do with the fruitless deeds of darkness, but rather expose them" (Ephesians 5:11). "Let the light of your holy life expose their evil."

2. The positive part of the apostle's exhortation: **"Be holy."** This includes the former, the renouncing of the evil desires and pollutions of the world, both in heart and life. Now that they have been evicted, they must be replaced with the beautifying graces of God's Spirit. These graces are to permeate one's private and public life.

But just as he who called you is holy. "Consider whom you belong to, and then you will not be able to deny that you should be holy. Think about how closely related you are to the holy God." This is expressed in two ways, namely, as . . . children, and as he who called you. This is like saying, "He gave birth to you." The outward calling of those who profess Christ presses holiness upon them, but the inner calling does so even more. "You were heading for destruction in your life of sin, and then you heard the voice of the Gospel preached, which spoke to your heart and called you back from the way of death to the way of holiness, which is the only way of life. Christ has separated you from the profane world and picked you out to be a jewel for himself. He has set you apart for this purpose, that you may be **holy** to him."

The Hebrew word for holiness means "setting apart" or making suitable for a particular use. "So do not be untrue to Christ's purpose for you." "For God did not call us to be impure, but to live a holy life" (1 Thessalonians 4:7). Therefore, "**be holy.**" "It is a sacrilege if you allow yourself to run after the impure ways of the world since you are consecrated to God himself."

As . . . children. This links with verse 3 where we give thanks to God because "he has given us new birth." The **therefore** of verse 13 turns this into an exhortation. "Seeing that you are, through a spiritual and new birth, the children of so great and good a Father, who commands you to be holy, be **obedient children** and **be holy.** Since God himself is most holy, be like him as his children. **Be holy, because I am holy.**"

As obedient children. The opposite phrase is used by the apostle Paul: "those who are disobedient" (Ephesians 2:2). This Hebrew way of speaking—children of obedience and children of disobedience—indicates a high degree of obedience or disobedience most emphatically. Of all children, the children of God are most obligated to obedience, for God is both the wisest and most loving of fathers, and the sum of all his commands is for their glory and happiness, that they might endeavor to be like him, to resemble their heavenly Father. Our Saviour says, "Be perfect, therefore, as your heavenly Father is perfect" (Matthew 5:48). And here the apostle is quoting the law: "I am the LORD your God; consecrate yourselves and be holy, because I am holy" (Leviticus 11:44). Law and Gospel agree about this.

Again, children who resemble their fathers become more like them as they grow up. Thus the children of God increase in their likeness to the heavenly Father and are daily more and more renewed after his likeness. There is in them an innate likeness because of his image stamped upon them. There is a constant increase of this likeness through their pious imitation of him, which they are exhorted to do here.

The imitation of vicious people and the corrupt world is forbidden here. The imitation of people's ungodly customs is base and servile, but the imitation of the virtues of good people is commendable. But the imitation of this highest pattern, of the goodness of the most holy God, is the supreme way of living. The essence of true religion consists in the imitation of him whom we worship. All of us offer him some kind of worship, but few seriously study and endeavor to attain this blessed conformity.

There is unquestionably among those who profess to be God's people a select number who are indeed his children and bear his image in their hearts and in their lives. This stamp of holiness is on their souls and their way of living. But most people have only "a form of godliness ... denying its power" (2 Timothy 3:5). We speak about holiness, we hear about holiness, and we may commend holiness, but we do not act holy. Or if we do, it is just an act, like an impersonation on a stage. A child is genuinely like his father when his face not only looks like him but, more importantly, when his mind or inner disposition is like him. Thus the true children of God are like their heavenly Father in their words and in their actions, but most of all in their heart.

It does not matter that the profane world, which hates God so much that it cannot endure his image, mocks and reviles us. It is our honor to be, as David said, "more undignified" (2 Samuel 6:22) as we grow still more like God in holiness. The worldly man may think we are odd and too narrow-minded, but it is because he does not know anything except the model of holiness he has set himself, and so he approves nothing that is higher than that. He does not know God and so does not discern and esteem what is most like him.

"Because I am holy." People compare themselves with other people, and usually with the worst people, and so flatter themselves that they are better than they really are. Looking into the muddy waters of the lives of evil people is not the right way to see our faults. Instead, we should look into the clear fountain of the Word. Considering the infinite holiness of God will humble us in the dust. When Isaiah saw the glory of the Lord and heard the seraphim cry, "Holy, holy, holy," he cried out about his own and the people's unholiness, "Woe to me! . . . I am ruined! For I am a man of unclean lips, and I live among a people of unclean lips, and my eyes have seen the King, the LORD Almighty" (Isaiah 6:3, 5).

Verse 17

Since you call on a Father who judges each man's work impartially, live your lives as strangers here in reverent fear.

The temptations that meet Christians in the world, to turn them away from the path of obedience and holiness, either present the hope of some apparent good, to draw them from the right way, or the fear of some evil, to drive them from their path. Therefore the Word of God often strengthens the Christian mind against these two tendencies. It does this through pointing to the hopes and fears of a higher nature, which far surpass sin's lures or fears. The most frequent attacks of temptation are on these two passions of the mind—hope and fear. So they are defended with a hope and a fear so strong that they are able to resist all attacks. Thus our apostle here urges, first, the **hope** of that glory that the Gospel expounds (verse 13), which is more than the world can ever offer, both in the greatness and in the certainty of its promises; and, second, the fear of God, the most just Judge, **who judges** and who alone is to be feared and reverenced. The worst anger in all the world is nothing compared with God's tiniest displeasure. In verse 17 we have, first, this fear, second, the reason enforcing it, and, third, its term or continuance.

1. The fear itself: **in reverent fear.** How does this link up with the previous verses and the assured hope of love and joy and inexpressible glory? All these excellencies fall, as it were, into a dungeon when **fear** is mentioned after them. Did not the apostle John say that "perfect love drives out fear" (1 John 4:18)? Is not fear completely counter to perfect or assured hope, and to faith and joy as well?

In actuality this **fear** is no handicap but rather preserves those other graces and the comfort and the joy that come from them. They all agree so well with it that they naturally help each other.

It is superfluous to insist on a definition of this passion of **fear** with the countless distinctions that philosophers and theologians have made. The **fear** that is commended here is, undoubtedly, a holy fear of offending God. This is not merely made up of assured hope of salvation along with faith, love, and spiritual joy, but is their inseparable companion. All divine graces are linked together, and they grow or die together. The more a Christian believes and loves and rejoices in God's love, the more reluctant he is to displease God. This **fear** is the right way to live—running away from sin and from temptations to sin, and resisting all temptation when it attacks. This is a guard for the soul that keeps a lookout for all enemies and anything that may disturb the soul. Thus inner peace is preserved, the assurance of faith and hope is unmolested, and joy remains untouched. But all this is in danger when a proper **fear** disappears, for then some great sin or other easily breaks in, puts everything into confusion, and makes it seem as if these graces do not exist.

It is no wonder, then, that the apostle, having stirred up his Christian brothers to seek to be rich in these jewels of faith, hope, love, and spiritual joy and then, considering that they journey through a world of thieves and robbers—no wonder, I say, that he adds this thought of keeping the jewels they have in their possession, under God, under the trustworthy and watchful grace of godly **fear.** Having earnestly exhorted them to holiness, he quite rightly moves on to this particular **fear** that is such an integral part of holiness that it is often substituted for it in Scripture.

Solomon calls this fear of and reverence for God "the beginning of wisdom" (Proverbs 9:10). The word *fear* there signifies both fear and wisdom. The beginning of it is the beginning of wisdom, and the progress and increase of it is the increase of wisdom. That hardy rashness that some count as valor is the companion of ignorance; and of all rashness, boldness to sin is the most foolish. There is in this fear of God, as in all fear, an understanding of evil, of which we are daily in danger. The godly man judges wisely, seeing the truth that sin is the greatest of evils and the reason for all other evils or difficulties. It is a breaking of God's just law and so provokes his just anger and the punishments, temporal, spiritual, and eternal, that he inflicts. Considering how certain he is to punish, considering both the power and the reach of his hand, that it is both very strong and unavoidable, all these things may and should produce this **fear.**

Though it is not restricted to this, the genuine fear of God's children, who call him Father, does not exclude the consideration of his justice and the punishment of sin that his justice inflicts. We see here, as a great incentive for this fear, that he **judges each man's work impartially.** David, in the Psalms, when he speaks about the sweet affections of love, hope, and delight in God and his Word, also speaks all the time about the justice of God. "My flesh trembles in fear of you; I stand in awe of your laws" (Psalm 119:120). The body should be in awe of divine judgment, even though the higher and purer part of the soul is strongly and freely tied with the cords of love. Temporal corrections are not feared so much in themselves except insofar as they are impressions of wrath that may come upon us for our sins. "O LORD, do not rebuke me in your anger or discipline me in your wrath" (Psalm 6:1). This is the main matter of believers' fear, because their happiness is in God's love and the light of his countenance. They do not worry about what the world thinks of them. They do not care who frowns on them, for no enemy or evil in the world can deprive them of spiritual health except their own sin. Therefore, that is what they fear most.

The Christian has good reason to fear that he is in danger, considering the number and strength of his enemies. He realizes he is unable to resist them in his own strength. His sad experience in being often foiled teaches him that this is the case. He discovers how often even his own resolve deceives him. Certainly a godly man is sometimes driven to wonder at his own frailty and inconstancy. To the unspiritual man it seems an odd kind of logic that the apostle Paul should say, "Work out your own salvation with fear and trembling, for it is God who works in you to will and to act according to his good purpose" (Philippians 2:12-13). Such a person thinks that you may stop working and sit still, or if you do work, you must work fearlessly. But the apostle Paul puts the two together.

Why should the person who is certain about his salvation fear? If there is truth in his assurance, nothing can disappoint him, not even sin itself. This is true, but it is no less true that if he has no fear of sinning, there is no truth in his assurance. From this **fear** have sprung all the patient sufferings of the saints and martyrs of God. Because they dare not sin against God, they are prepared to be imprisoned, impoverished, and tortured and even to die for him. Thus the prophet Isaiah sets earthly and godly fear as opposites: "Do not call conspiracy everything that these people call conspiracy; do not fear what they fear, and do not dread it. The LORD Almighty is the one you are to regard as holy, he is the one you are to fear, he is the one you are to dread" (Isaiah 8:12-13).

Our Saviour has said, "I tell you, my friends, do not be afraid of those who kill the body and after that can do no more. But I will show you whom you should fear: Fear him who, after the killing of the body, has power to throw you into hell. Yes, I tell you, fear him" (Luke 12:4-5). "Fear not, but fear. Fear, so that you may not fear." Moses was bold and fearless when dealing with a proud and wicked king, but when God appeared he said, "I am trembling with fear" (Hebrews 12:21).

2. The reason we have to convince Christians about this **fear** is twofold:

First, our relationship to God as Father and Judge: **Since you call on a Father who judges** . . . "Because you call him Father and profess to be his children, born again by him"—this verse looks back to that expression— "it becomes you, as obedient children, to stand in awe and fear of him, so that you will not offend him, a Father who is so full of goodness and tender love. He is the best Father, but remember that he is also the greatest and most just Judge, **who judges each man's work impartially**."

God always sees and discerns men and all their deeds, and he **judges**, that is, takes account of them. He sometimes pronounces his judgment on them in this life. But the most solemn judgment of all is reserved for that great day that he has appointed. "For he has set a day when he will judge the world with justice by the man he has appointed" (Acts 17:31).

Who judges each man's work impartially. We see here the sovereignty of this Judge, the universality of his judgment, and the fairness of his judgment. Everyone must answer at his great court. He is supreme Judge of the world. He made the world and therefore has the unquestionable right to judge it. He **judges each man's work**, and his judgment is the most righteous judgment in two ways. First, it is based on an exact and perfect knowledge of everyone's deeds; second, it is impartial judgment. Totally unlike the crooked rule of human judgment, it will be impartial. ". . . who shows no partiality to princes and does not favor the rich over the poor" (Job 34:19). The reason for this is then given: "for they are all the work of his hands." God made everyone, so he does not think of them in the same way that we do. We make great distinctions between palaces and cottages, between a prince's robes and a beggar's cloak. But to God they are all one.

All these petty differences vanish in comparison with his own greatness. People are great and small when they are compared with each other. But they amount to nothing when compared with God. We find high mountains and low valleys on this earth, but compared with the vast expanse of the heavens, it is all but a dot and is not great at all.

Who judges each man's work. This includes all actions and words, as well as all thoughts. In the great judgment all secret things will be revealed. As all secret things are already open to the eye of this Judge, so they will then be opened to all people and angels. May we let the all-seeing Judge, and the great judgment day, wean our hearts from sin and make us **fear.** "For we must all appear before the judgment seat of Christ, that each one may receive what is due him for the things done while in the body, whether good or bad. Since, then, we know what it is to fear the Lord, we try to persuade men" (2 Corinthians 5:10-11). If you want to have confidence on that day and not fear it when it comes, fear it now, so that you avoid sin. Those who tremble now will, when judgment comes, lift up their faces with joy. Those who do not fear this now will on judgment day be overwhelmed with fear and terror.

Live your lives as strangers here in reverent fear. There is another reason implied here why Christians should fear: it is because of their relationship with this world. They are **strangers.** This is not their permanent home. Thus watchful fear is appropriate for their journey. Perfect peace and security are reserved for them in heaven, and that is the end result of this **fear.** Throughout this life this **fear** continues, and it will end only when we die.

3. This, then, is the term or continuance of this fear: "Blessed is the man who always fears the LORD," says Solomon (Proverbs 28:14). He should fear God when he is with others, when he is in his own house, and when he is in God's house. We must hear the Word with fear and preach it with fear. We must "serve the LORD with fear and rejoice," yet "with trembling" (Psalm 2:11). This should be so not only when we feel our own weakness most, but when we find ourselves at our strongest. Nobody is so far advanced spiritually here below that he has outgrown his need for this grace. But when our journey is over, and we have arrived home at our Father's house above, then there will be no more fearing. There will be nothing to fear there, and therefore there will be no fear. We shall indeed then, most of all, have a holy reverence of the majesty of God, as the angels have because they see him most clearly and because the more he is known, the more he is reverenced. But the fear that relates to danger will then vanish, for in heaven there is no sin, no sorrow over sin, and no temptation to sin. There are then no more conflicts, but after a final victory only eternal peace and everlasting triumph. Not only fear but faith and hope imply imperfection, which is inconsistent with that blessed state. So all of them,

having achieved their purpose, will end. Faith ends in sight, hope in possession, and fear in perfect safety. Everlasting love and delight will fill the whole soul in a vision of God.

Verses 18-19

For you know that it was not with perishable things such as silver or gold that you were redeemed from the empty way of life handed down to you from your forefathers, but with the precious blood of Christ, a lamb without blemish or defect.

We have here, first, the evil we are delivered from and, second, an exhortation.

1. Our former evil is called **the empty way of life.**

2. **Handed down to you from your forefathers.** This includes not only the superstitions and vain devices in religion, which abounded among the Jews through tradition, but also all the corrupt and sinful habits of their lives. The prophet Ezekiel observes this especially about the Jews: "they had not obeyed my laws but had rejected my decrees and desecrated my Sabbaths, and their eyes lusted after their fathers' idols" (Ezekiel 20:24). This was in spite of a previous warning: "I said to their children in the desert, 'Do not follow the statutes of your fathers or keep their laws or defile yourselves with their idols'" (verse 18). This was the great quarrel the non-Christians had against the Christian religion, that it was new and not known to their fathers. The Church of Rome levels the same accusation against reformed religion. But this is a foolish diversion from the truth.

God's voice makes people leave everything and follow him, as Abraham did. He was called from his family and his father's house to journey toward the land God had promised him. This is what is said to the church, and to each believing soul, by God's Spirit: "Listen, O daughter, consider and give ear: Forget your people and your father's house. The king is enthralled by your beauty; honor him, for he is your lord" (Psalm 45:10-11). Do not pay any attention to what other people think, even if they are closest friends, but only work to please God, and then you will indeed please him.

This exhortation is against all sinful and unholy conversation. The apostle states this very strongly in the words **the empty way of life.** The human mind, the guide and source of human actions, while it is cut off from God is nothing but a center of vanity. The apostle Paul says of the Gentiles that "although they knew God, they neither glorified him as God nor gave thanks to him, but their thinking became futile and their foolish hearts were darkened" (Romans 1:21). This included all their philosophers. The more they tried to be wise, the more foolish they became. This is also said in Ephesians 4:17: "So I tell you this, and insist on it in the Lord, that you must no longer live as the Gentiles do, in the futility of their thinking." In the same way the Lord complains through his prophet Isaiah about the extreme folly of his people: "he feeds on ashes, a deluded heart misleads him" (Isaiah 44:20). Jeremiah has a similar statement: "O Jerusalem, wash the evil from your heart and be saved. How long will you harbor wicked thoughts?" (Jeremiah 4:14).

These are the things that cause **the empty way of life.** As the apostle Paul says, "What benefit did you reap at that time from the things you are now ashamed of? Those things result in death!" (Romans 6:21). Either reckon that shame that comes out of them as their fruit, or confess that they do not have any fruit at all. Therefore, they are called "the fruitless deeds of darkness" (Ephesians 5:11). It is a terrible thing indeed to be deluded for one's whole life by a false dream. "Their land is full of idols; they bow down to the work of their hands, to what their fingers have made" (Isaiah 2:8). The apostle Peter says here, **you were redeemed from the empty way of life.** As the word **empty** implies a fruitless life, so **redeemed** implies they were escaping from a life of slavery. This is the madness of the sinner, that he fancies liberty in what is the worst situation. Those poor frantic people, lying in rags, bound in chains, still manage to imagine that they are kings. They think that their irons are chains of gold, their rags are robes, and their filthy living-place a palace. As it is miserable to live under the sentence of death, so it is slavery to be subject to the dominion of sin. The person who is delivered from one is also delivered from the other. There is a single redemption from both.

The person who is redeemed from destruction by the blood of Christ is also redeemed from that vain and unholy way of life that leads to it. "Who gave himself for us to redeem us from all wickedness and to purify for himself a people that are his very own, eager to do what is good" (Titus 2:14). Our Redeemer was anointed for this reason, not to free the captives from the death sentence but leave them in prison, but to "preach good news to the poor. He has sent me to bind up the brokenhearted, to proclaim freedom for the captives and release for the prisoners" (Isaiah 61:1).

You may easily persuade yourself that Christ has died for you and redeemed you from hell. But you do not consider that if this is so, Christ has also redeemed you from your **empty way of life** and has set you free from serving sin. While you do not experience this, you can have no assurance about the first. If the chains of sin are still around you, for all you know these chains bind you over to other chains of darkness. "For . . . God did not spare angels when they sinned, but sent them to hell, putting them into gloomy dungeons to be held for judgment" (2 Peter 2:4). Let us not delude ourselves. If we find the love of sin and love for the world stronger in our hearts than the love of Christ, we are not yet taking part in his redemption.

But if we have indeed taken hold of Christ as our Redeemer, then we are redeemed from serving sin. "It is for freedom that Christ has set us free. Stand firm, then, and do not let yourselves be burdened again by a yoke of slavery" (Galatians 5:1).

It was not with perishable things such as silver or gold that you were redeemed. In view of the high price of our redemption, the apostle urges us to value it. First, he states this in a negative way: **not with perishable things.** How foolish we are when we search after such items as if they were incorruptible and everlasting treasures. Even the best of them, those that people value most highly, **such as silver or gold**, are of no value at all in ransoming souls. They cannot buy off the death of the body, nor can they purchase any extension to temporal life; much less can they attain the value of spiritual and eternal life.

Second, he states it positively: **but with the precious blood of Christ.** The precious soul could not be redeemed except by blood, and that only by the blood of the spotless Lamb, Jesus Christ, who is God, equal with the Father. No wonder the apostle calls this blood **precious.** It surpasses everything in the whole world as far as value is concerned. Therefore, do not make void the sufferings of Christ for you. If he shed his blood to redeem you from sin, do not be false to his purpose.

A lamb without blemish or defect. Christ is the great and everlasting sacrifice who gave value and virtue to all the sacrifices made under the law. Their blood could not purge sin except through being linked to Christ's blood. The laws about the choice of the paschal lamb or the lambs for other sacrifices were but obscure and imperfect shadows of Christ's purity and perfections, who is the undefiled Lamb of God. "John saw Jesus coming toward him and said, 'Look, the Lamb of God, who takes away the sin of the world!'" (John 1:29). This lamb came meekly and in silence. "He was oppressed and afflicted, yet he did not open his mouth; he was led like a lamb to the slaughter, and as a sheep before her shearers is silent, so he did not open his mouth" (Isaiah 53:7).

For you know. This is what makes all this effective. "You do know it already, but I want you to know it better, more deeply and more personally. Turn it over frequently in your mind, and study it more, and meditate on it more. It is a mystery so deep that you will never fathom it. It is so useful that you will always benefit from it." Our foolishness is that we hanker after new things and so in effect become ignorant about the things we think we know best. That learned apostle Paul, who knew so much, said, "For I resolved to know nothing while I was with you except Jesus Christ and him crucified" (1 Corinthians 2:2). Again, he said that his primary ambition was, "I want to know Christ and the power of his resurrection and the fellowship of sharing in his sufferings, becoming like him in his death" (Philippians 3:10). The person who does not have his evil desires mortified and his heart weaned from the world, even though he knows all the history of the death and sufferings of Jesus Christ and can speak about them, does not truly know about them.

If you want to increase greatly in holiness and be strong against the temptations to sin, this is the only way to achieve it. Look at Christ's death often, and so seek to know about his death. Consider often how much it cost for us to be redeemed from sin, and offer this answer to all the entice-ments of sin and the world: "Except you can offer my soul something greater than the price that was given for it on the cross, I cannot listen to you." "Far be it from me," will a Christian say who considers his redemp-tion, "that I should ever prefer a base evil desire or anything in this world or all of it to him who gave himself to die for me and paid my ransom with his blood. His matchless love has freed me from the miserable captivity of sin and has forever linked me to the sweet yoke of his obedience. Let Christ alone live and rule in me, and never let him leave my heart who for my sake refused to come down from the cross."

Verse 20

He was chosen before the creation of the world, but was revealed in these last times for your sake.

Out of all the considerations, and there are many, that may move peo-ple to obedience, none convinces them more strongly than the sense of God's goodness and mercy toward them. And among all the evidence for this, there is nothing to equal the sending and giving of God's Son for our redemption. Therefore the apostle, having mentioned this, insists on it again. Here he states, first, its purpose, second, its performance, and third, its application.

1. The purpose: **chosen before the creation of the world.** "By faith we understand that the universe was formed at God's command, so that what is seen was not made out of what was visible" (Hebrews 11:3). If we want to understand heavenly things, we must learn them from the Word of God. We must be persuaded of the truth of God's Word by the Spirit of God. The whole world and everything in it was made out of nothing by God's almighty power. God is the fountain and source of all things.

Creation of the world. In the word **creation** or "foundation" is clearly intimated the comparison of the world to a building. Such a building reflects the greatness of him who made it. The world was created by the wisdom and power of God. "When I consider your heavens, the work of your fingers . . ." (Psalm 8:3). Job says that among the wonderful works of God, an evidence of his power, "he suspends the earth over nothing" (Job

26:7). Before there was time or place or any creature, God, the blessed Trinity, was completely happy in himself. But he wanted to communicate his goodness. Among all the deeds he planned before time, to be revealed in time, is his masterpiece—**chosen before the creation of the world**— namely, the manifesting of God in the flesh for man's redemption.

2. We are told the reason for this: **was revealed in the last times for your sake.** Christ was manifested through his incarnation. According to the apostle Paul, "he appeared in a body" (1 Timothy 3:16) and was manifested through his wonderful deeds and teaching. Christ was also revealed through his sufferings, death, resurrection, and ascension and through the sending of the Holy Spirit as he had promised and through the preaching of the Gospel.

The times of the Gospel are often called the **last times** by the prophets. The abolishing of the Jewish priesthood and ceremonies was succeeded by what would remain until the end of the world (see Matthew 28:20). In addition to this, the time of our Saviour's incarnation may be called the **last times** because, while it may not be close to the end of time by many ages, yet in all probability it is much closer to the end of time than to the beginning of time.

3. The application of this revelation: **for your sake.** The apostle says that the things he is writing about particularly apply to his readers, though they also apply to those before and after them. Christ who is here said to be **chosen before the creation of the world** is also called "the Lamb that was slain from the creation of the world" (Revelation 13:8). The virtue of his death looks backward to all preceding ages, whose faith and sacrifices looked forward to it. That same death is of perpetual value until the end of the world. "But when this priest had offered for all time one sacrifice for sins, he sat down at the right hand of God . . . because by one sacrifice he has made perfect forever those who are being made holy" (Hebrews 10:12, 14). The cross on which Christ was stretched points in its length to heaven and earth, reconciling them, and in its breadth to previous and following ages, as bringing salvation equally to both. It is not the general contemplation of Christ but the special possession of Christ that brings both comfort and motivation to obey and be holy, which is the apostle's particular interest here.

Verse 21

Through him you believe in God, who raised him from the dead and glorified him, and so your faith and hope are in God.

1. The complete object of faith. Our Saviour takes the sin between us and God out of the way and puts himself between our sins and God. The Father cannot look on his well-beloved Son except in a gracious way. God

looks on us, if we are outside Christ, as rebels, fit to be condemned. But when Christ is between us and God, God looks on us in Christ as justified, and we look at God in Christ as pacified and see the smiles of his favorable countenance. Take Christ out and everything is terrible; put Christ between us and God, and everything is full of peace. Therefore always place him between us and God, and through him we shall believe in God.

2. The ground for believing in God through Christ. God **raised him from the dead and glorified him.** It is for this reason that our **faith and hope are in God.** All of Christ's work, his humiliation and his exaltation, may be claimed for our benefit. Since Christ has paid everything that was necessary and so is set free from death, we are acquitted and have nothing to pay. Since Christ was exalted to glory, so will we be. Christ has taken possession of that glory for us. Like Stephen in his vision, faith in a spiritual way looks through the visible heavens and sees Christ at the Father's right hand. "If I go and prepare a place for you, I will come back and take you to be with me that you also may be where I am" (John 14:3).

Verse 22

Now that you have purified yourselves by obeying the truth so that you have sincere love for your brothers, love one another deeply, from the heart.

"Christ Jesus, who has become for us wisdom from God—that is, our righteousness, holiness and redemption" (1 Corinthians 1:30). It is a well-known truth, and yet one that we need to remember, that redemption and holiness are inseparable companions. We were redeemed so we would be holy. This is the point of what the apostle is saying here. Having made that point in a general way, he now exhorts us to exercise the Christian grace of brotherly love.

Our Saviour often told his disciples to do this. He says that will be the way we will be recognized as his disciples: "All men will know that you are my disciples, if you love one another" (John 13:35). St. Paul frequently extols and exhorts his readers to excel in this grace. "Be devoted to one another in brotherly love. Honor one another above yourselves" (Romans 12:10). "Let no debt remain outstanding, except the continuing debt to love one another, for he who loves his fellow man has fulfilled the law" (Romans 13:8). "You, my brothers, were called to be free. But do not use your freedom to indulge the sinful nature; rather, serve one another in love" (Galatians 5:13). "Be completely humble and gentle; be patient, bearing with one another in love" (Ephesians 4:2).

Love must be **sincere.** Dissimulation is a widespread disease. The apostle Paul uses the same word: "Love must be sincere" (Romans 12:9). The apostle John exhorts us in the same way: "Dear children, let us not love with words or tongue but with actions and in truth" (1 John 3:18). He who commands this love looks mainly within us and seeks it there; and he will judge those who merely pretend to possess it.

Love for your brothers. "Therefore, as we have opportunity, let us do good to all people, especially to those who belong to the family of believers" (Galatians 6:10). "You are brothers through the same new birth, born into the same inheritance; so there should be no strife among you. All your harps should be tuned to the same song, which you will sing forever. Let that love begin here that will never end."

Now that you have purified yourselves by obeying the truth. Sanctification renews and purifies the whole person. "Let us draw near to God with a sincere heart in full assurance of faith, having our hearts sprinkled to cleanse us from a guilty conscience and having our bodies washed with pure water" (Hebrews 10:22). "Since we have these promises, dear friends, let us purify ourselves from everything that contaminates body and spirit, perfecting holiness out of reverence for God" (2 Corinthians 7:1). The way to purity is through obeying the truth of the Word of God. It is true and pure in itself, and it brings truth and purity to the heart, through teaching it about the holy and pure nature of God. It shows us that God's holy will is his rule of purity, and it shows us Jesus Christ as the fountain of our purity and renewal, from whom we may receive grace upon grace (see John 1:16).

The reason there is so little mutual love among those who call themselves Christians is because there is so little purifying obedience to the truth, from which love flows. Genuine faith brings genuine love. Men may exhort each other to both, but only the hand of God will make them active in the heart.

Verse 23

For you have been born again, not of perishable seed, but of imperishable, through the living and enduring word of God.

The two things that comprise the apostle's exhortation sum up the Christian's duty. They are to walk as obedient children of God and to have love toward the brothers. In order to emphasize this, the apostle Peter here says they **have been born again** to make them God's children, and so they are brothers to other Christians. We will speak about regeneration, and then the **seed.**

1. Regeneration itself. It is the great dignity of believers that they are sons of God (see John 1:12), and this is proof of God's love (see 1 John 3:1). This divine adoption is often said to be a regeneration or a new birth in Scripture: "children born not of natural descent, nor of human decision

or a husband's will, but born of God" (John 1:13). "If you know that he is righteous, you know that everyone who does what is right has been born of him" (1 John 2:29). A new being, a spiritual life, is given to them. They have in them their Father's Spirit. This is derived from Christ and so is called his Spirit. "Because you are sons, God sent the Spirit of his Son into our hearts, the Spirit who calls out, 'Abba, Father'" (Galatians 4:6). They are not only said to be in God's family through adoption, but through this new birth they are his children and take part in the divine nature. "Through these he has given us his very great and precious promises, so that through them you may participate in the divine nature and escape the corruption in the world caused by evil desires" (2 Peter 1:4). The psalmist compares this generation of the sons of God to the dew: "from the womb of the dawn you will receive the dew of your youth" (Psalm 110:3). "Unless a man is born again, he cannot see the kingdom of God" (John 3:3). This is the special work of the Spirit of God. He himself speaks of the dew to Job: "Does the rain have a father: Who fathers the drops of dew?" (Job 38:28).

2. We are **born again . . . through the . . . word of God.** Ministers of the Word dispense the new birth through the Scriptures and so are called God's fellow workers. But the work of the Father remains untouched. The Father gives new birth to the same spirits he created. No matter how powerful a preacher is, all he can do is place the seed in the ear. He can do no more. The hearer, by paying attention, can convey the seed to his head. But it is the supreme Father and Teacher above who carries it into the heart, which is the only soil where it can live and bear fruit. One man cannot reach the heart of another. So how can he renew its fruitfulness? Natural birth has always been acknowledged as belonging to God's prerogative: "Sons are a heritage from the LORD, children a reward from him" (Psalm 127:3). How much more is the new birth completely dependent on God's hand!

This **word** gives birth, and **word** here means the Gospel. The Word is the seed of this new birth because it contains and declares that other Word, the Son of God, as our life. Moses says, "Let my teaching fall like rain and my words descend like dew, like showers on new grass, like abundant rain on tender plants" (Deuteronomy 32:2). The Word, like heavenly dew, drops into the heart through the hand of God's own Spirit and so makes it all become spiritual and heavenly.

In hearing the Word, men look too much to men and forget from what spring the Word derives its power. So we must learn that true conversion is no light matter. It is not an outward change of some bad customs, called "a reformed man." It is a new birth, a new creation. Children of disobedience and heirs of wrath become children of God and heirs of glory. They have a new spirit given to them, and this spirits acts in their life and actions.

Not of perishable seed. The Word of God is not only a living Word in itself, but it is an abiding Word, an incorruptible seed, which directly relates to regeneration. The eternal nature of the Word and the spiritual life that it brings is contrasted with the frailty and shortness of natural life. This the apostle speaks about in the words of Isaiah in the next verse.

Verses 24-25a

For, "All men are like grass, and all their glory is like the flowers of the field; the grass withers and the flowers fall, but the word of the Lord stands forever."

People's natural life is compared to vanity. Here it is called **grass.** Generations of people have been compared with the leaves of trees. The light of Scripture teaches us this lesson. "Teach us to number our days aright, that we may gain a heart of wisdom" (Psalm 90:12), says Moses. David said, "Show me, O LORD, my life's end and the number of my days; let me know how fleeting is my life" (Psalm 39:4). The apostle James asks, "What is your life?" And he replies, "You are a mist that appears for a little while and then vanishes" (James 4:14). In this verse in Peter, life is **like grass.** Job says, "Man born of woman is of few days and full of trouble. He springs up like a flower and withers away; like a fleeting shadow, he does not endure" (Job 14:1-2). Our life is like grass that at the cut of a scythe disappears for good.

"All their glory." There seems to be a great deal of difference between the outward circumstances of different people. Are the rich and beautiful and healthy the same as the poor and the ill? Are all **grass?** Are we to make no distinctions between categories of people? No. **"All men are like grass."** The best flower of the field decays. **Their glory** soon withers. The great projects of kings and princes turn to dust in a moment. "When their spirit departs, they return to the ground; on that very day their plans come to nothing" (Psalm 146:4). Archimedes was killed in the middle of one of his demonstrations.

So learn the foolishness and pride of man who can glory and please himself in the frail and wretched existence he has here. He dotes on this poor and natural life and cannot be persuaded to think on a higher and more permanent life, even though all his experiences tell him that all flesh is grass (see Isaiah 40:6). The life that never ends, which begins here, is the new spiritual life, of which the Word of God is the immortal seed. This is contrasted with a corruptible seed and transient human life. The frailty of human life is mentioned here so that our affections may be drawn away from it to the spiritual life that is not subject to death.

Verse 25b

And this is the word that was preached to you.
The Word of God is so like God himself and carries so plainly the image of his power and wisdom that when they are spoken about together, it is sometimes difficult to know if the expression refers to God or to his Word. "The word of God is living and active" (Hebrews 4:12). Here, however, I think these words refer to the written Word.

Preached to you. It is not enough to have these thoughts about the Word of God in a general way if we do not know what that Word is. We must be sure that the Word that is preached to us is this very Word of God, which is so excellent. We must be convinced that it is imperishable and endures forever and thus surpasses all the world and all the glory in the world. Although this Word is passed on through weak people, it does not lose any of its virtue. For its power depends on its first Owner and Author, the everlasting God, who through it brings to life his chosen ones.

So this is what we should learn to hear, receive, esteem, and love—this holy, living Word. We should despise all the glittering vanities of this perishing life, all outward pomp, and all inner wisdom and natural endowments of mind. We should be prepared to lose all that in favor of the heavenly light of the Gospel that is preached to us. The only treasure that should live in our hearts is that treasure of glory kept for us in heaven. May God in his infinite mercy bring us to that blessed state. Amen.

1 Peter
Chapter 2

Verses 1-2

Therefore, rid yourselves of all malice and all deceit, hypocrisy, envy, and slander of every kind. Like newborn babies, crave pure spiritual milk, so that by it you may grow up in your salvation.

The same power and goodness of God that shows itself in bringing life to his creatures also sustains and preserves them. This is true of both the first creation and the second creation. In the first creation God provided the necessary nourishment for life. "Then God said, 'Let the land produce vegetation: seed-bearing plants and trees on the land that bear fruit with seed in it, according to their various kinds'" (Genesis 1:11). In the same way at the end of 1 Peter 1 we find the doctrine of the new birth and life of a Christian, where the needed food is given. The same Word by which we are born also gives life. So Christians are here exhorted by the apostle Peter to make use of this Word. This is the main purpose of these two verses.

No matter how much the world may despise this Word, we know that "the message of the cross is foolishness to those who are perishing, but to us who are being saved it is the power of God" (1 Corinthians 1:18). If you want to experience this, and if you want life and growth from the Word, you must look beyond the poor worthless messenger and request the help of the almighty Lord of life. You should present the blindness of your minds and the deadness of your hearts to God and say, "Lord, here is an opportunity for you to show the power of your Word. I want to find life and strength in it. But I cannot do this, nor can the preacher do this. Only you have the prerogative to do this. You just have to say the word and it will be done." "And God said, 'Let there be light,' and there was light" (Genesis 1:3).

In this exhortation this apostle continues to use the analogy of the new birth that he mentioned in chapter 1.

Like newborn babies. Do not be content until you find evidence of this new supernatural life in yourself. Our Saviour says, "I tell you the truth, unless a man is born again, he cannot see the kingdom of God" (John 3:3). Surely those who are not born again will one day wish they had never been born. How wretched this life is that we have here. If we want to share in a happier life after this life, it must begin here. Grace and glory are one and the same life. The only difference is that one is the start and the other is the completion. Or if we do call them two different lives, the one is the undoubted pledge of the other. Remarkably, even a heathen said, "That day of death we fear so, is the birthday of eternity" (Seneca). It is the same with those who are born again here. This new birth of grace is the definite guarantee of the birthday of glory. Why do we not work to make sure we possess the new birth now? Is it not a fearful thing to spend our days in vanity and then lie down in darkness and sorrow forever?

But this new life removes us from the danger and fear of that eternal death. As St. John says, speaking about those who are born again, "We know that we have passed from death to life" (1 John 3:14). Once this has happened, there is no going back from this life to death again.

This new birth is the same as that which St. John calls the "first resurrection," and he says about those who share in this, "Blessed and holy are those who have part in the first resurrection" (Revelation 20:6).

The weak start of grace, weak in comparison with the later strength it attains in this life, is sometimes pictured in terms of its infancy. But believers should not continue to be infants. If they do, they should be reproved. "Then we will no longer be infants, tossed back and forth by the waves, blown here and there by every wind of teaching and by the cunning and craftiness of men in their deceitful scheming" (Ephesians 4:14). "Brothers, stop thinking like children. In regard to evil be infants, but in your thinking be adults" (1 Corinthians 14:20). "In fact, though by this time you ought to be teachers, you need someone to teach you the elementary truths of God's word all over again" (Hebrews 5:12). Although the apostle writes to new converts, and so may possibly imply the tenderness of their beginnings of grace, I think infancy here should be understood in such a way that it depicts the Christian life as a whole. In the same way **milk** is recommended here, and this is suitable for infants. But here it signifies the whole Word of God and all its wholesome and saving truths as the proper nourishment for God's children. And so the apostle's words are a lasting exhortation for all Christians at all stages in their Christian lives.

The whole course of their spiritual life is here called **newborn babies**. This is not contrasted with the corruption and wickedness of the old nature but signifies its weakness and imperfection in this life when compared with the life to come. All our knowledge here is like the ignorance of infants, and all our expressions of God and his praises are but like the first stammers of children in comparison with the knowledge that we will have of Christ in the next life, when we will know him as he knows us.

For we know in part and we prophesy in part, but when perfection comes, the imperfect disappears. When I was a child, I talked like a child, I thought like a child, I reasoned like a child. When I became a man, I put childish ways behind me. Now we see but a poor reflection; then we shall see face to face. Now I know in part; then I shall know fully, even as I am fully known.

—1 Corinthians 13:9-12

It is the wonder of divine grace that it takes such small beginnings to a height of perfection that we cannot conceive, that a little spark of true grace, which is not only indiscernible to others but often to a Christian himself, should be the beginning of that condition by which he shines brighter than the sun in the sky. In our natural life, some who struggle in infancy later excel in knowledge and grow up to command great armies or to be kings. But it is a much greater matter that **newborn babies**, the small beginnings of grace, grow into perfection and full knowledge.

If God's children are to grow by the Word of God, the apostle Peter requires two things from them. First, the innocency of children; second, the appetite of children. For this expression **newborn babies**, as I see it, relates not only to the desiring of the milk of the Word (**crave pure spiritual milk**, verse 2), but also to the removal of malice (**rid yourselves of all malice**, verse 1). Similarly, the apostle Paul exhorts, "In regard to evil be infants" (1 Corinthians 14:20).

Therefore, rid yourselves of all malice and all deceit, hypocrisy, envy, and slander of every kind. This implies that we are naturally given over to these evils, and so we are told to rid ourselves of them. Our hearts are by nature cages for those unclean birds—**malice, deceit, hypocrisy, envy, and slander.** The apostle sometimes mentions some of these evils, and at other times he mentions others. But they cannot be separated from each other. They are all one set of clothes and are all included in that one term "old self" (Ephesians 4:22), which the apostle Paul tells them to "put off." Here throwing out these base habits is shown to be a necessary evidence of their new birth, as well as for their future spiritual growth. Filthy habits do not become children of God. They are the marks of an unrenewed mind, the very character of the children of Satan, for they constitute his image. His very names denote **malice, deceit,** and **slander.** Satan means "the adversary or enemy." Devil, *diabolos,* means "the envious accuser or slanderer." Satan is that great hypocrite and deceiver who "masquerades as an angel of light" (2 Corinthians 11:14).

In contrast, the Spirit of God who dwells in God's children is the spirit of meekness, love, and truth. That dove-like Spirit who descended on our

Saviour is given by him to believers. It is the greatest impudence to pretend to be Christians and still cling to hatred and envy, for our Saviour lavishes his love upon our hearts by his Spirit. "Take from the devil envy, pride and arrogance, and what evil is there in him? Take from the elect love, meekness and humility, and what goodness is there in them?" (Dr. H. More).

Rid yourselves of all malice. *Kakia* may be taken generally, but I think it means what we call **malice.** Study shows that **malice** and **envy** are two branches growing out of the same bitter root—self-love. **Slander** is the fruit that **malice** and **envy** bear. **Malice** wishes evil on another person, while **envy** is jealous of his goodness. Both **malice** and **envy** express themselves by speaking evil about a person. This infernal fire within smokes and flashes out through the tongue, which James says "is itself set on fire by hell" (James 3:6). These evils of **malice, envy, slander,** and the like should not be hidden by us in ourselves and carried around under better appearances. They should be thrown out. So the apostle commands us here to throw off also the outer garment and cloak of the others—namely, **hypocrisy.** What advantage is it to wear this mask? A person may in the sight of men act this part well, but we know there is an Eye that sees through this, and a Hand that, if we will not take the mask off, will pull it off to our shame, either here in the sight of men or on the appointed day when all hypocrites will be unveiled and be seen for what they are before men and angels.

It is tragic to be approved and applauded by men but condemned by God, for all people stand or fall before God's sentence. Seek to be approved and justified by God, and who will be able to condemn you? (See Romans 8:34.) We may bear the dislike of all the world if God declares himself to be well pleased with us. "I care very little if I am judged by you or by any human court" (1 Corinthians 4:3).

But the evils mentioned here are especially to be thrown off, as they prevent the profitable receiving of the Word of God. This part of the exhortation (**rid**) leads to that which follows (**crave**) and should be carefully noted. This is the double task of true religion. When a person begins the Christian life, he is not only to be taught the true religion but also has to reject the errors and wickedness that are deeply rooted in his mind, which he has not only learned through the corrupt world, but that he himself brought into the world. These evil seeds are originally in our nature and grow with the influence of the surrounding world. No one comes to the school of Christ, in the words of Aristotle, "as blank paper." On the contrary, everyone is scribbled upon and blurred with such base habits as **malice, envy, hypocrisy,** and so on.

Therefore, the first task is to cleanse and purify these blots and foul characters from the heart so that it may receive God's image. Because it is the Word of God that starts and carries on the work, in order to receive this Word rightly the heart must be purged of such impurities as **malice**, **envy**, and **hypocrisy**. These dispositions are so opposed to receiving the Word of God profitably that, while they possess and rule the soul, it cannot embrace these divine truths at all. While it is filled with such guests there is no room to entertain the Word.

These foul impulses and the attributes of Christian character cannot live together because of their contradictory natures. The saving nature of the Word of God in the soul is what is spoken of in Hebrews 4:2: "For we also have had the gospel preached to us, just as they did; but the message they heard was of no value to them, because those who heard did not combine it with faith." Can there be anything more opposed to the good Word of God than **slander**, or anything so opposed to God as a person's life and words full of poison? As the apostle James says, "No man can tame the tongue. It is a restless evil, full of deadly poison" (James 3:8). **Hypocrisy** and **deceit** are directly opposed to the Word of truth. How can the gall of **malice** and **pure spiritual milk** agree?

There are two conditions for good nourishment. First, good and wholesome food; second, a good inner constitution in those who eat the food. **Spiritual milk** is the only proper nourishment for the spiritual life. But most listeners are inwardly infected, being full of the evil diseases mentioned here, as well as with other evils. So they have no appetite for the Word but rather feed on such rubbish as suits their disposition. This evil of **envy** and **slander** possesses their minds in such a way that they are unable to be nourished by the Word they hear.

In the same way the hypocrite uses all that he hears from the Word not to renew his inner mind and alter what is wrong there, but to enable him to better play the part of an expert hypocrite. He seeks to appear to be a Christian and to be known as a Christian in the eyes of others, but he does not use the Word to grow as a Christian. As these evils are so natural to men and so opposed to the nature of the Word of God, it is very necessary that they be purged out, so that the Word may be effectively received. The apostle James gives a similar exhortation but uses a different metaphor: "Therefore, get rid of all moral filth and the evil that is so prevalent, and humbly accept the word planted in you, which can save you" (James 1:21). James compares the Word to a plant of excellent virtue, the tree of life, "the word . . . which can save you." But the only soil this plant can grow in is a heart full of meekness, a heart that is purged from all those evil weeds that naturally grow. These weeds must be rooted out and thrown away so the Word can grow within us.

This is so necessary that the most respected teachers of wisdom, in a human way, have required this of their scholars. In order to make their minds capable of receiving wisdom, the students had to be purged from vice and wickedness. For this reason Aristotle judged that young men who were given over to their own passions were unfit hearers of moral philosophy. When anyone asked Socrates a question, seeking information from him, it was his custom before answering to ask them about their own way of living.

If people require a calm and purified disposition of mind to enable them to receive teaching, how much more is it necessary for learning God's teaching and those deep mysteries that his Word opens up. This is well expressed in the apocryphal book of the Wisdom of Solomon, 1:34: "For perverse thoughts separate people from God, and when his power is tested, it exposes the foolish; because wisdom will not enter a deceitful soul, or dwell in a body enslaved to sin." Even the heathen recognized that "The mind that is impure is not capable of God and divine things" (Seneca, Epistle 87). It is easy to see the reason why the book of Proverbs speaks so much about such wisdom. It requires, in its first chapter, that those who wish to listen to wisdom should cut out all their ungodly customs. What makes the Word ineffective is what is inside people. Indeed, how can the soul understand spiritual things and rise to heavenly thoughts when it has not been set free from its love of sin?

Our Saviour said, "Blessed are the pure in heart, for they will see God" (Matthew 5:8). Not only will they see him perfectly hereafter, but so far as they receive him, he will impart and make himself known to them here and now. "If anyone loves me, he will obey my teaching. My Father will love him, and we will come to him and make our home with him" (John 14:23). He will also, in his just judgment, hide himself and the saving truth of his Word from those who entertain and delight in sin. The sins they take delight in will obscure the light of the Gospel from them, so that although it shines as brilliantly as the noonday sun, they will be like those who live in a dungeon. They will not discern the Word.

If we want to know the main reason for fruitlessness regarding the Word, it is this: people do not bring meek and guileless spirits to the Word. They do not bring to the Word minds that have been purified, but rather minds full of **malice and all deceit, hypocrisy, envy, and slander of every kind.** Although they hear the Word frequently, they become weaker spiritually. Therefore, work hard to welcome the Word of truth, unlike those who perished because "they refused to love the truth and so be saved" (2 Thessalonians 2:10). Instead, "keep hold of the deep truths of the faith with a clear conscience" (1 Timothy 3:9). Be like David when he says, "I hate double-minded men, but I love your law" (Psalm 119:113). And as our apostle exhorts us here, **rid yourselves of all malice and all deceit, hypocrisy, envy, and slander of every kind.** Then you will be able to receive the Word.

Crave pure spiritual milk, so that by it you may grow up in your

salvation. Every real believer has received a life from heaven that is far greater than his natural life. This life has its own special desires and delights. The main one, similar to our natural life, is a desire for food. The natural result of eating this spiritual food is growth, since we are still imperfect here.

Pure spiritual milk. The life of grace is the proper life of the soul, and without it the soul is dead, just as the body is dead without the soul. This milk is **pure** because it is not contaminated. It is the **pure** Word of God without any impurities of error, and free from any human influences. The natural and genuine appetite of God's children is for the Word itself, **pure spiritual milk.** Those who are really God's children, like infants who like breast milk best, love the Word best, and wherever they find it they relish it. But natural men cannot love spiritual things and do not desire the Word for its sweetness. Before conversion, wit or eloquence may draw people to the Word and may possibly prove to be a successful bait in catching them, as Augustine says about listening to Ambrose; but once people are born again, they desire the milk itself.

Crave pure spiritual milk. Do not only listen to the Word out of habit, but desire it because it is your food. This is, first, a natural desire, like an infant's desire for milk. The desire comes from within and not as a result of exterior pressure. And because it is natural, it is, second, an earnest desire. This is no cold, indifferent wish. The Greek *epipothe sate signifies* vehement desire—like a baby who will not be satisfied until it has breast milk, even if you offered it gold and silver. The baby ignores these, for they do not meet its desire, which must be satisfied. Thus David said, "My soul is consumed with longing for your laws at all times" (Psalm 119:20), like a baby whose heart is broken from crying over its longing for milk. In the third place this desire should be constant. The baby does not tire of having breast milk every day. It desires it as if it had never had it before. In the same way, the child of God has an untiring appetite for the Word. It is fresh to him each day, and he takes his delight in it daily. With David the law became his meditation day and night (see Psalm 1:2). In contrast to this, the natural man quickly tires of the Word.

So that by it you may grow up in your salvation. The aim of the desire for God's **pure spiritual milk** is growth. **Crave** the Word not just to hear it, but to grow from hearing it. The ear is the mouth of the mind, but meat that goes no further than the mouth does not nourish. To desire the Word in order to increase in knowledge, while necessary and commendable, is not the true reason for listening to the Word. As the Word is the means for beginning the Christian life, so it is also the means for continuing the Christian life.

First, this will happen if we consider the nature of the Word in general, that it is spiritual and divine. The Gospel is called "light," and

God's children are also called "light." They are transformed by the Gospel and thus become even more enlightened the more they hear it, and so they **grow.**

Second, if we look more particularly at the nature of the Word, it will be seen that it is most fit for increasing the graces of the Spirit in a Christian, for there are truths in it that apply to them and through which they grow. It fans "into flame the gift of God" (2 Timothy 1:6). It does this by particular exhortations regarding the study and exercise of those graces, sometimes emphasizing one and sometimes another. The Word feeds faith by setting before it the free grace of God, his rich promises, and his power to carry them all out. The Word shows the strength of the new covenant, so that "through him the 'Amen' is spoken by us to the glory of God" (2 Corinthians 1:20). The Word feeds repentance by making the vileness and deformity of sin daily more clear and visible. The Word increases our love for God by opening up more and more of his infinite excellency and loveliness to us. The Word brings Jesus Christ into our view, not only as the perfect pattern, but as the fountain of all grace. As we contemplate him as God's perfect image, the soul sees him more clearly and can grow spiritually.

Thus the apostle Paul, speaking about the excellency of the ministry of the Gospel revealing Christ, wrote, "For God, who said, 'Let light shine out of darkness,' made his light shine in our hearts to give us the light of the knowledge of the glory of God in the face of Christ" (2 Corinthians 4:6). We may not only observe his grace but share it.

As far as spiritual growth is concerned, remember that it is not observable in people while they are growing, but only after they have grown. It may appear that you are not growing in grace, but if you grow more in self-denial and are humble about your slow growth, all is not lost. While the branches may not be shooting up as fast as you would wish, yet if the root grows deeper, that will be useful for future growth. The person who is still learning to be more in Jesus Christ and less in himself, and is seeking all his dependence and comfort in him, is doubtless a growing believer.

Many people wrongly conclude they are growing just because they are acquiring more knowledge. But the natural man is incapable of spiritual growth, for he is dead and does not have any of the new life to which this growth relates. Remember, Herod "liked to listen" to John (Mark 6:20).

Consider, then, what true delight we might have in this. You find it a pleasure to see your children growing as they begin to stand and walk. But for the soul to be in the process of becoming more like God is a pleasure beyond all other pleasures. To find pride, earthliness, and vanity abating, and faith, love, and spiritual-mindedness increasing is the greatest delight. "You have made known to me the path of life; you will fill me with joy in your presence, with eternal pleasures at your right hand" (Psalm 16:11).

Verse 3

Now that you have tasted that the Lord is good.

Our natural desire for food arises principally from its necessity for the nourishment of our bodies. In addition to this there is a sweetness and pleasantness as we eat it that serves to sharpen our desire, and nature has given it to us for this purpose. Thus God's children, in their spiritual life, naturally desire the means of their nourishment and growth, as in this life we are always in a growing state. In addition, there is a spiritual delight and sweetness in the Word, for it reveals God, and this adds to their desire and stirs up their appetite for it. By the Word we grow, and in the Word we taste the graciousness of God. David, in the psalm that he dedicates wholly to this subject, gives both of these as reasons for his appetite. "Oh, how I love your law!" (Psalm 119:97). He declares that by it he was made "wiser than my enemies. . . . I have more insight than all my teachers" (Psalm 119:98-99). He has been taught to keep his feet "from every evil path" (Psalm 119:101). He is taught by the Author of the Word, the Lord himself, to grow wiser and holier in divine ways. And then, in verse 103, he adds another reason: "How sweet are your words to my taste, sweeter than honey to my mouth!"

We will speak, first, about the goodness or graciousness of the Lord, second, about this taste, and, third, about the inference from these two things.

1. The goodness of God. **The Lord is good.** He has a bountiful, kind disposition. The Hebrew word *Tobin* in Psalm 34:8, from which this is taken, means "good": "Taste and see that the LORD is good; blessed is the man who takes refuge in him." The Septuagint renders this with the same word used by the apostle. Both words signify a kindness of nature. One of love's attributes is that it is kind, always compassionate, always ready to do good. "Love is kind" (1 Corinthians 13:4). God is naturally good; goodness is his nature. He is goodness and love itself. "Whoever does not love does not know God, because God is love" (1 John 4:8). All goodness is derived from God.

There is a common bounty of God in which he lavishes his goodness on everyone. In this sense "the earth is full of his unfailing love" (Psalm 33:5). But the goodness that the Gospel is full of is spoken about here. He is gracious to his people in freely forgiving their sins, in giving no less than himself to them. He frees them from all evils and fills them with all good. He "forgives all your sins and heals all your diseases . . . and . . . satisfies my desires with good things" (Psalm 103:3-5). So it follows with good reason that "the Lord is compassionate and gracious" (verse 8). His graciousness is further expressed in his gentleness and his being "slow to anger." He bears with the frailties of his own; "as a father has compassion on his children, so the LORD has compassion on those who fear him" (verse 13).

No friend is so kind and friendly and none so powerful. He is "an ever present help in trouble" (Psalm 46:1). He is ready to be found. Though others may be distant, he is always close by, and his presence always comforts us.

God is gracious in Christ; otherwise we could not find him so. So this verse speaks particularly about Jesus Christ, as becomes apparent in the following verses, through whom all the special kindness and love of God is conveyed to the soul, for it can come in no other way. Though God is mercy and goodness in himself, yet we cannot find him so for us unless we look through the Mediator. The main point of the goodness of God in the Gospel, which is so sweet to a humbled sinner, the forgiveness of sins, we know we cannot taste except in Christ. "In him we have redemption through his blood" (Ephesians 1:7).

The taste of the free grace of God was given in the promises, before Christ came in the flesh. But after he had come, the sweetness of grace was even stronger. When he was pierced on the cross and his blood was poured out for our redemption, his love was revealed in all its glory. "Through those holes of his wounds may we draw, and taste that the Lord is gracious," said Augustine.

2. Concerning this taste: **Now that you have tasted.** In order to taste Christ, there must be, first, a firm belief in the truth of the promises, in which the free grace of God is shown to us. Second, there must be a particular application of that grace to ourselves. Isaiah speaks about the promises contained in the Old and New Testaments in these terms: "For you will nurse and be satisfied at her [Jerusalem's] comforting breasts; you will drink deeply and delight in her overflowing abundance" (Isaiah 66:11). Third, there must be a sense of the sweetness of that grace being applied or drawn into the soul, and that constitutes this taste. No unrenewed person has any of these in reality. One person cannot make another person alive to the sweetness of divine grace. "The man without the Spirit does not accept the things that come from the Spirit of God, for they are foolishness to him, and he cannot understand them, because they are spiritually discerned" (1 Corinthians 2:14).

Even a spiritual person does not fully appreciate this sweetness. It is an infinite goodness, and he has only a taste of it. The peace of God, which is the main fruit of his goodness, "transcends all understanding" (Philippians 4:7), says the apostle Paul. This applies not just to our natural understanding, but to all understanding, including spiritual understanding. The godly man cannot appreciate it all, and what he does understand he cannot fully express, and what he does express the carnal mind cannot appreciate.

But for people who have indeed tasted this goodness, how insipid are the things the world calls sweet. The heart of Christian people is not set on earthly delights, for they find their rest in God.

3. The inference: If you have tasted, then **rid yourselves of all malice and all deceit, hypocrisy, envy, and slander of every kind.** Verse 3 looks back to the exhortation given in verse 1. "Surely if you have tasted the kindness and sweetness of God in Christ, it will compose your spirits and conform them to him. It will diffuse such a sweetness through your soul that there will be nothing but love, meekness, and singleness of heart." Therefore, those who have bitter, malicious spirits demonstrate that they have not tasted God's love. The Lord is good, and those who taste his goodness are made like him. "Be kind and compassionate to one another, forgiving each other, just as in Christ God forgave you" (Ephesians 4:32).

Again, if you have tasted, then you will desire more. The true evidence for this is if you constantly hunger and thirst after God's graciousness. If **you have tasted that the Lord is good,** then **crave pure spiritual milk** (verse 2). This is the sweetness of the Word, that it has in it the Lord's graciousness and gives us a knowledge of his love. People whose spiritual lives are nourished in this way discover that they have "trained themselves to distinguish good from evil" (Hebrews 5:14). The heart that clings to the Word of God and delights in it cannot but daily find in it new tastes of God's goodness.

Verses 4-5

As you come to him, the living Stone—rejected by men but chosen by God and precious to him—you also, like living stones, are being built into a spiritual house to be a holy priesthood, offering spiritual sacrifices acceptable to God through Jesus Christ.

The spring of all the dignities of Christians, and therefore the great motive of all their duties, is their close relationship to Jesus Christ. The apostle makes this the subject of his teaching, both to show his persecuted brothers their dignity in that respect, and to apply it to the necessary duties he commands. Having spoken about their spiritual life and growth in Christ, using the imagery of natural life, the apostle uses another comparison here that is also often used in Scripture. He compares the saints to a temple and to a priesthood.

We have in the first simile, first, the nature of the building, second, its materials, and, third, the structure of the building.

1. The nature of the building. It is a spiritual building. Our Saviour says about worshiping God, "God is spirit, and his worshipers must worship in spirit and in truth" (John 4:24). God's house must be a spiritual one because he is spirit. God's temple is his people. This building is the whole invisible church of God, and each Christian is a stone in this building. Each of these stones is called the whole temple. "Do you not know that your body is a temple of the Holy Spirit?" (1 Corinthians 6:19). The glory

of the church of God does not consist in stately temples, rich with furniture and full of pompous ceremonies. These do not agree with its spiritual nature. Its true beauty is to grow spiritually, to have more of God's presence and glory filling it like a cloud. It has been observed that the more the church grew in outward riches, the less she grew in spiritual excellence.

2. The materials of this building: **As you come to him, the living Stone—rejected by men but chosen by God and precious to him—you also, like living stones.** . . . The whole building is the mystical Christ, with the entire body of the elect. He is the foundation, and they are the stones built upon him. Christ is **the living Stone,** and they through union with him are **like living stones.** Christ has life in himself, as he says in John 6, and they derive their life from him. Christ is here called **the living Stone** not only because of his immortality and glorious resurrection, the Lamb who was killed but now lives forever, but because he is spiritual and eternal life for us, a living foundation that transfuses this life into the whole building and every stone in it. "In him the whole building is joined together and rises to become a holy temple in the Lord" (Ephesians 2:21). The Spirit flows from him, brings life to the building, and binds it together as a living body.

3. The structure of the building: **As you come to him.** First, we come, then we are built up. They come to Christ, not only out of the wicked world, but out of themselves. A great many who seem to come to Christ have not truly come to him because they have not left themselves. Coming to Christ means believing in him, handing over the soul to Christ, and living through him. "You refuse to come to me to have life," said our Saviour (John 5:40). Christ states this as if a wrong had been done to him, and it has, but the loss is ours. It is his glory to give us life who were dead, but it is our happiness to receive that life from him.

These stones **come** to their Foundation. The soul is moved to come to Christ through the Spirit. The will acts but is actuated and drawn by the Father. "No one can come to me unless the Father has enabled him" (John 6:65). The outward means of drawing is through the Word. Once united to Christ, believers are built up and grow into a holy temple. "Consequently, you are no longer foreigners and aliens, but fellow citizens with God's people and members of God's household, built on the foundation of the apostles and prophets, with Christ Jesus himself as the chief cornerstone. In him the whole building is joined together and rises to become a holy temple in the Lord" (Ephesians 2:19-21). To teach us the necessity of growth, believers are often compared to things that grow—trees planted in fruitful growing places, such as by rivers; cedars in Lebanon, the tallest of trees; the morning light; babies at the breast; and here, **living stones.**

If, then, you want to be certain about your union with Christ, see if you find your souls built on the strong foundation of Christ. Make sure you are not resting on yourself or on anything either within you or outside you, but are supported by Christ alone. See if you are drawing life from him through your union with him, as from a living foundation. "I have been crucified with Christ and I no longer live, but Christ lives in me. The life I live in the body, I live by faith in the Son of God, who loved me and gave himself for me" (Galatians 2:20).

As these **stones** are built on Christ by faith, so they are cemented to each other through love. Therefore, where there is no love, it is a delusion to think they are part of this building. Because these **stones** are **living**, they grow in the life of grace, for they are a **spiritual** building. So if we do not find this in our lives, and if our hearts are still carnal and absorbed with earthly things, that is evidence that we are not part of this building. Base lusts are still ruling within us, and our hearts are like cages keeping unclean birds and filthy spirits within us.

Consider it your happiness to form part of this building, and consider the empty nature of other comforts and privileges. Happy indeed are those God chooses to be **living stones** in this **spiritual house** or temple. Even though they are hammered and hewn in order to be polished for it through afflictions and the inner work of mortification and repentance, it is worth enduring everything in order to be made suitable for this building. Such people are happier than all others, even though they are not laden with honors, kingdoms, or wealth. For all other buildings, and all the parts of them, will be demolished and will come to nothing, from the foundation to the copingstone. All your houses, both cottages and palaces, "the elements will" destroy "by fire" (2 Peter 3:10). But this spiritual building will grow up in heaven. When it has been perfected, it will abide forever in beauty and glory. In it will be found nothing impure and no unclean people. "Nothing impure will ever enter it, nor will anyone who does what is shameful or deceitful, but only those whose names are written in the Lamb's book of life" (Revelation 21:27).

To be a holy priesthood. The worship and ceremonies of the Jewish church were all shadows of Jesus Christ and fulfillment in him. The priesthood of the law represented Christ as the great High Priest who offered himself for our sins, and that priesthood cannot be passed on to anyone else. "Unlike other high priests, he does not need to offer sacrifices day after day, first for his own sins, and then for the sins of the people. He sacrificed for their sins once for all when he offered himself" (Hebrews 7:27). There is no special office of priesthood for offering sacrifices in the Christian church; we need Christ's alone. But this dignity that is mentioned here, a **holy priesthood, offering spiritual sacrifices,** is common to all those who are in Christ. As they are **living stones** built on Christ into a **spiritual** temple, so they are priests of that same temple made by him:

"... has made us to be a kingdom and priests to serve his God and Father" (Revelation 1:6). As Christ was, in a transcendent manner, temple, priest, and sacrifice, so Christians in their kind are all three through Christ. And by his Spirit who is in them, their offerings through him are made **acceptable**.

We have here, first, the office, second, the service of that office, and, third, the success of that service.

1. The office: **a holy priesthood.** The death of Jesus Christ, being in every way powerful for reconciliation and union, did not only break down the partition wall of guilt that stood between God and man, but the wall of ceremonies that stood between the Jews and the Gentiles. It made all who believe one with God and united them to one another. "For he himself is our peace, who has made the two one and has destroyed the barrier, the dividing wall of hostility" (Ephesians 2:14). The way of salvation was made known not to one nation only, but to all people. So whereas the knowledge of God was before confined to one little corner, it is now diffused through the nations. Whereas the dignity of the Old Testament priesthood was invested in a few people, all those who believe are now priests to God the Father. This was signified by the tearing of the curtain of the temple at our Saviour's death. So not only were these ceremonies and sacrifices to cease, being all fulfilled in Christ, but the people of God, previously kept in the outer court and cut off by the curtain, were now allowed into the Holy Place, since they were all priests and fit to offer sacrifices.

The priesthood of the law was holy, and its holiness was signified by many outer things such as anointings, washings, and special clothes. But in this spiritual priesthood of the Gospel, holiness itself replaces all of these things. The children of God are all anointed, purified, and clothed with holiness.

2. The purpose of this office: **offering spiritual sacrifices.** There is no priesthood without sacrifice. Because the **priesthood** spoken about here is completely spiritual, its **sacrifices** must be **spiritual** as well. **Offering spiritual sacrifices.** We are saved the pains and cost of bringing bullocks and rams and other sacrifices. **Spiritual sacrifices** replace these. "There is a change of the priesthood" (Hebrews 7:12). So in the priesthood of Christians, there is also a change of the kind of sacrifice offered. All sacrifice is not done away with, but it is changed from the offering of those things formerly in use to **spiritual sacrifices.** These are to be preferred in every way. They are easier and cheaper for us, and yet more precious and **acceptable to God. Even when the other sacrifices were made, these** spiritual sacrifices always took precedence in God's account. Without **spiritual sacrifices** God hated and despised all burnt offerings. How much more should we abound in spiritual sacrifice.

With what shall I come before the LORD and how down before the exalted God? Shall I come before him with burnt offerings, with calves a year old? Will the LORD be pleased with thousands of rams, with ten thousand rivers of oil? Shall I offer my firstborn for my transgression, the fruit of my body for the sin of my soul? He has showed you, O man, what is good. And what does the LORD require of you? To act justly and to love mercy and to walk humbly with your God.

—Micah 6:6-8

Although the spiritual sacrificing is easier in its own way, because of the corrupt nature of man it is much harder. Men prefer all the toil and the cost of the former way, if they were allowed to choose. This was the sin of the Jews in those days, that their souls leaned on the body's service too much and desired to do enough of that to dispense with spiritual service. Hence the Lord frequently reproved them (see Psalm 50 and Isaiah 1). Hence the willingness, in popery, for outward work, for penances and satisfactions of body and purse, anything of that kind if it might serve, rather than the inner work of repentance and mortification, outward service, and sacrifices of the soul.

One spiritual sacrifice is the prayers of the saints. The book of Revelation mentions "golden bowls full of incense, which are the prayers of the saints" (Revelation 5:8). Similarly, David says, "May my prayer be set before you like incense; may the lifting up of my hands be like the evening sacrifice" (Psalm 141:2). It is not the composition of prayer or the eloquence of expression that is seen as sweet in God's sight, but the desire of the heart. That is what makes a spiritual sacrifice. Otherwise, it is carnal, dead, and worthless in God's sight.

Praise is also a sacrifice. This involves making respectful and honorable mention of the name of God and of his goodness, to bless him humbly and with the whole heart. "Sacrifice thank offerings to God, fulfill your vows to the Most High, and call upon me in the day of trouble; I will deliver you, and you will honor me" (Psalm 50:14-15). "He who sacrifices thank offerings honors me, and he prepares the way so that I may show him the salvation of God" (Psalm 50:23). "Through Jesus, therefore, let us continually offer to God a sacrifice of praise—the fruit of lips that confess his name" (Hebrews 13:15). This sacrifice will never end but will continue in heaven through all eternity.

A holy life is also called a sacrifice of righteousness. Our bodies are to be presented as "living sacrifices" (Romans 12:1). "My son, give me your heart, and let your eyes keep to my ways" (Proverbs 23:26). The heart, given to God, makes the eyes, ears, tongue, hands, and everything else holy, as God' s special property. Once these are consecrated to him, it is a sacrilege to turn them to any unholy use. This makes a man delight to hear and speak of things that concern God and to think about him often, to be holy in his secret thoughts and in all his ways. In everything we bring God, every thanksgiving and prayer we offer, he looks to see if our heart is coming with our offering; and if God does not see it, he does not care about the rest but throws it back again.

The heart must be offered with every spiritual sacrifice. The whole heart must be offered and given over to God, just as Christ offered up his whole self for us. In another sense, which does not contradict the first, the heart must not be whole but broken. "The sacrifices of God are a broken spirit; a broken and contrite heart, O God, you will not despise" (Psalm 51:17). If your heart is not broken, give it to God so it can be broken. And if it is broken when you give it to God, he will break it more and will melt it, but you will not be sorry for giving it to him. He breaks and melts your heart so that he may refine it and make it new, press his own image on it, and make it holy and so like himself.

Let us then give God ourselves or nothing. To give ourselves to him is not for God's benefit, but for ours. As the philosopher Seneca said to a poor pupil who, when others gave him great gifts, told him he had nothing but himself to give, "It is well, and I will endeavor to give you back to yourself better than I received from you." God treats us in the same way if we daily make this spiritual sacrifice. The Christian gives himself to God every day and receives it back every day in a better condition. The more he sacrifices, the more sanctified he becomes.

The way we offer all **spiritual sacrifices**, including ourselves, is with love. That is the holy fire that burns up everything and sends up our prayers, our hearts, and our whole selves as whole burnt offerings to God. Like the fire on the altar, it is originally from heaven, being kindled by God's own love for us. The fire that fell from heaven (Leviticus 9:24) was to be kept burning all the time on the altar and never allowed to go out, and no other fire was allowed to be used in sacrifices.

How far from this are most of us, even though we profess to be Christians! How many consider their holy calling? Just as the special holiness of the ministry should be much in the thoughts of those who are called to it, so all who are Christians ought to remember that they are priests to God. As we are called **a holy priesthood**, we ought to be holy. But if we are saying what we are, we must rather say we are an unholy priesthood, a shame to that name and holy profession. Instead of the sacrifice of a godly life and the incense of prayer and praise, in families and alone, what do we see in many but the profane speaking of a profane life? But you who have once offered up yourselves to God and are still doing so, continue to do so, and be assured that no matter how unworthy you and your offerings are, you will not be rejected.

3. The success of that work: **acceptable to God through Jesus Christ.**

The children of God delight in offering sacrifices to him. But if they did not know they were being well received, they might be greatly discouraged. Therefore, this is added: the sacrifices are **acceptable to God through Jesus Christ.** How often do the godly find it in their sweet experience that when they come to pray, God welcomes them and gives them such evidences of his love that they would not exchange it for all the pleasures of the world. And when this does not appear to be the case, they nevertheless believe it is the case. God accepts them and their ways when offered in sincerity, even when they have no more to offer than a sigh or a groan. This is most properly a spiritual sacrifice.

Do not stray away because you and the gifts you offer are inferior to the offerings of others. No one is excluded for that reason. Only give what you have, and act with affection, for that is what God looks for most of all. Under the law, those who did not have a lamb were welcomed when they brought a pair of pigeons. So the Christian must say, "What I am, Lord, I offer to you, to be wholly yours. And had I a thousand times more of outward and inner gifts, all would still be yours. Had I a greater estate or more wit or learning or power, I would endeavor to serve you with everything. What I have, I offer to you, and it is most truly yours. I am only giving to you what you already own." Nobody needs to stop sacrificing because he is poor, for what God desires is the heart. Nobody is so poor that he cannot give his heart to God.

But we must also offer our own guilt. Our prayers and service are polluted, but our acceptance does not depend on ourselves, but on the One who is not guilty at all. We are **acceptable to God through Jesus Christ.** In him we are clothed with righteousness. All our other sacrifices, our prayers and service, if we offer them through Christ and put them into his hand to offer to the Father, we need not doubt that they will be accepted in Christ, for the phrase **through Jesus Christ** refers both to our offerings and to our acceptance. We should not offer anything except through Christ. "Through Jesus, therefore, let us continually offer to God a sacrifice of praise—the fruit of lips that confess his name" (Hebrews 13:15). In this way we are viewed by the Father as hidden in his Son, for Christ is God's one and only, well-loved Son, in whom his soul delights. Not only is the Father delighted and pleased with the Son but, in Christ, with all things and people that appear with him and are presented by Christ.

This alone answers all our doubts, for we may see many wanderings in prayer, so much deadness, that would make us doubtful about being accepted by God. With Job we might say, "Even if I summoned him and he responded, I do not believe he would give me a hearing" (Job 9:16). But we must remember that all our prayers and our sacrifices pass through Christ's hand. He is that "angel, who had a golden censer, [who] came and stood at the altar. He was given much incense to offer, with the prayers of all the saints" (Revelation 8:3). Christ purifies our prayers and sacrifices with his own merits and intercession, and so makes them pleasing to the Father. How our hearts ought to be united to him through whom we are brought into favor with God and kept in favor with him, in whom we obtain all the good we receive, and in whom all we offer is accepted. In him are all our supplies of grace and our hopes of glory.

Verse 6

For in Scripture it says: "See, I lay a stone in Zion, a chosen and precious cornerstone, and the one who trusts in him will never be put to shame."

God's most important work is, quite reasonably, the chief subject of his Word—namely, the saving of lost humankind through his Son. "These are the Scriptures that testify about me," said Jesus Christ himself (John 5:39). The "Scriptures" at that time were the Old Testament, as only those books had been written then.

In the previous verse the apostle explained the happy position of Christians. They were a **spiritual house** or temple, and they were a **spiritual priesthood.** Now he amplifies and confirms both from the writings of the prophets—the former in verses 6-8, the latter in verse 9. The passages that he quotes from concerning the building are pertinent, for they include the foundation and the edifice. The first of these comes from Isaiah: "'See, I lay a stone in Zion, a tested stone, a precious cornerstone for a sure foundation'" (Isaiah 28:16).

Let it commend the Scriptures much to our diligence and affection that their great theme is our Redeemer and the redemption wrought by him. Were we more versed in them, we would daily see more of him in them, and so of necessity love him more. We must look within them. We must study them, as Christ requires. If we dug into these gold mines we would find treasures of comfort that cannot be spent but that would help us in the hardest times.

The prophecy cited here comes from the middle of a very sad denunciation of judgment against the Jews. This is normal with the prophets, particularly with the preaching prophet Isaiah, who lifts up the spirits of the godly in the worst times with this one great consolation, the promise of the Messiah. There is "a precious cornerstone for a sure foundation" laid in Zion on which those who build will not be confounded.

There are five things to note in Peter's words. First, the cornerstone; second, the laying of the cornerstone; third, building on the cornerstone; fourth, the strength of the building; fifth, the greatness of the work.

1. The **cornerstone.** This is the foundation stone, "a precious cornerstone for a sure foundation." Although the prophet's words are not

quoted exactly, the substance and sense of them are the same. In Isaiah 28:16 both expressions, "cornerstone" and "foundation," are used. The cornerstone in the foundation is the main support of the building, and throughout the building the cornerstones unite and hold the building together. Therefore this same word, "a corner," is frequently used in Scripture for princes or heads of nations (see Judges 20:2; 1 Samuel 14:38) because good governors and government uphold and unite groups of people in states or kingdoms as one building. And Jesus Christ is indeed the only Head and King of his church and thus gives it laws and rules it with wisdom and righteousness. If we believe what Peter himself teaches here, it is not built on Peter, much less his supposed successors. Jesus Christ alone is the Rock on which his church is built. Jesus Christ is the foundation and cornerstone who knits together the Jews and Gentiles ("who has made the two one," Ephesians 2:14) and who unites all the believers into one everlasting temple and bears the weight of the whole fabric.

Chosen. Christ was chosen for this purpose and was completely suited for it. Isaiah says he was "a tested stone" or a tried stone. Among humans the best things are chosen after they have been tried and tested. Jesus Christ was known by the Father and suited for the work for which he was chosen.

All the combined strength of the angels was not enough for this work. But the wise Architect of this building knew what it would cost and what foundation was necessary to bear so great and lasting a structure as he intended. Since sin had defaced and demolished the first building of man in the integrity of his creation, it was God's plan to take the ruins of the fallen building and raise a more lasting edifice than the previous one. This new building must not be prone to decay, and therefore God gave it a foundation that would last forever. A sure foundation is the most important part of a permanent building. So God chose his own Son. Christ was God, and so a strong foundation. Christ was man and so suited the nature of the stones of which the building consisted, and thus it would cement together.

Precious. The **cornerstone** was inestimably **precious.** It was rare, had inner excellence, and was most useful. That Christ was rare and unique there is no doubt. Nobody ever came to the world like him. Therefore he is called by the same prophet "Wonderful" (Isaiah 9:6), full of wonders. Christ has the power of God and the frailty of man living together in his person. The "Ancient of Days" (Daniel 7:22) became a baby. He who "stretches out the heavens" (Psalm 104:2) was wrapped in swaddling clothes in his infancy and in his prime of life was stretched out on a cross. He was completely pure and innocent, but he endured not merely the unjust cruelties of men, but the just wrath of God his Father. The Lord of life died! Christ's excellency appears in that he is the Lord of life, God blessed forever, equal with the Father. The sparkling brightness of this **pre-**

cious stone is none other than that he is "the radiance of God's glory" (Hebrews 1:3). He shines so brightly that people could not look at his appearing. Therefore, he veiled it with our flesh, and yet it shone and sparkled so much through that flesh that the apostle John says about himself and others that they had their eyes opened and looked right at him. "The Word . . . lived for a while among us" and had a tent like ours, and yet through that "we have seen his glory, the glory of the one and only Son, who came from the Father, full of grace and truth" (John 1:14).

Deity filled Christ's human nature with grace. And Christ is not only excellent in himself, but his precious virtue was given to others. Just a touch from him and spiritual diseases were cured. People talk about some stones possessing strange virtues, but it is certain that this **precious cornerstone** possessed virtue not only to heal the sick but to raise the dead. He raised dead bodies while he lived on earth, and he still raises dead souls through the power of his Word. The prophet Malachi calls him "the sun of righteousness" (Malachi 4:2), referring to this excellence and rarity.

2. The laying of the foundation: **"I lay a stone in Zion"**—that is, it is laid in God's church. It was first laid in **Zion**, the center of the church and of true religion. He was laid there in his manifestation in the flesh—suffering, dying, and rising again. Afterwards, as he was preached about throughout the world, he became the foundation of his church wherever he was received. He "became a huge mountain and filled the whole earth," as Daniel 2:35 says.

Isaiah the prophet says, "See, I lay a stone in Zion" (Isaiah 28:16). God says, "I lay" because God the Father first thought of this great work. It was in his mind from eternity, and it was accomplished by his almighty power in his Son's birth, life, death, and resurrection.

3. The building on this foundation. To be built on Christ is plainly to believe in Christ. But in this matter most people deceive themselves. They hear about the great privileges and happiness in Christ, and then imagine that this is all theirs without any more ado. Consider that madman of Athens, Thrasyllus, who thought all the ships that entered the harbor belonged to him. When his brother Crito tried to show him the error of his thinking, he bitterly mourned the loss of his happy delusion. Much of our knowledge is like the poor philosopher who defined riches exactly and spoke about their nature but possessed none of them. We are like the mapmaker who can measure land exactly in all its dimensions but does not possess a foot of it.

Truly it is but a lifeless, unsavory knowledge that people have of Christ through books and study until Christ reveals himself and persuades the heart to believe in him. Then, indeed, when it sees him and is made one with him, it says of all the reports it had heard, "I heard much, yet only the half was told me." There is in living faith, when it is infused into the soul, a clearer knowledge of Christ and his excellency than before. Even if I am surrounded on all sides, accused by the law, accused by my own conscience, accused by Satan, and am unable to reply to all these accusations, I am certain that in Christ is salvation, and there is salvation nowhere else. God has laid this precious stone in Zion so that weary souls may rest on it.

Do not think it is enough to know that this stone is laid, but make sure you are built on it by faith. Countless professing believers exist, but they are never the better nor the surer for that, any more than stones that lie loose in heaps near a foundation are joined to it. There is no benefit for us through Christ unless we are united to him. Many who think they believe are, on the contrary, like those about whom the prophet speaks as being hardened in sin, who have a "covenant with death" and "an agreement with the grave" (Isaiah 28:18).

4. The strength of this building: **the one who trusts in him will never be put to shame.** This strength of belief is mirrored by the nature of the foundation. It is a simple mistake to think it is being presumptuous to be certain of one's perseverance. Those people who have this assurance are far from building on themselves, since it is their foundation that makes them sure. That foundation not only remains firm itself but supports all who are built on it. The prophet Isaiah says, "the one who trusts will never be dismayed." Those who are disappointed by their own hopes run to and fro seeking after some new resource, but those who go to Christ do not need to do this. Our sure Foundation is laid for us, so that our souls may be established on it and be as "Mount Zion, which cannot be shaken" (Psalm 125:1). Times may come that will shake all other supports, but our Foundation rides all the storms. "Therefore we will not fear, though the earth give way" (Psalm 46:2). Even when the structure of the world is cracking around our ears, we may listen to it without fear, since we are built on this Foundation.

Why then do we choose to build on sand? Wherever we put our confidence other than in Christ, we will sooner or later repent of it and be ashamed. Remember that we must die and "must all appear before the judgment seat of Christ" (2 Corinthians 5:10). That will be "a day of darkness and gloom, a day of clouds and blackness" (Joel 2:2), when "every face turns pale" (verse 6) for all who have neglected Christ; it will nevertheless be a happy day for those who have trusted in him, for **the one who trusts in him will never be put to shame.** There is a double negative in the original—"by no means." They will be "more than conquerors through him who loved us" (Romans 8:37).

5. The greatness of this excellent work: **"See," "Behold."** Turn your wandering eyes this way. Look at this **precious cornerstone.** Do not just give him an idle glance, but behold him so that you lay hold of him. He is presented so that we may **trust in him** through whom we **will never be**

put to shame. All other unions are dissoluble. A man may be taken from his home and lands, or his home and lands may be taken from him, no matter how good his title is to them. The closest of friends may be separated, including husbands and wives, if not during their lifetime, certainly at death. But nothing can separate us from Christ. "For I am convinced that neither death nor life, neither angels nor demons, neither the present nor the future, nor any powers, neither height nor depth, nor anything else in all creation, will be able to separate us from the love of God that is in Christ Jesus our Lord" (Romans 8:38-39).

Two mistakes are made about faith. On the one hand, some people are completely without faith, and they go around flattering themselves that they possess it. On the other hand, those who do possess faith misjudge their own condition and so deprive themselves of much comfort that they should derive from their belief.

The former is the worst state and is the most common evil. What is said of wisdom is true of faith: "Many try to seek after it and attain it, if they did not falsely imagine that they have attained it already" (Seneca). There is nothing more contrary to the living nature of faith than for the soul not to be at all occupied with the thoughts of its own spiritual condition, and this is exactly the state of unbelief that many people are in. They have no doubts because they do not think about their condition. Their minds are not on these things at all. They are not awake to seek diligently after Jesus, refusing to rest until they find him. They are well enough without him. It satisfies them to hear about him, and they do not ask themselves, Is he mine? If this is all they think, they are like the wild animals.

We must note two things about spiritual doubts. There is a solicitous care of the soul about its own welfare that is praiseworthy, for it is a genuine work of the Spirit of God. But there is also doubt and distrust that stems from darkness and weakness in the soul. Where there is a great deal of smoke and no clear flame, that suggests there is a great deal of moisture in the fire. Therefore, dubious questioning of a man concerning himself is much better evidence than senseless deadness that most take for believing. People who know nothing have no doubts. The person who is not first of all aware of unbelief will never truly believe. "Never be afraid to doubt," said Coleridge, "if only you have this disposition to believe, and doubt in order that you may end in believing the truth." The Spirit's first work in the world is to "convict the world of guilt." And the sin is this, that "men do not believe" (John 16:8-9). If your faith grew out of your natural heart, you can be certain it is only a weed. The genuine plant of faith is always set by God's own hand, and it is watered and preserved by him. Because it is exposed to many hazards, he watches over it day and night. "I, the LORD, watch over it; I water it continually. I guard it day and night so that no one may harm it" (Isaiah 27:3).

The truly believing soul who is brought to Jesus Christ and united to him by God's own hand abides in him and never leaves him. For these people, what the Gospels say about Christ is more than just historical fact. They possess another knowledge and evidence that earthly people do not have; they have "the knowledge of the secrets of the kingdom of heaven" (Matthew 13:11). This is the basis for all their faith, which persuades people to rest in Christ. Christ is an able Redeemer, a sufficient Saviour, "able to save completely those who come to God through him" (Hebrews 7:25). Convinced of this, the heart believes that "whoever believes in him shall not perish but have eternal life" (John 3:16).

I am to deliberate no longer. This is the thing I must do: I must lay my soul on him, on One who is an almighty Redeemer. In myself there is nothing but shame, but in Christ there is nothing but glory; he endured shame so that we might not be ashamed. We cannot distrust ourselves enough, nor trust enough in Christ. This assurance is given me for my comfort, that whoever **trusts in him will never be put to shame.**

Verses 7-8

Now to you who believe, this stone is precious. But to those who do not believe, "The stone the builders rejected has become the capstone," and, "A stone that causes men to stumble and a rock that makes them fall." They stumble because they disobey the message—which is also what they were destined for.

Besides all the opposition that confronts faith from inside our hearts, faith also has great opposition from the world's opinion. So it is in special need, particularly where it is weak, of being strengthened against this.

Now to you who believe. "Do not be surprised that other people reject Christ, but be more convinced in your own belief as you see that the Word is true, even if they do not believe it." It is fulfilled and verified by their very rejecting it as false. Whatever worldly people think about Christ does not matter, since they do not know him.

We consider here, first, the opposition of the people and, second, the opposition of the things spoken about them.

The Opposition of the People

1. Unbelief is the supreme disobedience, for "the work of God is this: to believe in the one he has sent" (John 6:29). Therefore, the apostle Paul calls this "the obedience that comes from faith" (Romans 1:5). There is nothing more worthy of the name of obedience than for the mind to receive and believe the supernatural truths that the Gospel teaches about Jesus Christ. "You wholeheartedly obeyed the form of teaching to which you were entrusted" (Romans 6:17). The word used in 1 Peter 2:7 for **not believe**

signifies "refused persuasion." Nothing can express unbelief better than that. It is the nature of our corrupt hearts. We are children who "are disobedient" (Ephesians 2:2), altogether incredulous toward God, who is Truth itself, and therefore we are pliable as wax in Satan's hand "who is now at work" in such people (Ephesians 2:2). Such people find it easy to believe in the devil, who is the father of lies. "You belong to your father, the devil, and you want to carry out your father's desire. He was a murderer from the beginning, not holding to the truth, for there is no truth in him. When he lies, he speaks his native language, for he is a liar and the father of lies" (John 8:44).

2. Unbelief is at the root of all other disobedience, and all disobedience flows from unbelief. It is the bitter root of all the ungodliness that is rife among us. A living conviction in the heart about Jesus Christ alters all of this. "We demolish arguments and every pretension that sets itself up against the knowledge of God, and we take captive every thought to make it obedient to Christ" (2 Corinthians 10:4-5).

The Opposition of the Things Spoken About These Disobedient Unbelievers

These two testimonies taken together have in them three things: first, their rejection of Christ; second, their folly; and, third, their misery in this action.

1. Their rejection of Christ. They did not receive him, though the Father had appointed and designed him as the Foundation, **the capstone.** They slighted him and threw him out as being unfit for the building. This was done not only by the ignorant crowds but by **the builders.** Those who professed to have the skill and the office or power—the lawyers, the scribes, the Pharisees, and the chief priests—rejected Christ. "Has any of the rulers or of the Pharisees believed in him?" (John 7:48).

We should not be surprised, then, that it is not only the powers of the world who are usually enemies of Christ and those who form policies who leave Christ out of the building, but that the supposed builders of the church of God, even though they use Christ's name, still reject him and oppose the power of his spiritual kingdom. They may be learned and have a great deal of knowledge about Scripture, but they still hate Christ and the power of godliness. It is the spirit of humility and obedience and saving faith that teaches people to esteem Christ and build on him.

2. But the vanity and folly of those builders' opinion appears in that they are overpowered by the great Architect of the church, whose purpose stands. Despite their rejection of Christ, he is still made **the capstone.** They rejected him and handed him over to be crucified and then caused a stone to be rolled on this **stone,** so that it might no longer be seen, and so they thought they were safe. But he rose and **has become the capstone.**

3. The unhappiness of those who do not believe is expressed in the

words, **"A stone that causes men to stumble and a rock that makes them fall."** Because they will not be saved through Christ, they will stumble and fall and be broken to pieces on him. How does this happen? How does he who came to save destroy people? How does he whose name is salvation turn out to be people's destruction? His primary and proper purpose is to be a foundation for souls to build on and to rest on. But some, instead of building on him, will stumble and fall on him, as he is such a strong stone. Thus we see the evil of unbelief in that as other sins undermined the law, so this sin undermines the Gospel that saves us and turns life itself into death for us. And this is the misery, not of a few, but of many. Many who hear about Christ through the preaching of the Gospel will regret that they ever heard this sound and will wish they had lived and died without it as they find that they are so miserable because they neglected such a great salvation. They **stumble** over the Word because it testifies about Christ, whom they will not work hard to understand but prefer to slight and misrepresent.

The Jews stumbled over the humility of Christ's birth and life and the ignominy of his death and did not judge him according to the Scriptures. And we, in another way, think we have some kind of belief that he is the Saviour of the world; and yet because we do not allow the Scriptures to rule our thoughts about him, many of us stumble and break our necks on this rock. We think of him as Saviour of the world in general but do not embrace him ourselves as the Mediator of the new covenant.

What they were destined for. This the apostle adds in order to explain how it is that so many reject Christ and stumble over him. He tells them plainly that the secret purpose of God is accomplished in this. God has determined to glorify his justice with impenitent sinners even as he shows his rich mercy on those who believe. Here it is easier to lead you into a deep trough than to bring you out again. I prefer to stand on the shore and silently admire it rather than enter it. This is certain: God's thoughts are all no less just in themselves than deep and unfathomable by us. His justice is clear for all to see. People's destruction always comes about as a result of their own sin. What is certain is that God is not bound to give us more details about these things, and we are not entitled to ask for more information. Let two passages, as Augustine says, answer all. "But who are you, O man, to talk back to God? Shall what is formed say to him who formed it, 'Why did you make me like this?'" (Romans 9:20). "Oh, the depth of the riches of the wisdom and knowledge of God! How unsearchable his judgments, and his paths beyond tracing out!" (Romans 11:33).

The only definite way to know that our names are not on that dreadful list and to be sure that God has chosen us to be saved by his Son is this: to know that we have chosen him and are built on him by faith, which is the fruit of his love, who first chose us.

To you who believe. Faith is absolutely necessary to make a right estimate of Christ.

1. Faith is the seeing faculty of the soul in relation to Christ. That inner light must be infused from above, to make Christ visible to us. Without this light, even though Christ is beautiful, we remain blind and so cannot love him on account of his beauty. But by faith we see in Christ "the glory of the one and only Son, who came from the Father" (John 1:14). Then it is impossible for us not to give the entire affection of our hearts to him.

2. Faith, as it is this that discerns Christ, makes him ours. Faith starts by discovering Christ's excellencies, which we could not previously see. Then faith goes on to make Christ ours and gives us complete possession of Christ—all that he has and is. Once we possess Christ, faith looks at all his sufferings as endured especially for this end and benefits from them. Faith will say, "I cannot choose but to view Christ as precious, he who suffered shame that I might not be ashamed and suffered death that I might not die, who took that bitter cup of the Father's wrath and drank it, that I might be free of it."

Do not think about believing unless you want your hearts to be taken up by Christ and want him to possess your soul. Do not think about believing if you cannot despise and trample on all advantages that you either have or want to have. Everything, in comparison to knowing Christ, is rubbish. "I consider everything a loss compared to the surpassing greatness of knowing Christ Jesus my Lord, for whose sake I have lost all things. I consider them rubbish that I may gain Christ" (Philippians 3:8).

Verse 9

But you are a chosen people, a royal priesthood, a holy nation, a people belonging to God, that you may declare the praises of him who called you out of darkness into his wonderful light.

It is a cause of great consolation for Christians to know what they are as Christians. This letter dwells a great deal and frequently on this point, for two reasons. First, so as they reflect on their position in Christ they may be upheld and comforted as they suffer for him; and second, so this may help them to lead a life that honors Christ. This has been illustrated as a building, a spiritual temple, and a suitable priesthood.

The former is confirmed by testimonies of Scripture in the preceding verses; the latter in this verse, in which, though it is not directly quoted, yet it is clear that the apostle is referring to Exodus 19:5-6, where this priesthood is ascribed to all of God's chosen people. In Exodus the promise is made to the nation of the Jews, but here it is rightly applied to believing Jews, to whom he especially writes. "You who have laid your

souls on Christ by believing have shown that God has chosen you to be a
people belonging to God, yes, a **royal priesthood**, through Christ."

We have to consider here, first, the position of Christians, in the words
by which they are here described; second, how this is opposite to the state
of unbelievers; and, third, the result of this.

The State of Christians

First, they are described as **a chosen people**. This is also the case in
Psalm 24, where the psalmist speaks of God's universal sovereignty and
then about his particular choice. "The earth is the LORD's" (verse 1), but
there is a select group of people appointed to "stand in his holy place" and
"ascend the hill of the LORD" (verse 3). They are described as "the generation of those who seek him" (verse 6). We see also this in Deuteronomy
10:14-15 and Exodus 19:5, from which this passage is taken. All the earth
is the Lord's, and the nation that stands for the elect of all nations is God's
special people, beyond all others in the world. "To the LORD your God
belong the heavens, even the highest heavens, the earth and everything in
it. Yet the LORD set his affection on your forefathers and loved them, and
he chose you, their descendants, above all the nations, as it is today"
(Deuteronomy 10:14-15).

Chosen here indicates the work of effectual calling, or the separating of
believers from the rest. It indicates a difference in their present state. This
election is complete, keeping with God's eternal decree. He is drawing into
this kingly priesthood those whose names were specifically written for this
purpose in the book of life.

A royal priesthood. The worth of the holy function of believers is
emphasized by these two words (**royal** and **priesthood**) being put
together. By analogy this shows the importance of the ministry of the
Gospel, which God has placed in his church in place of the priesthood of
the law. So this title of spiritual priesthood rightly signifies a great privilege
and honor that Christians are given. They are linked to royalty because the
office of priesthood was so honorable. Those who are called to this holy
service should view themselves correctly. They should not puff themselves
up but be humble. They should compare their own worthlessness with
this great work and wonder at God's dispensation, by which he has honored them in this way. As St. Paul says of himself, "Although I am less
than the least of all God's people, this grace was given me" (Ephesians 3:8).
So the more people extol this calling, the more they humble themselves
under its weight.

There is no doubt that this kingly priesthood is the common possession
of all believers. "This is the glory of all his saints" (Psalm 149:9). They are
kings, having victory and dominion given to them to have power over the
powers of darkness and the desires of their own hearts.

Believers are not shut out from God as they were before but, being in

Christ, are brought near to him and have free access to the throne of his grace. "Since we have a great priest over the house of God, let us draw near to God with a sincere heart in full assurance of faith, having our hearts sprinkled to cleanse us from a guilty conscience and having our bodies washed with pure water" (Hebrews 10:21-22). They very clearly resemble, in their spiritual state, the priesthood under the law, first, in their consecration, second, in their service, and, third, in their laws of living.

1. Their consecration. First, the Levitical priests were washed. Therefore it is stated that he has "washed us from our sins in his own blood" (Revelation 1:5, KJV), and then follows, "and has made us to be a kingdom and priests to serve his God and Father" (Revelation 1:5). It would not be possible to draw close to God in his holy service as his priests unless we had been cleansed from our guilt and the pollution of our sins. That is done by the pure and purifying blood of Jesus, and in that way alone. None of all the blood of the sacrifices made under the law (see Hebrews 9:12) but only the blood of the pure Lamb takes away the sin of the world (see John 1:29).

Second, this is the case with that other ceremony of the priest's consecration, which was by sacrifice as well as by washing. Christ both offered himself as our sacrifice and poured out his blood for our washing. With good reason it is said that he "loved us" before it goes on to say that we are "washed" (Revelation 1:5, KJV) in his blood. That precious stream of his blood that flowed for our washing showed clearly that his heart was full of indescribable love.

Third, an anointing—namely, the graces of the Spirit—is conferred on believers, flowing to them from Christ. "From the fullness of his grace we have all received one blessing after another" (John 1:16). As the apostle Paul wrote, God "anointed us" (2 Corinthians 1:21) after he made us stand firm in Christ. This was poured on Christ as our Head and runs down from him to us. Thus he is called Christ, and we are called Christians, for we share his anointing. The consecrating oil that the priests used was made from the richest ointments and spices, to show how precious the graces of God's Spirit are that are bestowed on these spiritual priests. As that holy oil was not for general use, nor for any other people to be anointed with except for the priests, so the Spirit of grace is a special gift to believers. Natural men may have very great gifts of judgment and learning and eloquence and moral virtues, but they do not have any of this precious oil— namely, the Spirit of Christ—given to them. This anointing is said to teach believers all things: "As for you, the anointing you received from him remains in you, and you do not need anyone to teach you. But as his anointing teaches you about all things and as that anointing is real, not counterfeit—just as it has taught you, remain in him" (1 John 2:27).

Fourth, the clothes the priests wore in their services do not shine as brightly as the purity and holiness with which all saints are clothed, and in particular do not shine as brightly as the imputed righteousness of Christ. These are the pure robes that those who appear before Christ wear. "Then one of the elders asked me, 'These in white robes—who are they, and where did they come from?' I answered, 'Sir, you know.' And he said, 'These are they who have come out of the great tribulation; they have washed their robes and made them white in the blood of the Lamb'" (Revelation 7:13-14). Christ's priests are indeed clothed with righteousness. "May your priests be clothed with righteousness; may your saints sing for joy" (Psalm 132:9).

Fifth, the priests had offerings placed in their hands, and this filling of the hand signified consecration to the priesthood. Thus does Jesus Christ, who consecrates priests, put into their hands through his Spirit the offerings they are to present to God. He furnishes them with prayers and praises and all other oblations that are to be offered by them. He also gives them themselves, which they are to offer as living sacrifices, rescuing them from the usurped possession of Satan and sin.

2. Their work. This was of different kinds. First, they were in charge of the sanctuary and the vessels in it and the lamps they had to keep lit. Thus the heart of every Christian is made a temple of the Holy Spirit, and he, as a priest consecrated to God, is to obey the Spirit diligently. He has the light of spiritual knowledge within him, and he must nourish this light by continually drawing on fresh supplies from Christ.

Second, the priests were to bless the people. This is truly a spiritual priesthood, **chosen people** who procure blessings on the rest of the world and particularly on the places where they live. They are daily to offer the incense of prayer and other spiritual sacrifices to God, as the apostle says in verse 5. As the priests offered up prayers not just for themselves but for the people, so Christians are to extend their prayers and entreat God's blessings for others. As the Lord's priests, they are to offer up those praises to God that are his due from other creatures, which praise him indeed. This is put into the hands of these priests, namely, the godly, to do.

3. Their lives. We find that the rules given to the priests under the law were stricter than others, to avoid pollution. And from these this spiritual priesthood must learn an exact, holy fellowship, keeping themselves from the stain of the world. Here it follows that they are of necessity **a holy nation**. If there is a priesthood, it must be a holy one. They are indeed bought to be **a people belonging to God** (see Exodus 19:5). God did not spare his only Son, nor did the Son spare himself, and so these priests ought to be the Lord's special people. All believers are God's clergy. And as they are his portion, so he is theirs. The "clergy" or clerics are so called from the word *kleros,* a lot or portion, because they are allotted and consecrated to God, and he is their lot and inheritance (see Numbers 8:14;

18:20). The priests were not given any inheritance among their brothers, for the Lord was their inheritance (see Deuteronomy 10:9). Whatever a Christian possesses in the world, if he belongs to this spiritual priesthood, he is to have it as if it was not his to keep (see 1 Corinthians 7:30). What he has set his mind on, how he may enjoy God and find a clear conscience—that is his inheritance.

It is not such a contemptible thing to be a Christian as we might think. It is a holy, honorable, happy position. All who share this life will study to live in the correct way and not fail to love the Lord Jesus who has bought all this for them, yes, who has humbled himself so they can be exalted.

The Contrast Between the State of Christians and That of Unbelievers

As far as outward condition is concerned, we would complain less if we thought about the sad condition many other people are in. That would make us not only content, but cheerful and thankful. Not only unspiritual people but even those who have a spiritual life in them, when they forget who they are, tend to look on the things before them with an unspiritual eye and to doubt God's goodness. But when they view the situation correctly, they are no longer taken in by appearances. When they think of unbelievers as strangers, yes, as enemies of God and slaves of Satan fastened in the chains of their own impenitence and unbelief, and by these bound over to eternal death, when they see themselves called to the freedom of the children of God, partakers of the honor of the one and only Son in whom they have believed and have been made kings and priests, then they no longer envy but pity the ungodly. It makes them say with David, "The boundary lines have fallen for me in pleasant places; surely I have a delightful inheritance" (Psalm 16:6). It makes them endure all their sufferings and disgraces with patience, indeed with joy, and think more about praising than complaining.

The Purpose of Their Calling

That purpose is **that you may declare the praises of him who called you out of darkness into his wonderful light.** So that we may understand more fully the position into which we have been called, it is spoken about in different ways. To magnify the grace of God the more, we have here, first, both the terms of this change (from where and to what), and, second, its principle, the calling of God.

First, regarding the terms of this change, **out of darkness.** There is nothing more usual, not only in divine but in human writings, than to use outward visible things to express things understood with the mind. Among such expressions there is nothing more frequent than that of light and darkness. They stand for good and evil and for outward prosperity or adversity. Truth is rightly called light because it is the chief ornament of the rational world, just as light is of the visible. As light, because of its beauty, is refreshing and comfortable to those who look at it, so truth is a most delightful thing to the soul who rightly apprehends it.

This may help us to appreciate the spiritual sense in which it is spoken about here. The position of lost mankind is indeed nothing but **darkness**, being destitute of all spiritual truth and comfort and leading to utter and everlasting darkness.

And it is like this because through sin the soul is cut off from God, who is the first and highest Light, the first and foremost Truth. He is light in himself, as the apostle John tells us: "God is light; in him there is no darkness at all" (1 John 1:5). God is also light to man's soul, as David said, "The LORD is my light" (Psalm 27:1).

Since the soul is made capable of receiving divine light, it cannot be happy without it. Give it whatever other light you will, it remains in darkness so long as it is without God, since he is the special light and life of the soul. And as truth is united with the soul that understands it, and light with the visual faculty, so, in order that the soul may have God as its light, it has to be in union with God. Sin has broken that union and thus cut off the soul from its light and plunged it into spiritual darkness. Our souls are filled with darkness and also with uncleanness, a companion of darkness. They are not only dark as dungeons, but as filthy as dungeons used to be. "They are darkened in their understanding and separated from the life of God because of the ignorance that is in them due to the hardening of their hearts. Having lost all sensitivity, they have given themselves over to sensuality so as to indulge in every kind of impurity, with a continual lust for more" (Ephesians 4:18-19). Again, in this state they have no light or solid comfort. Our great comfort here is not in anything present but in hope. Now, if we are without Christ and without God, we have no hope (see Ephesians 2:12).

Into his wonderful light. As the state from which we are called by grace is rightly called **darkness**, so that to which it calls us is correctly named **light**. In the same way Christ, who came to bring our deliverance, is frequently called "light" in Scripture. "The true light that gives light to every man was coming into the world" (John 1:9). "In him was life, and that life was the light of men" (John 1:4). Similarly, Christ is called "the Word" and "the wisdom of God," not just in regard to his own knowledge, but as revealing God to us (see John 1:14 and 1 Corinthians 1:24, and compare with 1 Corinthians 1:30). Malachi calls him "the sun of righteousness" (4:2). Now the sun does not light itself up, but it gives light to the world (see Genesis 1:15).

Christ is our Light, as opposed to all kinds of **darkness.** He is our light, in contrast with the dark shadows of the ceremonial law, which may be meant here as part of that **darkness** from which the apostle writes that these Jews were delivered through the knowledge of Christ. Christ is our

Light, in contrast with the **darkness** of Gentile superstitions and idolatries. That is why Simeon said Christ was "a light for revelation to the Gentiles and for glory to your people Israel" (Luke 2:32). To all who believe, to both Jews and Gentiles, Christ is light, as opposed to the ignorance, slavery, and misery of their natural state, teaching them through his Spirit the things of God and reuniting them with God, who is the Light of the soul. Jesus said, "I am the light of the world. Whoever follows me will never walk in darkness, but will have the light of life" (John 8:12).

That mysterious union of the soul with God in Christ, which the unspiritual man understands so little about, is the reason for all the spiritual light of grace that a believer enjoys. There is no correct knowledge about God once a person has fallen from it, except in his Son. There is no comfort in beholding God, except through Christ. There is nothing but anger and wrath seen in God's looks unless we view him through Christ, in whom God is well pleased. "For God, who said, 'Let light shine out of darkness,' made his light shine in our hearts to give us the light of the knowledge of the glory of God in the face of Christ" (2 Corinthians 4:6). Therefore the kingdom of light, as opposed to the kingdom of darkness, is called "the kingdom of the Son he loves" (see Colossians 1:13).

A spirit of light and knowledge flows from Jesus Christ into the souls of believers and acquaints them with the mysteries of the kingdom of God, which cannot be known in any other way. This spirit of knowledge is also a spirit of holiness, for purity and holiness are both signified by this light. He took away that huge, dark body of sin that was between us and the Father and that hid him from us. The light of his countenance sanctifies us through the truth. It is a light that has heat in it and that influences our affections and warms them toward God and divine things. The **darkness** here is indeed the shadow of death, and those who do not have Christ are said to sit "in darkness and in the shadow of death" until Christ visits them (see Luke 1:79). So this "light" is "life" (see John 1:4) for the soul.

Two things are said about this Light to commend it. First, it is **his . . . light**—that is, it is God's light; and, second, it is **wonderful.** All light is from God. He is called "the Father of the heavenly lights" (James 1:17). But this **light** of grace is special. It is a light beyond the reach of nature, infused into the soul in a supernatural way, the light of the elect world, where God especially and graciously lives. Unspiritual people may know a great deal about unspiritual things, and they may know much about spiritual things but in an unspiritual way. They may speak about Christ, but it is in the dark. They do not see him, and therefore they do not love him. But the soul that has Christ's light, God's special light, sees Jesus Christ and loves and delights in him and walks with him. A little of this light is worth much more than all other knowledge. It is superior in kind and in origin, for it is from heaven. One beam of the sun is worth more than the light of 10,000 torches. It is a pure, heavenly light that never fades, whereas the other light is earthly and lasts for only a moment. So we must not think it incredible that a poor uneducated Christian may know more about God than the wisest unspiritual man. For the one knows God by man's light, the other by God's light, and that is the only right knowledge. As the sun cannot be seen except by its own light, so God cannot be known as Saviour unless he reveals himself.

Since this **light** is especially God's, it is not surprising that it is **wonderful**. The common light of the world is so as well, but because it is so common, we think it is not. The Lord is wonderful in wisdom and in power, in all his deeds of creation and providence. But above all, he is wonderful as he brings his grace to us. This **light** is not known to the world. It is **wonderful**, but few take part in it. Since this **light** of grace is so **wonderful**, how much more wonderful will be the light of glory in which it ends.

Hence, first, learn to esteem highly the Gospel, in which this light shines to us. The apostle calls it, therefore, "the light of the gospel of the glory of Christ" (2 Corinthians 4:4). Surely we have no reason to be ashamed of it, except for ourselves being so unlike it.

Second, do not think, you who are so ignorant about God and his Son and the mysteries of salvation, that you have any share in his grace. The first characteristic of his renewed image in the soul, as it was his first deed in the material world, is light. A house that is shut and does not allow any light in, even though it is daytime outside, remains dark inside.

Third, consider your delight in the deeds of darkness, and be in awe of God's great condemnation: "This is the verdict: Light has come into the world, but men loved darkness instead of light because their deeds were evil" (John 3:19).

Fourth, you who do indeed participate in this happy change, let your hearts be a place where this light lives. "Have nothing to do with the fruitless deeds of darkness, but rather expose them" (Ephesians 5:11). Study a great deal to increase your spiritual light and knowledge, with holiness and obedience. Reflect on God's rich love, and remember his **wonderful light**. As "you were once darkness, but you are now light in the Lord," I beseech you, as did the apostle Paul, and through him the Spirit of God, "Live as children of light" (Ephesians 5:8).

We now move on to speak about the other parts of this verse and to the main part of this charge, to God's calling: **who called you.** The main point of wisdom in a man is to consider who he is, who created him, and for what purpose he exists. While a Christian sometimes thinks about this as an unspiritual person, he must also remember that he is a spiritual being, since he is a new creature because he is a Christian. This is clearly shown in the words of this verse. First, he is told what he is. Christians are **a chosen people, a royal priesthood, a holy nation, a people belonging to God.**

Second, this verse says where Christians come from. They are **called out of darkness** by God. The God who is the author of every kind of being has **called you out of darkness into his wonderful light.** You "have been chosen according to the foreknowledge of God" (1 Peter 1:2). If you are **a royal priesthood,** you know that it is he who has anointed you. If you are **a holy nation,** God has sanctified you (see John 17:17). If you are **a people belonging to God,** it is because he has bought you (see 1 Corinthians 6:20). All this is included in this calling, and they are all one thing.

Third, this verse says for what purpose we exist: **that you may declare the praises** of God. We have already looked at the first of these three things, and now we will consider the other two.

Who called you. Those who live in society and profess the faith of Christians are called to the **light** of the Gospel that shines in the church of God. Now, this is no small favor and privilege, as many people are left in **darkness** and in the shadow of death. What is here termed a calling in regard to the way of God's working with the soul is termed a rescue elsewhere. The apostle Paul speaks about it in these terms: "For he has rescued us from the dominion of darkness and brought us into the kingdom of the Son he loves" (Colossians 1:13). That rescue is this calling. It is from the power of **darkness,** a powerful force that keeps the soul captive. As there are chains of eternal **darkness** on damned spirits that will never be taken off and that are said to be reserved for the day of judgment, so there are chains of spiritual **darkness** on the unconverted soul that can be only be taken off by God's powerful hand. When God calls the sinner to come out, the chains fall off and enable the soul to come into the **light.**

It is an operative word that carries out the command, as in creation: "And God said, 'Let there be light,' and there was light" (Genesis 1:3). The apostle Paul refers to this when he writes, "For God, who said, 'Let light shine out of darkness,' made his light shine in our hearts to give us the light of the knowledge of the glory of God in the face of Christ" (2 Corinthians 4:6). God calls man. He works with him as with a reasonable creature, but he works as an almighty Creator. "The voice of the LORD is powerful; the voice of the LORD is majestic" (Psalm 29:4). The work of grace, like oil, to which it is often compared, penetrates and sinks into the soul. That word of God's own calling frees the heart from all its nets, as it did the disciples from theirs, to follow Christ. The call that brought St. Matthew from his tax-collecting work made him reject worldly gains and pleasures and follow Christ (see Matthew 9:9).

Every believer is ready to acknowledge how rebellious his heart was and what his miserable love of darkness was and that the gracious yet mighty call of God drew him out of this. Therefore, he willingly assents to the third thing to be considered, which is that it becomes him, as being the end of his calling, to **declare the praises** of God who has so mercifully and so powerfully called him from such misery to so happy a state.

This is logical, first, because it is God's purpose in calling us to communicate his goodness to us, so that he may be given the glory. The top agent cannot work except for the highest goal. In particular, the calling and exalting of a number of lost mankind to this great honor and happiness happens through God's rich grace. The apostle Paul refers to this when he says, "to the praise of his glorious grace, which he has freely given us in the One he loves" (Ephesians 1:6), and "in order that we, who were the first to hope in Christ, might be for the praise of his glory" (verse 12).

Second, as this is God's purpose, it should be ours. This is his purpose in calling us, and therefore it is our great duty, being thus called, to **declare his praises.** This is God's due, and it is most profitable for us in all things to seek his praises. It is the most excellent intent to have the same thought as God, the same purpose as his, and to aim at nothing less than his glory.

Verse 10

Once you were not a people, but now you are the people of God; once you had not received mercy, but now you have received mercy.

The love of God for his children is the great subject both of his Word and of their thoughts, and therefore his Word (the rule of their thoughts and their whole lives) speaks so much about that love, so that they may highly esteem it and walk in it. This is the scope of St. Paul's doctrine to the Ephesians, and his prime concern for them. "So that Christ may dwell in your hearts through faith. And I pray that you, being rooted and established in love . . . may be filled to the measure of all the fullness of God" (Ephesians 3:17, 19). And this is the aim of the apostle Peter here. He began this letter to the believing Jews by contrasting their election in heaven with their dispersion on earth, and the same consideration runs through the rest of the letter. Here he is showing them the great fruit of that love, the happy and privileged state to which they are called in Christ.

The choosing of Christ and of believers is like one deed, and they both have the same objective—one glorious temple, with Christ as its foundation and **cornerstone** (verse 6), and with them as the **stones** (verse 5). Christ is the King of kings and the great High Priest, and they, through him, are made kings and priests to God the Father, **a royal priesthood** (verse 9). Christ is the Light of the world, and they, through him, are the children of light. Now that this is their privileged state, the apostle emphasizes it with a double contrast. First, by showing the misery under which others exist and, second, by showing that this was the miserable state they were in before they were called.

The former misery is spoken about in the previous verse as **darkness.** In this verse it is more fully and plainly set out. These words are taken from the prophet Hosea: "I will plant her for myself in the land; I will show my love to the one I called 'Not my loved one.' I will say to those called 'Not my people,' 'You are my people'; and they will say, 'You are my God'" (Hosea 2:23). Here, as is usual with the prophets, Hosea is raised up by God's Spirit from the temporal troubles and deliverances of the Israelites to consider and foretell that great restoration brought by Jesus Christ in purchasing a new people for himself, made up of both Jews and Gentiles who believe. Therefore this prophecy applies to both groups of people. St. Paul too uses this prophecy about the calling of the Gentiles: "As he says in Hosea: 'I will call them "my people" who are not my people; and I will call her "my loved one" who is not my loved one'" (Romans 9:25).

Their previous misery, in contrast with their present happiness, is here expressed in two ways. They were, first, **not a people;** and, second, they **had not received mercy.** When they were not God's people they were so miserable that they were not worthy of the name of a people at all. "I will make them envious by those who are not a people" (Deuteronomy 32:21).

There is a divine kind of being, a life that the soul has through a special union with God, and therefore in that sense the soul without God is dead, as is the body without the soul. "As for you, you were dead in your transgressions and sins" (Ephesians 2:1). As the body, separated from the soul, is not only a lifeless lump but putrefies, so the soul, separated from God, is subject to a vile putrefaction. "All have turned aside, they have together become corrupt; there is no one who does good, not even one" (Psalm 14:3). People who are still unbelievers are **not a people** but rather a heap of filthy carcasses.

Captive sinners lack that happiness that flows from God to the souls who are united to him. "As the whole life of the body is the soul, so the happy life of the soul is God" (Augustine). God's people are the only people in the world worthy of being called "a people." The rest are but dross and rubbish. Yet in the world's judgment, the people of God are merely a company of foolish creatures. "Up to this moment we have become the scum of the earth, the refuse of the world," states the apostle Paul (1 Corinthians 4:13). But in God's sight his people are the only people, and the rest of the world are as nothing.

The people of God. "I will say to those called 'Not my people,' 'You are my people'; and they will say, 'You are my God'" (Hosea 2:23). That mutual interest and possession is the very foundation of all our comfort. He is the first chooser. He first says, "my people." He calls them his, and he makes them this; then they say, "You are my God." This is therefore a relationship that will endure and will not break because it is founded on God's choice, and God does not change his mind.

Once you had not received mercy. The mercies of the Lord to his chosen people are from everlasting. Yet, as long as God's decree of mercy stays hidden and is not discovered by those whom it affects, they are said not to have **received mercy.** When it begins to work in their effectual calling, then they find it to be theirs. It was in a secret way moving toward them, just as the sun after midnight is coming closer to us, although we are not aware of it until dawn.

But now you have received mercy. God's mercy is both free and tender. As God's mercy is said to have been free to the Jews in choosing them before the rest of the world, so it is for the spiritual Israel of God and to everyone belonging to that company. "The Lord did not set his affection on you and choose you because you were more numerous than other peoples, for you were the fewest of all peoples. But it was because the LORD loved you and kept the oath he swore to your forefathers that he brought you out with a mighty hand and redeemed you from the land of slavery, from the power of Pharaoh king of Egypt" (Deuteronomy 7:7-8). As well as being free mercy, it is tender mercy. The prophet Jeremiah speaks about this tenderness or compassion. The mercies of our God toward us are like the love of a compassionate father. "'Is not Ephraim my dear son, the child in whom I delight? Though I often speak against him, I still remember him. Therefore my heart yearns for him; I have great compassion for him,' declares the LORD" (Jeremiah 31:20). "As a father has compassion on his children, so the LORD has compassion on those who fear him" (Psalm 103:13). And if you do not think this shows enough tenderness, God's tenderness is also said to be like the tenderness of a mother, and even greater than a mother's love. "Can a mother forget the baby at her breast and have no compassion on the child she has borne? Though she may forget, I will not forget you!" (Isaiah 49:15). This is rich mercy. It is a constant, unalterable mercy, a stream still running.

In both these expressions the apostle draws the attention of believers to reflect on their former misery and to view it together with their present state. This occurs very frequently in the Scriptures. "So I will establish my covenant with you, and you will know that I am the LORD. Then, when I make atonement for you for all you have done, you will remember and be ashamed and never again open your mouth because of your humiliation, declares the Sovereign LORD" (Ezekiel 16:62-63). "Do you not know that the wicked will not inherit the kingdom of God? Do not be deceived: Neither the sexually immoral nor idolaters nor adulterers nor male prostitutes nor homosexual offenders nor thieves nor the greedy nor drunkards nor slanderers nor swindlers will inherit the kingdom of God. And that is what some of you were. But you were washed, you were sanctified, you were justified in the name of the Lord Jesus Christ and by the Spirit of our God" (1 Corinthians 6:9-11). This is most useful. It helps to make the Christian humble in his soul. It helps to make him love and be grateful and obedient. It cannot but make him abase himself and magnify the free grace and love of God. This may be one reason why it pleases the Lord to delay the conversion of some people, so that after they have experienced years of sin, they appreciate all the more the riches and glory of God's grace and the freeness of his choice.

Remember that you have been pulled out of everlasting destruction. "He lifted me out of the slimy pit, out of the mud and mire; he set my feet on a rock and gave me a firm place to stand" (Psalm 40:2-3). Remember from what you have been delivered and to what you have been raised up. "He raises the poor from the dust and lifts the needy from the ash heap; he seats them with princes, with the princes of their people" (Psalm 113:7). Joshua the high priest was stripped of his filthy clothes, and a clean turban was put on his head, and those who belong to this priesthood are treated in the same way. "Now Joshua was dressed in filthy clothes as he stood before the angel. The angel said to those who were standing before him, 'Take off his filthy clothes.' Then he said to Joshua, 'See, I have taken away your sin, and I will put rich garments on you.' Then I said, 'Put a clean turban on his head.' So they put a clean turban on his head and clothed him, while the angel of the LORD stood by" (Zechariah 3:3-5). Let us look back, as the apostle Peter says we should, and reflect on how God has called us **out of darkness into his wonderful light.**

Verse 11

Dear friends, I urge you, as aliens and strangers in the world, to abstain from sinful desires, which war against your soul.

In this letter we find the apostle combining divine doctrine with most useful practical exhortations; see 1:13, 22; 2:1. This occurs again in this verse. Ministers of the Gospel should base their teaching on this model. They should both teach and exhort. They should exhort people to holiness and the duties of a Christian life, as well as teach them the doctrines of the Christian faith. To hear about the mercies of God is very pleasing. But to have this followed by **abstain from sinful desires** is not so pleasant. But it must be like this. Those who want to share in God's mercy and happiness must **abstain from sinful desires.**

Dear friends, I urge you. The apostles frequently use this appeal. "Therefore, I urge you, brothers, in view of God's mercy, to offer your bodies as living sacrifices, holy and pleasing to God" (Romans 12:1). The apostle Peter calls his readers **dear friends.** What is known to stem from love cannot but readily be received and accepted. "Here is the advice of a friend, one who genuinely loves you and aims at nothing other than your good. It is because I love you that **I urge you.**"

Abstain. Epictetus made a very wise summary of philosophy when he said, "Bear and forbear." Stoic philosophy was summarized as: "to bear with the troubles and to abstain from the pleasures of life." These are truly the two main duties that our apostle recommends to his Christian brothers in this letter. We will, first, explain what these **sinful desires** are and then consider the exhortation to **abstain from** them.

Unchaste desires are particularly given this name, but to see these only in this passage is doubtless too narrow. Any undue desire and use of earthly things and all the corrupt affections of our unspiritual minds is what is meant here.

In that sense these **sinful desires** encompass a great deal of sin. The three that the apostle John speaks of, the world's accursed trinity, are included in this title **sinful desires.** "For everything in the world—the cravings of sinful man, the lust of his eyes and the boasting of what he has and does—comes not from the Father but from the world" (1 John 2:16). A crew of base, imperious masters they are, to which the unspiritual man is a slave. "At one time we too were foolish, disobedient, deceived and enslaved by all kinds of sinful passions and pleasures" (Titus 3:3). Some people are more addicted to one kind of lust than to another, but all are unhappy, as they are God's enemies. "Get rid of all bitterness, rage and anger, brawling and slander, along with every form of malice" (Ephesians 4:31).

To **abstain** from these **sinful desires** is to hate them, and if overtaken by them to kill them then and there. In a word, we are to **abstain** not only from serving things that are forbidden, but also from desiring and delighting in them. As the honor of a Christian's state is far above these base desires, so the happiness of his state sets him above the need for the pleasures of sin. The apostle has already said, **Like newborn babies, crave pure spiritual milk, so that by it you may grow up in your salvation, now that you have tasted that the Lord is good** (verses 2-3).

The real reason why we remain servants of these evil desires is that we are still strangers to God's love and to those pure pleasures that are in him. The pleasures of this earth are not worthy of being followed, but since people know no other, they stay with what they know. Aristotle gives this as the reason why people are so set on sensual delights, because they are ignorant of the higher pleasures that are appropriate for the soul. It is in vain to tell people to **abstain from sinful desires** unless they have received mercy and experienced the gracious love of Christ. Oh, that we would seek the knowledge of this love. For seeking it, we would find it; and finding it, we would throw away sinful pleasures. We are barred from having fellowship with the unfruitful deeds of darkness so that we may have fellowship with the Father and with his Son, Jesus Christ (see 1 John 1:3, 7). The apostle dissuades us from following these **sinful desires** by speaking, first, about the condition of Christians and, second, about the condition of those **sinful desires.**

1. The condition of Christians: they are **aliens and strangers in the world.** These dispersed Jews were strangers scattered in different countries—"scattered throughout Pontus, Galatia, Cappadocia, Asia and Bithynia" (1:1)—but that is not what is meant here. They are called **strangers** in the spiritual sense that applies to all saints. If Christians would consider how little, and for how little a time, they need to concern themselves with the affairs of this life, they might indulge in **sinful desires** in order "to gratify the desires of the sinful nature" (Romans 13:14). This is not the place to rest or take delight in. We are to live as **strangers** on this earth.

2. The apostle argues from the condition of those lusts. It is bad enough that **sinful desires** are far inferior to the soul, so that they can never satisfy the soul. But that is not all. These **sinful desires** also **war against your soul.** And their fight against the soul is made up of cunning and deceit. They embrace the soul in order to strangle it. The godly know well from their own sad experience that their hearts often deceive them, harboring and hiding such things as deprive them of the joy of grace and the comforts of the Holy Spirit that they would otherwise attain.

This **war against your soul** involves breaking God's law and becoming subject to his wrath. The apostle Peter says this to drive home his point. "In addition to these **sinful desires** being unworthy of you, the truth is, if you Christians serve your **sinful desires** you kill your souls." "For if you live according to the sinful nature, you will die; but if by the Spirit you put to death the misdeeds of the body, you will live" (Romans 8:13).

Consider, when people are on their deathbeds and are close to entering eternity, what they think about their work on this earth and about serving their own hearts and **sinful desires.** Then they see that nothing remains of all these ways except the guilt of their sin and their accusing conscience and the wrath of God.

Oh, that you would be convinced to esteem your precious souls and not wound them as you do, but to fight for them against those **sinful desires** that attack them. The service of Jesus Christ is alone appropriate for the soul's loyalty. The only honorable way for a soul to live is to serve Christ as its Lord, and to serve him alone, for he has bought it at such a high price.

Verse 12

Live such good lives among the pagans that, though they accuse you of doing wrong, they may see your good deeds and glorify God on the day he visits us.

There are two things that unspiritual people take least account of but are of all things most highly prized by Christians—their own souls and God's glory. So there are no more important things for them to be interested in than these. The apostle uses them to exhort Christians to live a holy and blameless life. His advice here, and his exhortation in the previous verse, are the same. A truly good life lived among the pagans can only be a spiritual one that is not defiled with the **sinful desires, which war against the soul.** The inner disposition of the heart and the outward living of our lives are inseparably linked.

I will speak about the former first, as the spring of the latter. "Above all else, guard your heart, for it is the wellspring of life" (Proverbs 4:23). All else follows from that, and if you do this, the tongue, eyes, and feet will follow. "Put away perversity from your mouth; keep corrupt talk far from your lips. Let your eyes look straight ahead, fix your gaze directly before you. Make level paths for your feet and take only ways that are firm. Do not swerve to the right or the left; keep your foot from evil" (Proverbs 4:24-27). For impure streams to stop flowing, the corrupt spring must dry up. This is the correct approach, according to our Saviour's teaching. "By their fruit you will recognize them. Do people pick grapes from thornbushes, or figs from thistles? Likewise every good tree bears good fruit, but a bad tree bears bad fruit" (Matthew 7:16-17). Some good outward actions avail nothing if the soul is not renewed. You may stick some figs or hang some clusters of grapes on a thornbush, but they cannot grow on it.

In this people deceive themselves. When they fall into sin and are reproved for it, they possibly think, "I will reform myself. I will not be guilty of this again." But because they go no deeper, they fall in the same way again. If they do not commit the same sin again, they substitute another one for it. They are starting at the wrong place. They must first of all purify the heart. Evil desires are the source of evil words and evil deeds. "What causes fights and quarrels among you? Don't they come from your desires that battle within you?" (James 4:1).

So then, according to the order of the apostle's exhortation, the only true principle of all good and Christian behavior in the world is to put to death all earthly and sinful desires in the heart. As long as they possess the heart, they clog it up and constrict its flow toward God and his ways. But when the heart is freed from them, it is enlarged, and then, says David, a person may not only walk but "run in the path of [God's] commands" (Psalm 119:32). Unless the heart is freed in this way, a person will always lead an inconsistent life. He will take one step like a Christian, and the next step like a worldly person. The solution for this is to have our **sinful desires** put to death. "For we know that our old self was crucified with him so that the body of sin might be rendered powerless, that we should no longer be slaves to sin" (Romans 6:6).

The text states three things: first, one result of Christians' ordinary behavior in the world is to be accused of wrongdoing (**though they accuse you of doing wrong**); second, their good use of that evil—they may do better because of it; and, third, the good goal and certain result of doing this, the glory of God (**glorify God**).

1. **Though they accuse you of doing wrong.** This is in general the disease of people's corrupt nature. In addition to this general bias toward speaking evil about people, there is a particular malice in the world against those who are born of God. The evil tongue is always on fire, and it is seven times as hot against Christians. "The tongue also is a fire, a world of evil among the parts of the body. It corrupts the whole person, sets the whole course of his life on fire, and is itself set on fire by hell" (James 3:6). There are three reasons for this. First, as people naturally hate God and are unable to reach him, it is little wonder that they vent their malice against those who are in his image, God's children. Second, because they themselves are neither able nor willing to be pure or lead a holy life, they attempt to prevent Christians from doing so. Third, the reproaches they cast on those who follow pure religion [the Puritans] are aimed at religion itself.

2. **Live such good lives among the pagans.** As the sovereign power of drawing good out of evil resides in God, so he teaches his own children to copy him in this. He teaches them to draw sweetness out of their bitterest affliction and increase inner peace from outward troubles. David says, "Lead me, O LORD, in your righteousness because of my enemies—make straight your way before me" (Psalm 5:8). The word for "enemies" is "observers" or those who scan my ways, every step I take. If there is a single slip, they will be sure to note it. So we depend on the Spirit of God to be our guide and to enable us to lead a holy and blameless life.

Good lives. The word *kalon* means "goodness and beauty." A Christian has beauty. When those who do not know God discover such beauty, they cannot but love it. But where it does not evoke love, it brings opposition. Let us all, therefore, resolve to follow the apostle's exhortation, so that we may conduct ourselves "in a manner worthy of the gospel of Christ" (Philippians 1:27). And if you live among godless people, do not worry if they speak evil about you. Let your life answer for you as you lead your **good** life.

3. **Glorify God on the day he visits us.** Peter does not say that they will praise or commend you, but that they should **glorify God.** However **the day he visits us** is understood, the result is the same: they should **glorify God.** It is this that the apostle keeps in their sight. He does not teach them to be concerned about their own esteem but about God's glory. In everything the Christian says, "Let God be glorified," and that is sufficient. This is the sum of his desires. He is far from glorying in himself or seeking to

raise himself, for he knows that of himself he is nothing, but through the free grace of God he is what he is. "Whence any glorying to thee, rottenness and dust?" says St. Bernard. "What is it to you if you are holy? Is it not the Holy Spirit that has sanctified you? If you could perform miracles, even if they were done by your hand, it would still not be by your power, but by the power of God."

David says, "You turned my wailing into dancing; you removed my sackcloth and clothed me with joy, that my heart may sing to you and not be silent. O LORD my God, I will give you thanks forever" (Psalm 30:11-12). What we are to do in the world as God's creatures, his new creatures, his creatures created for good works, is to bring glory to him. Our dominant thought should be, How can I best advance God's glory?

The day he visits us. As they see your good deeds, they may embrace religion and God, whom they reject at present. Whether this happens or not, they will be visited by the same light and grace from above that has sanctified you. This, I believe, is the sense of this word, although it may be interpreted in different ways. Your good lives may be one of the means of their conversion. But for this to be effective God must visit them.

Verses 13-14

Submit yourselves for the Lord's sake to every authority instituted among men: whether to the king, as the supreme authority, or to governors, who are sent by him to punish those who do wrong and to commend those who do right.

One of the most false yet common prejudices the world has had against true religion is that it is an enemy of civil power and government. The enemies of the Jews made this accusation as Jerusalem was being rebuilt: "In these records you will find that this city is a rebellious city, troublesome to kings and provinces, a place of rebellion from ancient times. That is why this city was destroyed" (Ezra 4:15). The Jews leveled this charge against Christian preachers as well. "These men who have caused trouble all over the world have now come here, and Jason has welcomed them into his house. They are all defying Caesar's decrees, saying that there is another king, one called Jesus" (Acts 17:6-7). Generally speaking, the enemies of the Christians in the early days accused them of rebelling against authority. Therefore our apostle, coming to particular rules for Christian living, begins with this one: **Submit yourselves . . .** This verse teaches, first, the extent of this duty and, second, the basis of this duty.

1. The extent of the duty. This extends to all civil power, to **every authority instituted among men.** There is no need to question the origin of civil power. If you look at those great monarchies in Daniel's vision, you see that one of them is built on another, and all of them are like terri-

ble, devouring beasts of monstrous shape. Whether this verse in 1 Peter refers to the Roman Empire or not, it teaches that the apostle's brothers are to be submissive to its authority. God has been more specific in the officers and government of his own house, his church. But civil societies he has left to be free to choose their type of government. Even though they will be defective, it is specifically stated here that we are to submit to their authority.

2. The ground of this duty. The main reason for submitting to human authority is the interest that divine authority has in it. God has appointed civil government as a common good among men and has especially commanded his people to obey it, "for the Lord's sake." First, God has in general instituted civil government for the good of human society, and there is good in it, no matter how depraved it is. Tyranny is better than anarchy.

Second, it is through God's providence that men come to places of authority. "No one from the east or the west or from the desert can exalt a man. But it is God who judges: He brings one down, he exalts another" (Psalm 75:6-7). "You will be driven away from people and will live with the wild animals; you will eat grass like cattle and be drenched with the dew of heaven. Seven times will pass by for you until you acknowledge that the Most High is sovereign over the kingdoms of men and gives them to anyone he wishes" (Daniel 4:25). "Jesus answered, 'You would have no power over me if it were not given to you from above'" (John 19:11).

Third, God commands that these powers be obeyed. "Everyone must submit himself to the governing authorities, for there is no authority except that which God has established" (Romans 13:1). "Remind the people to be subject to rulers and authorities, to be obedient, to be ready to do whatever is good" (Titus 3:1). The subjection that is commanded here is to be subject, as it were, in your rank, just as you remain subordinate to God. It is the pride and self-love of our nature that brings about disobedience in inferiors and violence and injustice in superiors. Just government and due obedience are special gifts from God's own hand and a prime blessing on states and kingdoms.

Verses 15-16

For it is God's will that by doing good you should silence the ignorant talk of foolish men. Live as free men, but do not use your freedom as a cover-up for evil; live as servants of God.

This continues the same reason for the same duty. If Christians will obey the Lord, then they must obey civil powers, for that is his will, and they will not deny their obligation to him, for they are **servants of God.** The point of civil obedience is here recommended to Christians as conforming to God's will and as being most in keeping with Christian freedom.

For it is God's will. The strongest and most binding reason that can guide a Christian mind is having **God's will** as its law. A Christian's renewed frame of mind, through which a man may renounce the world and himself and his sinful ways, longs to follow God's will. "Do not conform any longer to the pattern of this world, but be transformed by the renewing of your mind. Then you will be able to test and approve what God's will is—his good, pleasing and perfect will" (Romans 12:2). The task of the Christian is to understand and do God's will. "Therefore do not be foolish, but understand what the Lord's will is" (Ephesians 5:17). He is to walk so that he pleases God. The apostle exhorts the Thessalonians, "Finally, brothers, we instructed you how to live in order to please God," and then he adds, "It is God's will that you should be holy" (1 Thessalonians 4:1, 3).

Let it, then, be your aim to have your will crucified to everything that is sinful. In a word, you must say, "This is the will of God, and therefore it is mine."

That by doing good you should silence the ignorant talk of foolish men. The duties of the second half of the Ten Commandments, which relate to our actions toward other people, are seen by unspiritual people to be more devoid of religion than those that refer to God. And, therefore, as in other letters, the apostle is here particular about these things that vindicate religion in the eyes of outsiders. Ignorance is usually loud and prattling, making a great deal of noise, and so needs a muzzle to silence it, as the word *phimoun* implies. They are called **ignorant** because they were prepared to speak evil of religion. There was a perverseness in their ignorance that the word *aphronon* indicates. Generally all kinds of speaking evil and uncharitable censures reveal foolish, worthless minds and as such belong to a great number of people. The wise Christian reaction to this, instead of impatiently fretting at people's wrongdoings, is to remain calm and silent. Be like a rock over which the waves foam and roar.

Live as free men. The apostle adds this in case anyone should misunderstand the nature of their Christian freedom. God gives this freedom, and he wants them to understand it correctly. This is only mentioned in passing, but free they are, and only they participate in this liberty. "So if the Son sets you free, you will be free indeed" (John 8:36). All others are slaves to Satan, the world, and their own sinful desires. They are like the Israelites in Egypt, working in the clay under hard taskmasters.

A cover-up for evil. Beware that you do not bring in, under the specious name of liberty, anything that does not belong to it. Do not let it become **a cover-up for evil.** It is too precious a garment for such a base use. Freedom is indeed Christ's provision to all his followers. But to live in freedom is not to live in wickedness or disobedience of any kind, but in obedience and holiness. You are called to be **servants of God**; this is your **freedom**.

The apostles of this Gospel of freedom gloried in the title, "the servants of Jesus Christ." David, now settled on his throne, before a psalm of praise for his victories, prefixes that title as more important than everything else: "David the servant of the LORD" (Psalm 18:1, introduction). The only true happiness, both of kings and their subjects, is to be God's subjects. It is the glory of the angels to be God's ministering spirits. The more we serve God cheerfully and diligently, the more we will experience this spiritual **freedom**. Oh, that we would live as God's **servants**, making it our overriding aim to seek the advancement of God's glory.

Verse 17

Show proper respect to everyone: Love the brotherhood of believers, fear God, honor the king.

This is a precious cluster of divine precepts. The whole face of the heavens is adorned with stars, but they differ from one another. It is the same in the Holy Scriptures. In fact, these are the two books that the psalmist opens before us in Psalm 19. The heavens instruct us, and the Word of God gives us even clearer teaching. Chrysostom also mentions a two-volume book of God—the book of the creatures and the book of the Scriptures. "The heavens declare the glory of God; the skies proclaim the work of his hands" (Psalm 19:1). "The law of the LORD is perfect, reviving the soul" (Psalm 19:7). Here in 1 Peter we see a constellation of very bright stars close to each other. They sum up our duty to God and to men. To men in general: **Show proper respect to everyone**; and in special relationships, in their Christian or religious relationships, **love the brotherhood of believers**; and in their chief civil relationship, **honor the king**. Concerning our whole duty to God, we are to **fear God**. This is placed in the middle of these instructions, as they constitute the common spring for our duty to other people and the sovereign rule by which it is to be regulated.

Show proper respect to everyone. "Honor all people." Instead of walking by this rule of showing respect to everyone, what is most common is a perverse inclination to dishonor one another. Everyone is ready to dishonor everyone, so that he may pay tribute to himself. That is why we find mutual defamation filling almost every society. The bitter root of this iniquity is that wicked self-love that lives in us. Every man is naturally his own grand idol who will ruin the reputation of others in order to promote himself. But because the humble man is more aware of this divine rule, he respects other people and is not in competition with them. Therefore, learn more about this excellent grace of humility; then you will obey this word. As humility is a precious grace, so it preserves all other graces, and without it, they would be like a box of precious powder carried in the wind, in danger of being blown away. "To those who by persistence in doing good seek glory, honor and immortality, he will give eternal life" (Romans 2:7). "So we make it our goal to please him, whether we are at home in the body or away from it" (2 Corinthians 5:9).

Love the brotherhood of believers. A love due to everyone is included in **show respect to everyone**, but there is also a special love for Christian brothers, whom the apostle Paul refers to in a similar way ("the family of believers," Galatians 6:10).

Christian brothers are united by a threefold cord, two of which are common to other people; but the third is the strongest and belongs only to them. Their bodies are descended from the same man and their souls from the same God, but their new life, through which they are brothers, is derived from the same God-man, Jesus Christ. Indeed, in him they are all one body, receiving life from him, their glorious head. "For those God foreknew he also predestined to be conformed to the likeness of his Son, that he might be the firstborn among many brothers" (Romans 8:29). As his indescribable love was the source of this new being and brotherhood, it cannot but produce indissoluble love among those who share in it. This is the badge that Christ has left his brothers: "All men will know that you are my disciples if you love one another" (John 13:35).

How often the beloved disciple John emphasized this. He drank deep from that wellspring of love that was in the heart of the one on whom he leaned, and, if the story is accurate, he died with these words on his lips: "love one another." Oh, that there were more of this love of Christ in our hearts, arising from his love for us, that we would teach this mutual love more effectively. Do we accept what the love of Christ did for us and suffered for us? And are we prepared to do nothing for him—not forgive an injury for Christ's sake and love the one who wronged us, whoever he is, but especially if he is one of our brothers in this spiritual sense?

Fear God. All the rules of love among people flow from a higher principle and depend on it. Therefore, the principle of obedience is rightly inserted here among these rules. The first obligation of man is to the sovereign majesty of God who made him, and all the mutual duties to each other stem from this. A person may indeed from moral principles be civil toward everybody. But this does not answer the divine rule required here. The spiritual and religious observance of these duties toward other people springs from a respect toward God. It all begins and ends in God. And generally all obedience to God's commands, which regulate our behavior toward him and toward other people, stems from a holy fear of his name. Therefore, this fear of God, on which necessarily follows the keeping of his commandments, is said by Solomon to be the sum of our duty: "Here is the conclusion of the matter: Fear God and keep his commandments, for this is the whole duty of man" (Ecclesiastes 12:13). After Solomon had made his discoveries about everything under the sun, he announced that the whole duty of man is to "fear God" and to "keep his commandments." In the same way Job, after his quest for wisdom, searching for its vein as men do in gold and silver mines, concluded, "The fear of the Lord—that is wisdom, and to shun evil is understanding" (Job 28:28).

This fear encompasses all religion, both inward and outward, all the worship and service of God and all the observance of his commandments. Do not think of this as a trivial matter, but learn from it as our great lesson for living on earth.

This **fear** has in it chiefly several things. First, a reverential esteem of God's majesty. This is a fundamental thing in religion, and it molds the heart most powerfully to obey God's will. Second, a firm belief in God's purity and in his power and justice. God loves holiness and hates all sin and can and will punish it. Third, a right understanding of the intensity of his wrath and the sweetness of his love. Life is the name of the sweetest good we know, and yet God's loving-kindness is better than life (see Psalm 63:3). Fourth, it supposes the sovereign love of God, his own infinite goodness. Fifth, from all these springs a most earnest desire to please God in all things and an unwillingness to offend him in anything.

Honor the king. This should be qualified in no other way than the text qualifies it. It is regulated by the preceding command, **fear God.** We must never think of any such obedience and **honor** due to kings that opposes the **fear** due to God. Let kings and subjects and everyone else know that they are bound absolutely to honor God first. This command is given to kings: "Therefore, you kings, . . . Serve the LORD with fear" (Psalm 2:10-11). Shall a worm, whose breath is in his nostrils, compete with the ever-living God? "Woe to him who quarrels with his Maker, to him who is but a potsherd among the potsherds on the ground. Does the clay say to the potter, 'What are you making?'" (Isaiah 45:9). As we conclude in the debate with the Church of Rome about the honor due to saints and angels, honor let them have, with good reason, but not divine honor, not God's special honor. Similarly, in the subject before us, "Give to Caesar what is Caesar's, and to God what is God's" (Matthew 22:21). It is a miserable position for a kingdom to err in this matter. All are happy when kings and people concur to honor God. "Those who honor me I will honor, but those who despise me will be disdained" (1 Samuel 2:30).

Verses 18-20

Slaves, submit yourselves to your masters with all respect, not only to those who are good and considerate, but also to those who are harsh.

For it is commendable if a man bears up under the pain of unjust suffering because he is conscious of God. But how is it to your credit if you receive a beating for doing wrong and endure it? But if you suffer for doing good and you endure it, this is commendable before God.

"Your word," says the psalmist, "is a lamp to my feet and a light for my path" (Psalm 119:105). It is not just a light to please our eyes but a lamp to guide our feet by the precepts and rules of life that it gives. We are taught about spiritual knowledge through the Word of God. The Son, the eternal Word, when he came to live with men, brought life and wisdom and all heavenly blessings with him from heaven. He taught the people through his teaching and by his perfect example of how to live. His apostles have this as their goal in their holy writings, linking the mysteries of faith with those rules of life that point people along the paths of happiness.

With regard to **slaves**, we have here, first, their duty, second, the extent of their duty, and, third, the principle that governs this duty.

1. Their duty: **submit yourselves.** "Keep your place under your master, and that **with all respect** and inner reverence of mind." Their obedience includes diligence and patient suffering, as both these qualities are included in the word **submit.** "Carry out faithfully, to the best of your ability, what is entrusted to you. Obey all their just commands, and suffer patiently their unjust severities."

2. The extent of this duty: **to those who are harsh.** How can the person who has servants under him expect their obedience when he cannot rule his own passion but is a slave to it? The apostle Paul says to masters about their slaves, "Do not threaten them, since you know that he who is both their Master and yours is in heaven, and there is no favoritism with him" (Ephesians 6:9). Masters should remember, therefore, that when they appear before the judgment seat of God, they will be judged. However, the Christian slave who falls into the hands of a **harsh** master should not become disobedient on account of all the wrong treatment he receives but rather take this as an opportunity to exercise more obedience and patience, as the apostle exhorts here. The person who seeks lasting glory and thanks must turn in a different direction. They need to seek God's praise, not man's (see Romans 2:29). The least of all graces will not lose its reward, in whomever it appears. "Because you know that the Lord will reward everyone for whatever good he does, whether he is slave or free" (Ephesians 6:8).

This is the bounty of the great Master we serve. For who are we and what can we do that we should receive any reward? Yet not a poor prayer, nor a tear, nor a sigh poured out before God will be missed. No cross, whether directly from God's own hand or coming through man's hand, that is borne patiently, yes, and welcomed and embraced for God's sake, will go unnoticed. Happy are those who, whether servants or masters, are determined to serve the Lord. "My reward is with me, and I will give to everyone according to what he has done" (Revelation 22:12).

3. The principle of this obedience and patience: **Because he is conscious of God.** This speaks about knowledge of God and of his will and of the respect for him that is the guiding principle for right actions and suffering.

Observe, first, that this declares that God's grace is given without any reference to people's outward standing. God often bestows the riches of his grace on people who are very poor. It is supposed here that being **conscious of God,** this saving knowledge and fear of God's name, is to be found in slaves. Such people are included in the apostle's opening greeting of this letter: "To God's elect . . . who have been chosen according to the foreknowledge of God the Father" (1 Peter 1:1-2). Slaves are also part of "a chosen people" (2:9). The honor of a spiritual royalty may be concealed under the dull ordinariness of a servant. Furthermore, this grace may be conferred on the servant and denied to the master, as is here supposed. God has chosen the people we would least imagine (see Matthew 11:25; 1 Corinthians 1:27).

Observe, second, that grace finds a way to exert itself and regulates the soul according to the particular duties of its position. Whether grace finds a man in a high or low position, a master or servant, it does not require that he change his position but works a change in his heart and teaches him how to live in it. The same Spirit who makes a Christian master pious and gentle and prudent in commanding makes a Christian servant faithful and diligent in obeying. A skillful engraver can make a statue out of wood, stone, or marble. In the same way, grace makes people walk in a Christian way in whatever position they are in.

Observe, third, that as a corrupt mind debases the best and most excellent callings and actions, so the lowest are raised above themselves and are ennobled by a spiritual mind. A sincere Christian may elevate his low calling by being **conscious of God,** observing his will and intending his glory in it. The spiritual mind has that alchemy of turning base metals into gold, earthly employments into heavenly. The work of a servant who keeps his eyes on God is much holier than the prayer of a hypocrite. A slave who endures harshness from his master patiently **because he is conscious of God** is more acceptable to God than those who may endure much for a good cause but do not have a good and upright heart. Slaves will offer up the hardships they suffer as a sacrifice to God and say, "Lord, this is the station in which you have placed me in the world, and I desire to serve you here. What I do is for you, and what I suffer I desire to bear patiently and cheerfully for your sake, in submission and obedience to your will."

Verses 21-23

To this you were called, because Christ suffered for you, leaving you an example, that you should follow in his steps. "He committed no sin, and no deceit was found in his mouth." When they hurled their insults at him, he did not retaliate; when he suffered, he made no threats. Instead, he entrusted himself to him who judges justly.

The rules that God has given people to live by are universally just, and there is a universal obligation on all people to obey them. But as they are especially addressed to his own people in his Word, those persons are especially bound to obey them. Christians have the highest possible motivation for this because they are following the example of Jesus Christ himself: **Because Christ suffered for you, leaving you an example.** Christians should behave in this way because it is the very thing they are called to, that is, to be like Jesus Christ.

To this you were called. This, in a general way, is a thing that should always be in your mind. Consider the nature and purpose of your calling, and endeavor in everything to behave in line with this calling. As every event happens, think, What does the calling of a Christian require me to do in this situation? In reality, we rarely do this. We profess ourselves to be Christians but seldom think what kind of behavior this obliges us to. "For God did not call us to be impure, but to live a holy life" (1 Thessalonians 4:7). We do not strive to live up to this holy calling, and therefore we live lives that are out of step with the Gospel. "If we claim to have fellowship with him yet walk in the darkness, we lie and do not live by the truth" (1 John 1:6). Our actions belie our supposed beliefs.

The particular things that Christians are called to here are suffering and patience. This is not confined to slaves but is generally true of all Christians. "In fact, everyone who wants to live a godly life in Christ Jesus will be persecuted" (2 Timothy 3:12). Everyone who follows Christ must take up his cross. This is a very harsh and unpleasant part of the Gospel to an unspiritual mind, but the Scriptures do not hide it. People are not led blindfolded into sufferings but are frequently warned about them. Our Saviour told his disciples about this quite openly: "All this I have told you so that you will not go astray" (John 16:1). It is as if he said, "I have shown you the rigors of your path, so that you will not stumble as you travel, thinking it will be a smooth path."

But when this is spoken about, it is usually mentioned alongside the comforts that accompany these sufferings and the glory that follows them. The teaching of the apostles, which was confirmed in their own lives, was this: "We must go through many hardships to enter the kingdom of God" (Acts 14:22). It is an unpleasant way if you do not look to see where it is leading, for it leads to "the kingdom of God." Understanding this will transform the most bitter pain. While it is true that the righteous undergo many afflictions, it is also true that the Lord delivers them from them all (see Psalm 34:19). So our Saviour said, "In me you may have peace" (John 16:33), even though in the world we "will have trouble."

We are called to suffer, and to suffer in this particular way, says the apostle most clearly. The supreme example of this is that of our Lord Jesus Christ, for the sum of our calling is to follow him. In both these matters, suffering and suffering innocently and patiently, the whole Gospel testifies that Christ is our pattern. And the apostle gives us here a summary and a clear account of that.

We see here two things: first, the perfection of this example and, second, our obligation to follow it.

The Perfect Example

The apostle sets the example out very fully, first, in regard to the greatness of our Saviour's sufferings and, second, in regard to his patience in suffering.

1. The greatness of his sufferings: **Christ suffered** (verse 21). Later, in verse 24, his crucifixion and his wounds are specifically mentioned.

This is sufficient reason for Christians being called to suffer. They see the Lord and Author of that calling who suffered so much himself. "The author of their salvation [was made] perfect through suffering" (Hebrews 2:10). If he is the Leader of our salvation, must we not follow him wherever he leads us? To start with, the disciples found it hard to believe this was Christ's way. And we find it hard to believe that it is our way. "How foolish you are, and how slow of heart to believe all that the prophets have spoken! Did not the Christ have to suffer these things and then enter his glory?" (Luke 24:25-26). Do you want to share in your Leader's glory without following your Leader along the only path that leads to it? Is it possible for the servant to be greater than his Master? (See John 13:16.) Remember, if they hate you, they also hated Christ (see John 15:18).

The way to be like Christ is to follow him in this way. "We always carry around in our body the death of Jesus," says the great apostle (2 Corinthians 4:10). In addition to this, there is the unspeakable advantage that is yet to come, which is linked to suffering—namely, that "if we endure, we will also reign with him" (2 Timothy 2:12). As the good Duke of Lower Lorraine, Godfrey of Bouillon, said, when they wanted to crown him king of Jerusalem, "No, by no means; I will not wear a crown of gold where Jesus was crowned with thorns."

2. Christ's spotlessness and patience in suffering—the one in verse 22, the other in verse 23. When you feel like complaining about all the injustice you endure, let me ask you, are you more just and innocent than the One set before you here? **"He committed no sin, and no deceit was found in his mouth."** This highlights his perfect holiness and is confirmed by the words of James: "We all stumble in many ways. If anyone is never

at fault in what he says, he is a perfect man, able to keep his whole body in check" (James 3:2). All of Christ's words, as well as his actions and thoughts, flowed from a pure spring that was undefiled. This is the main ground for our confidence in him—that he is "such a high priest [who] meets our need—one who is holy, blameless, pure, set apart from sinners, exalted above the heavens" (Hebrews 7:26). The more sinful we are, the more we need our High Priest to be sinless. Then we can build on his perfection, and his righteousness is invested in us.

In addition to this, **"no deceit was found in his mouth."** This convinces us that all the promises he made are true. "All that the Father gives me will come to me, and whoever comes to me I will never drive away" is one of his promises (John 6:37). So you need not be afraid, no matter how unworthy and vile you are. Just come to Christ, and you have his word that he will not close the door on you. And as he has promised access, so he has further promised rest for the souls who do come. "Come to me, all you who are weary and burdened, and I will give you rest. Take my yoke upon you and learn from me, for I am gentle and humble in heart, and you will find rest for your souls" (Matthew 11:28-29).

When they hurled insults at him, he did not retaliate (verse 23). The spotless Lamb of God was a Lamb both in guiltlessness and in silence. The prophet Isaiah speaks of this: "He was oppressed and afflicted, yet he did not open his mouth; he was led like a lamb to the slaughter, and as a sheep before her shearers is silent, so he did open his mouth" (Isaiah 53:7). All the torments on the cross only drew from Christ, "Father, forgive them, for they do not know what they are doing" (Luke 23:34).

He entrusted himself to him who judges justly. This is the true method of Christian patience, which calms the mind and keeps it from thoughts of revenge and puts the whole matter into God's hands. Our Saviour during the time of his humiliation and suffering **entrusted himself** and his cause **to him who judges justly.** We learn from this that during unjust suffering we should be like him and not reply with angry words, as is our custom. People who are full of pride think it is ridiculous simply to suffer in this way, but their way makes for great strife and contention. You may think it greatness of spirit to bear nothing, to put up with no wrong, whereas that is in fact great weakness and baseness. It is true greatness of spirit to despise most of those things that make us angry with other people. Oh, that we had less of the spirit of the dragon among us, and more of the spirit of the dove.

Our Obligation to Follow Christ's Example

This is seen here, first, in the purpose of his behavior, which is to be our example, and, second, our interest in him and in his sufferings.

1. His behavior was intended to be an example to us: **Leaving you an example, that you should follow in his steps** (verse 21). He left his foot-

steps as a copy (as the word in the original Greek, *hupogrammon*, indicates) to be followed by us. Every step of his, we are to copy. The particular point here is his suffering. He gave us a pure and perfect copy of obedience, in clear and great letters, in his own blood.

Christ's whole life is our rule. Not his miraculous deeds, like walking on water, but his obedience and holiness, his meekness and humility, we are to copy, and we should continually endeavor to do so. The best and most effective way of teaching, they say, is by example. Christ's matchless example is the happiest way of teaching us. He said, "Whoever follows me will never walk in darkness" (John 8:12). Imitating people in worthless things is useless. Imitating people's virtues is commendable, but if we aim no higher than this, it is both imperfect and unsafe. The apostle Paul links imitation with our supreme Pattern: "Follow my example, as I follow the example of Christ" (1 Corinthians 11:1). There is "a great cloud of witnesses" and examples (see Hebrews 12:1), but we must look beyond them, to him who is as far above them as the sun is above the clouds. We must not only see Christ as "full of grace and truth" (see John 1:14) but must also receive this grace from him: "From the fullness of his grace we have all received one blessing after another" (verse 16).

2. Our interest in Christ and his sufferings: **Christ suffered for you** (verse 21). The apostle returns to this in verse 24. Observe from linking these two verses together that if we neglect Christ's example, we cannot enjoy any assurance of his suffering for us. But if we try seriously to follow him, we may be sure we will receive life through his death and that the steps we take will lead us to where he is.

Verse 24

He himself bore our sins in his body on the tree, so that we might die to sins and live for righteousness; by his wounds you have been healed.

What is deepest in our hearts is most often in our mouths. Thus the apostles in their writings, when they mention Christ's suffering for us, love to delight in it. That is the case here. The apostle has spoken about Christ in the previous verses, recommending him to Christian slaves and to all suffering Christians as their example. This will encourage them as they suffer so much and will help them to be innocent and patient in their afflictions. The apostle tells them to follow Christ as their example in this. But he cannot leave it at that. He enlarges on this topic, using some of the words of that evangelist among the prophets, Isaiah: "He was oppressed and afflicted, yet he did not open his mouth; he was led like a lamb to the slaughter, and as a sheep before her shearers is silent, so he did not open his mouth" (Isaiah 53:7).

This is a most apt quotation for the point the apostle wishes to drive home, for it is most reasonable that we should willingly conform to Christ in suffering, as he would never have had to be such an example of suffering or be subject to such suffering had it not been for us. That Jesus Christ in this suffering is our supreme and unequaled example, and that he came in order to be this, is the truth. But that he is no more than this and that he came for no other purpose is the height of falsehood. For how could we be enabled to follow the example of obedience unless there was more than just an example in what Christ did? Christ **himself bore our sins in his body on the tree.** For this purpose he had "a body . . . prepared for" him (Hebrews 10:5). "And by that will," says the apostle, "we have been made holy through the sacrifice of the body of Jesus Christ once for all" (Hebrews 10:10).

It was Christ's work not only to rectify sinful man by his example but to redeem us through his blood. We have in this verse two great points, and in the same order in which the words come. First we see the nature and quality of the sufferings of Jesus Christ, and, second, we see their purpose.

The Nature and Quality of Christ's Sufferings

We consider, first, the exchange of persons—**he himself** for us (**our sins**); second, the work undertaken and performed—**he . . . bore our sins in his body on the tree.**

1. The act or sentence of the law when it was broken was death, the consequence of sin. Christ implies in his prayer in Matthew 26:39 that it was impossible that he could escape that cup. Justice might have seized rebellious man and laid the pronounced punishment of death on him. Mercy might have freely acquitted him and pardoned everyone. But in Jesus Christ mercy and justice met. "Love and faithfulness meet together; righteousness and peace kiss each other" (Psalm 85:10). This was the only way both justice and mercy could be satisfied. God's just hatred of sin was seen in punishing his one and only Son, so that the whole human race did not have to suffer eternally. Mercy is seen at its most wonderful in that God did not just forgive us, but did so through his own, co-eternal Son.

Consider what Christ is and what we are. He is the Son of God's love, and we are God's enemies. Therefore it is emphatically expressed that **He himself bore our sins** and that God so loved the world (see John 3:16). God's love was so great that he gave his Son. It is impossible to express how wonderful this love is. "But God demonstrates his own love for us in this: While we were still sinners, Christ died for us" (Romans 5:8).

2. The work of redemption itself: **He himself bore our sins in his body on the tree.** In addition to Christ's suffering, the visible kind of death inflicted on him, the fact that he was hanging on the tree of the cross was an analogy ordered by the Lord. Christ died in this way for us. "Christ

127

redeemed us from the curse of the law by becoming a curse for us, for it is written: 'Cursed is everyone who is hung on a tree'" (Galatians 3:13).

But the most important part of Christ's sufferings was not visible to those who watched him die. **He himself bore our sins.** There are three things here: first, the weight of sin; second, the transferring of sin to Christ; and, third, Christ bearing the sin.

The weight of sin. Christ bore sin as a heavy burden. The word **bore** implies carrying a heavy load. Isaiah 53:4 says that he "took up our infirmities and carried our sorrows," as if he were bearing and taking away some great heavy load. And that is what sin is, for it has the wrath of an offended God bearing down upon it. The smallest sin will press a man down forever, and he will not be able to recover. "Who can stand before you when you are angry?" (Psalm 76:7). The prophet Jeremiah urged Israel to return to God to avoid God's wrath falling on her as a great weight, like a millstone, to crush the soul: "'Return, faithless Israel,' declares the LORD, 'I will frown on you no longer'" (Jeremiah 3:12; "I will not cause mine anger to fall upon thee," KJV).

Sin is such a burden that it makes the frame of heaven and earth, the whole creation, crack and groan (see Romans 8:22). Sin was a heavy load upon Jesus Christ, causing him to cry out, "My God, my God, why have you forsaken me?" (Matthew 27:46).

Sin transferred to Christ. It became his debt, and Christ became responsible for it. "Seeing you have accepted this matter according to my will," we may imagine the Father saying to the Son, "you must go through with it. You knew what it would cost you, and yet, like me, you are willing to undertake it. Now the moment has come that I must lay on you the sins of all those people, and you must bear them—the sins of all those believers who lived before and all who are to come after, to the end of the world." "The LORD has laid on him the iniquity of us all" (Isaiah 53:6). The sins of all people, in all ages before and after, who were to be saved, all their guilt, fell on Christ's back on the cross. "God made him who had no sin to be sin for us, so that in him we might become the righteousness of God" (2 Corinthians 5:21). "Such we are in the sight of God the Father, as is the very Son of God himself. Let it be counted folly or frenzy, or whatever; it is our wisdom and our comfort. We care for no knowledge in the world but this, that man has sinned, and God has suffered; that God has made himself the sin of men, and that men are made the righteousness of God" (Hooker).

Christ carried our sins. Christ **bore our sins** suggests that he was active and willing in his suffering for us. It was not a constrained offering. John tells us that Jesus said, "I lay [my life] down of my own accord" (John 10:18). This expression **he bore** implies that Christ willingly took this burden from us onto himself. This bearing is spoken about by St. John—

"who takes away the sin of the world!" (John 1:29). Christ, the great anti-type, answers to both goats of Leviticus 16—the sin-offering and the scapegoat. He did bear our sins on the cross, and then he bore them away to his grave, and there they were buried. So those whose sins he bore, took away, and buried hear no more about them being theirs to bear. So is not Christ rightly viewed as the Lamb of God? "The next day John saw Jesus coming toward him and said, 'Look, the Lamb of God, who takes away the sin of the world!'" (John 1:29).

The Goal of These Sufferings

So that we might die to sins and live for righteousness. Being dead to sin involves an inner and universal alienation of the heart from all sin and an antipathy to the most beloved sin. The believer must not only forbear sin but hate it. This is the true character of a Christian—he is dead to sin. But, alas, where is this Christian to be found? And yet, everyone who partici-pates in Christ really is dead to sin. The apostle Paul says that the believer is buried with Christ. "We were therefore buried with him through bap-tism into death in order that, just as Christ was raised from the dead through the glory of the Father, we too may live a new life" (Romans 6:4). Death and burial is a very unpleasant subject if you talk about it in isola-tion, as if there was no more life. But **live for righteousness** follows the mention of dying to sin. The apostle Paul says, "When you were slaves to sin, you were free from the control of righteousness" (Romans 6:20). While you were alive to sin, you were dead to righteousness. But when a new breath of life from heaven has been breathed on the soul, it lives indeed, for it is one with God, loves him, and delights in his will. This indeed is to **live for righteousness**, which in a comprehensive sense encompasses the whole Christian life, and all of its duties toward God and toward men.

By his wounds you have been healed. The misery of fallen man and the mercy of his deliverance are both so deep that no one expression, or any number of expressions, can fathom them. We have here a variety of very significant expressions. First, the guilt of sin as an intolerable burden, pressing the soul and sinking it, is transferred and laid on a stronger back: **He himself bore our sins.** Second, the same wretchedness, under the image of a strange disease, incurable by any other remedy, is **healed . . . by his wounds.** And, third, this is again represented by the forlorn condition of a wandering sheep (verse 25), with our salvation only to be found in the love and wisdom of our great Shepherd. All these images are borrowed from that sweet and clear prophecy in Isaiah 53.

The polluted nature of man is none other than a bundle of desperate diseases. He is spiritually dead, as the Scriptures often teach. Because he is in such a miserable condition, he is rightly said to be dead. No amount of thinking or logic can cure this situation, but only faith in Jesus Christ, namely, in his **wounds**, through which we are **healed**. These **wounds**, and the blood that flowed from them, are a sound cure. Applied to the soul, they take away the guilt of sin and death and free us from God's wrath. They cleanse our corrupt nature by showing us the way of repentance. Now, for this cure to be effective, it must be applied. The best prescriptions from a doctor are worthless if they are not taken. In order to be healed we must receive the divine remedy.

His wounds. It is one of the wonders of the great work of redemption that the sovereign Lord of all, who binds and looses at his pleasure the influences of heaven, would himself in our flesh be thus bound—the only Son bound as a slave and scourged as a malefactor! And his willing obedience made this an acceptable and expiating sacrifice. "I offered my back to those who beat me. . . . I did not hide my face from mocking and spitting" (Isaiah 50:6). No one who is healed through this remedy can again take constant delight in sin. Consider **his wounds**. Reflect on this, those of you who are not healed, in order that you may be healed. And those of you who are healed, continue to apply the remedy to effect a perfect and complete cure.

There is a sweet mixture of sorrow and joy in contemplating these wounds—sorrow that they were on Christ, and joy that they brought our healing. Christians are not mindful enough of this and maybe are guilty, along with Ephraim, of the accusation, "they did not realize that it was I who healed them" (Hosea 11:3).

Verse 25

For you were like sheep going astray, but now you have returned to the Shepherd and Overseer of your souls.

In these words we have a brief and yet clear presentation of the wretchedness of our natural condition and of our happiness in Christ. It is borrowed from Isaiah 53:6: "We all, like sheep, have gone astray, each of us has turned to his own way; and the Lord has laid on him the iniquity of us all." So that we may know that no one is exempt from the guilt and misery of this wandering, the prophet is explicit about its universality. "We all, like sheep, have gone astray." There is an inbred propensity to stray in all sheep; each person wants to go his own way.

Now you have returned. We stray from God in many ways, but all our wanderings originate in the aversion of the heart from God, which results in disquiet and an unsettled state. This shift and change finds no rest until it returns. "'If you will return, O Israel, return to me,' declares the LORD" (Jeremiah 4:1). This is not merely changing one of your habits for another. To "return to me" is your salvation. We find in our own experience of wanderings and perplexities why we do not return to God.

There is wisdom in David's message, "Be at rest once more, O my soul, for the LORD has been good to you" (Psalm 116:7). Is not the God in whom we expect rest incensed against us for our wandering? Is he not, being offended, a consuming fire? This is true. But the way to find acceptance and peace and the comfort of returning is to come first to **the Shepherd and Overseer of your souls**, to Jesus Christ, and, through him, to the Father.

The Shepherd and Overseer. Kings were called shepherds. But this great **Shepherd and Overseer** is especially worthy of these names. He alone is the universal **Shepherd and Overseer**. From Christ's guidance, power, and love flows all the comfort of his flock. When his sheep consider their own folly and weakness, the only fact that gives them confidence is that his hand is guiding them; they believe in his strength far more than in the roaring lion (see John 10:28-30), and in his wisdom in knowing their particular state and their weakness, and in his tender love in caring for them. This **Shepherd** is perfect in every way. "He tends his flock like a shepherd: He gathers the lambs in his arms and carries them close to his heart; he gently leads those that have young" (Isaiah 40:11). Young and weak Christians, and also older ones when weak and weighed down with problems, are led gently and with the tenderness that their weakness requires. The **Shepherd** provides for his flock, heals them when they are injured, washes them, and makes them fruitful. "My sheep listen to my voice; I know them, and they follow me. I give them eternal life, and they shall never perish; no one can snatch them out of my hand" (John 10:27-28). To follow Christ is to follow life, for he is the Life.

1 Peter
Chapter 3

Verse 1

Wives, in the same way be submissive to your husbands so that, if any of them do not believe the word, they may be won over without talk by the behavior of their wives.

The apostle gives instructions here for **wives** and **husbands.**

Be submissive to your husbands. The common spring of all mutual duties, on both sides, is here to be supposed—namely, love. The special conjugal love that makes them one will infuse a sweetness into the authority of the husband and the obedience of the wife that will make their lives harmonious. Love is the basis of everything. But because its particular character, as appropriate for the wife, is conjugal obedience and subjection, it is therefore usually specified, as it is here and as it is in Ephesians 5:22: "Wives, submit to your husbands as to the Lord." This obedience arises out of a special kind of love, and the wife should remember that it must not be forced, uncheerful obedience. And the husband should remember that he should not insist on base and servile obedience. For both such attitudes oppose that love in which this obedience should be carried out. All will be right where love commands and love obeys. This subjection, as always, is qualified by "in the Lord." The Lord's authority is primary and binds first, and everything else stems from this. Therefore, he is supremely and absolutely to be observed in everything. If the husband wants to draw the wife into an irreligious way of life, he should not be followed in this, but in all things of no consequence this obedience holds.

If any of them do not believe the word. This supposes a special case and takes for granted that a believing wife will cheerfully observe and respect a believing husband. But if he is an unbeliever, a particular good may result from obedience. By the behavior of their wives the husbands **may be won over.** This does not give Christians freedom to choose to be joined to an unbeliever, but it teaches them, if they are matched in this way, how they should behave. In the early days of Christianity it often happened that the Gospel was preached, and the husband might be converted from Judaism or paganism and not the wife, or, as is supposed in this case, the wife was converted and not the husband.

What is said here about **the behavior of their wives** is equally true for a husband in a similar case and, in general of all Christians with reference to those they are in contact with. The pure, holy lives they live as Christians, and in their special positions as Christian husbands or wives or friends, is a very likely and hopeful means for converting others who do not believe. People who are prejudiced observe actions a great deal more than words. The blameless lives of Christians, especially in those early days, did much to increase their number.

Work hard, you wives and others, to adorn and commend the religion you profess to others, especially to those closest to you, who are opposed to Christianity. Strive to be holy, and pray much for this. "If any of you lacks wisdom, he should ask God, who gives generously to all without finding fault, and it will be given to him" (James 1:5).

If wives and other Christians are under such an obligation, how much more are ministers of the Word! Oh, that we could remember our deep commitment to holiness of life! Nazianzen rightly said, "Either teach none, or let your life teach too." The Sunday's sermon lasts for only an hour or two, but holiness of life is a sermon that lasts all week long.

They may be won over without talk. The conversion of a soul is an inestimable gain. Oh, how precious the soul is, but how undervalued by most! Wives and husbands and parents and friends, if they are themselves converted, should consider seriously and pray a great deal for their unconverted relations, for by nature such people are dead and need to receive life.

Verse 2

When they see the purity and reverence of your lives.

As all graces are linked to each other, so they are used for the purpose that the apostle propounds here—for the conversion of those who are strangers to religion. This is summed up by the words **the behavior** of their wives in verse 1, as well as in the specific duties in their lives—subjection, chastity, fear, modesty in dressing, and the inner ornaments of meekness and quietness of spirit. Such qualities enable a wife to be the successful means of converting her husband.

Purity. It is a characteristic of Christians to work hard to be pure in all things. The particular **purity** in mind here is that of chastity. It is the pure whiteness of the soul to be chaste, to abhor the filth of sinful desire. We are called to this state as Christians. "For God did not call us to be impure, but to live a holy life" (1 Thessalonians 4:7).

Reverence. This either means reverent respect to their husbands or the fear of God. From reverence for God flow all other observances, in married life and in the Christian life.

Verses 3-4

Your beauty should not come from outward adornment, such as braided hair and the wearing of gold jewelry and fine clothes. Instead, it should be that of your inner self, the unfading beauty of a gentle and quiet spirit, which is of great worth in God's sight.

So that a Christian wife may lack nothing, she is told how she should dress herself. **Your beauty should not come from outward adornment, such as braided hair and the wearing of gold jewelry and fine clothes.** Our perverse, crooked hearts turn everything we use into chaos. How few people know how to use the two necessities of life—food and clothes. For the mind to be pleased with such things is foolish and childish. This is a disease that few escape. It is strange what poor things men and women become vain about, thinking they are somebody. The soul that departs from God has lost its true worth and beauty, and so it descends to concentrating on how it may indulge and dress the body. God alone is the beauty of their soul. "Does a maiden forget her jewelry, a bride her wedding ornaments? Yet my people have forgotten me, days without number" (Jeremiah 2:32).

The apostle deliberately forbids vanity and excess in dress and too much delight in lawful ornaments, but his main purpose is to recommend an ornament of the soul, **your inner self** (verse 4). The particular grace the apostle commends is especially suited to the subject at hand, the duties wives have in marriage—**a gentle and quiet spirit.** But this should apply to every Christian. Moses was a great general, and yet his greatest virtue was his meekness. "Now Moses was a very humble man, more humble than anyone else on the face of the earth" (Numbers 12:3). The spirit of meekness may not be fashionable in the world, but it is in the court of heaven. It is the King's own fashion: "Learn from me, for I am gentle and humble in heart" (Matthew 11:29). It is never right to abide by the opinion of men and not seek God's approbation.

Verses 5-6

For this is the way the holy women of the past who put their hope in God used to make themselves beautiful. They were submissive to their own husbands, like Sarah, who obeyed Abraham and called him her

master. **You are her daughters if you do what is right and do not give way to fear.**

The apostle supports his teaching with an example. The correct way to use the Scriptures is to order our lives according to them. This is why a great deal of the Bible is historical. There is in the saints a oneness of soul, for they share the same Spirit in all ages. Hence pious and obedient wives are here called **daughters** of Sarah. Such women are here set before us because they are holy, believing, and resolute. They **do not give way to fear.** While they may be fearful by nature, they have undaunted spirits through a holy, clean, and pure conscience. Believing wives who fear God are not frightened. Their minds are established in obeying God and also their husbands.

Verse 7

Husbands, in the same way be considerate as you live with your wives, and treat them with respect as the weaker partner and as heirs with you of the gracious gift of life, so that nothing will hinder your prayers.

"Your wives are subject to you, but you, in the same way, are subject to the Word, by which everyone ought to be directed, no matter what their station in life. One day all will be judged by this Word. You are **in the same way** subject, just as wives are." This exhortation includes parents as well as children, masters as well as servants, and kings as well as subjects.

Treat them with respect. This is a due conjugal esteem for wives. Husbands are to respect their wives, not vilify or despise them, which is liable to exasperate them. Husbands are not to talk about their wives' weaknesses to other people or to themselves concentrate too closely on them, but rather to hide them from others and from their own sight by love. They should not see those flaws more than love requires. The reasons for this are appropriate. This sounds at first a little incongruous: **treat them with respect** because they are **the weaker partner.** But this is not the case when we consider the kind of respect ordered here. It is not the honor due to a superior but esteem and respect without which love cannot exist. We cannot love what we do not in some way respect. Care should be taken that the wives are not slighted, even though they are **weaker,** for of all injuries, contempt is one of the most stinging that can be inflicted, especially on weak people.

As heirs with you of the gracious gift of life. This strongly binds all these duties on the hearts of husbands and wives, and binds their hearts to each other and makes them one. If each is reconciled to God in Christ as an heir of life, one with God, then they are truly one with each other in God. This is the surest and sweetest union possible. Natural love is very strong with some husbands and wives, but the highest natural love falls very far short of that which comes from God. Hearts concentrating on God are the most united hearts. Love that is bonded by youth and beauty fades when youth and beauty decay. Ignorance and disregard of this teaching is a great cause for much bitterness and for so little true sweetness in the life of most married people. When God is ignored, they do not live as one in him.

Heirs with you. People who have been bought with the precious blood of the same Redeemer will be loath to grieve or despise each other. As they have been brought into peace with God, they will have true peace between themselves and will not allow anything to disturb this. They have the hope of a day when there will be nothing but perfect concord and peace, and they live as **heirs** of that life now and make their present state as like heaven as they can.

Life. A sweet word, but sweetest of all in this sense—**the gracious gift of life.** Life above is indeed alone worthy of the name, and what we have here, in comparison, is more of a constant dying, an incessant journey toward the grave. If only that blessed life were more known, it would be more desired.

Gracious gift. The tenor of this heirship is free grace. This life is a free gift. "For the wages of sin is death, but the gift of God is eternal life in Christ Jesus our Lord" (Romans 6:23). No life is completely pure, inside or outside marriage. If we consider who we are, we will quickly agree with this. Then we will be very content to hold, as a gift, the grace that God bestows on us.

So that nothing will hinder your prayers. The apostle supposes in Christians the frequent use of prayer. He takes it for granted that the **heirs** of **life** cannot live without prayer. These **heirs,** if they are alone, pray alone; if **heirs** together and living together, they pray together. Can the husband and wife have that love, wisdom, and meekness that may make their life happy, and neglect God who is the giver of all these things? Those who pray together should have hearts turned to each other for prayer, and this is especially true of husbands and wives.

Verse 8

Finally, all of you, live in harmony with one another; be sympathetic, love as brothers, be compassionate and humble.

The apostle now directs his instructions to all Christians. The universal nature of his exhortation is seen in the words, **finally** and **all of you.** Most people hear these exhortations, think they refer to somebody else, and never apply them to themselves. But they are addressed to every Christian, so that each one may live life as directed by these teachings. This verse has a cluster of five Christian graces or virtues. The central grace, as the stalk or root of the others, is **love as brothers**, and the others grow out of this, two on each side—unanimity and sympathy on the one side, and pity and humility on the other. We will take them in the order in which they come.

Live in harmony with one another. "Be of one mind." This not only means union in judgment but extends also to affection and action. I think it embraces an agreement of minds and affections among Christians and progressive agreements among them, especially in spiritual things.

We consider, first, what this is not. It is not a careless indifference about the matters being presented. It is not an indication of a loving agreement not to be troubled about them at all and to make no judgment about them. That would be a dead stupidity, arising out of total spiritlessness. The unanimity required here needs to take account of the fact that some things are fundamental in religion. While no part of divine truth once clearly understood should be slighted, there are still some things that may be true but are of less importance than other things. This difference is carefully noted by wise Christians, especially in the context of the agreement that is recommended here.

We need to ask what this unanimity is. We may conclude that Christians should have a clear and unanimous belief about the mysteries and principles of faith. They should agree about these without any argument. They should also be diligent in seeking the truth in all things that concern faith and religion and should try to reach agreement in such things as far as possible. Perfect and universal agreement in all things is not attainable here, either between churches or between individual Christians within one church. While churches should seek unity through their synods and meetings, they should be careful to avoid trying to attain uniformity in everything. Leaving a latitude and indifference in things capable of it is often a stronger way of preserving peace and unity. But this is by the way. We will rather give a few rules that may be of use to every Christian concerning this common mind among Christians.

First, beware of two extremes that often cause division—being captive to custom on the one hand, and a tendency to continually indulge in novelty on the other hand.

Second, work hard to have a settled mind that will not be tossed about by every wind of doctrine or reason and be easily blown aside with false interpretations of Scripture.

Third, in unclear and doubtful things do not be obstinate. Some people imagine they are infallible, which makes them contentious, contrary to the apostle Paul's instruction: "Do nothing out of selfish ambition or vain conceit, but in humility consider others better than yourselves" (Philippians 2:3). Some people argue as strongly over the smallest detail as they do about a central article of faith.

There are some things about which we should have the same mind. First, in the defense of truth, as the Lord calls us, we should be of one mind, and all be as one. Satan acts by the maxim that all his followers use: divide and conquer. So let us hold to the other maxim: union based on truth is invincible. Second, in the practice of truth, we should agree as one person. The saying goes, "It is believed that united prayers ascend with greater efficacy." Our Saviour said, "For where two or three come together in my name, there am I with them" (Matthew 18:20). Being gathered together does not just mean being in the same building, but having united hearts. So our Lord speaks about Christians agreeing together and their prayers being answered: "If two of you on earth agree about anything you ask for, it will be done for you by my Father in heaven" (Matthew 18:19). But, alas, where is our agreement? The first Christians were in agreement with each other, and the church grew.

> When the day of Pentecost came, they were all together in one place.... All the believers were together and had everything in common.... Every day they continued to meet together in the temple courts. They broke bread in their homes and ate together with glad and sincere hearts, praising God and enjoying the favor of all the people. And the Lord added to their number daily those who were being saved.
>
> —Acts 2:1, 44, 46-47

Be sympathetic. "Have compassion." This shows that the badge of Christian unity is not a mere speculative agreement of opinions. There is a living sympathy among them, as making up one body, animated with one spirit. This is why the members of the body have a mutual feeling, even when they are separated by distance or social class. "Just as each of us has one body with many members, and these members do not all have the same function, so in Christ we who are many form one body, and each member belongs to all the others" (Romans 12:4-5). "Now the body is not made up of one part but of many. If the foot should say, 'Because I am not an eye, I do not belong to the body,' it would not for that reason cease to be part of the body" (1 Corinthians 12:14-15).

This living sense resides in every member of the body of Christ toward the whole and toward each individual. This makes Christians rejoice in the welfare and good of another as if it were their own, for the word **sympathetic** embraces all feelings, both joy and grief. "Remember those in prison as if you were their fellow prisoners, and those who are mistreated as if you yourselves were suffering" (Hebrews 13:3). "If one part suffers, every part suffers with it; if one part is honored, every part rejoices with it" (1 Corinthians 12:26). Where there is grace and the Spirit of Jesus Christ, there is sympathy. The apostle Paul, eminent in all grace, had a large share of this: "Who is weak, and I do not feel weak? Who is led into sin, and I do not inwardly burn?" (2 Corinthians 11:29). Grace does not sit in judgment over those who have fallen but sits down with them and mourns with them. This is the characteristic of stronger Christians found in the Scriptures. "We who are strong ought to bear with the failings of the weak and not to please ourselves" (Romans 15:1). "Brothers, if someone is caught in a sin, you who are spiritual should restore him gently" (Galatians 6:1). This holy and humble sympathy is evidence of a strong Christian. As Augustine wrote: "Nothing truly shows a spiritual man so much as the dealing with another man's sin."

Love as brothers. From love springs this feeling we are speaking about. Love is the foundation of union, and union brings about sympathy and that unanimity we mentioned before. Those who have the same spirit uniting and animating them cannot but have the same mind and the same feelings. And this spirit is derived from that Head, Christ, in whom Christians live and move and have their being, their new and excellent being; and so, living in Christ, they love him and are one in him. They are **brothers**. He is the Head of their fraternity, as he is "the firstborn among many brothers" (Romans 8:29). Men and women are **brothers** in two natural ways. Their bodies are made of the same earth, and their souls come from the same God. But this third fraternity, which is founded in Christ, is far more wonderful and lasting than the other two.

In Christ every believer is born of God, in his Son. And so they are not only brothers with each other, but Christ himself owns them as his brothers. "Both the one who makes men holy and those who are made holy are of the same family. So Jesus is not ashamed to call them brothers" (Hebrews 2:11). Seek to understand this more and more. Consider the source of this love: "How great is the love the Father has lavished on us, that we should be called children of God!" (1 John 3:1). The same apostle says that God is love and that God gave his one and only Son and that the Son gave himself. God sweetened Christ's bitter cup with his transcendent love, and this he recommended to us: "Love each other as I have loved you" (John 15:12). We know that we cannot attain to this height completely, but the more we look on it, the higher we will reach in this love. What starts here on earth will be completed in heaven.

Be compassionate and humble. The roots of plants are hidden under the ground, so that they themselves are not seen, though they appear in their branches, flowers, and fruits, demonstrating that they have a root and life in them. The graces of the Spirit planted in the soul, though themselves invisible, are revealed in a Christian's life, words, and actions. A truly Christian mind is compassionate to the miseries of everyone, especially the sick and poor. But it is most of all compassionate about the spiritual misery of ungodly people, their hardness of heart and unbelief, and earnestly desires their conversion. It longs for "the riches of his kindness, tolerance, and patience . . . realizing that God's kindness leads you toward repentance" (Romans 2:4). Being **humble** is a chief characteristic of a Christian. It receives grace from God, kills envy, and commands respect and goodwill from men. God gives grace to the lowly and loves to bestow it where there is most room to receive it. As much humility gains much grace, so it grows by it.

Verse 9

Do not repay evil with evil or insult with insult, but with blessing, because to this you were called so that you may inherit a blessing.

Opposition helps grace to become stronger. When Christian love does not encounter the world's hatred, it has a much easier task. But if Christian love overcomes attacks, it shines more brightly as a result, and it rises higher, for it does **not repay evil with evil.**

To repay good for evil is, so far as men are concerned, the worst sin. But the opposite reveals our universal guiltiness toward God. He multiplies mercies on us, and we respond by multiplying sins. The Lord complained that the more Israel increased, the more it sinned. But not to repay offenses, not repaying evil with evil, is the Christian's rule. More than this, to return good for evil and blessing for cursing is not only counseled but commanded. "Love your enemies and pray for those who persecute you" (Matthew 5:44). If you take revenge for injuries you have received, you usurp God's prerogative. "'It is mine to avenge; I will repay,' says the Lord" (Romans 12:19). Even if the world despises this, you must seek more of that dove-like spirit, the spirit of meekness. It is shameful to be vindictive in any way and to return evil for evil. "A man's wisdom gives him patience; it is to his glory to overlook an offense" (Proverbs 19:11).

God is our pattern in love and compassion. People rate some virtues higher than others and trample on virtues like love, compassion, and meekness. Although these violets grow low and are dark in color, they give a very sweet perfume. "You have heard that it was said, 'Love your neighbor and hate your enemy.' But I tell you: Love your enemies and pray for those who persecute you, that you may be sons of your Father in heaven" (Matthew 5:43-45). Be like that, no matter how other people behave.

Because to this you were called. We are called to a holy inheritance, and we are called to a holy way of life. We are called to an inheritance of light, and so we are called to walk as children of light. The Lord has spoken pardon to the soul instead of the curse due to our sin. He has blessed us with a title to glory; so the believer can easily and readily speak about pardon and even of blessing on those who upset him most. When we have been forgiven so many talents, will we not forgive a few pence?

So that you may inherit a blessing. Our calling does not exempt us from troubles and injuries here. We are not extolled by those in the world, but on the contrary we have to suffer their malice and scoffing. But all these curses cannot deprive us of our inheritance. Inheriting this **blessing** places on Christians the duty to bless others. It also encourages us to endure the worst the world can do to us. If the world should bless you and applaud you loudly, such blessings could never be called an inheritance. Such blessings have no substance and are only temporary. Our inheritance comes from "a kingdom that cannot be shaken" (see Hebrews 12:28). Ponder this blessed inheritance. Seek to have the right to it in Jesus Christ, and the evidences and seals of it from his Spirit. And insofar as you can, set your heart on it and live your lives conformed to it.

Verse 10

For, "Whoever would love life and see good days must keep his tongue from evil and his lips from deceitful speech."
The rich bounty of God diffuses itself throughout the world on everyone. Yet there are a select number who have special blessings from his right hand that the rest of the world do not share in. "Show the wonder of your great love, you who save by your right hand those who take refuge in you from their foes" (Psalm 17:7). Consider, first, the required qualification and, second, the blessing annexed. The purpose here is to recommend an exact rule in order to achieve an important and desirable good.

The apostle James said about this, "Likewise the tongue is a small part of the body, but it makes great boasts" (James 3:5). It needs a strong bridle (see verse 3). If we think about it, the consequences of how we use the tongue are very great, for it is the main outlet of what is in the heart. The bit that is made for people's mouths is made up of two halves—first, to keep it from speaking evil openly and, second, from speaking deceitfully.

"Keep his tongue from evil." The evil of the tongue is a large subject. It is "a world of evil" (James 3:6), extending throughout the world, covering every type of evil. It includes profane speech, which is clearly wicked. Impious words, which directly reflect on the glory and name of God, such as blasphemies, oaths, and curses, are so common among us that the land is full of them. Then there is the sin of speaking evil about people, even against close relatives. "You speak continually against your brother and slander your own mother's son" (Psalm 50:20). Our Saviour warns us that we will have to answer for our words: "But I tell you that men will have to give account on the day of judgment for every careless word they have spoken" (Matthew 12:36). For that very reason evil words are included in the "world of evil" of the tongue. We need to emulate our Saviour: "no deceit was found in his mouth" (1 Peter 2:22).

We will now add something about the remedy for this evil. It must be done in the heart or it will be an imaginary conquest. Our Saviour says, "out of the overflow of the heart the mouth speaks" (Matthew 12:34). What the heart is full of overflows into the tongue. If the heart is full of God, the tongue will delight to speak about him. If there is nothing but vanity and foolishness in the heart, then speech will be vain and have no purpose. "The mouth of the righteous man utters wisdom, and his tongue speaks what is just. The law of his God is in his heart; his feet do not slip" (Psalm 37:30-31). David says, "your law is within my heart" (Psalm 40:8). From this center it sends out rays of suitable words. A purified heart will teach the tongue not to utter impure words and will give it holy words. There is no greater task for the tongue than to extol God. "My tongue will speak of your righteousness and of your praises all day long" (Psalm 35:28). If a day was ten days long, there would still be no room for unholy speech. Those who praise God do not lose out, for God loves to speak peace to them. In place of the world's vain freedom with words, we have sweet fellowship with our Father.

Verse 11

"He must turn from evil and do good; he must seek peace and pursue it."

This is a full and complete rule. It is miserable folly to mistakenly embrace evil under the guise of good. We have been deluded so many times that we have not grown in wisdom. "He feeds on ashes, a deluded heart misleads him" (Isaiah 44:20).

"Turn from evil." The bias of the soul must be turned from sin and turned toward God. This is not just a dislike of evil but a loathing and hatred of it. "Hate what is evil" (Romans 12:9). "Let those who love the LORD hate evil" (Psalm 97:10). As you do this, you will know that love for God is upright and true.

Where there is this love, sin will be avoided, and people will walk in holiness, doing good. Avoiding sin involves being alert on all occasions. We should flee from sin as we would from a serpent. We should not toy with sin or go close to it. If you think you have the power and skill to handle evil without falling into danger, you should heed Solomon's words: "Keep to a path far from her [the adulteress], do not go near the door of her house" (Proverbs 5:8).

"Do good." This precept does not just concern outward actions. The main thing is to be inwardly principled for it and to have a heart stamped with God's love and his commandments, to love him and desire his glory. A good action, even the best kind of action by an evil hand and from an evil and unsanctified heart, is evil. To **"do good"** in the sense the apostle means, we must "delight" in the Lord and his ways (see Psalm 119:16).

From this follows constant obedience, which directly opposes the tendency toward wickedness in corrupt people's hearts. We should have a serious desire to do all the good that is within our calling and reach. What matters is not your position in life but your faithfulness. "You have been trustworthy in a very small matter, take charge of ten cities" (Luke 19:17). As we strive to do good, "Let us fix our eyes on Jesus, the author and perfecter of our faith" (Hebrews 12:2).

We see then our rule, and it is the rule of peace and happiness. We must apply this to our hearts. This is our work. Consider the thing in itself. First, the opposition of sin and obedience—**evil** and **good**; and, second, the composition of our rule in these expressions: **turn from** and **do**. If you consider **evil** and **good** in this way, you will know what to **turn from** and **do**.

If you are convinced about this, then, first, desire light from above, to discover what offends God and what pleases him. "Do not conform any longer to the pattern of this world, but be transformed by the renewing of your mind. Then you will be able to test and approve what God's will is— his good, pleasing and perfect will" (Romans 12:2). You must discover what is most adverse and repugnant to that will. Second, seek a renewed mind to hate that evil, even the evil that is closest to you and that you find most congenial. And love to **"do good,"** even when you find this to be most unnatural. Third, seek strength and skill from a Spirit other than your own, so you may **"turn from evil and do good."**

"Oh, but I am often entangled in evil," you reply, "and often frustrated in my thoughts against these evils and in my attempts to do good, which is my duty." Was not this Paul's condition? Are you not complaining with the same words he used? You will be happy if you obey God with the same strength of feeling. You will be glad to cry out about your wretchedness. "When I want to do good, evil is right there with me" (Romans 7:21). But remember, although your duty is to **"turn from evil and do good,"** your salvation is not founded on your own goodness. The perfection that answers to justice and the law is not required of you. You are to walk not after sinful desires, but after the Spirit. But in this walk, your comfort is not in yourself, but because "there is now no condemnation for those who are in Christ Jesus" (Romans 8:1). The apostle Paul ends the previous chapter by saying, "What a wretched man I am!" but in the same breath exclaims, "Thanks be to God through Jesus Christ our Lord!" (Romans 7:24-25).

So then, mourn over your sins with the apostle Paul, and rejoice with him, and go on with the same courage he exercised in order to fight the good fight of faith. When you fall into the mire, be ashamed and humbled, but then return and wash in the open fountain, and return and beg for new strength to walk more surely. Learn to trust yourself less and God more, and take action against your enemies. "Let us purify ourselves from everything that contaminates body and spirit, perfecting holiness out of reverence for God" (2 Corinthians 7:1). Do not imagine that your little is enough, or despair because you cannot do more, but "press on toward the goal to win the prize" (Philippians 3:14). Do not think everything is lost because you are at present foiled. The experienced soldier knows that he will often win the day after a fall or the day after he has been wounded. Be assured of this, after a short battle follows an eternity of triumph.

"He must seek peace and pursue it." Leaving aside the many meanings for the word peace, external peace with men is what I believe is especially meant here. This is to be sought. It is not just to be sought when it is easy to find, but when it appears to be most elusive. Remember, "peacemakers who sow in peace raise a harvest of righteousness" (James 3:18).

The life of a godly person, though short in comparison with nature's course, may be long in value, in that much spiritual good has been attained. Such a person may be said to live much in a little time, whereas those who spend their days in folly and sin live long but little. Or as Seneca puts it, "He did not live long, but existed long." And the good of the godly person's days, though unseen good, surpasses all the world's mirth and prosperity, which makes a noise but is hollow within. As Augustine says of Abraham, he had "good days in God, though evil days in his generation." A believer can make up an ill day with a good God; and enjoying him, he has solid peace. And then what abides and dwells in God's house is what "no eye has seen, no ear has heard" (1 Corinthians 2:9). There will come an everlasting day that does not need the light of the sun or the moon, for God's glory shines there because the Lamb is its light.

Verse 12

"For the eyes of the Lord are on the righteous and his ears are attentive to their prayer, but the face of the Lord is against those who do evil."

No knowledge causes such happiness as firmly believing the universal dependence of everything on the First and Highest Cause, the Cause of causes, the Spring of being and goodness, the wise and just Ruler of the world. The psalmist, like the apostle, gives the true link between holiness and happiness: "The eyes of the LORD are on the righteous and his ears are attentive to their cry; the face of the Lord is against those who do evil" (Psalm 34:15-16). There is a double contrast in these words, between people and their condition or portion.

1. People: the righteous and those who do evil. These two expressions are often used in the Scriptures, and particularly in the book of Psalms, to denote the godly and the wicked. This righteousness is not absolute perfection or sinlessness, nor is the contrasted evil every act of sin or breach

of God's law. But **the righteous**, since they are students of obedience and holiness who desire to walk as in the sight of God and to walk with God, as Enoch did, hate everything that pleases their corrupt nature. This is the kind of perfection meant here. "Not that I have already obtained all this, or have already been made perfect, but I press on to take hold of that for which Christ Jesus took hold of me" (Philippians 3:12).

On the other hand, **those who do evil** are those who commit sin with greediness, who walk in the way of sin and make it their way, who live in sin as their element, who "have delighted in wickedness" (2 Thessalonians 2:12). Their great faculty, their great delight, lies in sin. They are skillful and cheerful evildoers. No one man delights in all kinds of sin, as that is impossible. But sin spreads, and one sin leads to anther sin. Evil people do not resist sin or hate sin or worry that sin is hated by God.

2. Their contrasting conditions or portions. **"His ears are attentive to their prayer"** is the state of the righteous; but **"the face of the Lord is against those who do evil."** God shows his favor to the righteous by his open ear toward them. The wicked either do not pray or what they say is not really a prayer. So the Lord sets his face against them, and his ear is closed to them. Thus God says through Ezekiel, "Although they shout in my ears, I will not listen to them" (Ezekiel 8:18).

"The eyes of the Lord are on the righteous." This shows God's love and the disposition of his heart toward the righteous. The Lord is pleased to speak about his love to his own. He sees the whole world, but he looks on his people with special delight. God is ready to do them good, to supply their needs and order their affairs for them. He has his **eyes** upon them. He is thinking about what to do for them. "For the eyes of the LORD range throughout the earth to strengthen those whose hearts are fully committed to him" (2 Chronicles 16:9). This brings inexpressible comfort when a poor believer is in great trouble of any kind concerning his outer or spiritual condition. "I see no way of escape. I am blind about this; but there are eyes on me that see what is best. The Lord is caring for me and is bringing about everything for my advantage." "Yet I am poor and needy; may the LORD think of me. You are my help and my deliverer; O my God, do not delay" (Psalm 40:17). That tips the scales. Would you not think yourself happy if, even though you had nothing, some great prince was busily working out how to make you rich? How much greater happiness it is to have God, whose power is the greatest and whose thoughts always come about, watching over you and planning good for you!

"His ears are attentive to their prayer." Whatever requests you have, you may freely ask them. He will not refuse you anything that is for your good. Prayer may be thought of in the following three ways. First, prayer is a duty we owe God. As it is from him that we expect and receive everything, it is only reasonable that we should express our dependence on him.

So we will daily come before his throne and go to him for everything. Second, prayer is the delight of a spiritual mind, overjoyed at having close access to God and such freedom to speak to him. Third, prayer is a certain means, by divine appointment and promise, of obtaining from the hands of God those good things we need.

God's open ear to our prayers implies that he answers them. Understanding that God takes notice of prayer encourages our hearts to pray. Therefore, in the Psalms the hearing of prayer is often made a part of the song of praise. It endears both God and prayer to the soul. "I love the LORD, for he heard my voice; he heard my cry for mercy" (Psalm 116:1). "Because he turned his ear to me, I will call on him as long as I live" (Psalm 116:2). There is need for directions to be given in this, but too many rules may be more confusing than too few rules. Briefly then:

1. Slothful minds often neglect the answers of God even when they exactly match our requests. We are sometimes so preoccupied with asking God for more and more that we never think about what he has already done for us. This is one of the most common causes of ingratitude.

2. When the Lord changes our requests, through his answers, it is always for the better. God regards, according to Augustine, "our well more than our will." When we plead for deliverance, we are not unanswered if God gives patience and support.

3. We should always remember not to set bounds and limits on the Lord about time, and not tell him what day the answer must come. All God's deeds are done in their season. Believers should never regret having to wait for an answer to their prayers. After they have received their answer, they realize that God's time was best. "I waited patiently for the LORD; he turned to me and heard my cry" (Psalm 40:1).

When you are in great affliction, outward or inward, you may think God is not looking at you. But he is. You are his gold. He knows the moment to refine you and the moment to take you out of the furnace. He will not leave his work unfinished. "The LORD will fulfill his purpose for me; your love, O LORD, endures forever—do not abandon the works of your hands" (Psalm 138:8). His eye is on you, although you do not see him; his ear is open to your cry, even though at the moment he is not speaking to you as you want. The passage in 1 Peter does not say that God's children always see and hear him with their senses. But when they do not, God is looking at them and hearing them, and he will show himself to them and answer them at the right moment. David says, "O my God, I cry out by day, but you do not answer, by night, and am not silent" (Psalm 22:2). Yet David refuses to entertain harsh thoughts about God. On the contrary, he acknowledges, "You are . . . the Holy One" (Psalm 22:3). David states that God showed his favor to his people: "In you our fathers put their trust; they trusted and you delivered them" (Psalm 22:4).

Let the Lord's open ear persuade us to make much use of prayer. "It is the key of day and the lock of night."

But the face of the Lord is against those who do evil. Our happiness and misery are all in the Lord's face, the Lord's looks. There is nothing so comforting as God's favorable face, and nothing so terrible as his face full of anger. No matter how rich or beautiful or noble you are, if **the face of the Lord is against** you, you are to be pitied. The godly often do not see the Lord's favorable looks as he is eyeing them. In the same way, the wicked do not usually see or perceive or believe that the Lord's face is against them. If you are ungodly, forsake your ways. Do not flatter yourself that you will escape when you hear about the outward judgments on your neighbors and brethren, but tremble and be humbled. Remember our Saviour's words: "Or those eighteen who died when the tower of Siloam fell on them—do you think they were more guilty than all the others living in Jerusalem? I tell you, no! But unless you repent, you too will all perish" (Luke 13:4-5). These seemingly harsh words from the lips of him who is wisdom and sweetness are words spoken to the perishing, that they might not perish.

Your blessedness is not where most of you seek it, in things below. How is this possible? It requires a higher good to make you happy. While you labor and sweat for happiness under the sun, you are wasting all your efforts. You are seeking a happy life in the region of death. Only in the love and favor of God, in his favorable countenance and friendship, is blessedness. It can be found only in the ways of holiness.

Verse 13

Who is going to harm you if you are eager to do good?
The apostle adds as a further reason for the safety and happiness of the way he points out a reason drawn from its own nature. There is something about a meek, upright, holy carriage that is apt, in part, to free a man from many evils to which the ungodly are exposed. Your pure and harmless deportment will bind the hands of your enemies and sometimes somewhat allay and cool the malice of their hearts, so that they cannot rage against you as they might otherwise. It is rather monstrous to rage against the innocent. **Who is going to harm you?** We see here two things. First, the deportment of the godly and, second, the advantage of it.

Their Deportment

Eager to do good. They are followers of that which is **good**. The Greek word for *followers* is *mimetai*, imitators. Some people imitate wickedness by copying other people's sins. But it is always praiseworthy to imitate what is good. The ultimate pattern, of course, is not any human being but

God. A person full of God's grace has the closest likeness to God, and so we follow that example since it is from God.

The Word of God contains our perfect pattern, and it is very legible and clear. When our ways are regulated by the Word, we imitate what is good. Students of holiness, those who are **eager to do good**, study that perfect rule in the Scriptures, that highest and first Pattern there so often set before them, even the Author of that rule, the Lord himself. "Be imitators of God, therefore, as dearly loved children and live a life of love, just as Christ loved us and gave himself up for us as a fragrant offering and sacrifice to God" (Ephesians 5:1-2). Pythagoras says that "the end of man is to become like God." Children who are loved by their father, and who love and revere him, will be ambitious to be like him and will particularly aim to follow his virtues. Thus it is most reasonable that it should be like this with the children of God, for their Father is the highest and best.

But this excellent pattern is drawn even closer to their view in the Son, Jesus Christ. In Christ, we have the highest Example made low, without losing any of his perfection, so that we may study God in man. In him we may learn everything. Do you want to grow in all grace? Study Christ much, and you will not only find the pattern, but the strength and skill in him to follow him.

The Advantage

Who is going to harm you? Men, even evil men, will often be overcome by our blameless and harmless behavior.

1. In the life of a godly person, there is a sober beauty that often attracts some kind of reverence and respect, even from ungodly minds.

2. Although unspiritual people cannot love Christians spiritually, they may have a natural liking for some virtues that they see in Christians.

3. These and similar graces make a Christian life so calm that malice hardly knows where to attack. When pride and passion strike out, the result has to be a fire. But "a gentle answer turns away wrath" (Proverbs 15:1).

Verse 14

But even if you should suffer for what is right, you are blessed. "Do not fear what they fear; do not be frightened."

There are two things to note in this verse. First, even in the most blameless Christian life, suffering is assumed; and, second, happiness, even in suffering, is asserted.

1. Suffering is assumed. There will be suffering even for the righteous. This will not be unusual but the normal lot of Christians. Luther called it "the evil genius of the Gospel." As we have been warned about this, we should not pay attention to the false prophecies of self-love that sets out

what it wants. Do not think that any prudence will lead you safely past all oppositions and the malice of an ungodly world. Suffering and war with the world is a part of the godly person's portion here, which seems hard but, taken with everything else, is sweet. Nobody in his right mind would refuse the entire legacy: "I have told you these things, so that in me you may have peace. In this world you will have trouble. But take heart! I have overcome the world" (John 16:33).

Look around you and see if anyone is exempt from trouble. The greatest persons are usually subject to the greatest vexations, just as the largest bodies create the largest shadows. As we must suffer no matter what course we take, this kind of suffering, suffering for righteousness, is by far the best. What Julius Caesar said of doing ill, we may well say of suffering ill: if it must be, it is best for it to be for a kingdom. If we are to reign with Christ, it is certain that we must suffer with him. And if we suffer with him, it is certain that we will reign with him. "If we endure, we will also reign with him" (2 Timothy 2:12). Therefore, people who suffer in this way are **blessed** or happy.

2. Happiness in suffering is asserted. This will become apparent from the following considerations.

First, it is the happiness of Christians, until they attain perfection, to be advancing forward. They are daily being refined and are growing stronger in grace. Their hearts are being weaned away from earth and are being fixed on heaven. Their suffering for the sake of righteousness has a special place in that process. If the world should caress them and smile on them, they might quickly forget their heavenly home.

Second, persecuted Christians are happy in showing their love for God through their sufferings. The more Christians suffer for Christ, the more they love him; and the more they love Christ, the more they can suffer for him.

Third, they are happy to be conformed to Christ, which is love's ambition. Believers would be offended if the world was kind to them, yet cruel to their beloved Lord and Master. Are you not most willing to share with Christ in suffering for righteousness? As the apostle Paul said, who himself was an ambassador in chains, "May I never boast except in the cross of our Lord Jesus Christ, through which the world has been crucified to me, and I to the world" (Galatians 6:14).

Fourth, suffering Christians are happy in the rich supplies of spiritual comfort and joy that are normal in times of suffering. "For just as the sufferings of Christ flow over into our lives, so also through Christ our comfort overflows" (2 Corinthians 1:5). God speaks most peace to the soul when the world speaks most war and enmity against it, and this is abundant compensation. When Christians lay in one balance the greatest sufferings people can inflict and in the other balance the least glance of God's countenance, they say it is worth enduring everything for that joy. "They may curse, but you will bless" (Psalm 109:28). Let them frown, but let God smile. God usually acts in this way. He refreshes those who suffer for him with special visitations.

The world cannot but misjudge the state of suffering Christians. St. Bernard says that the world sees their crosses but not their anointings. Do you not think St. Stephen was happy in his enemies' hands? Was he afraid of the showers of stones falling all around him? He saw the heavens opened and Jesus standing on the Father's right hand. He was not troubled about being stoned. As the text says, in the middle of all this, "he fell asleep" (Acts 7:60).

Fifth, if our present sufferings are far outweighed by present comforts, how much more will the future weight of glory surpass these sufferings! "I consider that our present sufferings are not worth comparing with the glory that will be revealed in us" (Romans 8:18). We are happy in our present sufferings because they lead to future happiness, to the glory that is to come. The Hebrew word translated "glory" means "weight." Earthly glories are all lightweight when compared with the future weight of glory.

"Do not fear what they fear; do not be frightened." No time or place in the world is so far in favor of Christianity that it is unnecessary to arm the Christian mind against the outward oppositions and discouragements it meets on the way to heaven. This is the point the apostle makes here. He does it, first, with an assertion and, second, by an exhortation. The assertion is that in suffering for righteousness, they are happy. The exhortation agrees with this assertion: **"Do not fear."** Why should they fear anything when they are assured of happiness, especially since they will be even more happy on account of those very things that are supposed to frighten them?

The words are partly taken from the prophet Isaiah, who relates them as the Lord's words to him and to other godly people with him at that time. The prophet was speaking against their distrust of God and their fearfulness, which drove them to seek help from an ungodly king and people instead of from God. "Do not fear what they fear, and do not dread it. The LORD Almighty is the one you are to regard as holy, he is the one you are to fear, he is the one you are to dread" (Isaiah 8:12-13). This the apostle extends as a universal rule for Christians amidst their greatest troubles and dangers.

The things contrasted here are a perplexing, troubling fear of sufferings, as the soul's disease, and a sanctifying of God in the heart, as the sovereign cure for the fear and the true principle of a healthy, sound mind.

Natural fear is not evil in itself, and yet in unspiritual people it is out of control. We may speak of our natural passions as not sinful in their nature, and yet in us who are naturally sinful, in fact full of sin, our passions cannot escape being mixed with sin.

Sin has put the soul into universal disorder, so that it neither loves nor hates what it should. It does not have the right joy or sorrow or hope or fear. A very small matter stirs and troubles it. As water that is stirred (this is what the word translated **frightened** means) becomes muddy and impure because it has dregs in the bottom, so the soul, through carnal fear, is confused. It has neither quiet nor clarity in it. "But the wicked are like the tossing sea, which cannot rest, whose waves cast up mire and mud" (Isaiah 57:20). It is like this with a person's unrenewed heart. The least blasts disturb it and make it restless, and its own impurity makes it muddy. When troubles are faraway, we are prepared to relax. But when troubles suddenly overtake us, we become fearful. Is this not the condition with most people? Contemplatives have always noted this human disease and have attempted to cure it in many ways, without success. Divine light is needed here, and it is given us in the next verse.

Verse 15-16a

But in your hearts set apart Christ as Lord. Always be prepared to give an answer to everyone who asks you to give the reason for the hope that you have. But do this with gentleness and respect.

It is implied that the reason for all our fears and troubles is our ignorance and disregard for God. Acknowledging God properly is the only way to establish a strong mind. In these words we consider three things: first, respect for God as it is expressed here: **set apart Christ as Lord**; second, the center of this, **your hearts**; and, third, its fruit, the power that this sanctifying of God in the heart has to rid that heart of those fears and troubles.

Set apart Christ as Lord. He is holy, most holy, the fountain of holiness. It is he and he alone who powerfully sanctifies us; and then, and not until then, we sanctify him. When he has made us holy, we know and confess him to be holy, we worship and serve our holy God, we glorify him with our whole souls and all our affections. We sanctify him by acknowledging his greatness and power and goodness, and (which is here especially intended) we do this by a holy fear of him and faith in him. These emotions within us confess his greatness and power and goodness. The prophet Isaiah expressed it in this way: "The LORD Almighty is the one you are to regard as holy, he is the one you are to fear, he is the one you are to dread" (Isaiah 8:13). Then the prophet adds that if you sanctify him in this way, "he will be a sanctuary" (verse 14). You will regard him like this in believing in him and will find him protecting you. You will lean on him for safety. These ways especially cure the heart of undue fears.

But in your hearts. We are to be sanctified in our words and actions, but primarily in our **hearts**, the root and principle of the rest. He sanctifies his own throughout, makes their words and their lives holy, but first, and most of all, their **hearts**. And as he chiefly sanctifies the heart, the heart chiefly sanctifies him; it acknowledges and worships him often when the tongue and body do not and trusts in him, which the outward man cannot do though it does follow and is acted upon by these affections and so shares in them according to its capacity.

Beware of sanctifying God in an external and superficial way, which he will not accept. He will interpret that as profaning him and his name. "Do not be deceived; God cannot be mocked" (Galatians 6:7). But let your hearts sanctify him, and then he will strengthen and fortify your hearts.

This sanctifying of God in the heart composes the heart and frees it from fears.

First, in a general sense, the heart turns to consider God and turns away from those vain, empty things that make it fearful. The heart cannot be at rest until God comes in and throws these things out of it.

Second, fear and faith in the believer work in the following special way:

The fear of God nullifies all lesser fears. It tells the heart what it must do and what it must not do. It tells the heart that it is better to obey God rather than human beings. It is not necessary to have the favor of the world, nor to have riches, but it is necessary to hold firmly to the truth and to walk in a holy way, to sanctify the name of the Lord and honor him, both in life and in death.

Faith in God clears the mind and dispels earthly fears. It is the most sure help. "When I am afraid, I will trust in you," says David (Psalm 56:3). Faith says, "Even if everything fails, I know one thing that will not fail. I have a refuge that all the strength of nature and human scheming cannot break or demolish." "Find rest, O my soul, in God alone; my hope comes from him. He alone is my rock and my salvation; he is my fortress, I will not be shaken" (Psalm 62:5-6).

Seek to have the Lord **in your hearts,** and sanctify him there. He will make them strong and will carry them through all dangers. "Even though I walk through the valley of the shadow of death, I will fear no evil, for you are with me" (Psalm 23:4). "The LORD is my light and my salvation— whom shall I fear? The LORD is the stronghold of my life—of whom shall I be afraid?" (Psalm 27:1). What makes the church so firm and strong, "though the earth give way and the mountains fall into the heart of the sea"? It is this: "God is within her, she will not fall" (Psalm 46:2, 5). God is immovable, and therefore everyone he lives in, he makes strong. Work hard, then, to have God **in your hearts,** living in the midst of them, in the midst of all circumstances, and you will not be moved.

Always be prepared to give an answer. The real Christian is all for Christ and has given all of his own rights to his Lord and Master, to be his completely, and has chosen to suffer for him, and therefore he will surely not fail to speak for him on all occasions. If a Christian sanctifies Christ in his heart, the tongue will follow and will **be prepared to give an answer** (*pros apologian*), a defense or apology. There are four things to be noted here:

1. The need of it: people will call you to account.
2. The subject of it: **the hope that you have.**
3. The manner: **with gentleness and respect.**
4. The faculty for it: **be prepared.**

1. The need for a defense or apology. Religion is always under attack from the world. These attacks fall on those who love Christ. The saints, through their blameless actions and patient sufferings, may write or live out most convincing defenses. Yet sometimes it is necessary to add verbal defenses and to vindicate not so much themselves as their Lord and his truth from suffering reproach.

Christian prudence goes a long way in regulating this, for holy things are not to be thrown to dogs. Some people are not capable of receiving rational answers, especially in divine matters. The name Christian, in the early days of Christianity, was hated. Then, as now, we need to be ready to give a defense.

2. All that they are to give account of is contained in the words, **the hope that you have.** Faith is the root of all graces, of all obedience and holiness, and hope is so near in nature to it that the one is often called the other. The things that faith lays hold of as present in the truth of divine promises, hope looks for as things to come in certain performance. To believe a promise to be true before it is performed is nothing but believing that it will be performed, and hope looks forward to that.

Saints receive many rich and excellent things, even in their humble, despised condition here. But their **hope** is mentioned as the subject they may speak of and give account of with most advantage. So, then, the whole of religion is summed up in this phrase, **the hope that you have**, for two reasons. First, it does indeed resolve the things to come; and, second, it leads the soul toward them by all the graces it has. Hope aims mainly to keep that life to come in the believer's eye until he has it in his hand, and so it brings him to possess it. As one of the apostles says of faith, "faith is being sure of what we hope for" (Hebrews 11:1). The word *hope* concerning other things does not suit its meaning here, as there it sounds so uncertain. About all other hopes than Christian hope, Seneca was right to say that "hope is the name of an uncertain good." But the Gospel, being founded on faith, furnishes a hope that has substance and reality in it. And all its truths concentrate to give such a hope. Christians are prepared to endure suffering with joy because of the hope of glory that is laid up for us. "You . . . joyfully accepted the confiscation of your property, because you knew that you yourselves had better and lasting possessions" (Hebrews 10:34).

The hope. The total position of a believer lies in hope. He is born of God and has a crown that does not fade. He is rich in hope that surpasses all worldly hopes. It is a great comfort for Christians to look beyond all that they can possess or attain here. As for answering others about **the hope** they have, they give this answer to themselves about all their present griefs and wants: "I have a poor traveler's lot here, little friendship and many pressing problems, but still go cheerfully in the direction of home. When I reach home I will have riches and honor enough, and a palace and a crown that lasts forever. Here I find strong and cruel assaults of temptations breaking over me, but for all that, I have the certain hope of a complete victory, and then everlasting peace. I lift up my head because the day of my redemption is coming closer. I dare proclaim this to everyone and am not ashamed **to give an answer** about this blessed **hope.**"

3. As for the manner of this, it is to be done **with gentleness and respect**—**gentleness** toward other people and reverent fear toward God.

Gentleness. A Christian is not to be blustering and assaulting unbelievers with invectives just because he has a superior position on the question of hope. He is not to be like those people who think they are allowed to speak roughly because the truth is on their side. On the contrary, they should work hard to show **gentleness**, for the sake of the truth. The Spirit of truth is also the Spirit of gentleness, and as a dove he rested on that great Champion of Truth who is the Truth itself. Imprudence makes some Christians neutralize much of their labor in speaking for Christ and only serves to drive away those they are trying to draw in.

And respect. Divine things are never to be spoken about in a light, perfunctory way but always with a reverent, grave manner of spirit. The confidence that comes with this **hope** makes the believer not fear other people, whom he answers; but he still fears God, for whom he answers, and whose interest is the main purpose in everything he says. The soul that has a deep sense of spiritual things and the true knowledge of God is most afraid of answering wrongly and most wary about how he speaks when he is speaking of and for God.

4. We have the faculty for this defense: **be prepared.** In this are implied knowledge, affection, and courage. As far as knowledge is concerned, it is not required of every Christian to be able to answer obscure points of the Christian faith. But all Christians should know enough to be able to explain the hope that is in them and explain the main doctrine of grace and salvation, about which most people are lamentably ignorant. Affection inspires one to work. Whatever faculty the mind has, love not only will not allow it to be useless but hardens it against hazards in the defense of truth. The only way to know and love the truth, and to have the courage

to explain it, is to have the Lord sanctified in your heart. People may argue strongly against popery and errors, and yet be strangers to God and this **hope**. Surely the liveliest defense comes from the soul's special interest in God and in those truths and **the hope** that is being questioned. This will animate you when you make your defense, not for a hope you have read and heard about in a vague way but for a **hope** within you, not merely a hope in believers in general but in you. Put all your hope in Christ, and when attacked, take all your answers from him, for it is "Christ in you" who is "the hope of glory" (Colossians 1:27).

Verse 16b

Keeping a clear conscience, so that those who speak maliciously against your good behavior in Christ may be ashamed of their slander.

"The complacency of fools will destroy them" (Proverbs 1:32). None of God's children die of the disease of too much ease. But God knows how to direct them so they overcome conflicts. One main thing, helping them in their support and victory, is what is here required in the saints and is accomplished in them by God's Spirit—**keeping a clear conscience.**

We have here two parties opposing each other— the evil tongues of the ungodly and the good conscience of the Christian—**those who speak maliciously against you,** but you have **a clear conscience.**

1. The outcome of the contest: the good conscience prevails, and the evil speakers are **ashamed.**

The parties engaged: **Those who speak maliciously.** This is a general evil in corrupt human nature, though in some people it rises to a greater height than in others. Are not tables and chambers, and almost all societies and meetings, full of it? Satan, as the Syriac calls him, is an eater of calumnies. This evil tongue has its root in the heart, in a perverse constitution, in pride and self-love. Self-love makes people seek recognition, and this makes them attack other people and speak ill of them.

But this bent of the unrenewed heart and tongue to speak evil is mostly against those who do not walk in the ways of this world. Against such people this furnace of the tongue, "set on fire by hell" (James 3:6), is made seven times hotter than normal. They call sincere Christians "a company of hypocrites who pretend to be godly but are malicious and proud." If believers are cheerful in society, they are said to have more freedom than suits their profession; if they have a serious disposition, they are accused of being sullen. In a similar way John the Baptist and Christ were perversely censured by the Jews (see Matthew 11:18-19).

Search yourselves to see that you do not possess any of this malicious talk. Remember that we will be called to give an account of our words. Learn to be more humble and to censure yourselves. Ensure that people only meet with charity at your hands. Because those hissings are the natural voice of the descendants of serpents, expect them as you follow Christ, and do as you are directed here: **keeping a clear conscience.** In the Scriptures conscience is the mind in reference to ourselves and our own actions. There is a double goodness in the conscience—purity and tranquillity. The latter flows from the former; so the former is the thing we should primarily study, and the latter will then naturally follow.

The goodness of **conscience** recommended here is the integrity and holiness of the whole inner nature of a Christian. The ingredients of this are, first, a due light or knowledge that, like the lamps in the temple, must always be burning within, for filthiness is always the companion of darkness. So if you want to have a good **conscience,** you must by all means have so much light, so much knowledge of the will of God, that it will regulate you and show you the way and teach you how to act, speak, and think as in God's presence.

Second, you must have a constant regard and use of this light, applying it to every area of your life. Continue to seek a closer conformity with the known will of God. Daily order the affections by it. We must not spare anything that is out of step with this within ourselves. Then our hearts will be polished and in the right frame of mind. It is the daily, inner work of Christians, their great business, to purify themselves, just as God is pure (see 1 John 3:3).

Third, to make progress in this work it is necessary to search our hearts and actions frequently, to consider not only what we are to do in the future, but what we have done in the past. These inquiries, as they are the main part of the conscience's work, are a chief means of making and keeping a good conscience. Do this by familiarizing the soul with its own state and with the inclinations toward which it most naturally inclines. Then stir it up to work out and purge away by repentance the pollution it has contracted by any outward act or inner sin. This search enables the conscience to be more watchful and teaches it how to avoid similar errors in the future. God uses our previous lapses to keep us from falling in the future and makes a medicine out of this poison.

So, if the conscience is to be good, it must be enlightened, and it must be watchful.

The other thing in this verse is the advantage of this **clear conscience.** First, even external success accompanies it in respect to the malicious, ungodly world. The accusers will **be ashamed of their slander.** This is often clear to people. They acknowledge the victory of silent innocency, and false accusers hide their heads. Thus without stirring, the integrity of a Christian conquers, just as a rock, unmoved, breaks the waters that are crashing against it. Punishing evil speakers by doing good is not only a lawful but a laudable way of revenge. It shows the falseness of the accusers. This is the most powerful defense and refutation. But without this **clear conscience**, we cut ourselves short of other defenses for true religion, no matter how much we say. One unchristian action will disgrace our faith more than we can repair by the largest and best-framed speeches on its behalf.

Let those, therefore, who have given their names to Christ honor him and their holy profession most in this way. Speak for Christ as occasion requires. Why should we not, provided it is **with gentleness and respect**, as the apostle requires? But let this be the main defense of religion: live in a way that will commend it. Everyone who calls himself a Christian should live in this way. They should adorn that holy profession with holy conversation. But most people are nothing more than spots and blots, some wallowing in the mire, and provoking one another to all uncleanness. Oh, the unchristian life of Christians! This is an evil to be greatly lamented, more than all the troubles we sustain! These people deny Christ and declare that they do not belong to him. Let us strive to honor that name that they disgrace. And if they reproach you because you do not walk with them, take no notice, but go on your way. Do not be troubled by false accusations. Shame them by your blameless life.

2. There is an intrinsic good in **keeping a clear conscience** that sweetens all suffering, as seen in succeeding verses.

Verse 17

It is better, if it is God's will, to suffer for doing good than for doing evil.

Suffering results from the path you choose to travel along. If you choose the way of wickedness, you will not escape suffering. With that in mind, it is far better to **suffer for doing good than for doing evil.**

The way of the ungodly is not exempt from suffering, even at present. Setting aside the judgment and wrath to come, they often suffer from the hands of men, whether justly or unjustly, and often from the immediate hand of God, who is always just, both in this and in causing the sinner to "be filled with the fruit of their schemes" (Proverbs 1:31). When profane, ungodly people wrong one another, God is being just with them both, since both of them are unjust. They are both rebelling against God, and so God sets them against each other. The wicked profess their combined enmity against the children of God, and yet they are not always at peace among themselves. They often revile and defame each other. The godly do not copy them, as they are to be like their Lord, who did not issue threats when he suffered (see 1 Peter 2:23).

If it is God's will. The Christian seeks to do God's sovereign will. Nothing quiets the mind more than this. We must suffer **if it is God's will.**

If we will what God wills, even in suffering, that makes it sweet and easy. When our mind goes along with God's, we willingly move with the stream of providence, which will carry us with it, even when we row against it, which will bring toil and tiredness from our pains. God's children, convinced of their Father's love and wisdom, know that his will is always best for them. Sufferings are unpleasant to the flesh, and it will grumble. But the voice of God's Spirit in his children is similar to that of good king Hezekiah: "The word of the LORD you have spoken is good" (Isaiah 39:8). "Let God do with me as seems best in his sight. My foolish heart might think that the things I suffer should cease, but my wise and heavenly Father thinks otherwise. Though I desire the light of his countenance above everything in the world, yet if God sees fit to hide it sometimes, if that is his will, let me not murmur." No soul will enjoy anything as much as when he has renounced himself and only has God's will.

Verse 18

For Christ died for sins once for all, the righteous for the unrighteous, to bring you to God. He was put to death in the body but made alive by the Spirit.

The whole of life for a Christian is aiming to be conformed to Christ. So in anything, whether doing or suffering, we are to follow Christ's example. The apostle frequently says this. Here he says, **For Christ died.** While the doctrine of Christian suffering is the occasion of his speaking about Christ's suffering, he insists on it for its own sake as well, and because it has additional usefulness. So we will consider the double capacity of Christ's sufferings—first, as an encouragement and engagement for Christians to suffer and, second, as the great point of their faith, on which all their hopes and happiness depend.

An Encouragement to Suffer

The correct consideration of Christ's sufferings greatly assists Christians in their own sufferings, especially in those that are directly for Christ.

It is a comfort to the mind in any distress to look at examples of other people in greater distress, both in the past and in the present. This diverts the eye from continual concentration on our own suffering, which, when we return to view it again, seems less of a weight to bear. Public, spiritual troubles are lessened, and particularly the sufferings and temptations of the godly, by the consideration of it as their common lot, not new to anyone. "No temptation has seized you except what is common to man" (1 Corinthians 10:13). If we follow the lives of the most eminent saints, will we not find that every notable step is marked with a new cross, one trouble following another, as the waves do in incessant succession? Is this not clear in the life of Abraham and Jacob and the rest of God's followers in the Scriptures? And does this not make it unreasonable to imagine that we can be an exception to this? Do you want a new path cut for you that is free of thorns and flowers? Do you expect to meet with no contradictions and no hard times from the world? This can never be the situation. It is a universal conclusion that "Everyone who wants to live a godly life in Christ Jesus will be persecuted" (2 Timothy 3:12). This is the path that leads to the kingdom, along which all the children of God, heirs of the kingdom, have traveled. It is the road that even Christ trod. As Augustine said, "One Son without sin, but not one without suffering." **For Christ died.**

The example and company of the saints in suffering is worthy of our contemplation and study, but the example of Christ is more worthy of this than any other person, indeed than all others put together. Another apostle writes, "Let us run with perseverance the race marked out for us" (Hebrews 12:1). He tells us about "a great cloud of witnesses," made up of believers who suffered before us; the heat of the day in which we run is cooled through that cloud of witnesses surrounding us. But the main strength of our comfort lies in this: "Let us fix our eyes on Jesus" (verse 2) and view his sufferings and their result. Considering Christ is the strongest cordial and will keep you from growing weary or losing heart (see Hebrews 12:3).

The singular power of this example lies in many details that are worth considering. To specify some important things briefly in the steps of the present words, consider, first, the greatness of the Example, **Christ**, who is singled out for us in the expression, *kai Christos*, **For Christ.** There is no higher example. Not only are the sons of adoption sufferers, but so was the one and only Son, the eternal Heir of glory, from whom everyone else derives their inheritance. So who will complain about their suffering? Will the wretched sons of men refuse to suffer as the glorious Son of God suffered? As St. Bernard said about pride, "After Majesty, Highest Majesty, to teach us humility, has so humbled himself, how wicked and impudent a thing it would be for a worm to swell with pride and become conceited." Since our Lord has taught us by suffering himself and has dignified suffering in this way, we should not be afraid to suffer but be keen to endure it.

Second, consider the greatness and the continuance of Christ's sufferings. The apostle says here, **Christ died . . . once.** Christ did suffer at one particular moment; but his whole life may be viewed as suffering, up to his death on the cross. If you are killed in a violent way or cut off in the prime of your life, you can look on Christ as the One who went before you in both these respects. He was scourged, buffeted, and spat on. He endured everything. He gave his back to the smiters. Furthermore, as the prophet says, he "was numbered with the transgressors" (Isaiah 53:12). They subjected him to all that shame, even hanging him between two thieves. As they passed him, they hurled taunts at him, as at a target fixed to the cross. "Let us fix our eyes on Jesus, the author and perfecter of our faith, who for the joy set before him endured the cross, scorning its shame ..." (Hebrews 12:2). As St. Bernard said, "They truly do not feel their own wounds who contemplate Christ's."

We will now take a closer look at the details that the apostle sets out. We note, first, the cause of Christ's sufferings and, second, their kind.

The Cause

We observe both their meritorious cause and their final cause.

1. The meritorious cause, what in us brought sufferings on Christ: **Christ died for sins ... the righteous for the unrighteous.** The evil of sin has the evil of punishment inseparably connected with it. We are under a natural obligation of obedience to God, and he justly urges it. Where the command of God's law is broken, its curse will follow.

Thus the angels who did not stay in their station fell from grace and fell into a dungeon where they were "kept in darkness, bound with everlasting chains for judgment on the great Day" (Jude 6). Mankind also fell under the sentence of death. Mankind fell as one person, so that everyone fell together, and thus no one in the race could escape condemnation unless some other way of escape could be found. And here it is: **Christ died ... the righteous for the unrighteous.** The Son says to the Father, "You granted him [Christ] authority over all people that he might give eternal life to all those you have given him" (John 17:2). And, "All I have is yours, and all you have is mine. And glory has come to me through them" (John 17:10).

Christ suffered for the sins of these people. He stood in their place. All the sins of all the elect were parceled up into one huge bundle and bound to his shoulders. The prophet speaks about them in this way: "The punishment that brought us peace was upon him" (Isaiah 53:5). He had spoken about many ways of sinning and said, "Each of us has turned to his own way ... he was pierced for our transgressions, he was crushed for our iniquities" (Isaiah 53:5-6). Christ binds up everything in that word "iniquities." The one transgression of the first Adam, which brought the curse onto his seed, was borne by the Second Adam to take it away from all who are his seed, who are now in him as their root.

2. The final cause of his sufferings: **To bring you to God.** You who are still strangers to God, who declare yourselves to be so by living as strangers far off from him, do not continue to behave in this evil way. Most of you seem to think that our Lord Jesus suffered so that we might neglect God and disobey him, rather than be restored to him! Has Christ bought you so that you are free to sin? Or is deliverance from sin, which alone is true freedom, what Christ purposed and laid down his life for?

Why let his blood still run in vain for us? He has through it opened up our way to God, and yet we refuse to make use of it. Those who are brought to God and are received into friendship with him relish that friendship, delight in his company, and love to be constantly with him. Is this so with us? By being so close, they become like him, know his will better every day, and grow more like him. But, alas, there is nothing like this in most people. Remember this for your comfort, that as you are brought to God through Jesus Christ, so you are kept in that union by him. It is a firmer knot than at first. No power of hell can dissolve it. Christ suffered once to bring us to God, never to depart again. As Christ suffered once for all, so we are brought to God once for all. We may feel we are closer to Christ at certain times than at other times, but we are never cut off once we are united to him. "For I am convinced that neither death nor life, neither angels nor demons, neither the present nor the future, nor any powers, neither height nor depth, nor anything else in all creation, will be able to separate us from the love of God that is in Christ Jesus our Lord" (Romans 8:38-39).

Regarding the kind of our Lord's sufferings, **he was put to death in the body but made alive by the Spirit.** The true life of a Christian is to see Christ in every step of his life. We look to Christ as our pattern both in living and in suffering, and we draw power from Christ for both. The apostle has mentioned Christ's suffering in general, but here he specifies how he died (**He was put to death in the body**), and then he adds that this resulted in his being **made alive by the Spirit.** This is a great encouragement to Christians. Was Christ, our Head, crowned with thorns, and shall we look for garlands? Are we redeemed from hell and condemnation by Christ, and can we refuse any service Christ calls us to? Those who are washed in the Lamb's blood "follow the Lamb wherever he goes" (Revelation 14:4).

Remove sin, and all suffering is light. And that has happened, for **Christ died for sins once for all.** Those who are in him will not hear any more talk of being condemned or suffering the wrath that is due because of sin. This puts invincible strength into the soul for enduring all other things, no matter how hard they are.

Put to death. This is the point that startles people: Christ's life ended in a violent way.

In the body refers to Christ's human nature. The whole person suffers death. But death, or the taking away of life and sense, applies particularly to the flesh or body. But the spirit, in contrast with the body, has a higher nature and power than the human soul, which cannot of itself return to live in and bring life to the body.

Christ's death was both voluntary and violent. The same power that restored his life could have prevented his being killed. But Christ's death was planned. Christ took on a human body like ours in order to die in this way and to offer himself up as a sacrifice, which, if it was to be accepted, had to be voluntary. In that sense he is said to have died even by that same Spirit who here is said to give him life. "How much more, then, will the blood of Christ, who through the eternal Spirit offered himself unblemished to God, cleanse our consciences!" (Hebrews 9:14).

Made alive by the Spirit. Christ was too big for the grave to devour. It looked as if Christ had been defeated. His disciples were at the point of giving up when they said, "We had hoped that he was the one who was going to redeem Israel" (Luke 24:21). But that body that was entombed was united to the spring of life, to the divine Spirit of the Godhead who had given it life.

In the same way the church, which is Christ's body, when it seems to be defeated, when it is brought to the lowest position, through its mystical union with Jesus Christ will be preserved from destruction. The church will be delivered and raised up in due time. As Christ was closest to his exaltation in the lowest step of his humiliation, so it is with his church. When things are most hopeless, light will arise out of darkness. "When the tale of bricks is doubled, Moses comes."

Do you want to be cured of that common disease, the fear of death? Look to Christ, and you will find more than you seek. You will be taught not only not to fear but to love it. Consider Christ's death. **Christ died.** Through that, you who received him as your life may be sure of this, that you are by his death freed from the second death. "He who is our life descended here and bore our death, killing it by the abundance of his life" (Augustine). And that is the great point. The second death is removed. The death that you must pass through is beautified and sweetened. Its ugly features become pleasant when you look on it in Christ and in the light of his death. The believer longs to lie down in that bed of rest since his Lord lay in it and has warmed that cold bed and purified it with his fragrant body. Jesus often reiterates in John 6 that he is himself the living and life-giving Bread for believers. He also promises that he will raise them up on the last day.

Verses 19-21

Through whom also he went and preached to the spirits in prison who disobeyed long ago when God waited patiently in the days of Noah while the ark was being built. In it only a few people, eight in all, were saved through water, and this water symbolizes baptism that now saves you also—not the removal of dirt from the body but the pledge of a good conscience toward God. It saves you by the resurrection of Jesus Christ.

A Christian desires nothing more than to know the excellency of Jesus

Christ, his person and his deeds. The apostle Peter, having spoken about this Spirit and his power that raised Christ from the dead, now takes the opportunity to speak about another work of that Spirit. His subject now is the proclamation of God's teaching. He is not talking about something new that followed Christ's death and resurrection, but about something that was told to the first inhabitants of the world. The same Spirit **went and preached to the spirits in prison.**

This passage is rather obscure. As is usually the case, the interpreters make it even more obscure with all their loud opinions. Those who dream of the descent of Christ's soul into hell think this text sounds like that. But when these verses are examined, it is seen that this cannot refer to that. Why? First, Christ went there to preach, and they do not admit this. Second, they say Christ's purpose was to be with the spirits of the faithful dead before his coming again. But this verse talks about the disobedient. Third, Christ's Spirit here is the same as meant by the previous words, which do not refer to his soul. Fourth, it is not to "the spirits who were in prison," as they read it, but to **the spirits in prison.** This clearly refers to their present condition, the just consequence of their disobedience.

The assertion about Christ preaching and the people he preached to in these verses must be taken together. **Through whom he also went and preached to the spirits in prison who disobeyed long ago.** In these words we have a preacher and his hearers. With regard to the preacher, we will find here, first, Christ's ability and, second, Christ's activity in the use of it.

1. Christ's ability is matchless, as it stems from the Spirit of wisdom himself, for he is the coeternal Son of God. The Spirit Christ preached by was the same as that by whom he was raised from the dead. Without the Spirit there is no preaching. Noah was, as our apostle calls him, "a preacher of righteousness" (2 Peter 2:5), but this was by this same Spirit, who preached through him. The Spirit flows from Christ and is in those through whom he preaches.

To Christ, then, everyone must come to be rightly supplied and enabled for that work. It is impossible to speak properly for him in any measure except by his Spirit. There must be particular access, instructions must be received from him, and his Spirit must be transfused into ours. If this happened all the time, how sweet it would be to speak about him! To be much in prayer, much in dependence on him, and drawing from him would be much better than reading, studying, and seeking after the arts, tongues, and common knowledge. These, indeed, are not to be despised nor neglected. As Bernard says, "Reading is good, learning is good, but above all, anointing is necessary, that anointing that teaches us all things." You must be earnest with the Lord, so that your messages are full of his Spirit.

2. We have the activity of Christ as a preacher. By the Spirit, it is said here, he **preached.** Not only did he do this during his time on earth, but he

did this at all times, both before and after that. He never left his church completely destitute of saving light, which he dispensed himself and conveyed through the hands of his servants. Since he **preached**, there is no excuse for the times after he ascended into heaven, nor for the times before he descended to the earth in human flesh. Though he did not preach then, nor does he now in his body, yet by his Spirit he then preached and still does. So, through what was chief in him he was still present with his church and preaching in it, and he will be to the end of the world, for his infinite Spirit is everywhere.

Yet it is said here, **through whom he also went and preached**, signifying the remarkable clearness of his administration in that way. When God appears eminently in any work of his own or in taking notice of our works, he is sometimes said to come down (as in reference to the cities of Babel and Sodom, "But the Lord came down to see the city and the tower" [Genesis 11:5, 7; 18:21; see also Exodus 3:8]). And here Christ clearly admonished them through Noah, coming, as it were, himself on purpose to declare his mind to them. This word, I believe, is used to show what equality there is in this. He came indeed visibly and dwelt among people when he became flesh; yet before that he visited them by his Spirit. And in later times, after he himself had ascended, "he came and preached peace to you who were far away" (Ephesians 2:17). And he continues to do this in the ministry of his Word. Therefore, he says, "He who listens to you listens to me" (Luke 10:16). Bearing this in mind would result in greater respect for the Word and greater acceptance of it. Do you think that in his Word Christ speaks through the eternal Spirit, yes, that he comes and preaches and addresses himself particularly to you in it? Will you slight him in this and turn away from him and refuse to listen to him?

Who disobeyed long ago. If you look at the visible, subordinate preacher mentioned here—Noah—you find that he was a holy man and an able and diligent preacher of righteousness, both in his teaching and in his living. So it seems strange that his preaching prevailed so little. But it appears much more so if we look higher, to the height at which the apostle points: the almighty Spirit of Christ was preached to them, and yet they were disobedient. The Greek means "they were not persuaded." This signifies both unbelief and disobedience. Unbelief is in itself the grand disobedience. It is the mind not yielding to divine truth, and so it is the spring of all disobedience in affection and action. This root of bitterness, this unbelief, is deeply embedded in our natural hearts. Unless they change, they cannot be good.

It may seem strange that the Gospel is so fruitless among us—that neither Word nor rod, both preaching aloud to us the doctrine of humility and repentance, persuades us to return or so much as to turn inward and question ourselves and say, "What have I done?" But it will be like this until the Spirit is poured from on high to open and soften hearts. This is to be desired. But were it there, that would not be enough unless a similar work in the heart meets the Word. For here we find that the Spirit went and preached, but the spirits of the hearers remained unbelieving and disobedient.

The spirits in prison. This is now their position, and because he refers to them in this position, he calls them **spirits.** It is their **spirits** that are in that **prison.** If disobedience follows the preaching of the Word, **prison** follows that disobedience. The Word by which they would not be bound to obedience binds them over to that **prison** from which they will never escape or ever be released.

Take note of this and know that you have been warned, you who will not receive salvation. You are every day in the way of disobedience, hastening to this perpetual imprisonment. Christ is still following us with his entreaties, "crying aloud by his words, by his deeds, by his death, by his life, by his coming down from heaven, by his ascension into it, crying to us to return to him" (Augustine). Though you may be happy in your own prison, unless you are released you will be placed in chains of everlasting darkness and kept there until the great judgment day. But if you will receive Jesus Christ, you will receive liberty and life. "So if the Son sets you free, you will be free indeed" (John 8:36).

When Christ Preached and How God Dealt with the People He Preached To

When God waited patiently in the days of Noah. There are two outstanding wonders in the world—the bounty of God and the disloyalty of man. One great example of this is set before us here. On God's part there is much patience, and yet on man's part, invincible disobedience. Here we see two things—first, the Lord's general dealing with the world of the ungodly at that time and, second, God's special way with his chosen, Noah and his family.

Observe, first, the time designated for this—**in the days of Noah.** There were doubtless many greater people than Noah in those days, and yet they perished in the Flood, and their names drowned with them. The name and memory of the righteous is ever sweet and delightful, like the name of Abraham, the father of the faithful, and those of Isaac and Jacob. Thus Noah was preferred by God and became "heir of the righteousness that comes by faith" (Hebrews 11:7).

The Lord's dealing with the wicked in those times, before he swept them away by the Flood, is seen in two ways—first, long-suffering and, second, clear warning.

1. Long-suffering: **God waited patiently.** The Hebrew term translated "slow to anger" (for example, in Exodus 34:6) supposes both great provocation and continuing patience. Here we see the goodness of God.

Considering how he hates sin, and how strongly he punishes it, he could easily cut off all the ungodly in a moment. Yet he bears with them and does not punish them. And he continues to send his common mercies upon them (see Acts 14:17).

2. But this was not just unvoiced patience; it combined a constant warning and teaching. We see that they did not lack the choicest of preaching. The Son of God, by his eternal Spirit, **went and preached** to them. It was Christ's truth in Noah's mouth. There was a real sermon, expressed in this verse: **while the ark was being built.** That action spoke God's mind; every hammer blow used in the building of the ark preached to them about the impending judgment, exhorting them to escape it. That is why Peter adds that **God waited**, expecting that his Word would be believed and they would turn from their wickedness. But we see that no such thing followed. They took their own course, and therefore the Lord took his. They had polluted the world with their wickedness, and now the Lord wanted it to be cleansed by repentance. But since this was denied, it had to happen in another way, through a flood. They would not let go of their sins, and so they and their sins, being inseparable, had to be cleansed away together.

Impenitence, after much patience on God's part, makes judgment full and complete. Has not the Lord been equally patient with us? Has he not spared us and warned us, and have not the spiritual riches of the Gospel been opened to us?

While the ark was being built. The delay of the Lord's determined judgment on the ungodly did indeed show his patience toward them. And for Noah and his family he provided preservation. The patience that the ungodly enjoy usually benefits the godly as well. Notice here, first, the work (which is appointed by God and carried out by Noah's obedience) and, second, the goal of the work.

The Work

1. The work, in the first place, consisted in preparing the ark, by God's appointment. His power did not perform it, but his wisdom chose it. He who steered the course of the ark safely all that time could have preserved those he designed it for without it. But it usually pleases the Lord to combine his most wonderful deliverances with some selected means. In this way we are called on to be obedient.

2. The work, in the second place, consisted of Noah's obedience. If we look at the difficulties in this work and the way in which the eight were preserved through it, we would see just how remarkable this was. Think of the size of the task and the great effort that was involved in providing the materials in the teeth of opposition from the surrounding ungodly people. "What," they would say, "does this old man think he is doing? Who is going to make such a huge voyage?" But Noah continued to obey God through all these attacks. The apostle Paul tells us what the root of this

was: "By his faith he condemned the world" (Hebrews 11:7). There is no living and lasting obedience except for what springs from that root. Noah believed what the Lord said about judging the ungodly world, and from belief in this arose what is specifically mentioned in Hebrews. "By faith Noah . . . built an ark" (Hebrews 11:7). He firmly believed that he would finish the ark and that he would be saved by that ark.

Its Goal

The goal of this work was to save Noah and his family from the flood in which all the rest perished. **In it only a few people, eight in all, were saved through water.** If so few people are saved, we should ask ourselves if we belong to this **few.** Further, those of you who are indeed seeking the way of life should not be discouraged by how few people are involved. It has always been like this. You see here how **few** of the whole world were saved. Is it not better to be one of the **few** in the ark than one of the multitude in the waters?

The main truth I want to leave you with is this: look on Jesus Christ as the Ark, of whom this was a figure, and believe that apart from him there is nothing but certain destruction, a deluge of wrath, all over the world, on those who are outside Christ. Our life, our only safety, is to be in him. But these things are not often believed. People think they believe them but do not. Were it believed that we are under the sentence of eternal death in our natural state, and that there is no escape except to run to Christ, what a great crowd would throng around him. Christ invites and calls, but how few are persuaded to follow him! Noah believed the Lord's word of judgment against the world; he believed God's promise to him and prepared an ark. Is it not a sign of unbelief that though there is an ark of everlasting salvation prepared for us, we will not come to it? Are you persuaded that the door of the ark stands open? Christ's offer to you is free. Come and you will see that you are not turned away (see John 6:37).

The ark is also a good way to instruct Christians about the rule of Christianity. **This water symbolizes baptism that now saves you also.**

In these words we have, first, the goal of baptism, second, its virtue or efficacy for that end, and, third, a resemblance in both these to Noah's preservation in the Flood.

The Goal of Baptism

The end of baptism is to save us. This is the common goal of all of God's ordinances. The common mistake concerning God's ordinances is that they are not used for this purpose. We come and sit awhile and, if we can keep awake, give the Word a hearing. But how few of us receive it as "the word planted in you, which can save you" (James 1:21). If it were accepted in this way, how sweet it would be found to be. In the same way, if the sacraments were seen as seals of this inheritance, annexed to its great charter, seals of salvation, this would greatly increase our appetite for the Lord's Supper. It would teach us to think more often about our own baptism. An unspiritual eye looks on bread and wine and water and sees the outward difference in their use, that they are set apart from their normal use. But it does not see the most important part of the difference, in which their excellency lies, since only the eye of faith perceives salvation under them. We should aspire to know the hidden rich things of God that are wrapped up in his ordinances. Let us be more earnest with him who has appointed them and made it their end to save us. Let us seriously seek salvation in them from God's own hand, and we shall find it.

It saves us. The salvation of Noah and his family from the Flood, and all outward deliverances and salvations, are but dark shadows of this. They should not be spoken of, these reprieves in this present life, in comparison with the deliverance of the soul from death, the second death. You can hardly compare the prolonging of a moment with eternity. Those who have escaped a danger of this kind are apt to rest there, as if nothing else was to be feared. How did wicked Ham benefit from outliving the Flood, since he inherited a curse after it? Think about this seriously. What will be the end of all your temporary safety and preservation if you do not share in this salvation and find yourself sealed and marked for it?

The Efficacy of Baptism

That baptism has power is expressly stated: **baptism that now saves you.** What kind of power this is, is equally clear from the way it is here expressed. It is not by a natural force of the element. Even when it is used sacramentally it can only wash away the dirt of the body, as its physical power reaches no further. But since it is in the hand of the Spirit of God, as other sacraments are and as the Word itself is, it can purify the conscience and convey grace and salvation to the soul through its reference to and union with what it represents. It saves by **the pledge of a good conscience toward God**, and that **by the resurrection of Jesus Christ.**

Thus, we have a true account of this power, and so of other sacraments, and we find the error of two extremes. First, that of those who ascribe too much to them, as if they worked through a natural, inherent value and carried grace in them inseparably. Second, the error of those who ascribe too little to them, making them only signs and badges of our profession. Signs they are, but more than signs that merely represent something. They are the means exhibiting and seals confirming grace to the faithful. But the working of faith and the conveying of Christ into the soul are not put into them to accomplish in themselves but are still in the supreme hand that appointed them. God causes the souls of his own to receive these seals of his with faith and makes them effectual to confirm the faith that receives them in this way. They are then, in a word, neither empty signs to those who believe, nor effectual causes of grace to those who do not believe.

The pledge of a good conscience toward God. The taking away of spiritual filthiness as the true and saving effect of baptism, the apostle here expresses by what is the further result and effect of it—**the pledge of a good conscience toward God.** Now, **a good conscience**, in its full sense, is a pure conscience and a peaceable conscience. It cannot be at peace if it is not pure. The purified and good condition of the whole soul may well, as here it does, go under the name of **a good conscience**, for it is the prime faculty for it. Therefore, the efficacy of the blood of Christ is expressed in this way. It "cleanse[s] our consciences from acts that lead to death" (Hebrews 9:14). This is a similar expression to the one here.

This **pledge of a good conscience toward God** touches two great points that are of the utmost importance to the soul—its justification and its sanctification. For baptism is the seal of both and purifies the conscience in both respects. **This water** is the figure both of the blood and the water, the justifying blood of Christ and the pure water of the sanctifying Spirit of Christ. Christ takes away the condemnation and guilt of sin by the one and polluting filthiness by the other.

The conscience of a true believer inquiring within, upon right discovery, will make this answer to God: "Lord, I have found that there is no standing before you, for the soul in itself is overwhelmed with a world of guiltiness. But I find a blood sprinkled on it that has, I am sure, virtue enough to purge all my guilt away and to present my soul pure to you. And I know that wherever you find that blood sprinkled, your anger is quenched and appeased immediately upon the sight of it. Your hand cannot strike where you see that blood." And the Lord agrees with this and authorizes the conscience, upon this account, to reply with an answer of safety and peace to the soul.

By the resurrection of Jesus Christ. Baptism does all this, not of itself, but by virtue of **the resurrection of Jesus Christ**, which refers both to the distant effect, salvation, and to the nearer effect as a means and pledge of that, the purifying of the conscience.

By this Christ's death and the effusion of his blood in his sufferings are not excluded but are included in it. His resurrection is the evidence of that whole work of expiation, both completed and accepted. Full payment has been made by our Surety, and his freedom is the cause and assurance of ours. Our apostle shows us the value of our living hope in the resurrection: "Praise be to the God and Father of our Lord Jesus Christ! In his great mercy he has given us new birth into a living hope through the resurrection of Jesus Christ from the dead" (1 Peter 1:3).

Now, baptism applies and seals to the believer his interest in the death and resurrection of Christ, as the apostle Paul teaches: "We were therefore buried with him through baptism into death in order that, just as Christ was raised from the dead through the glory of the Father, we too may live a new life" (Romans 6:4). The dipping into the waters represents our dying with Christ; and the return from there represents our rising with him.

The Resemblance of Baptism to the Saving of Noah

And this water symbolizes baptism. This relates to what we have just said, for when Noah went into the ark, it looked as if he were entering a grave rather than a safeguard of life. Yet, being buried there, he rose again, as it were, in his coming out to begin a new world. The waters of the Flood drowned the ungodly as a heap of filthiness washed them away, them and their sin together as one, being inseparable. But on the same waters the ark floated, and so preserved Noah and his family. Thus the waters of baptism are intended as a deluge to drown sin and to save the believer, who by faith is separated both from the world and from his sin. Sin sinks, and the believer is saved.

There is another thing specified by the apostle that, although it is a little hard, is his main parallel—the small number of those who are saved in both instances. Though many are sprinkled with water in baptism, so few attain through it **a good conscience toward God** and live by participating in the resurrection life of Christ.

You see the world perishing in a deluge of wrath and are now most thoughtful about this. How are you going to escape? Run to Christ for your safety, and rest secure there! You will find life in his death, and that life also brings to you his rising again. You have such a complete and clear title to life in these two events that you can challenge all adversities. You are unconquerable while you stand on this ground. You may speak in the same way as the apostle does in his challenge, "It is God who justifies. Who is he that condemns?" How do you know that God justifies? "Christ Jesus, who died—more than that, who was raised to life—is at the right hand of God and is also interceding for us" (Romans 8:33-34). This alludes to Isaiah 50:8, where Christ speaks of himself, but in the name of all who adhere to him: "He who vindicates me is near. Who then will bring charges against me?" What Christ says there, the apostle, with good reason, imparts to each believer in Christ. If no more is to be laid to Christ's charge, he is now acquitted; this is clear through his rising again. If you are clothed with him and are one with him, then you are free from any charges against you.

This is the great answer of the **good conscience.** It is the point of being justified before God. What has anyone to say against you? Your debt is paid by Christ, and thus you are free. Answer all accusations with this: Christ is risen.

Then, for the mortifying of sin and the strengthening of your graces, look daily on that death and resurrection. Study them, set your eye on them, until they are impressed on your heart. "And we, who with unveiled faces all reflect the Lord's glory, are being transformed into his likeness with ever-increasing glory, which comes from the Lord, who is the Spirit" (2 Corinthians 3:18). This is where all our peace and happiness come from. It is worth your time and trouble to become interested in this. It is the only thing worthy of your highest diligence. And yet most people run around, distracted by all they are doing, not knowing why they are doing it. They are deceived, though unwillingly, in those things that at their best only deceive them when all is done. They are content with shadows of faith, false touches of sorrow, and false flashes of joy. They are not building on Christ. They do not have him as their treasure, their righteousness, their all, their answer to God the Father. If this is your state, let go of everything and lay hold of Christ. Give your souls over to him and never leave him. He is the tried Foundation Stone, and the person who trusts in him will not be confounded.

Verse 22

Who has gone into heaven and is at God's right hand—with angels, authorities and powers in submission to him.
This is added to show us further who Christ is and what a glorious Saviour we have.

We have here four pointers or steps of the exaltation of Christ:

1. Resurrection from the dead.
2. Ascension into heaven.
3. Sitting at the right hand of God.
4. In that position, his royal authority over the angels.

The details are clear in themselves. Sitting at God's right hand is a borrowed expression of which you are not ignorant. It is drawn from earth to heaven, to bring down some idea about heaven for us. It shows us in our language the supreme dignity of Jesus Christ, who is God and man, the Mediator of the new covenant. It shows his matchless closeness to his Father and the sovereignty given him over heaven and earth. The subjection of angels is a further detail, specifying Christ's dignity and power. As he is enthroned at the Father's right hand, and as the angels are the most elevated and glorious creatures, so Christ's authority over all the world is implied in that subjection of the highest and noblest. His victory and triumph over the angels of darkness is further evidence of his invincible power and greatness and is a comfort to his saints. But here the apostle means Christ's supremacy over the glorious elect angels.

Here we see Christ's dignity and authority over them.

1. Christ's dignity over the angels. Such is Christ's dignity that even that nature that he stooped below them to take on, he has carried up and raised above them. Human flesh, being exalted in the person of Christ above all

those heavenly spirits, has been clothed with transcendent glory. The parcel of clay is made so bright and set so high that it outshines those bright, flaming spirits.

This those angels look upon with perpetual wonder but not with envy. Among them no such thing is to be found. They rejoice in the infinite wisdom of God and in his infinite love to poor, lost mankind. It is wonderful, indeed, to see Christ filling the space left by their fallen brothers with new guests from earth, yes, with such as are born heirs of hell. Not only would sinful people thus be raised to participate in glory with the spotless ones, these sinless spirits, but their flesh, in their Redeemer, would be dignified with a glory far beyond them. This is the mystery the angels are intent on looking and prying into; they cannot, nor ever will, see its bottom, for it has none.

2. Jesus Christ is not only exalted above the angels in absolute dignity, but also in relative authority over them. He is made Captain over their heavenly bands. They are all under his command for all services in which he desires to employ them. They are engaged in serving Christ's church. "Are not all angels ministering spirits sent to serve those who will inherit salvation?" (Hebrews 1:14). They are Christ's servants and at his appointment are the servants of every believer. Concerning the danger of overvaluing them or the inclination to worship them, thinking correctly about them will move us away from such errors. St. John tells us, "At this I fell at his feet to worship him. But he said to me, 'Do not do it! I am a fellow servant with you and with your brothers who hold to the testimony of Jesus. Worship God! For the testimony of Jesus is the spirit of prophecy'" (Revelation 19:10). They are servants to us, but they are not inferior. Yet they are certainly inferior to our Head and serve his mystical body, for it belongs to Christ.

Reflection 1

The height of our Saviour's glory will appear the more if we reflect on the descent from which he ascended to it. Oh, how low did he bring down so high a majesty into the pit in which we had fallen, and he did this by climbing higher than he had set us. It was high indeed, as we were fallen so low, and yet he against whom our sin was committed came down to help us up and to take hold of us (see Hebrews 2:17). He "made himself nothing" (literally, "emptied himself" of his glory) (Philippians 2:7). Furthermore, after he had descended to earth and took on our flesh, in it he "became obedient to death—even death on a cross!" (Philippians 2:8). He then descended into the grave. By these steps he was walking toward that glory in which he now is. "Therefore God exalted him to the highest place" (Philippians 2:9). So Christ says of himself, "Did not the Christ have to suffer these things and then enter his glory?" (Luke 24:26). This, indeed, is important to consider. The apostle is here writing about Christ's suffering. That is his theme, and that is why he is so particular about Christ ascending to his glory. Who of those who would go there will refuse to follow Christ in the way in which he has led? He is "the author and perfecter of our faith" (Hebrews 12:2). Who of those who would follow Christ there will not love and delight to follow him through any way, even the lowest and darkest?

Reflection 2

Do not consider it strange that the Lord's methods with his church often bring her to so low and desperate a position. Can she be in a condition more desperate than her Head was in? Not only did he suffer ignominious sufferings, but he was killed and lay dead in the grave, with the stone rolled across the tomb, sealing it. And yet Christ rose and ascended and now sits in glory until all his enemies become his footstool. Do not fear for Christ. Nobody is able to reach him, as he is exalted so high, higher than the heavens. Do not fear for his church, which is his body. If her Head is safe and alive, the church cannot but partake of safety and live with him. "But your dead will live; their bodies will rise. You who dwell in the dust, wake up and shout for joy. Your dew is like the dew of the morning; the earth will give birth to her dead" (Isaiah 26:19). The deeper the church's distress, the higher she will rise on her day of deliverance.

Thus, concerning Christ's dealing with a soul, observe the Lord's method. Do not think it strange that he brings a soul low, very low, for he intends to comfort and exalt it very high in grace and glory. "The way to heaven lies by the gates of hell" (John Bunyan, *The Pilgrim's Progress*).

Reflection 3

Turn your thoughts more frequently to this excellent subject, the glorious state of our great High Priest. The angels admire this mystery, but we slight it! They rejoice in it, and yet we, whom it certainly more closely concerns, are not moved by it. We do not draw that comfort and instruction from it that it plentifully affords if it is sought after. It would comfort us against all troubles and fears to reflect, Is Christ not on high, who has undertaken for us? Does anything happen to us unless it is allowed by heaven? And shall anything pass there to hurt us? Christ sits there and is the One who has loved us and given himself for us. Yes, he descended from there for us and in the same way ascended there again for us. He has made our inheritance that he bought certain for us, taking possession for us and in our name, since he is there not only as the Son of God but as our Surety and as our Head. And so the believer may think he has already possessed this right, inasmuch as his Christ is there. The saints are glorified already in their Head. "Where Christ reigns, there I believe myself to reign" (Augustine).

Consider further, in all your troubles, outward and inner, that you are not hidden from Christ. He knows them and feels them, your compassionate High Priest. He has a gracious sense of your frailties and griefs, your fears and temptations, and will not allow you to be overwhelmed. He is still presenting your state to the Father and is using the interest and power that he has for your good. What more could you want? Do you wish in your heart to rest on him and cling to him? You are united to him so that his resurrection and glory secure yours. His life and yours are not two lives but one, like that of the head and members of the human body. And if he could not be overcome by death, neither can you. Oh, that sweet word, "Because I live, you also will live" (John 14:19)!

Let your thoughts and life be molded by this contemplation. Always look on your exalted Head. Consider his glory. Look down on sin and the world with a holy disdain, being united to Christ who is so exalted and so glorious. "Since, then, you have been raised with Christ, set your hearts on things above, where Christ is seated at the right hand of God" (Colossians 3:1). What will you do? Will you let go of your interest in this once crucified and now glorified Jesus? If not, why do you not conform more to it? Why does it not possess your heart more? It should not be like this. Should not our hearts be where our treasure is, where our blessed Head is? Oh, how much we may be ashamed to have any room in our hearts for thoughts, desires, or delights that are about anything other than Christ.

If this was deeply buried in the hearts of those who have a right to it, would they have any attachments to things that are passing away? Would death be a terrifying word? Would it not, indeed, be one of the sweetest thoughts to make us rejoice, to bring our hearts solace and rest, as we look forward to the day of freedom? This infectious disease may stay here all winter and break out more strongly again next year. [A plague ravaged Lothian in 1645 and first appeared at Newbattle in July 1645 and did not end until the end of 1646.—Editor's note.] Do not flatter yourselves and think it has passed. But consider how Christ wishes us to contemplate our union with him. Will it not be our earnest wish, as it is his, to be with him? "Father, I want those you have given me to be with me where I am, and to see my glory" (John 17:24). Let us look forward to this with patient submission, yet strive and be on the lookout for our release from this body of sin and death.

1 Peter
Chapter 4

Verse 1

Therefore, since Christ suffered in his body, arm yourselves also with the same attitude, because he who has suffered in his body is done with sin.

The main part of a Christian's duty lies in these two things—patience in suffering and avoidance of sin. They affect each other. Affliction, when it is borne humbly, encourages the heart to become disentangled from sin and weans it away from the world. But awareness of sin and carelessness toward sin weaken the soul. Therefore the apostle has good reason to insist often on these two points in this letter and to interweave them.

As the things agree in their nature, so do they also in their great pattern and principle, Jesus Christ. The apostle still draws both lessons from there—patience (3:18) and holiness (4:1).

Therefore, since Christ suffered in his body, arm yourselves. The chief study of Christians, and the very thing that makes them Christians, is conformity to Christ. "This is the sum of religion," said the wise heathen Pythagoras, "to be like him whom you worship." This example is in itself too sublime, and so it is brought down to our view in Christ. The brightness of God is veiled, and veiled in our own flesh, that we may be able to look at it. The inaccessible light of the Deity is seen in the humanity of Christ, so that we may learn from him and direct our steps from his example. That is the only way to live. All other ways are nothing but wandering and perishing, darkness and misery. "Whoever follows me will never walk in darkness" (John 8:12). Therefore Christ is presented to us in the Gospel in clear and living colors, so that our whole lives may be like him.

Consider here:

1. The highest engagement of this conformity.
2. Its nature.
3. Living it out.

1. The engagement: **Christ suffered** for us. We have already spoken about this. Here we will just observe that had Christ come down, as some have falsely imagined, only to show a perfect way of obedience and give us an example of it in our own nature, that would have been a great deal. The Son of God indeed descended to teach wretched human beings; the great King descended into man and lived in a tabernacle of clay, to set up a school in it, for such ignorant, accursed creatures, and in his own person performed the hardest lessons, both doing and suffering. But the matter goes much further than this. Oh, how much higher has he suffered, not simply as our model, but as our Surety and in our place! **Christ suffered in his body.** We are under obligation to make his suffering our example because it was for us more than an example. It was our ransom.

This makes the conformity reasonable in a double way. First, we are bound to follow him who went ahead as the Captain of our salvation. Thus we should follow him in suffering and doing, seeing that both were for us. It is wonderful how some armies have attached themselves to their leader so as to be at his call night and day, in summer and winter, and refuse no work in order to achieve his ambition. In addition to Christ being our Lord and Leader, he also suffered for us and endured great hatred from men and wrath from God the Father. He went through death, such a vile death, to procure our life. So what can be too much to endure or forsake to follow him? If we thought aright concerning this, would we cling to our sinful desires or to our ease? Should we not be willing to go through fire and water, and even through death itself—even through many deaths, if that were possible—to follow Christ?

Second, consider that as this conformity is due, so it is made easy through Christ's suffering for us. Our burden that pressed us to hell is taken away, and everything that remains is nothing in comparison with that. Our chains that bound us over to eternal death are struck off. So will we not walk and run in his ways? Think about that burden and yoke that Christ has taken from us, how heavy and unbearable it was, and then we will see that what he says is true: "My yoke is easy and my burden is light" (Matthew 11:30). What a happy change this is, to be rescued from the vilest slavery and called to be in fellowship with the Son of God.

2. The nature of this conformity (to show the closeness of it) is expressed in the same terms as in the Pattern: it is not a remote resemblance but the same thing—suffering in the body. **Christ suffered in his body.** The suffering that is meant here is clearly connected with a ceasing from sin—**is done with sin.** So suffering in the body here is not simply the enduring of affliction, which is a part of the Christian's conformity to his

Head, Christ (see Romans 8:29), but implies an inner and spiritual suffering. It is the suffering and the dying of our corruption, the taking away of the life of sin by the death of Christ. This death of Christ's sinless body works in the believer the death of sinful flesh, that is, the corruption of his nature, which is so often called flesh in Scripture. Sin makes people base, drowns them in evil desires, makes the soul become earthly, and turns it, as it were, to flesh. So the apostle calls the unrenewed mind "the sinful mind" (Romans 8:7).

And what does the mind of unspiritual people hunt after and run after day after day and year after year? Is it not the things of this base world and preoccupation with the flesh? They are consumed by earthly things. Most of your efforts and time and strongest desires and most serious thoughts are about your worldly condition. So you must put on the Lord Jesus Christ (see Romans 13:14), and then everything else will easily come, as seen in the words that follow: "do not think about how to gratify the desires of the sinful nature." Once in Christ, your necessary general care for this natural life will be regulated and moderated by the Spirit. You will be able to stop making provision for all unlawful and wrong desires of your human nature. Instead, you will make room for the life of Christ in the sense that you now live for and serve a guest. Those who are in Christ are freed from the drudgery of sin. **He who has suffered in his body has done with sin.**

Done with sin. He is at rest from it, a good death, just as those who die in the Lord "rest from their labor" (see Revelation 14:13). He who has suffered in the body and is dead to it dies in the Lord and rests from the base turmoil of sin. It is no longer his master. As our sin was the reason for Christ's death, his death is the death of sin in us. And this is not just because he bore our moral pattern, but because his death affects the soul and kills it in regard to sin. The apostle Paul says, "I have been crucified with Christ" (Galatians 2:20). Faith looks on Christ's death in such a way that his sacrifice settles into the heart and kills its bondage to sin. Christ and the believer do not only become one in law, so that his death stands for theirs, but one in nature, so that his death for sin causes their death to sin as well. They are "baptized into his death" (see Romans 6:3).

I beseech you, seek to have your hearts set against sin, to hate it, to wound it, and to die to it daily. Do not be content unless you feel that it is leaving you and that the divine life is growing in you. This suffering in the flesh, we may safely say with the apostle, speaks of sufferings with and for Christ (see Romans 8:17). Those who share these sufferings are joint heirs of glory with Christ. "If indeed we share in his sufferings in order that we may also share in his glory" (Romans 8:17). If we die with Christ, we will live with him forever.

3. Living out this conformity: **Arm yourselves also with the same atti-**

tude to this mortification. Death, taken naturally, in its proper sense, being an entire privation of life, has no degrees attached to it. But this figurative death, this mortification of the flesh in Christians, is gradual. Insofar as we are renewed and animated through the Spirit of Christ, we are thoroughly mortified (for this death and that new life linked with it go together and grow together). But we are not totally renewed, and there is in us the remains of the corruption that is here called the **body**, and so it is our great task to be overcoming and mortifying it every day. There are frequent exhortations in Scripture to do this. "Put to death, therefore, whatever belongs to your earthly nature" (Colossians 3:5). "Count yourselves dead to sin but alive to God in Christ Jesus" (Romans 6:11). Thus here we read, **arm yourselves with the same attitude** or with this very thought. Consider and apply Christ's suffering in your **body**, so that you suffer with him in the body and so cease from sin. Accept that this is how it should be, and work to make it happen.

Arm yourselves. Although you are **done with sin**, yet there is still fighting, and sin will be molesting you. Although sin is mortally wounded, it still struggles for life and seeks to wound its enemy. It will assault the graces that are in you. Do not think, if it is hit once, it will no longer stir. So long as you live in the body, traces of your natural corruption remain. So you must be armed against it. Sin will not give you any rest as long as there is one spark of life left in it. This will continue as long as you have life here. This old man is stout and will fight to the death.

God's children often find that this is true, to their grief. The corruptions they thought had been killed and did not stir, and therefore they no longer thought about, revive so much that they attack them and possibly defeat them once again. Therefore, it is necessary to be in a constant state of alert and not to remove any armor until the day you die, until you put off the **body** and are altogether free of it. You may take the Lord's promise for victory to apply to the end, and it will not fail. But do not promise yourself an easy way, for that will not happen. If you are sometimes under great attack, do not think all is lost. Those who have been wounded in the fight have often won the day. Do not think that just because you will have the victory, there will be no fight.

The only growing and thriving life comes through a living contemplation and application of Jesus Christ. You must be constantly studying him and conversing with him and drawing grace from him (see John 1:16). Do you want great power against sin? Do you desire to increase in holiness? Let your eye be on Christ all the time. Set your heart on him. Let it dwell in him and be still with him. When any kind of sin threatens to prevail, go to Christ, and tell him about this attack and your inability to resist it. Ask him to defeat it. If your heart inclines toward sin, lay this before Christ. His beams of love will eat out the fire of those sinful desires. Do you want your pride, passions, love of the world, and self-love to be killed? Seek the virtue of Christ's death, and it will be so. Seek to imitate his spirit, the spirit of meekness and humility and divine love. Look on Christ, and he will draw your heart toward heaven and unite it to himself and make it like himself. Is this not the one thing you desire?

Verses 2-3

As a result, he does not live the rest of his earthly life for evil human desires, but rather for the will of God. For you have spent enough time in the past doing what pagans choose to do—living in debauchery, lust, drunkenness, orgies, carousing and detestable idolatry.

The chains of sin are so strong and so bind our nature that there is no power in us to break free from them until a stronger spirit than our own comes into us. The Spirit of Christ dropped into the soul enables it to leap over a wall. "With your help I can advance against a troop; with my God I can scale a wall" (Psalm 18:29). David said this about himself when he was equipped by God's strength. Human resolutions achieve nothing. If we tell people to free themselves but do not point them to Christ, we are telling them to attempt the impossible. But a look to Christ makes it possible and easy. Faith in Christ and the love for him that it brings break through and surmount all difficulties. It is the powerful love of Christ that kills the love of sin and kindles the love of holiness in the soul. It makes the soul willing to share in Christ's death and so partake of his life, for that always follows. **He who has suffered in the body is done with sin** (verse 1). He is crucified and dead to sin, but he does not lose anything. It is his great gain to lose that deadly life of the flesh for a new spiritual life, living for God.

He dies to sin, so that he may live. The person who is one with Christ, through believing in him, is one with him in every way, in death and in life. As Christ rose from the dead, so he who is dead to sin with him, through the power of his death, rises to new life with him through the power of his resurrection. And these two constitute our sanctification; whoever partakes of Christ and is found in him will certainly draw from him. They are linked in this way. "Count yourselves dead to sin but alive to God in Christ Jesus" (Romans 6:11).

All those who really come to Jesus Christ, coming to him as their Saviour to be clothed with him and made righteous by him, come to him as the Sanctifier, that they might be made new and holy. They follow the Lamb wherever he goes, through the worst sufferings and even death itself. And this spiritual suffering and dying with Christ is the universal way of all his followers. They are all martyrs in the crucifying of sinful flesh, thus dying for him and with him. It is with Christ that they go into his death, just as they go into life with Christ's life.

First the apostle sets before his Christian brothers the dignity of their new life, and then he particularly reflects on the former life and emphasizes the change. The former life he calls living for **evil human desires**, this new spiritual life living **for the will of God.**

He does not live the rest of his earthly life for evil human desires. Such **desires** are normal for corrupt human nature. Everyone has them and can see them in others. The apostle, especially in verse 3, specifies the kinds of people who were most notorious for possessing these sinful **desires.** Writing to the scattered Jews, he calls these **doing what pagans choose to do.** The apostle implies that these corrupt **desires** were not suited to their previous lives as Jews; so how less suitable are they now that they are Christians. Some of the worst corrupt **desires** he names, but he includes all others in them. These sins are not to be interpreted, as some people have done, as if they are worse than "more refined" sins. Everyone sins, though not to an equal degree; yet all sin stems from the same unholy nature of man and is ever contrary to the holy nature and will of God.

1. Those who walk in these ways of impiety but still want to be called Christians shame the Christians. They are enemies of Jesus Christ. They appear to have taken on his name for no other purpose but to shame it and disgrace it. But Christ will vindicate himself and will blot out these impudent people who dare show themselves in God's church as part of it. In reality they are nothing other than spots and blots. They dare to pretend to worship God as his people, and yet remain unclean, profane people. How can you say, "There goes the drunk Christian" or, "There goes the earthly minded Christian"? **Idolatry** is named last in the apostle's list, but not because it is the least important sin. The apostle Paul warns us against the same sin. "Put to death, therefore, whatever belongs to your earthly nature: sexual immorality, impurity, lust, evil desires and greed, which is idolatry" (Colossians 3:5).

2. People who are partly exempt from the blot of these foul impieties may still remain slaves to sin, alive to it and dead to God, alive to corrupt **human desires** and dead to the will of God. They please other people and themselves, but they displease God. The smoothest, best bred, and most moral unspiritual people are in such base thralldom. They are made even more miserable because they dream of freedom when they are in the middle of chains. They think that they are well by looking at those who wallow in greater wickedness. They measure themselves against the most crooked people imaginable. But they do not measure themselves against God's straight rule.

I advise you to see if you are not still living in your own sinful **desires** instead of in God's will. See if you are seeking your own will or God's.

You do not want to believe that you are so evil. You do not want to face up to this unpleasant truth about yourself. But this is part of your own self-pleasing. We please ourselves so much that we do not see our own evil actions and **evil . . . desires.** And even in these we seek nothing but our own pleasure. We are either after our own safety or our own peace. We are either trying to silence the cry of our consciences or we are trying to escape the divine wrath that is to come.

The unspiritual mind is in the dark and does not see its own vileness in living for itself. It never confesses that this is its miserable state. But when God comes into the soul, he lets it see itself and all its idols and forces it to abhor and loathe itself for all its abominations. Once the soul has discovered its filthiness in itself, then God purges and cleanses it for himself. "I will sprinkle clean water on you, and you will be clean; I will cleanse you from all your impurities and from all your idols" (Ezekiel 36:25). According to God's own promise, he enters and takes possession of the person for himself and enthrones himself in the heart. The person is never right or happy until this is done.

But rather for the will of God. We are too ready to take any little change for true conversion, but how mistaken we can be. This new life does not just knock off some apparent enormities but casts everything into a new mold, alters the whole frame of the heart and life, kills people, and makes them alive again. And this new life is opposed to the old life, for a complete change is made, so that they no longer live to satisfy their own corrupt desires but to do God's will. They are new creatures. They now have a new outlook on everything and so have new thoughts and new actions. "The old has gone, the new has come!" (2 Corinthians 5:17).

For this to happen, they must, first, live wholly **for the will of God.** We must know what God's will is. People who are entirely ignorant about God's will cannot live in a way that pleases him. We cannot "claim to have fellowship with him yet walk in the darkness," for "he is in the light" (1 John 1:6-7). This applies to many of us who have little idea about God's will. Knowing God's will is not gained from mere human teaching or effort. It is a beam from God himself that enlightens the whole soul. It stirs the affections into action. The more we walk according to what we know of God's will, the more we will discover about it. "Do not conform any longer to the pattern of this world, but be transformed by the renewing of your mind. Then you will be able to test and approve what God's will is— his good, pleasing and perfect will" (Romans 12:2). Christ says the same: "If anyone chooses to do God's will, he will find out whether my teaching comes from God or whether I speak on my own" (John 7:17). When we do not follow the truth we know, we reduce our knowledge of God and our fellowship with him.

The second thing about knowing God's will, when it is spiritual and from God himself, concerns the transformation of the heart by it. "They perish because they refused to love the truth and so be saved" (2 Thessalonians 2:10). The heart does not now follow God's will out of obedience, but because it is moved by the love in its heart. It is governed by God's love and so is governed by his will.

Third, as divine knowledge brings this affection, so this affection will bring action in the form of real obedience. These three are linked to each other, and each is dependent on the others. The affection is not blind but flows from knowledge. Obedience flows from affection, and affection is not idle, for it brings obedience. Nor is knowledge dead, for it produces affection.

Thus the renewed, living Christian is all for God, a sacrifice entirely offered up to him, a living sacrifice who lives for God. He takes no more notice of his own unspiritual will. He has renounced that in order to embrace God's holy will. Therefore, though there is an opposing law and will in him, he does not generally acknowledge it but only the law of Christ that is established in him. This is the law of love through which he is willingly led. In everything he gives real obedience. He no longer consults flesh and blood and what will please them, but only asks what will please his God. Knowing God's mind, he will do God's will, without needing to know anything more than this. "My Lord wills it; therefore in his strength I will do it. For now I live to do his will, since my life is given over to him."

We know what the true character of the redeemed in Christ is. They are free from serving themselves and the world. They are dead to themselves and the world and have no life except for God's.

Let it, then, be our ambition to receive this and to grow in it. Each day we must be further freed from all other ways and desires and more completely given over to the will of our God. We should be displeased when we find anything else stirring in us.

1. Because we know that God's sovereign will brings glory to his name (and most justly so), therefore we are not to rest until this is our entire view, our end in all things. We are to account all our plausible actions as hateful (as indeed they are) if they are not aimed at this end.

2. As living for God's will is in all things to be our goal, so every step we take along this path ought to be governed by this rule, for we cannot attain this goal unless we do so in God's way. I daily aspire and aim at having no will of my own but God's will in me. This is a pledge of the whole of heaven. This is indeed the life of Christ—not only like his but one with his. It is the work of his Spirit, his life in the soul. In this is the perseverance of the saints. Because they have one life with Christ, they are alive to God once and for all, forever.

It is true that the previous habit of sin fights against grace to keep its old possession. The apostle implies this here when he says, **For you have spent enough time in the past doing what pagans choose to do.** But he now urges us to turn away from all this and to reason like this: "True, you did have us for a long time, to our sorrow and shame, but this is no longer the case."

The rest of his earthly life is not to be spent in the same way as his previous way of living, **for evil human desires,** like the rest of the world. But as the Christian looks back on that, he finds that it spurs him to be more earnest and wholly given over in living for God, having lived so against God for much of his life.

"Now," says the Christian, "corrupt lusts and deluding world, I have served you for too long. The rest of my life must be given over to the Lord, to live for him through whom I live. What strength I have, and what time I have, through his grace will be wholly his." When any Christian is resolved to live this way, he will live for his God and in him without any defect, forever.

Spiritual things, once they are discerned by the spiritually alive, bring the whole soul along with them. The ways of holiness are never truly sweet until they are thoroughly embraced and until all the things that are contrary to them are completely renounced. All his previous ways of wandering from God are hated by a Christian who has genuinely returned to God and been brought home. A sight of Christ overwhelms the heart and makes it break free from all the entanglements both of its own lusts and of the surrounding profane world. These are the two things the apostle aims at here. He exhorts Christians to concentrate on the newness of life and shows how necessary this is. He points out that they cannot be Christians without this. He refers to their previous habits in these verses and to the opinion of the world in the following verses. Both of these will attack a man, especially while he is still weak and has recently entered into this new position.

As far as the first is concerned, his old habits, his previous sinful **desires,** will still be active and will attack him. They will remind him of their long-standing friendship. But the Christian, following the principles of his new being, will not entertain any long discussion with them but will cut them short and tell them of the change he has made. He tells them that he is happy now that his previous delights do not have any possibility of recapturing him. If they dress up in their best possible light and put on all their ornaments and say, "I am the same as I was," the Christian will answer, "I am not as I was."

This is the only way he will resist the pleas of his previous acquaintance with sin. He will say, "The longer I was so deluded, the greater reason I now have to be wiser. The time I have misspent is all the more reason for me to redeem it now. I have lived for too long in that vile slavery.

Everything I fed on was but husks. 'Why spend money on what is not bread, and your labor on what does not satisfy?' (Isaiah 55:2). Now I am following what I am sure will satisfy, and will satisfy the deepest longings of my soul. I will now live more for my new Lord, the living God, and sacrifice my time and strength and my whole self for him."

If we were more used to entertaining holy thoughts in our ordinary ways, it would keep our hearts in a sweet temper all day long and have an excellent influence on all our actions. Our hearts would be near those holy thoughts, not far off because we neglect to keep close to God. If you really want to live for God, look to him all the time. This is what David did. "I have set the LORD always before me. Because he is at my right hand, I will not be shaken" (Psalm 16:8).

You who have not started to do this, think how patient God is. Though you have slighted so many calls, you can still at last begin to seek him and live for him. All the time you lived without God, how wretched life was, if it can be called life at all when God is excluded. To live to sin is to live in a dungeon, but to live for the will of God is to walk in freedom. It is to walk in the light of God's presence.

Verses 4-5

They think it strange that you do not plunge with them into the same flood of dissipation, and they heap abuse on you. But they will have to give account to him who is ready to judge the living and the dead.

Grace, until it reaches its home and goal in glory, is still in conflict. There is a restless party within and without; indeed, the whole world is against grace. Grace is a stranger here and is accounted as such.

They think it strange that you do not plunge with them into the same flood of dissipation. These wondering thoughts they vent in reproaching words. In these two verses we have these three things:

1. The Christian's opposite course to that of the world.
2. The world's opposing thoughts and words.
3. The supreme and final judgment of both.

1. The Christian's opposite course. We see in the world their running to excess in luxury and unrestrained revelry, in which we cannot go along with them. Though all unspiritual people are not equally guilty of this, they all in some way or other waste their days by indulging in the delights of sin. Our Lord warned about this when he said, "Be careful, or your hearts will be weighed down with dissipation, drunkenness and the anxieties of life" (Luke 21:34). Whatever draws our hearts away from God, for whatever plausible reason, destroys us. We are ruined, as the word *asotias*, **dissipation**, indicates. The other word, *anachusis*, **flood of**, signifies pro-

186

fusion and dissolute lavishing, a pouring out of the affections on vanity. Those affections are scattered and defiled like water that is spilled on the ground, which cannot be cleaned or collected again. Indeed, it passes our skill and strength to recover and recollect our hearts for God. Only he can do it. He who made the heart can cleanse it, make it new again, and unite it to himself. Oh, what a scattered, broken, unstable thing is the unspiritual heart, until it is changed. It falls in love with every folly it meets. It can dream and muse on these long enough, upon anything that feeds the earthliness of its pride. It can waste hours and let out floods of thoughts where even a little is too much. It does not give one thought in the whole day to God.

Truly, the overflow of the heart is constant drunkenness and madness. It is not capable of reason and will not be stopped. "It is a land of idols" (Jeremiah 50:38). You may as well ask a river to stop flowing as to speak to an impenitent sinner who is engrossed in his sin. But there is a Hand that can stop both and turn the most impetuous torrent of the heart.

Because the ungodly world naturally moves so quickly in this direction, it is said to **plunge** into a **flood of dissipation.** Everybody is naturally carried away by the stream of sin that is in the world. This is their course, but **you do not plunge with them.** The godly are a small and weak group of people, and yet they run counter to the torrent of the world opposing them. There is a Spirit within them through whom they receive the strength to swim against the tide of ungodly opinions, a Spirit strong enough to make them resist all the combined weight of the ungodly. "The one who is in you is greater than the one who is in the world" (1 John 4:4). When Lot was in Sodom, his righteous soul was not carried along with the rest of them.

The believer has the example of Christ, who opposed the world, and is also indwelt by the Spirit of Christ, who resisted the world. Believers are far stronger than any power in the world. Faith looks to Christ and draws strength from him, enabling the soul to overcome all discouragements and oppositions. "Let us fix our eyes on Jesus, the author and perfecter of our faith, who for the joy set before him endured the cross, scorning its shame, and sat down at the right hand of the throne of God. Consider him who endured such opposition from sinful men, so that you will not grow weary and lose heart" (Hebrews 12:2-3). Christ is not only our Example—he is our Head, from whom we derive our strength; so we follow him, the author and perfecter of our faith. We read in 1 John 5:4, "This is the victory that has overcome the world, even our faith."

The Spirit of God clearly shows men both the baseness of the ways of sin and the wretched measure of their end. Divine light reveals the false blush of the pleasures of sin, that there is nothing beneath them except deformity and rottenness, which the deluded world does not see but takes the outward appearance as being true beauty, and so is enamored with a false picture. As the unredeemed see the vileness of their love of sin, they see the final unhappiness of it, that its ways lead to the chambers of death. I think of the believer as a person who stands on a high tower, who sees the way the world runs in a valley toward an unavoidable precipice, with a steep edge hanging over the bottomless pit, where all who are not reclaimed fall over before they are aware. People, in their low position, do not see what is happening and therefore walk and run on in the smooth pleasures of it toward their perdition. But the person who sees the end will not run with them.

Since believers have the light of the Spirit, they have good reason for taking another route. By that same Spirit they have a bias toward going a different direction, so that they cannot be one with the ungodly. Although they are weighed down by the flesh that clings to them, yet in the strength of their new nature they overcome this and go on until they attain the end. All the difficulties they encounter along the way are forgotten. This makes amends for every weary step, so that all those who walk in that way will appear "before God in Zion" (Psalm 84:6).

2. The world's opposing thoughts and words. **They think it strange that you do not plunge with them into the same flood of dissipation, and they heap abuse on you.** Their thoughts, **they think it strange,** and their words, **they heap abuse on you,** are both mentioned in this verse. Christians and unspiritual people are amazed at each other. Unspiritual people wonder when they see Christians walk so strictly and deny themselves those sinful desires that most people consider so necessary that they think they could not live without them. And the Christian thinks it strange that people should be so bewitched and still remain children in the vanity of their turmoil, wearying and distracting themselves from morning to night, running after stories and fancies, always busy doing nothing. They are absorbed in entertaining themselves and pleasing people and constantly refuse to listen to Jesus Christ. They will not turn from their life, and thus they choose to be miserable; indeed they take much trouble to make themselves miserable.

Christians know how blind and depraved man's nature is. They know because they were once like it. But now they see in a strong light the unreasonableness and frenzy of that way of living, so that they cannot but wonder at those woeful mistakes. But ungodly people wonder far more at Christians, not knowing the inner reason for their different choice and way. Believers are on the top of the hill. They are going up and are looking back on those in the valley; they see that their way is going toward and will end in death. They call them as loudly as they can to change paths.

> I beheld then, that they all went on till they came to the foot of the Hill Difficulty; at the bottom of which was a spring. There were also

in the same place two other ways besides that which came straight from the gate; one turned to the left hand and the other to the right, at the bottom of the hill. Now the name of one of those ways was Danger, and the name of the other was Destruction. But the narrow way lay right up the hill. Christian now went to the spring, and drank from it to refresh himself, and then began to go up the Hill. (*Pilgrim's Progress*)

The believer tells them about the danger, but they either do not hear or they do not understand his language or they refuse to believe him. They are content with the ease and delight of their way, and they are not at all suspicious about its end. They think the believer is the fool, for he will not share with them and take the way the multitudes go. These unredeemed prefer their own way, with its horses, coaches, and all their pomp, to the craggy steep hill that a few poor creatures like Pilgrim take. They do not believe that at the top of the hill is that glorious city, the new Jerusalem, of which he is a citizen. They do not realize that the believer knows the end of both routes. The world thinks it strange that a Christian can spend so much time in secret prayer, not knowing, nor being able to conceive, the sweetness of the communion with God that he attains in that way. Even now he feels how sweet it is, beyond the world's enjoyments, simply to be seeking after it and waiting for it. Oh, the delight that there is in the bitterest exercise of repentance, in the very tears, and much more in the succeeding harvest of joy. As Aristotle said, "The intemperate are strangers to true pleasure." It is strange to an unspiritual man to see the child of God disdain the pleasures of sin. He does not know the higher and purer delights and pleasures that Christians are called to—part of which believers have now, but that they have completely in certain hope.

The strangeness of the world's way to Christians, and of their way to the world, though it is somewhat unnatural, affects both groups differently. The Christian looks on deluded sinners with pity, while they look on him with hatred. Their part, expressed here as wondering, overflows into reviling: **they heap abuse on you.** But this does not trouble composed Christian minds at all. Though wild dogs snarl and bark around them, the sober travelers go on their way and pay no attention. Those who are acquainted with the way of holiness not only endure these revilings but think of them as their glory and their riches. Thus Moses "regarded disgrace for the sake of Christ as of greater value than the treasures of Egypt, because he was looking ahead to his reward" (Hebrews 11:26).

3. The supreme and final judgment: **But they will have to give account to him who is ready to judge the living and the dead.** The day has been set—**who is ready to judge.** It will definitely come, though you may think it is far away.

Though the wicked forget their scoffing against the godly, and though the Christian slights them and lets them pass, they do not just pass by. They are all registered, and in the great court God will call the wicked to account for all these excesses and for all their reproaching of the godly, who would not run with them in these ways. Tremble, then, you despisers and mockers of holiness. What will you do when those you reviled appear glorious in your sight, and their King's glory is their joy but is all terror to you? Oh, at that time all faces that looked disdainfully on true religion will turn dark and be covered with shame, and the despised saints of God will shout for joy.

You who would rejoice, then, at the appearing of that holy Lord and Judge of the world, let your way now be the way of holiness. Avoid and hate the common ways of the wicked world. The ungodly live according to their own foolish opinion but will quickly end, and the sentence of that day will stand forever.

Verse 6

For this is the reason the gospel was preached even to those who are now dead, so that they might be judged according to men in regard to the body, but live according to God in regard to the spirit.

It is a primary concern for Christ's followers to be rightly informed of and often to remember the true state and nature of being a Christian. This is something that most of those who call themselves by the name Christian either do not know or often forget. They are carried away with the vain fancies and mistakes of the world. The apostle has characterized Christianity very clearly for us in this passage by that which is its very nature—conformity with Christ. The necessary consequence of this is lack of conformity with the world. As the nature and natural properties of things hold universally, those who in all ages are effectually called by the Gospel are thus molded and framed by it. Thus it was, says the apostle, with your brothers who are now at rest, all those who earlier received the Gospel. The reason it was preached to them was that **they might be judged according to men in regard to the body, but live according to God in regard to the spirit.**

We have here, first, the preaching of the Gospel as the suitable means to a certain end and, second, the express nature of that end.

1. The preaching of the Gospel as a suitable means to a certain end: **For this reason the gospel was preached.** There is a particular end, and a very important one, for which the preaching of the Gospel is intended. So do not listen to the Gospel as if it had no purpose, and do not preach the Gospel as if it had no purpose. This should be carefully considered by those who preach this Gospel, that they may aim correctly at the right goal and at no other—no selfish end. The priests under the law were not allowed to

have "any eye defect" (Leviticus 21:20). In the same way evangelical ministers must not have any defect with their sight, looking for gain or applause. They should also work hard to discover this living God in themselves. Otherwise, they cannot faithfully apply their gifts to work this effect on their hearers. Therefore, acquaintance with God is most necessary.

It appears to many of us that some people use the preaching of the Gospel as if it were a beautifully written story, and they entertain us with it. Their purpose is to delight us. But this is not the purpose of the most serious and glorious of all messages. It must not be turned into an empty sound. If we wake up and give it a hearing, that is good. If I have a dead heart, I will go to the Word of Life, that it may come alive in me. My heart is frozen; I will lay it before the warm beams of that Sun who shines in the Gospel. My corruptions are mighty and strong, and grace, if there is any in my heart, is exceedingly weak. But there is in the Gospel a power to weaken and kill sin, and to strengthen grace. In this way my heart is refined and spiritualized, and my affections for divine things are enlarged. I will then have a greater hatred of sin and a greater love for God and communion with him.

Ask yourselves about previous times, "How did I come to be where I am [at church]? What did I have in my eye and desire this morning or on my way? What was my goal?" Just mentioning this in prayer is not enough, for much prayer, like other things that we do from habit, has no spiritual power, none of David's panting after God. Such desires will not be satisfied without a measure of attainment, like the child's desire for the breast, as our apostle says: "Like newborn babies, crave pure spiritual milk" (1 Peter 2:2). Further, now that you have returned home, reflect on your hearts. Much has been heard, but has anything been done? Ask yourself, "Have I succeeded in my aims? It was not just to while away a few hours that I went to church, or to spend some time listening with delight. It was not to have my ear pleased, but to have my heart changed. It was not to learn some new ideas and to carry them cold in my head, but to be brought to life and purified and to have my spirit renewed. Did this occur? Do I now think with greater esteem of Christ and the life of faith and the happiness of a Christian? And are such thoughts firm and abiding with me? What sin have I left behind? What grace of the Spirit have I brought home?"

It is a strange folly in many of us to set ourselves no goals and to listen to the Gospel with no end in mind. The trader does not just sail for the enjoyment of sailing, but in order to trade and become rich. The farmer plows, not just to keep himself busy, but in order to sow and then reap the harvest. Will we do the most excellent and fruitful work fruitlessly, listening just in order to hear, but looking no further? It is indeed a great vanity and a great misery to gain nothing from it.

Now, when you go to church, it is not simply to listen to a sermon and enjoy or dislike what you hear. It is a matter of life and death—eternal life and eternal death. Spiritual life is born and nourished by the Word, and this is the beginning of eternal life.

To those who are now dead. I believe the apostle means by this people who have heard and believed the Gospel, when it came to them, but are now dead. And this, I think, he does in order to strengthen those brothers to whom he writes. He commends the Gospel so that they might not think that its goal is too hard. Our Saviour softens the matter of outward sufferings in this way: "Rejoice and be glad, because great is your reward in heaven, for in the same way they persecuted the prophets who were before you" (Matthew 5:12). The apostle uses the same reasoning later on in this chapter (see verses 12-19). So here, in order that they might not think his point of mortification to be so grievous, as people naturally do, he tells them it is the goal of the Gospel. He says that those who have been saved by it went the same way as this. "Those who went before you and are now dead died in this same way that I now emphasize. The Gospel was preached to them for this very end."

People pass away, and others follow them, but the Gospel is still the same; it has the same tenor and substance, the same ends. Similarly, Solomon says of the heavens and earth that they remain the same: "generations come and generations go, but the earth remains forever" (Ecclesiastes 1:4). The Gospel surpasses both heavens and earth in its stability, as our Saviour testifies: "I tell you the truth, until heaven and earth disappear, not the smallest letter, not the least stroke of a pen, will by any means disappear from the Law until everything is accomplished" (Matthew 5:18). People age, but the Gospel remains, from one age to another, unaltered, with the same vigor and power that it had at the beginning.

Those who previously received the Gospel received it on these terms. So do not think this is a hard way. And they **are now dead.** All the difficulty of that work of dying to sin is now over for them. If they had not died to their sins by the Gospel, they would have died in them later, and so would have died eternally. It is therefore a wise, preventative measure to have sin judged and put to death in us before we die. If we do not part with sin, if we die in it and with it, we and our sin perish together. But if it dies first, before us, then we live forever.

What do you think of your unspiritual will and all the delights of sin? What is the longest term of its life? It is uncertain, but most certainly it is very short. You and these pleasures will be severed and parted within a little time. However, you must die, and then they die, and you will never meet again. Now, is it not the wisest course of action to part with them a little sooner and let them die before you, so that you may inherit eternal life and eternal delights, pleasures forevermore? This is the only wise bargain. Therefore delay in this no longer.

This is our season for enjoying the sweetness of the Gospel. Others heard it before us in the places where we now stand. And now they are taken away, and we will also soon be removed and leave our places for others to speak and listen. It is high time we were considering what we do here, to what end we speak and listen. It is high time to lay hold of that salvation that is offered to us. We must cling to it and let go of our hold on sin and of those who are perishing. Do those who are dead, who heard and obeyed the Gospel, now repent of their repentance and the mortifying of the flesh? Or rather do they not think 10,000 more pains, were it for many ages, all too little for a moment of that which they now enjoy and will enjoy for eternity? And those who are dead, who heard the Gospel and slighted it, what would they give for one of those opportunities that we now have daily, and daily lose?

You have recently seen, at least many of you have, many people dying in a short space of time, and whole families swept away by the stroke of God's hand. [The plague of 1645-1646 is being referred to here.—Editor's note.] And yet who has taken this to heart? Therefore, today, as long as it is called Today, do not harden your hearts. Though the pestilence does not frighten you so much now, you remain mortal, and the decay of these earthly days tells us that shortly we will cease to preach and hear the Gospel. If we only thought about this, it would excite us to be more earnest in our search after eternal life, which is set before us in the Gospel. We would seek that spiritual life that is the beginning of eternal life within us and is brought by the Gospel to all the heirs of salvation.

Think wisely, therefore, about these two things—the real goal of the Gospel and the approaching end of your days. And let your certainty about this latter point drive you to seek the former more certainly, that you may partake of it. And this will make the thoughts of the other sweet to you. That visage of death that is so terrible to unchanged sinners will be amiable to your eye. Having found a life in the Gospel as happy and lasting as this is miserable and vanishing, and seeing the perfection of that life on the other side of death, you will long for the passage.

Be more serious in this matter of listening to the Gospel every day. Consider why it is sent to you and what it brings, and think, "For too long I have slighted its message. Many who have done so are now dead and will hear it no more. Once more it is inviting me, and this may be the last invitation I receive." And with these thoughts, bow your knee to the Father of spirits, that this one thing may be granted you, that your souls may find at last the living and mighty power of God's Spirit upon you as you listen to the Gospel. Then you will **be judged according to men in regard to the body, but live according to God in regard to the spirit.**

2. The particular nature of the goal that is expressed. I believe the apostle's meaning is none other than dying to the world and sin and living to

God. This is his main subject and scope in the previous passage. That death was previously called suffering in the body (see verse 1), which is in effect the same, and therefore though the words may be seen in another way, it is still strange that commentators have been so wide of the mark in interpretations.

To be judged according to men in regard to the body, in the present sense, is to die to sin, or that sin dies in us. First, this is expressed according to its nature. To the flesh this is a violent death and occurs according to a sentence judicially pronounced upon it. The Gospel sentences that guilty and miserable life of sin to death. The arrest and sentence is clear and full. "For we know that our old self was crucified with him so that the body of sin might be rendered powerless, that we should no longer be slaves to sin" (Romans 6:6). "For if you live according to the sinful nature, you will die; but if by the Spirit you put to death the misdeeds of the body, you will live, because those who are led by the Spirit of God are sons of God" (Romans 8:13-14). Sin must die in order that the soul may live. It must be crucified in us, and we to it, that we may share the life of Christ and happiness in him. The execution of this sentence is called being **judged according to men in regard to the spirit.**

Second, the thing spoken about here as being **judged** stands in contrast to the judgment mentioned immediately before (verse 5), the last judgment of the living and the dead. To **be judged according to men** is added, I think, to signify how fitting man's life of sin is to his present corrupt nature. People do indeed judge it a death, and a cruel death, to be severed and pulled from their sins. And the sentence of it in the Gospel is a heavy sentence, a hard saying to an unspiritual heart. The ungodly man must give up all his sinful delights. He must indeed die in self-denial and must be separated from himself. He has to die if he wants to be united with Christ and live in him. Thus people think they are sentenced to a painful death by the sentence of the Gospel. Although they will truly and happily live, they do not appreciate this. They see only the death, the parting with sin and all its pleasures. They do not see the life, nor can they know about this until they share in it. It is known only to those in whom it exists. "Your life is now hidden with Christ in God" (Colossians 3:3). Therefore, the contrast here is very apt. Death is **according to men** in the flesh, but life is **according to God** in the **spirit.**

As Christians are sentenced to this death in the flesh by the Gospel, so they are viewed by unspiritual people as dead. For believers do not enjoy with the ungodly what those ungodly value in life and what they think they could not exist without. A person who cannot carouse and swear with profane men is a silly dead creature, good for nothing. He who can bear wrongs and love the person who injured him is a poor spiritless fool and has no mettle or life in him in the eyes of the world. Thus is he **judged**

according to men. He is a dead man. But he lives **according to God in regard to the spirit.** He is dead to men but alive to God. **He does not live the rest of his earthly life for evil human desires, but rather for the will of God** (verse 2).

Now, if this life is in you, it will act. All life is in motion, but most active of all is this most excellent and, as I call it, most living life. It will be moving toward God, often seeking him, and exerting itself in holy, affectionate thoughts about him. Sometimes he will dwell on one of his sweet attributes, sometimes on another, like the bee among the flowers. And as this life will thus act within, it will look for opportunities to be of service to the Lord. In a word, the constant thought of the believing soul is: "It is good for me to draw near to God, the only Good."

The purpose of those who have this life is to strengthen it and care for it.

1. Beware of omitting and interrupting those spiritual means that nourish it. Little neglects of that kind will become bigger neglects. Take care not to use holy things coldly, without affection. This makes them fruitless, and your life will not benefit from them unless they are used in a living way. Be active in all good that is within your reach. This is a sign of spiritual life, and it helps your spiritual life become stronger. A slothful life will become an unhealthy life. Movement toward and for God purifies and sharpens the spirit and makes people robust and vigorous.

2. Beware of having anything to do with any sin. Do not even look in its direction. It will certainly diminish grace within you and obstruct your communion with God. You know, if you have any knowledge at all of this life, that you cannot go to God with the freedom you used to have after you have been tampering with your old loves. Do not make foolish bargains with sin, to the detriment of your spiritual life. The greatest and longest enjoyments of sin only last for a season.

3. Do you want to grow in your spiritual life? Have much recourse to Jesus Christ your Head, the Spring who brings life to your soul. Do you want to know more about God? Christ reveals the Father as his Father and your Father. Do you want more victory over your corrupt desires? Our victory comes from Christ. Apply his conquest: "in all these things we are more than conquerors through him who loved us" (Romans 8:37). Do you want to be more replenished with grace and spiritual affections? Christ's fullness is for that purpose, and it is open to us. There is life in him and for us. He came "that they may have life, and have it to the full" (John 10:10).

Verse 7

The end of all things is near. Therefore be clear minded and self-controlled so that you can pray.

The heart of a true Christian is truly separate from the world and set toward heaven. Yet, while the believer is still in the body, there is so much to drag him down unless he is constantly elevated to spiritual activity. Thus the apostle in this letter, and particularly in this verse, concentrates on three things: a threefold duty recommended; the mutual relationship that binds these duties to one another; the reason to find them in a Christian.

1. A threefold duty recommended—sobriety, watchfulness, and prayer. Out of these three the last mentioned is evidently the most important, as the first two are subservient to prayer. So I start with prayer.

To speak and hear about this duty often brings new sweetness and usefulness to us, provided our hearts are given over to it. A living experience of prayer is superior to skill in being able to define it exactly.

Prayer is not just smooth expression or a well-contrived form of words. Prayer is not the product of a ready memory. The movement of the heart toward God makes prayer real, living, and acceptable to the living God, to whom it is presented. Pouring out your heart to him who made it and therefore hears it and understands what it says and how it is moved and affected—that is real prayer. It is not the gilded paper and clever writing of a petition that prevails with a king but the moving sense of it. And to that King who discerns the heart, heart sense is the sense of everything, and the only thing he takes notice of. All other excellence in prayer is useless if it does not contain this life. Prayer eases the soul in times of distress, when it is oppressed with griefs and fears; but more, it gives those fears and griefs vent, emptying them into the heart of God.

God cannot be compared with any of our friends, as he is more affectionate and more powerful. Isaiah speaks about his compassion and salvation: "In all their distress he too was distressed, and the angel of his presence saved them. In his love and mercy he redeemed them; he lifted them up and carried them all the days of old" (Isaiah 63:9). And so, resting on his love, power, and gracious promises, the soul quiets itself in God. It is assured that it is not in vain to seek God, for he does not despise "the oppression of the weak and the groaning of the needy" (Psalm 12:5).

The soul is more spiritually affected with its own condition by laying it open before the Lord. It becomes more deeply aware of sin and ashamed in God's sight in confessing it before him. The soul is also more disposed to observe the Lord in answered prayer and to bless him and trust him for taking note of its distresses and desires.

All the graces of the Spirit are stirred and exercised through prayer, and through exercise strengthened and increased. Faith applies the divine promises, which are the ground on which the soul goes to God. Hope looks to their fulfillment. Love especially expresses itself in sweet converse and finds that all the hours spent in prayer are too short. Oh, how the soul is thus refreshed with freedom of speech with its beloved Lord. And as it delights in that, it continually grows at each meeting. It beholds the excellency of God, delighting in the pure and sublime pleasures that are to be found in close communion with him. Looking on the Father in the face of Christ and using the Saviour as a mediator in prayer, the soul is drawn to greater admiration of that endless Love. David expresses his love for God in the Psalms, and doubtless his love for God grew as he did this.

Through prayer supplies of grace are received, as well as all other necessary mercies. "And I will do whatever you ask in my name, so that the Son may bring glory to the Father" (John 14:13). God, having established this fellowship, has engaged his truth and goodness in it, so that if his people call on him, they will be heard and answered. If they prepare their heart to call, he will incline his ear to hear. Our Saviour has assured us that we may build on his goodness, upon the affection of a father in him. "If you, then, though you are evil, know how to give good gifts to your children, how much more will your Father in heaven give good gifts to those who ask him!" (Matthew 7:11). And Luke adds, "and give the Holy Spirit to those who ask him" (Luke 11:13). Prayer for grace sets the mouth of the soul to the spring, draws from Jesus Christ, and is replenished out of his fullness, thirsting after it and drawing from it in that way.

For this reason our Saviour and, following his example, the apostles, highly recommend prayer. "Watch and pray," says our Saviour (Matthew 26:41). "Pray continually," says the apostle Paul (1 Thessalonians 5:17). Here Peter particularly specifies this as the great means of attaining that likeness with Christ that he exhorts. This is the road to it: **be clear minded and self-controlled so that you can pray.** Those who pray much will grow rich in grace. The people who thrive and increase most are those who are busiest in this.

2. The reason that binds on us these duties: **The end of all things is near.** We need to be reminded about this often, for even believers are all too ready to forget it. The general goal of everything **is near,** even though many generations have passed since the apostle wrote this. We must note, first, that the apostles usually speak about the whole time after the coming of Jesus Christ in the flesh as the last time. Among the Jews there is an ancient tradition that the duration of the world would correspond with the six days of creation, a day being with the Lord as a thousand years, and a thousand years as one day. They divided the whole into three periods— 2,000 years before the Law, 2,000 years under the Law, and 2,000 years under the Gospel. The seventh period was to be the sabbath of sabbaths, the blessed rest of eternity. It seems from various expressions that the apostles thought **the end** was not far off. Thus St. Paul says, "After that, we who are still alive and are left will be caught up together with them in the clouds to meet the Lord in the air" (1 Thessalonians 4:17). He speaks as if it was not impossible that might come about in their time.

Second, we note that this might always have been said. In comparison with eternity, the whole duration of the world is not considerable. And to the eternal Lord who made it and has appointed its period, a thousand years are but as a day. We think 1,000 years a great matter when compared with our short life. But what is the greatest length of time when compared with eternity?

Third, we see that for each person **the end of all things is near.** When we die, the world ends for us. This consideration fits the subject and helps the argument. Seeing all things will quickly come to an end, even the frame of heaven and earth, why should we, knowing this and having higher hopes, spend so much of our energies on those things that are passing away? It is not difficult to understand that we should be sober and watchful and prayerful, since we exist for such a short time. Why should our hearts cling to those things from which we will soon be separated? **The end of all things is near.** An end of a few poor delights and the many vexations of this wretched life will soon come. Then temptations and sins and the worst of all evils will be at an end as well. Even prayer petitions themselves will end and will be replaced with a new song of endless praises.

Verse 8

Above all, love each other deeply, because love covers over a multitude of sins.

The graces of the Spirit are an entire frame making up the new creature, and none of them can be lacking. Therefore, the teaching and exhortation of the apostles speak of them usually not only as inseparable but as one. But there is among them none so comprehensive as this one—**love.** St. Paul calls it "the fulfillment of the law" (Romans 13:10). Love toward God is the sum of all requirements relative to him, and so likewise is it toward our brothers. Love toward God is what makes us live for him and be wholly his. What most powerfully weans us from this world and causes us delight in communion with him in holy mediation and prayer is our love for God. The apostle, adding here the duty of Christians to one another, gives this as the primary duty, the sum of all: **Above all, love each other deeply.**

Consider first its nature, then its eminent degree, and finally its excellent fruit.

The Nature of This Love

1. It is a union, and therefore it is called a bond or a chain that links things together.

2. It is not a mere external union that holds in customs or words, but a union of hearts.

3. It is here not a natural but a spiritual, supernatural union; it is the mutual love of Christians as brothers. There is a common benevolence and goodwill due to all. But there is a more particular uniting affection among Christians that makes them one. The devil, an apostate spirit who revolted and became separated from God, naturally causes division. This was his first exploit, and it is still his great plan and business in the world. He first divided us from God. He put us at enmity with each other through the first sin of our first parents. Then we read that their first child was at war with his brother. So Satan is called by our Saviour, justly, "a liar" and "a murderer" (see John 8:44). He murdered by lying. The devil's work is division, but Christ's work is union. He came "to destroy the devil's work" (1 John 3:8) through an opposing work. Christ came to make everyone friends. He came to re-collect and reunite man to God, and man to man. Both those hold in Christ by virtue of the marvelous union of natures in his person and the mysterious union of believers with him as their Head. The apostle Paul says, "And he made known to us the mystery of his will according to his good pleasure, which he purposed in Christ, to be put into effect when the times will have reached their fulfillment—to bring all things in heaven and on earth together under one head, even Christ" (Ephesians 1:9-10).

This was Christ's great project in all. This he died and suffered for, and this he prayed for (see John 17). And this union with Christ is stronger and above all other ties, natural or civil. If natural friendship can be called "one spirit in two bodies," how much more can Christian union, for there is indeed one Spirit that makes them one body. They are only different members of that one body.

Now, this love of our brothers is not separate from the love of God. It is the reflection of God's love, streaming from God himself. Jesus Christ sent his Spirit into our hearts to unite us to God in himself by love. This is loving God with all our heart, mind, soul, and strength. And that same love, first wholly carried to God, is not diverted by the love of our brothers, as this is only derived from our love of God. God allows, in fact commands, in fact causes, this love to stream out from him. It is directed at Christians, who remain in his love, just as he is its source and center. It begins with God and returns to God. We are to love our brothers in God and for him, not only because he commands us to love them, but because that love of God naturally extends itself in this way. In loving our brothers in a spiritual, Christian way, we love God.

Loving God makes us one with God and so gives us an impression of his divine bounty in his Spirit. And his love, the work of his Spirit, dwelling in the heart, enlarges and dilates it, just as self-love contracts and narrows it. So as self-love is completely opposite to the love of God, it is likewise so to brotherly love. It shuts out and undoes both. And where the love of God is rekindled and enters the heart, it destroys and burns up self-love, and so carries the affection up to God himself, and in him carries it out to our brothers.

The bitter root of all human enmity against God and against one another is self—our heart turned from God toward ourselves. The work of renewing grace is to annul and destroy self and to replace God in his right position, so that the heart and all its affections may be at God's disposal. Instead of self-will and self-love, which ruled before, now the will of God and the love of God command all.

And where this occurs, there this *philadelphia*, this love of our brothers, will be sincere. Why are there so many wars and conflicts? It is because people love themselves, and nothing but themselves. That is the standard and the rule. Self-interest rules everything, and so there is strife and bitterness against one another. But the Spirit of Christ comes in and undoes all selfishness. And what is according to God, what he wills and loves, that is law, and a powerful law, written on the heart, the law of love. We obey this law not because we are forced to, but with delight. To forgive a wrong, to love even your enemy for Christ's sake, is now not only feasible but delectable, although a little while ago you thought it would be totally impossible.

The Spirit of Christ, which is all sweetness and love, so calms and composes the heart that peace with God and that inexpressible blessed love of Christ so fills the soul with loving-kindness and sweetness that it can breathe nothing else. It hates nothing but sin. It pities the sinner and bears towards the worst a love of goodwill, desiring their return and salvation. And as for those in whom the image of their Father appears, their heart clings to them as brothers indeed. No natural advantages of birth, beauty, or wit draw a Christian's love so much as the likeness of Christ. Wherever that is found, it is lovely to the soul that loves Christ. Much communion with God sweetens and calms the mind and cures passion and pride, which are the avowed enemies of love.

Prayer disposes people toward this love. "Whoever does not love does not know God," says the apostle John, "because God is love" (1 John 4:8). The person who is the most conversant with love cannot but have the fullest measure of it. It flows from God into the hearts of Christians, and from there to their brothers. It transforms the soul into Christ's likeness, making it merciful and loving and ready to forgive, as Christ is.

Love each other deeply. That is the point here—the special love that saints have for each other, as they rejoice and glory in the same Father. These people love each other as brothers. You who are brothers and united by that pure and strong tie, being one in your Head, in your life derived from him, in your hopes of glory with him, seek to be more united in heart. Have fervent love for one another in Christ. Consider the way wicked people combine against Christ and his little flock, and let this encourage you to more united affection. Shall the scales of Leviathan stick so close together, and will not the members of Christ be closer and undivided? Bewail your present divisions. Long earnestly for the one Spirit to work more powerfully in the hearts of his people.

The Eminent Degree of This Love

1. Its eminency among the graces: **above all.**
2. The high measure required of it: **love each other deeply.** The word **deeply,** *ektene,* means something that acts strongly and carries a long way.
3. This love is eminent, that which indeed among Christians preserves all and knits all together, and therefore it is called the bond of perfection: "which binds them all together in perfect unity" (Colossians 3:14). All is bound up by it. How can they pray together, how can they promote the name of their God, or keep in and stir up grace in one another, unless they are united in love? How can they have access to God or fellowship with him who is love, as St. John says, if instead of this sweet temper, there is rancor and bitterness among them? So, then, lack of charity and divisions among Christians not only hinder their civil good, but hinder their spiritual good much more. Where the heart entertains either bitter malice or uncharitable prejudices, there will be a decay of spirituality in the whole soul.
4. This is not a cold indifference, a negative love as I may call it. It must be fervent, active love. For if it is fervent, it will be active, a fire that will not be smothered but that will find a way to spread.

The Fruits of His Love

1. Covering evil (in this verse).
2. Doing good (in verse 9 and onward).

Love covers over a multitude of sins. This is taken from Solomon: "Hatred stirs up dissension, but love covers over all wrongs" (Proverbs 10:12). As covering sins is represented as a main act of love, so love is commended by it, as it is a most useful and laudable act. Love covers sins, **a multitude of sins.** Solomon says, "hatred stirs up dissension," aggravating and making everything worse, "but love covers over all wrongs." It does not delight in the undue disclosing of brothers' failings and does not willingly expose them for other people to see.

There is a great deal of spiritual art and skill in dealing with another person's sin. It requires a spiritual mind, much prudence, much love, and a mind free from passion. For passion blinds the eye and makes the hand rough, so that we do not see properly or handle the sore we are trying to cure in the right way. Many are lost through the ignorance that is brought to this work. People think otherwise, but they are mistaken. "Brothers, if someone is caught in a sin, you who are spiritual should restore him gently. But watch yourself, or you also may be tempted" (Galatians 6:1). Bernard quotes a story of an old man who, having heard that one of his brothers had sinned, wept bitterly and said, "He fell today, and I may fall tomorrow."

For yourself, as an offense overtakes you, learn to delight as much in the divine way of forgiveness as unspiritual minds do in the base, inhuman way of revenge. It is not, as they think, a glory to swagger about everything, but it is the glory of man to pass by a transgression; it makes him godlike. "A man's wisdom gives him patience; it is to his glory to overlook an offense" (Proverbs 19:11). Consider often the love that covers all your sins, the blood that was shed to wash off your guilt. Need any more be said to show that in this one thing, love, everything that is required of you is included?

The other fruit of love, doing good, is first expressed in one particular (verse 9) and then expanded to a general rule (verse 19).

Verse 9

Offer hospitality to one another without grumbling.

Hospitality, or kindness to strangers, is mentioned here as an important fruit of love. It was particularly necessary in those times among Christians who used to travel a great deal because of the heat and general persecutions. But I think this word should also include all other supply of the needs of our brothers in outward things.

This must indeed be done according to people's circumstances and ability, but certainly being tight-fisted in these things is more from a closed heart than from lack of means. A large heart with a small amount of money will do a great deal with cheerfulness, while hearts glued to the poor riches they possess, or rather are possessed by, can scarcely part with anything until it is pulled from them. Seneca says, "Most men have riches in the same way that men are said to have the ague, when the fact is, the ague has them."

One practical way to supply the necessities of our brothers is to cut back on our own excesses. Turn the stream into that channel where it will refresh your brothers and enrich yourself, and let it not run into the Dead Sea. Your vain excessive entertainments, your gaudy variety of clothing, these you do not question, for you think they are yours. But as verse 10 says, **Each one should use whatever gift he has received to serve others.** You are a steward of all your possessions. If you do not share them, you are committing robbery. You are robbing your poor brothers who lack the necessities of life while you lavish on yourself what you do not need. Such a feast, such an outfit of clothes, is direct robbery in the eyes of the Lord. And the poor may cry, "That is mine that you so vainly throw away. We might both have benefited from it." "Do not withhold good from those who deserve it, when it is in your power to act. Do not say to your neighbor, 'Come back later, I'll give it tomorrow'—when you now have it with you" (Proverbs 3:27-28).

Without grumbling. Some look to the actions, but few to the intention of the mind in the actions. And yet this is the most important part of any action. Even we to some extent are able to perceive other people's motives. It is much more the case with the Lord, who can always perceive everything. God delights in the good he does to his creatures and wants them to behave in the same way to each other. He especially wants his children to bear this trait of his. See then, when you give money or hospitality to a stranger, that you do not grumble under your breath or pander to your own self-seeking in the action. Do not let your left hand know what is happening, as our Saviour directs: "But when you give to the needy, do not let your left hand know what your right hand is doing" (Matthew 6:3). Let your **hospitality** not be to please other people or to please yourself or simply out of natural pity. Here is a superior principle to move you: love for God, and for your brother in and for God. This will make your giving cheerful and pleasant for yourself, and well pleasing to God for whom you do it. We lose much in actions that in themselves are good, but our hearts are not in them. Nothing will make us look more on our hearts than this: to look more on Christ who looks on our hearts and judges and accepts everything according to them.

Although all the sins of previous ages collect and fall into the latter times, the great evil that is pointed to is the lack of love. The apostle Paul says, ". . . in the last days. People will be . . . lovers of pleasure rather than lovers of God" (2 Timothy 3:1, 4). Where does all this evil come from? The source of everything is mentioned first, and that is the complete opposite to Christian love: "People will be lovers of themselves" (verse 2). This is what kills the love of God and the love of our brothers and kindles that infernal fire of loving to please ourselves. This makes people "lovers of money, boastful, proud, abusive, disobedient to their parents, ungrateful, unholy, without love, unforgiving, slanderous, without self-control, brutal, not lovers of the good, treacherous, rash, conceited" (verses 2-3). Many sins abound, but the sin of coldness of love is especially seen. Answering the question, "What will be the sign of your coming and of the end of the age?" our Saviour replied, "Because of the increase of wickedness, the love of most will grow cold" (Matthew 24:3, 12).

The only happy people will be those in whom the world is burnt up beforehand by another fire, the divine fire of the love of God kindled in their hearts. Be restless until you find your hearts possessed by this excellent grace of love, that you may have it and use it, so that it may grow by being used. In addition, there is in this love so much peace and sweetness, whereas pride and malice fill the ungodly heart with constant disquiet. Aspire to be wholly set not only to hurt no one, but to seek everyone's good. As far as those who are in Christ are concerned, surely that will unite your heart to them. You will want to do them good as part of the body of Christ, to which you also belong.

Verse 10

Each one should use whatever gift he has received to serve others, faithfully administering God's grace in its various forms.
Concerning the gifts and graces bestowed on men, we have here:

1. Their difference in kind and measure.
2. Their agreement in source and use.

1. Their difference in kind and measure is expressed in the first clause: **Each one should use whatever gift he has received.** It comes again in the last clause, **grace in its various forms.** *Charis,* **grace,** is the same as the former *charisma,* **gift.** It is taken in a general way for all kinds of endowments through which people are enabled to do good for people's welfare. One person has riches, another authority and command, another wit or eloquence or learning. And some, although eminent in one, have many gifts.

2. This difference accords well with what is said here about their common origin and use, for the variety of these many gifts comes from the riches and wisdom of their one Giver. The usefulness of the variety of these gifts reflects the bounty and wisdom of the Giver. The **gift** and **God's grace** here tie in with "the manifold wisdom of God" (Ephesians 3:10) mentioned by the apostle Paul.

There is such admirable beauty in this variety. These diverse gifts are from the same Spirit. They are a kind of embroidering of many colors mixed together, as the word **various** indicates. Every person's gift is suitable to use for the good of others.

Observation 1: The first thing that strikes us here is that it is very useful to know that all this is **received.** And what is **received** is a **gift,** a free gift, as the words indicate. This should check any grumbling from people who think they have received the least and prevent them from insulting those who have received the most. Whatever you have received, no matter how much or how little, praise God for it. Do not boast, but humbly bless your Lord. "For who makes you different from anyone else? What do you have that you did not receive? And if you did receive it, why do you boast as though you did not?" (1 Corinthians 4:7).

Observation 2: Everyone has received some **gift.** And nobody has received all the gifts. If you think about this properly, it keeps everyone in a more even temper. As in nature nothing is altogether useless, so also nothing is self-sufficient. This should keep those with the least gifts from complaining. Those who occupy the lowest ranks in most respects have still received something that not only benefits themselves but, if it is used properly, may be useful to other people as well. This should prevent those who have received many gifts from boasting. It will stop them from thinking that they are superior to those who have received few gifts.

Many poor Christians whom you perhaps despise may possess what is most useful to you. Yet you look on it and trample it underfoot. St. Paul acknowledges that he was comforted "by the coming of Titus" (see 2 Corinthians 7:6), even though that man was in terms of giftedness far inferior to the apostle. Sometimes a very uneducated Christian may speak more helpfully than a learned person.

Observation 3: As everything is **received**, and as there are various gifts, so the third consideration is that all who have received gifts should minister to each other. Nobody owns a received gift, for all are stewards of God's gifts. A steward in God's household is required to be faithful and prudent in using his gifts. Your graces are for the good of your brothers. Oh, that we would consider this and look back and mourn the fruitlessness of everything that we have had all our lives until now! If it has not been totally fruitless, yet how little fruit it has borne when compared with what it should have borne. Any little thing we do looks big in our own sight. We view it through a magnifying glass. But who must not acknowledge that their means and health and different types of opportunities for serving God and their brothers have for the most part been inactive? As Christians are defective in other duties of love, so are we in that most important duty of advancing each others' spiritual good. Even those who have grace do not duly use it for mutual edification. I do not ask anyone to go beyond the bounds of their calling or the rules of Christian prudence. But I fear lest unwary hands, throwing on water to quench that evil, have let some of it fall on those sparks that should have been stirred and blown up (see 2 Timothy 1:6).

Neither should the disproportion of gifts and graces hinder Christians from ministering to one another. It should neither move the weaker to envy the stronger, nor the stronger to despise the weaker. Rather, each in his place is to be of service to others, as the apostle Paul says: "If the foot should say, 'Because I am not a hand, I do not belong to the body,' it would not for that reason cease to be part of the body. . . . The eye cannot say to the hand, 'I don't need you!' And the head cannot say to the feet, 'I don't need you!'" (1 Corinthians 12:15, 21). There is no envy, no despising, in the natural body. What a pity that there is so much in the spiritual body! Were we more spiritual, less of this would be found.

In the meantime, if only we were more agreeable to each other. All the graces of the Spirit exist in some measure, yet not all in a like measure. One Christian is more eminent in meekness, another in humility, a third in zeal, and so on. By their spiritual converse one with another, each may gain from the other. In many ways Christians may promote the good of others with whom they live by timely admonitions, advice, and reproof sweetened with meekness, but most of all by holy example, which is most effective.

You who have greater gifts have more entrusted in your hand, and therefore you have the greater need to be faithful and diligent. People in high office and public service should stir themselves up by this thought, so that they are more watchful and zealous. And in private conversations with one another, we ought to be doing and receiving spiritual good. Are we not strangers to this? Is it not strange that we so often meet and part without saying a word about our future home or the way to it or our progress toward it? Christians should be trading with one another in spiritual things, and the person who faithfully uses most will receive most. This is included in our Saviour's words, "For everyone who has will be given more, and he will have an abundance. Whoever does not have, even what he has will be taken from him" (Matthew 25:29). Merchants can experience a dead time in their trading and complain seriously about it. But Christians in theirs either can suffer it and not see it, or see it and not complain, or, possibly, complain and yet not be fully aware of it.

Certainly it cannot be regretted enough that we are so fruitless in the Lord's work in this way. For when we are alone we do not work hard for this or seek it more in prayer, in order to know the true use of all we receive. Instead we trifle with our time. Instead of using our grace for mutual enrichment, we trade in vanity and are, as it were, children swapping shells and toys with each other.

This will surely weigh heavily on the conscience when we reflect on it. When we look forward to eternity and then look back over our days, we see how we have vainly wasted them and become worn out to no purpose. Oh, let us wake up ourselves and one another, in order to be more fruitful and more faithful, no matter how many gifts we have received.

Do not be discouraged. You will not be penalized for having little in your account. Great faithfulness in the use of small gifts has great acceptance and a great and certain reward. Great gifts should produce great returns and therefore require greater diligence. This is not just for the increase of the grace within but for the benefit of others. Private contemplation may be more pleasing, but due activity for God and his church is more profitable. Rachel was fair, but she was barren. Leah was "bleareyed" but fruitful. [see Genesis 29:17, where the *Geneva Bible* has the marginal reading "blear-eyed"—Editor's note.]

Verse 11

If anyone speaks, he should do it as one speaking the very words of God. If anyone serves, he should do it with the strength God provides, so that in all things God may be praised through Jesus Christ. To him be the glory and the power for ever and ever. Amen.

Every part of the body of Christ, as it shares life with the rest, serves the rest. But there are some more eminent and, so to speak, organic parts of this body, and these people are more eminently useful to the whole. Therefore, the apostle, having enlarged into a general precept, adds a word of special reference to these special parts—the preachers of the Word and the other assistant officers of the church of God (here, I think, meaning deacons or ministers).

These are co-ordained by Jesus Christ as Lord of his own house, to be of service to him in it. He equips and sanctifies for this great work all who are called to it by himself. They are directed to carry out this great work by a clear rule about the due manner and by the chief purpose for which it is appointed.

The Manner of Preaching

Particular rules for preaching the Word may be many, but the one the apostle gives is most comprehensive: **If anyone speaks, he should do it as one speaking the very words of God.** It is clear from this instruction what speaking is regulated. Anyone who speaks should speak **the very words of God.**

It is a top priority in all serious actions to understand their nature properly, for this regulates them and directs their performance. This is particularly true with regard to those things that are of the highest worth and greatest weight in spiritual employments. In these matters it is most dangerous to make mistakes. **If anyone speaks, he should do it as one speaking the very words of God.** Under this all the due qualifications of the holy work are comprised. I shall name just three of them, which are primary, and others may be easily deduced from these:

1. Faithfully.
2. In a holy way.
3. In a wise way.

1. First, faithfully. It is supposed that preachers should have a competent insight into and knowledge of the words of God. It is assumed that they have learned before they teach. Many of us have not done this, even though we have passed through schools and classes and through the books too in which these things are taught. Those who want to teach faithfully about God must be taught by God. They must be God-learned. "You

yourselves have been taught by God to love each other" (1 Thessalonians 4:9). This will help in everything else. It will help us to be faithful in delivering the message as we receive it, not adding to it or taking away from it or altering it. And as in setting it out in general truths, so it is when we drive particular sins home, declaring to people their sins and God's judgments following sin, especially in his own people.

2. A minister must speak in a holy way, with that high esteem and reverence that are due to the great Majesty whose message is carried, for the minister is carrying divine messages about deep mysteries that no created spirit can fathom. This would make us tremble as we dispense these **very words of God** and as we consider our impurities and weaknesses. We are not fit for such an elevated task. It has been said with good reason, "I am seized with amazement and horror whenever I begin to speak of God." And this humble reverence is to be linked with ardent love of our Lord, his truth, and his glory and of people's souls. These holy affections stand in contrast to our blind boldness in rushing on this sublime exercise as a common work and our dead coldness in speaking about things when our own hearts are not warmed by them. It is little wonder that what we say seldom reaches further than the ear or, at the furthest, to the understanding and memory of our hearers. It is the heart that speaks to the heart, just as the tongue speaks only to the ear.

Further, this holy attitude excludes all private passion in delivering divine truths. It greatly profanes God's name and holy things if we use them to further our private pleas and quarrels. Indeed, to reprove sin in this way is itself a heinous sin. To issue invectives that, though not expressed as such, are yet aimed as blows of self-revenge for injuries done to us, or for imaginary hurts, is to use the holy Word of God for our own unholy devices. Surely, this is not speaking the **very words of God.** This debases and abuses the Word of God. It is true that the Word is to be applied to reprove particular sins among people, but this is to be done not in anger but in love.

3. The Word is to be spoken wisely. By this I mean, it is to be delivered seriously and decently. Flippant remarks and unseemly gestures are to be avoided. You should speak with authority and mildness. Who is sufficient for such things?

You who hear should certainly meet and agree about this as well: anyone who hears should hear **the very words of God.** These words should reveal sin and death close to us and a Saviour who takes these away. Therefore, come to the Word with the necessary reverence, ardent desires, and hearts open to receive it. "Therefore, get rid of all moral filth and the evil that is so prevalent, and humbly accept the word planted in you, which can save you" (James 1:21). It would be well worth spending one day to take the trouble to learn how to speak and how to listen, so that in the future we would at least know how to speak and how to listen. We should especially speak and listen to **the very words of God.**

In the other instruction—**If anyone serves, he should do it with the strength God provides**—we observe, first, that ability is necessary and is received from God. There is no ability for any good work, let alone for the special work of God's spiritual ministry in his house, that is not received from God. And, second, we may observe that this ability received from God is to be used for other people.

Truly it is important for ministers, and for every Christian, to depend on the influence and strength of God and to do all his deeds in that strength. The humblest Christian, no matter how weak, is the strongest. There is a natural, wretched independence in our desire to be the authors of our own words and to do everything without God, without whom we can do nothing. Let us learn to go more out of ourselves, and we shall find more strength for our duties, and against our temptations. Faith's great work is to renounce self-power and to allow the power of God to be ours. Happy are those who are the weakest in themselves and know that this is the case. The apostle Paul's statement is a puzzle to the world but makes perfect sense to them: "That is why, for Christ's sake, I delight in weaknesses, in insults, in hardships, in persecutions, in difficulties. For when I am weak, then I am strong" (2 Corinthians 12:10).

The Purpose of Preaching

The purpose of this work is **so that in all things God may be praised through Jesus Christ.** Everything meets in this. It is most reasonable for God to be given what is due to him. God is the Author of everything—not just of good things, but of being itself; everything is from him, and so everything should be for him. **To him be the glory and the power for ever and ever. Amen.**

> *Oh, the depths of the riches of the wisdom and knowledge of God! How unsearchable his judgments, and his paths beyond tracing out! "Who has known the mind of the Lord? Or who has been his counselor?" "Who has ever given to God, that God should repay him?" For from him and through him and to him are all things. To him be the glory forever! Amen.*
>
> —Romans 11:33-36

As it is most just, so it is also most sweet to aim in everything that **God may be praised.** This is the only worthy and happy plan that fills the heart with heaven. It sets the heart beyond the clouds and storms of those passions that disquiet low, self-seeking minds. We are miserable, unsettled wretches if we cling to ourselves and forget God. When our plans fail, how can we look to God when we have looked to him so little in the past? May not God say, "Go to the gods whom you have served, and let them deliver and comfort you"? How appalling this would be! But if we rely on God, we may confidently say that the Lord is our portion. It is the Christian's aim to have nothing in himself, nor in anything else, so that everything is all for the glory of God—our possessions, family, abilities, and whole self, all we have and are. And as the love of God grows in the heart, this purpose grows. The higher the flame rises, the purer it is. The eye concentrates on it more strongly each day. It is more frequently in the mind as we go about doing ordinary things—eating, drinking, sleeping, and the work of our calling. All is for this end. It is this elixir that turns your ordinary deeds into gold.

Through Jesus Christ. The Christian in covenant with God receives everything in this way and returns everything in this way. And Christ possesses and has equal right with the Father to this glory, since he is equally the source of it with the Father. But it is all conveyed through Christ as Mediator; he obtains all the grace we receive. We return all the glory; all our praise, as our spiritual sacrifice, is put into Christ's hand. Being our High Priest, he offers up our sacrifices for us, so that they may be accepted.

The holy ardor of the apostle's affections, taken with the mention of this glory of God, leads him to a doxology, as we call it, a rendering of glory in the middle of his discourse. **To him be the glory and the power for ever and ever. Amen.** This is often done by the apostle Paul as well. The grandeur of man is poor and short-lived. Like ourselves, it is a shadow, nothing. But God's glory is lasting. It is supreme and abides forever. The apostles, full of divine affections, delight in this and cannot refrain from this at any time in their discourse. Spiritual minds are like this. Everyone should join in, acknowledging the greatness and goodness of God. This is our work, which never ends. At all times we should be saying, **To him be the glory and the power for ever and ever. Amen.**

Verses 12-13

Dear friends, do not be surprised at the painful trial you are suffering, as though something strange were happening to you. But rejoice that you participate in the sufferings of Christ, so that you may be overjoyed when his glory is revealed.

This fighting life, surely, when we consider it properly, should not persuade us not to love it. Rather, it points to our need to be strengthened with patience to go through and to fight on with courage and assurance of victory. We should fight with a greater strength than our own against sin within and troubles without. This is the great message of this letter, and the apostle often interchanges his advice and comfort with reference to these two things. Against sin he instructs us at the beginning of this chapter, urging us to "arm yourselves also with the same attitude" that was in Christ (verse 1), and here again, against suffering. In mortifying sin, we suffer with Christ, as the apostle teaches us (verse 1). In encountering affliction, we suffer with Christ, as it says in these verses. And so the same mind in the same sufferings will bring us to the same result. The words toward the end of the chapter also contain grounds for encouragement and consolation for God's children in sufferings, especially in suffering for God.

These two verses deal with the close connection of sufferings with the state of a Christian and the due composure of a Christian toward suffering.

The Close Connection of Suffering with the State of a Christian

It is no new and therefore no strange thing that sufferings, fiery ones, accompany religion. Besides the common miseries of human life, there are the troubles and hatreds for that holiness of life to which the children of God are called.

This was the lot of the church from her wicked neighbors; and within the church, this was the lot of the most holy and special servants of God from the profane multitude. "Alas, my mother, that you gave me birth, a man with whom the whole land strives and contends!" (Jer. 15:10). And our Saviour, in his sermon, says, "they persecuted the prophets who were before you" (Matthew 5:12). And later he tells them what they are to expect: "I am sending you out like sheep among wolves" (Matthew 10:16). In general there is no following Christ but with his badge and burden. We are to leave ourselves behind. "If anyone would come after me, he must deny himself and take up his cross and follow me" (Matthew 16:24). The apostle Paul gives his readers the universal lesson, as an infallible truth, that "everyone who wants to live a godly life in Christ Jesus will be persecuted" (2 Timothy 3:12).

Or look at the end of the list of believers who conquered in suffering. What a cluster of sufferings and torture they have: "Some faced jeers and flogging, while still others were chained and put in prison. They were stoned; they were sawn in two; they were put to death by the sword. They went about in sheepskins and goatskins, destitute, persecuted and mistreated—the world was not worthy of them. They wandered in deserts and mountains, and in caves and holes in the ground" (Hebrews 11:36-38). Thus in the early times the **trial**, literally a **painful trial**, continued over a long time. Those wicked emperors hated the very innocence of Christians. And the people, although they knew they were blameless, would still cry when any evil came, "The Christians to the lions!"

This is not strange—**do not be surprised.** The ungodly world hates holiness, despising the Light. And the more the children of God walk like their Father and their future home, the more unlike they must be, of neces-

sity, from the world around them. Therefore, they become the target of all
the malice of their enemies. And thus the godly, though the sons of peace,
are the occasion of much disturbance in the world. As their Lord, the
Prince of Peace, openly said of himself, "Do not suppose that I have come
to bring peace to the earth. I did not come to bring peace, but a sword. For
I have come to turn a man against his father, a daughter against her mother,
a daughter-in-law against her mother-in-law—a man's enemies will be the
members of his own household" (Matthew 10:34-36). If a member of a
family starts to inquire after God and withdraws from the profane and
dead way of ungodly relatives, what a clamor soon arises! "My son or
daughter or wife has become a complete fool!" And then everything is
done to make life miserable for them.

The holy walking of a Christian condemns the world around him. It
shows up the disorder and foulness of unbelievers' profane ways. Further,
the life of true religion, set next to dead formality, shows it to be a carcass.
There is in the life of a Christian a convicting light that shows the deformity of the works of darkness, and a piercing heat that scorches the
ungodly and stirs and troubles their consciences. They cannot endure this,
and hence there arises in them a wicked fire of hatred. Hence the godly are
subjected to **painful** trials. If they could remove these people out of their
way, they think, they might have more freedom.

As this is an infernal fire of enmity against God, so it is blown by that
spirit whose element it is. Satan stirs up the coal and raises the hatred of the
ungodly against Christians.

But while he and those in whom he powerfully works are thus working
for their vile ends in the persecution of the saints, God, who is sovereign
over all, is working in the same people to achieve his wise and gracious
ends. God succeeds in this and makes the malice of his enemies serve his
purposes. It is true that through the heat of persecution many are frightened away from embracing the Lord. People who love themselves and
their present ease are driven away from religion. Those who reject it or
revolt against it are those who do not have true knowledge of it or share in
it or in that happiness in which it ends. But those who are indeed united to
Jesus Christ cling all the more closely to him and seek to have their hearts
closer to him as a result of these trials. The love of Christ conquers and tri-
umphs in the worst sufferings of life, and even in death itself.

These **painful** trials have been the means of kindling faith in the hearts
of persecutors who have seen the victorious patience of the saints. They
watched the saints conquer death, as their Head did, and witnessed
patience triumph over cruelty.

Thus this **painful trial** makes faith shine more brightly, just as gold
shines brightest in the furnace. If any impurities are mixed with it, it is

refined and purified from them by these trials, and so it becomes, by means of this fire, purer than before.

One special advantage of these fires is the purifying of a Christian's heart from the love of the world and of present things. It is true the world at best is base, and yet there is something in believers that draws them into it. Thus the Lord makes the world displeasing to his own, so that they may turn to him and seek all their consolations in him.

The Composure of a Christian in Reference to Sufferings

1. Resolving to endure them, thinking about them properly: **do not be surprised.** This is not our natural reaction. We prefer to hear about peace and security and are glad to believe what we want to hear about. It is most important to think in the right way about Christianity. Many people do not do this. Such people either fall away quickly or walk on slowly and heavily. They do not take into account the sufferings Christians have to endure. Our Saviour warned, "If they persecuted me, they will persecute you also" (John 15:20).

Acquaint, therefore, your thoughts and hearts with sufferings, so that when they come, you and they will not be strangers. Do not burden yourself by worrying about future troubles. But do think ahead about the trials and sufferings you may undergo for Christ's sake, so that your mind is strong and prepared. Be humble and dependent on Christ's strength. In everything, both beforehand and during the time of trial, make your Lord Jesus all your strength. This is the only way to be "conquerors" in everything (see Romans 8:37).

As though something strange were happening to you. Again, **do not be surprised.** Align your thinking to the experience of all times and to the warnings that the Spirit of God has given us in the Scriptures and to our Saviour's words and thinking.

2. Accept them gladly: **but rejoice.** We may not think the sufferings are **strange,** but we may think that it is rather a strange instruction to **rejoice** in them. But this is just as reasonable as the other instruction was. They both rest on the same principle: **you participate in the sufferings of Christ.**

If God's children consider their trials properly, this will bring not only patience but rejoicing. But we add this, as it completes the reason for rejoicing in suffering: we are to **participate in the sufferings of Christ.**

So then, consider the link between the sufferings of Christ and the subsequent glory of Christ; and consider also the present joy, even in sufferings, springing from participating in Christ's sufferings.

I do not need to tell you that this communion in sufferings is not the expiation or satisfaction of divine justice, which was the special purpose of the sufferings of Christ. Christ "bore our sins in his own body on the tree" (1 Peter 2:24), and in bearing them, he took them away. We bear his sufferings as his body, the church, united to him by his Spirit. We participate in the sweet fruits that result from those sufferings that were his personal burden. We are acquitted as a result of them, but the endurance of them was Christ's task, which only he could do. Our communion in these sufferings, as fully completed by Christ in his physical body, is the ground of our comfort and joy in those sufferings that are completed in his mystical body, the church.

This is indeed our joy, that we might have the weight of our burden removed from our backs, and everything bound on Christ's cross. Our crosses, the badges of our conformity to Christ, are laid on our shoulders; but their great weight is held up by Christ's hand, and so they do not oppress us. The fires of our trials may be corrective and purge the remaining power of sin, and that is their purpose. But Jesus Christ alone, in the sufferings of his own cross, was the burnt offering, the propitiation for our sins.

Now although he has perfectly satisfied the penalty for sin for us and saved us by his sufferings, yet our conformity to him in the way of suffering is most reasonable. Our sufferings bear a likeness to Christ's, though in no way as an accession to his in expiation. Therefore, the apostle Paul says, even in this respect, we are "predestined to be conformed to the likeness of his Son" (Romans 8:29). This is the way we must follow or else resolve to leave Christ. The way of the cross is the royal way to the crown.

When his glory is revealed. Now that he is hidden, little of his glory is seen. It was hidden while he was on this earth, and now it is hidden in heaven, where Christ is. And as for his body here, his church, it has no pompous dress or outward splendor. The particular parts of it, the saints, are poor, despised creatures, human refuse in outward respects and common esteem. So Christ himself is not seen, and the more his followers are seen and looked on by the world, the more despised they appear. For the most part, Christ and his followers are covered with all the disgraces and ignominies the world can put on them. But a day will come when Christ will appear, and it is at hand: ". . . on the day he comes to be glorified in his holy people and to be marveled at among all those who have believed" (2 Thessalonians 1:10). How much more will the incomparable brightness of his glory then be! In the meantime Christ is hidden, and those who are in him are hidden also: "your life is now hidden with Christ in God" (Colossians 3:3). The world sees nothing of his glory and beauty, and even his own do not see much of this. They catch glimpses of him, and they are happy in him. But they know only a little about their privileged condition and what they are born to. But on that bright day Christ will shine forth in his royal dignity, and every eye will see him and be overcome with his splendor.

Then, our apostle says, you will be **overjoyed when his glory is**

revealed. On these grounds the admonition to **rejoice** even in **the sufferings of Christ** appears reasonable. This joy is based, first, in sufferings and, second, in glory.

First, this joy is based on the sufferings themselves. It is a sweet and joyful thing to share anything with Christ. All enjoyments without him are bitter, and all sufferings with him are sweet. What does the world by its hatred, persecutions, and revilings for the sake of Christ do but make me more like him and give me a greater share with Christ in what he so willingly underwent for me? "When he was sought for to be made a king," St. Bernard remarks, "he escaped; but when he was sought to be brought to the cross, he freely yielded himself." Will I shrink from what Christ calls me to suffer for his sake?

Second, this joy is grounded on the hope of glory. **When his glory is revealed.** When Christ is **revealed** in **his glory**, you will be filled with overflowing joy. You will be part of that **glory.** Therefore, rejoice now in the midst of your sufferings. By faith look beyond this moment and all that is in it to that day in which everlasting joy will be on your head, to the day when sorrow and mourning will flee away (see Isaiah 51:11). Believe in this day, and the victory is won!

What zeal for God this inspires! How soon will this pageant of the world vanish, which people gaze on. Instead they should give glory to God himself. He will be seen in full majesty, and all his brothers in glory with him will be dressed in their robes. And if you ask who they are, the answer is: "These are they who have come out of the great tribulation; they have washed their robes and made them white in the blood of the Lamb" (Revelation 7:14).

Verses 14-16

If you are insulted because of the name of Christ, you are blessed, for the Spirit of glory and of God rests on you. If you suffer, it should not be as a murderer or thief or any other kind of criminal, or even as a meddler. However, if you suffer as a Christian, do not be ashamed, but praise God that you bear that name.

The Word is the Christian's book for instruction and encouragement, both for doing and for suffering, and this letter is full of these two matters. What the apostle has said about suffering in general, he now specifies in the particular case of suffering insults. **If you are insulted.** This may not seem to be as bad as **the painful trial** mentioned in verse 12, but we will see that it is in fact a very acute trial.

If you are insulted. If we consider both the nature of this kind of suffering and how it comes in the Scriptures, we will find that insults are among the most painful types of suffering. When other types of persecution stop, insults remain. When all the fires of martyrdom are put out, insults burn on. People who do not dare to harm us physically let fly a taunt or a bitter word. Whereas other sufferings may be rarer, we meet with insults daily. ". . . my foes taunt me, saying to me all day long, 'Where is your God?'" (Psalm 42:10).

We see, then, how right it is to include insults among other sufferings. "Blessed are those who are persecuted because of righteousness, for theirs is the kingdom of heaven. Blessed are you when people insult you, persecute you and falsely say all kinds of evil against you because of me" (Matthew 5:10-11). Insults are mentioned among the ways of suffering for Christ in the Gospels, and even among the sufferings of Christ himself. "The people stood watching, and the rulers even sneered at him. They said, 'He saved others; let him save himself if he is the Christ of God, the Chosen One.' The soldiers also came up and mocked him" (Luke 23:35-36).

This is the lot of Christians, even as it was of Christ. Why should they expect more kindness and better treatment when their Lord was so vilified? The vain heart must be weaned from the fear of such things and follow Christ. "A student is not above his teacher, nor a servant above his master" (Matthew 10:24).

Since this is the case, the apostle instructs believers to make sure their sufferings are pure. Resolve to endure suffering, but also resolve that it will be on your part innocent suffering. Do not suffer as an evildoer. **If you suffer, it should not be as a murderer or thief or any other kind of criminal.** The rule here is that if you suffer, you must do so because you are a Christian. **If you suffer as a Christian.** Suffer as Christians in a holy and blameless way, so that your enemies are unable to take hold of you. Wrestlers anointed their bodies with oil so that opponents could not grip them with their hands, and believers are to walk and suffer as Christians anointed with the Spirit of Christ, so that their enemies cannot gain any hold on them.

To you, therefore, who love the Lord Jesus, I especially recommend this. Be careful that all the insults you receive are **because of the name of Christ,** and not for anything in you which is un-Christlike. Keep far away from all impure, unholy ways. **If you suffer, it should not be as a murderer or thief or any other kind of criminal, or even as a meddler.** Shun the appearances of evil. Walk warily and prudently in everything.

A spiritual mind does not swell with conceit, proud of its own courage or fortitude. This is the quickest route to its ruin. Everything must be acknowledged as a gift, even suffering. "For it has been granted to you on behalf of Christ not only to believe on him, but also to suffer for him" (Philippians 1:29). Love for Christ grows through suffering. "The apostles left the Sanhedrin, rejoicing because they had been counted worthy of suffering disgrace for the Name" (Acts 5:41). Remember, after only a short time the wicked and their insults will vanish. This shame and disgrace will soon be over, but the glory of Christ is eternal. So what if you are poor, mocked, and despised? The end of all this is at hand. This is now your part, but the scene will be changed. Kings here, real ones, are in deepest reality mere stage kings. [If, as there is good reason to believe, these words were written soon after the battle of Worcester, September 3, 1651, they have a special significance, referring to the dethronement and tragic end of Charles I.—Editor's note.] But when you are no longer the person you now are, how glorious will be the result. You appeared to be a fool for a moment, but you will truly be a king forever.

Verse 17

For it is time for judgment to begin with the family of God; and if it begins with us, what will the outcome be for those who do not obey the gospel of God?
There is perfect equity in all of God's ways, if we only have eyes to observe them. The apostle now sets before his brothers the **time for judgment.** In these words there is a parallel with the Lord's dealing with his own and with the wicked. This parallel is in the order and the measure of punishing. Concerning the order, it begins **with the family of God** and ends with the ungodly. And that carries in it this great difference in the measure—it passes from the one on whom it begins and rests on the other with whom it ends and on whom the full weight of it lies forever. It is said in this way: **What will the outcome be for those who do not obey the gospel of God?** Judgment will not only overtake them in the end—it will also be their end. They will come to an end in it, and it will endlessly be on them.

For it is time for judgment to begin. Indeed, the whole time of this present life is a time of judgment. It is a time of suffering and a time of being purified in the church. Whereas the wicked escape until their day of full payment, the children of God are in this life chastised with frequent afflictions. And so **time,** *ho kairos,* may here be taken as the apostle Paul does when he uses the same word: "I consider that our present sufferings . . ." (*pathemata tou nun kairou*) (Romans 8:18).

It seems to be implied here that there are particular set times when the Lord chooses to correct his church. The apostle probably means the times of those harsh persecutions that had just started. Those troubles threatened to make believers fall away. But believers, having the grace of God in their hearts, benefited from these hazards and sufferings. They held on to Christ with a firmer grip. They entered into the way of receiving Christ and his cross together.

Judgment to begin with the family of God. The church of God is punished, while the wicked are free and flourish in the world, possibly all their days. But if judgment does not reach them here, it will later, for judgment begins **with the family of God.** This applies to those who profess God's name and are the visible church, in contrast with those who are outside the church and are its avowed enemies. This judgment will be on those who desire a more religious way of living and lead a holy life within the church. The Lord touches such people with afflictions and corrects their wanderings.

We must not be so foolish as to think we will escape God's judgment on account of our relationship to him. We should rather see it as the start of a more severe judgment. Why do we not consider our proud, unpurified condition and tremble before the Lord? We must put a right construction on all God's dealings with his church and with our souls. With regard to God's church, there may be a time when you will see it not only tossed but, to your way of thinking, covered and swallowed up with tears. But wait a little, and it will arrive safely. This is a common stumbling-stone, but walk by the light of the Word and the eye of faith looking on it, and you will pass by and not stumble.

We read about Joseph hated, sold, and imprisoned, and all most unjustly; yet within a few pages we find him freed and exalted, and his brothers coming to ask for his help, and we are satisfied. But when we look on things that at the moment are cloudy and dark, our shortsighted, hasty spirits cannot learn to wait a little to see the other side and what end the Lord makes. We see that **judgment** begins **with the family of God,** and this perplexes us if we do not remember that **if it begins with us, what will the outcome be for those who do not obey the gospel of God?** God begins the judgment on his church for a short time, that it may end and rest on his enemies forever.

What will the outcome be for those who do not obey the gospel of God? The end of all the ungodly is terrible, but especially the end of those who heard the Gospel but did not receive and obey it.

The Greek word translated **do not obey** implies both unbelief and disobedience. These two things are inseparable. Unbelief is the main point of disobedience in itself and the spring of all other kinds of disobedience. The pity is that men will not believe this is the case. They think it is an easy and normal thing to believe. Who does not believe? Rather, who does believe? Were our own misery and the happiness that is in Christ believed, were the riches of Christ and the love of Christ believed, would not this persuade people to forsake their sins and the world in order to embrace God?

The gospel of God. This is God's embassy of peace to humankind. The riches of his mercy and free love are opened up and set out not simply to be viewed, but to be taken hold of. It concerns his own Son and his streaming blood that washes away uncleanness. And yet the Gospel is not obeyed! People love themselves and their evil desires and the present world and will not change, and so they perish. What is their end? I will answer only as the apostle does, and that is by asking the question again: **What will the outcome be for those who do not obey the gospel of God?** There is no description given. A curtain is drawn. Silent wonder expresses it best, telling us that it cannot be expressed. How then shall it be endured? It is true that there are resemblances used in Scripture, giving us a glance at this terrible destiny. We hear of a burning lake, a fire that cannot be put out, and a worm that does not die (see Isaiah 66:24; Mark 9:44; Revelation 21:8). But these are mere shadows of the real misery of **those who do not obey the gospel.** Oh, how awful to be filled with the wrath of God, the ever-living God, forever! What words or thoughts can capture this? Separated from God for eternity—eternity! Oh, that we did believe it!

The same parallel of the Lord's dealing with the righteous and the wicked is continued in the next verse in other terms, to make it clearer.

Verse 18

And, **"If it is hard for the righteous to be saved, what will become of the ungodly and the sinner?"**

It is true that **it is hard for the righteous to be saved.** Even for those who endeavor to walk uprightly in the ways of God, that is, **the righteous,** it **is hard . . . to be saved.** This does not mean the end result is in doubt. It means that there are great difficulties on the way—fightings without and fears within. What is most hurtful is that they sadden God's Spirit through their wanderings. If they stop striving for a short moment, they are carried along downstream. And yet through all this they are brought safely home, for the strength of Another bears them up and brings them through.

It is not an easy thing to come to heaven as most people imagine. And if the way of the righteous is so hard, then how hard will be the end of the ungodly sinner who walks in sin with delight!

What is the purpose of all this? It is so that you may be moved to think more deeply about your immortal souls. Oh, that you would be persuaded! Oh, that you would take yourself to Jesus Christ and seek salvation from him! Seek to be covered with his righteousness and to be led by his Spirit in the ways of righteousness. This will be your seal for a certain happy end and will overcome for you all the difficulties you encounter along the way. What is the Gospel of Christ preached for? What was the blood of Christ shed for? Was it so that by receiving him we might escape condemnation? Not that alone. This drew him from heaven: "I have come that they may have life, and have it to the full" (John 10:10).

Verse 19

So then, those who suffer according to God's will should commit themselves to their faithful Creator and continue to do good.

Nothing establishes the minds of believers in these turbulent times so much as an upward look and a forward look. The upward look is to the steady, good hand of God who rules them. The forward look is to that beautiful end toward which they are traveling. The apostle lays here the foundation of that patience and peace amid troubles that he wants all his brothers to experience. These words contain the true principles of Christian patience and tranquillity of mind in the sufferings of this life. He tells us where it comes from and what its basis is.

Where Our Peace Comes From

It comes from committing the soul to God: **should commit themselves to their faithful Creator.** If people want an inner peace in the midst of trouble, they must walk by the rule of peace and keep strictly to it. If you commit your soul to God's keeping, you must remember that he is a holy God, and an unholy soul that walks in any way of wickedness, whether known or secret, is not fit to be put into his pure hand to keep. You must walk so that you will not discredit your Protector and make him ashamed of you and disown you. Study pure and holy walking if you want to have confidence and boldness and joy in God. You will find that a little sin will shake your trust and disturb your peace more than the greatest sufferings.

Commit themselves to their faithful Creator. The Lord is a complete Protector. He keeps their bodies, in fact all that belongs to them, and, as much as is good for them, makes all safe. "A righteous man may have many troubles, but the LORD delivers him from them all; he protects all his bones, not one of them will be broken" (Psalm 34:19-20). Our Saviour agrees, saying, "even the very hairs of your head are all numbered" (Matthew 10:30). What is most precious both to believers and to God is committed and received into God's safekeeping—namely, their souls. If the soul is safe, all is well. It is riches enough. "What good is it for a man to gain the whole world, yet forfeit his soul?" (Mark 8:36). And so how will it harm us if we lose the whole world and gain our soul? Not at all.

From this learn what the proper act of faith is. It gives the soul to God. "Commit your way to the LORD" (Psalm 37:5). The Hebrew literally means, "Roll your way on the Lord." This is the only way to be quiet within. You may lose your possessions, your friends, and even life itself. But the most important thing is to keep your soul safe. "That is why I am suffering as I am. Yet I am not ashamed," says the apostle Paul. Why was he not ashamed? "Because I know whom I have believed, and am convinced that he is able to guard what I have entrusted to him for that day" (2 Timothy 1:12).

The Ground for This Confidence

The ground of our confidence is in these two things: the ability and the faithfulness of him in whom we trust. There is much strength in being persuaded of the power of God. Though few people think they question this, there is in us undiscovered unbelief. The Lord frequently mentions this in the prophets. "I clothe the sky with darkness and make sackcloth its covering. . . . Because the Sovereign LORD helps me, I will not be disgraced" (Isaiah 50:3, 7). Our apostle says that we are "shielded by God's power" (1:5). It is very necessary to consider this in regard to the many and great oppositions, dangers, and powerful enemies that seek our souls. "My Father who has given them to me, is greater than all; no one can snatch them out of my Father's hand" (John 10:29). This is what the apostle here implies with the word **Creator.** If he was able to give them being, surely he is able to keep them from perishing.

And as he is powerful, he is no less faithful. He is **their faithful Creator.** He is truth itself. Those who believe in him, he never deceives nor disappoints. Well might St. Paul say, "I know whom I have believed" (2 Timothy 1:12). Oh, the advantage of faith! It engages the truth and the power of God. God remains able and faithful to keep his Word, so that the soul will not perish.

There are in these words two other grounds for quietness of spirit in suffering. First, it is **according to God's will.** The believing soul, subjected and leveled to that **will,** complying with God's good pleasure in everything, cannot have a more powerful argument than this: it is all ordered by **God's will.** Having this settled in the heart makes it steadfast in all things.

And then consider him as your God and Father, who has taken special charge of you and of your soul. You have given it to him, and he has received it. Bearing this in mind, follow God's will in everything, and have no will but his. This is your duty. Nothing is to be gained from struggling; you will only harm yourself. It is the very secret, the mystery of solid peace within, to resign everything to his will, to be at his disposal, with no opposing thoughts. It is the sum of Christianity to have your will crucified, and the will of your Lord as your only desire. In joy or sorrow, in sickness or health, in life or death, in everything, "Your will be done."

1 Peter
Chapter 5

Verse 1

To the elders among you, I appeal as a fellow elder, a witness of Christ's sufferings and one who also will share in the glory to be revealed.

The church of Christ, being one body, is interested in the condition of each particular Christian, and in particular its more eminent members. Therefore the apostle, after giving many excellent directions for all his Christian brothers to whom he writes, now adds this exhortation for those who had oversight of the rest. **To the elders among you.** These words contain a particular definition of the people exhorted and the person exhorting.

1. The people exhorted: **To the elders among you.** Here **elders**, as in other places, is the name of an office. It does not mean the age of a person. But people who are called to this office, even if they are not aged, should be respected for their wisdom and gravity of mind. As St. Paul says, they should not be novices: "he must not be a recent convert, or he may become conceited and fall under the same judgment as the devil" (1 Timothy 3:6). An elder is not to be like young, unstable minds but like Timothy who, although young, was humble and diligent, as St. Paul testifies about him: "I have no one else like him, who takes a genuine interest in your welfare" (Philippians 2:20). "Don't let anyone look down on you because you are young, but set an example for the believers in speech, in life, in love, in faith and in purity" (1 Timothy 4:12).

The term ruling elders sometimes denotes civil rulers, sometimes pastors of the church. Among the Jews elders meant both of these things. Here it appears that pastors are meant, as the exhortation is to be **shepherds of God's flock** (verse 2). This sometimes means ruling, and here it may include that, but it mainly refers to teaching. The title given to Christ in the added encouragement confirms this interpretation: **the Chief Shepherd** (verse 4).

A due frame of spirit and behavior in the elders, particularly the apostles of the church, is primary concerning its welfare. It is one of the strongest threats when the Lord declares he will give a rebellious people the teachers and prophets they deserve and indeed desire: "If a liar and deceiver comes and says, 'I will prophesy for you plenty of wine and beer,' he would be just the prophet for this people!" (Micah 2:11). On the other hand, one of the sweetest promises of mercy is that the Lord will provide his people with plenty of faithful teachers. "Although the Lord gives you the bread of adversity and the water of affliction, your teachers will be hidden no more; with your own eyes you will see them" (Isaiah 30:20). Oh, how rich is Jeremiah's promise: "Then I will give you shepherds after my own heart" (Jeremiah 3:15). It is an inestimable blessing to have the saving light of the Gospel shining clearly through faithful and powerful ministers. The people thought so when they said of their worthy teacher Chrysostom that they would rather the sun did not shine than that he should not teach.

2. The person exhorting: **I appeal as a fellow elder.** The duty of mutual exhortation includes all Christians, but pastors should, as in some other duties, be particularly engaged in this. They should often be saying to one another, "Oh, let us remember to what we are called, to what holiness and diligence." They should be often sharpening one another through weighty and holy considerations.

A witness of Christ's sufferings. St. Peter did indeed give witness to Christ by suffering for him the hatred and persecutions of the world as he made known the Gospel, and I do not discount this. But what is particularly intended here is his definite knowledge of the sufferings of Christ. He was an eyewitness of them. In this letter he witnessed to what he had seen. "You are witnesses of these things" (Luke 24:48).

One who also will share in the glory to be revealed. As he was **a witness of Christ's sufferings**, so he will share in **the glory** purchased by those sufferings. As one who had insight and interest in what he spoke about, the apostle could rightly speak about the special duty that those **sufferings** and **glory** point to. He speaks as someone who shares in this. There is special force in a pastor's exhortation, either to his people or his brothers, when he brings a message written on his own heart, speaking about the guilt of sin and the sufferings of Christ for it, particularly feeling his own guilt and looking on those sufferings as taking it away. It is the same when Christians talk with each other. Everything is cold and dead if it does not flow from inner persuasion and experiential knowledge of divine things. But if it does flow from that, this gives a sweetness to Christian conversation—to be speaking of Jesus Christ not only as a King and as a Redeemer, but as their King and their Redeemer, as David did: "My King and my God."

In this way they talk of Christ's **sufferings** as theirs, applied by faith and acquitting them. As St. Paul puts it, "who loved me and give himself for me" (Galatians 2:20). "Nothing is more delightful," says Augustine, "to travelers in distant countries than the remembrance of their native land." And this ought to be the entertainment of Christians when they meet. Away with trifling vain discourses. Make everything give way to the refreshing memories of our future home. Were our hearts set on that rich inheritance above, it would be impossible for our tongues to be silent about it.

The glory to be revealed. It is hidden for the present, wholly unknown to the children of the world, and hardly known to the children of God, who are its heirs. Even those who know they are redeemed **share in** it, yet do not know much about it. They only know that it is above everything they know or can imagine. They may see things that make a great show here. They may hear about more than they see. They may think or imagine more than either they hear or see or can clearly conceive. But still they must think of this **glory** as superior to everything they know. If I see pompous shows or read or hear about them, I still say of them, "These are not like my inheritance; my inheritance far exceeds them." Indeed, my mind imagines things far beyond them—golden mountains and marble palaces; yet those fall short of my inheritance, which "'No eye has seen, no ear has heard, no mind has conceived what God has prepared for those who love him'" (1 Corinthians 2:9). Oh, the brightness of that glory when it will be **revealed**! If the heart dwelt a great deal on that **glory**, what in this perishing world could either lift it up or cast it down?

Verses 2-4

Be shepherds of God's flock that is under your care, serving as overseers—not because you must, but because you are willing, as God wants you to be; not greedy for money, but eager to serve; not lording it over those entrusted to you, but being examples to the flock. And when the Chief Shepherd appears, you will receive the crown of glory that will never fade away.

The Duty Commanded

That duty is, **Be shepherds of God's flock that is under your care, serving as overseers.**

We also see the necessary qualifications for this duty: **not because you must, but because you are willing, as God wants you to be; not greedy for money, but eager to serve; not lording it over those entrusted to you, but being examples to the flock.**

Further, we see the great advantage to be expected: **And when the Chief Shepherd appears, you will receive the crown of glory that will never fade away.**

Every step of the way our salvation is imprinted with infinite majesty, wisdom, and goodness. Yet poor, sinful people are used to bring Christ and souls together. Through the foolishness of preaching, the chosen of God are called, come to Jesus, and are made wise unto salvation. The life that is brought to them, the message of the word of life, is in the hands of poor people. This is the constant work of the ministry, and this is the command to those who are involved in this: **Be shepherds of God's flock that is under your care.** Jesus Christ descended to purchase a church and ascended to provide for it, to send down his Spirit. "He ascended on high . . . and gave gifts . . . some to be pastors and teachers, to prepare God's people for works of service" (Ephesians 4:7, 12). These gifts are to be used in feeding God's flock.

As we consider this, we note that the motivation springs from the fact that the flock is **God's flock.** This flock is not our own to use as we please, but is committed to our safekeeping by him who greatly loves his flock and will require us to give an account of our care for it. St. Paul uses similar thoughts about this flock being a purchased flock. "Guard yourselves and all the flock of which the Holy Spirit has made you overseers. Be shepherds of the church of God, which he bought with his own blood" (Acts 20:28). How reasonable it is that we should devote our strength and life to that flock for which our Lord laid down his life. We should be prepared to give our spirits for those for whom Christ shed his blood. "Had I," says that holy man, Bernard, "some of that blood poured out on the cross, how carefully I would carry it! And should I not be as careful of those souls that it was shed for?" If we valued what our Lord Jesus has done more, nothing would matter to us as much as other people's souls.

The Qualifications for Carrying out This Great Task

The apostle speaks about this negatively and positively. There are three evils the apostle wants to be removed from this work—reluctance, covetousness, and having the wrong kind of ambition. These should be replaced with willingness, an eagerness to serve, and exemplary behavior: **not because you must, but because you are willing, as God wants you to be; not greedy for money, but eager to serve; not lording it over those entrusted to you, but being examples to the flock.**

1. We are cautioned against being reluctant to serve the flock: **Not because you must.** We are warned against making our ministry into a trade that has to be followed rather than a calling that we choose to obey. We are to undertake this work with a **willing** heart.

2. **Not greedy for money.** A willing obedience to the Spirit of God within us moves every part of us in this holy work. The word **eager,** *prothumos,* indicates a mind that takes delight in carrying out its work and one in which love is expressed. Timothy took a genuine interest in the Philippians: "I have no one else like him, who takes a genuine interest in your welfare" (Philippians 2:20).

Nothing will give us the right motivation for this except loving Christ.

Our Lord Jesus asked Peter if he loved him, and then he told him to feed his sheep and to feed his lambs (see John 21:15-17). Love for Christ brings love for the souls of Christ's followers. Love is the great endowment of a shepherd of Christ's flock. Our Lord Jesus does not say to Peter, "Are you wise or learned or eloquent?" He asks, "Do you love me?"

3. The third evil is wrong ambition. This is either in having the wrong kind of authority or exercising authority in a tyrannical fashion, which is forbidden. "Jesus said to them, 'The kings of the Gentiles lord it over them; and those who exercise authority over them call themselves Benefactors. But you are not to be like that. Instead, the greatest among you should be like the youngest, and the one who rules like the one who serves'" (Luke 22:25-26). A ministerial sharpness is to be used in discipline. But lowliness and moderation must be dominant, not a domineering spirit. You should be examples to the flock in all holiness, and especially in humility and meekness. Our Lord Jesus is particularly an example for us: "Learn from me, for I am gentle and humble in heart" (Matthew 11:29).

But being examples to the flock. This is the pattern with which believers should stamp and print their spirits. "Follow my example, as I follow the example of Christ" (1 Corinthians 11:1). Without this, little fruit will follow from teaching. Nazianzen put it well when he said, "Either do not teach, or teach by living." The apostle Paul exhorts Timothy to "set an example for the believers in speech, in life, in love, in faith and in purity" (1 Timothy 4:12).

Some people may say this does away with all respect for learning. This is not the case. Rather, it removes poor, worthless encouragements and so makes way for one great one that is sufficient—namely, the **crown** that is spoken about in the next verse.

The High Advantage to Be Expected

And when the Chief Shepherd appears, you will receive the crown of glory that will never fade away. You will lose nothing by ignoring vain glory and worldly power. Let go of them, for a **crown** that is weightier than all of them put together and abides forever awaits you. Oh, how much more excellent this is. **The crown of glory** is pure glory and is not tainted with any pride or sinful vanity and is not in danger from such things. It is a crown **that will never fade away.** It is made of flowers that never wither, unlike temporary garlands that consist of fading flowers. "Woe to that wreath, the pride of Ephraim's drunkards," says the prophet Isaiah, "to the fading flower, his glorious beauty, set on the head of a fertile valley—to that city, the pride of those laid low by wine!" (Isaiah 28:1-2). But *this* **crown of glory** will remain fresh and in perfect luster for all eternity. Those who have this crown to look forward to may well trample on base gain and vain applause. All the pleasures of earth do not satisfy, but the heavenly pleasures do satisfy and last forever.

When the Chief Shepherd appears. This moment will come soon.

All effort for this **crown** is sweet. And what is there here to detain our hearts or that we should not most willingly let go of so we can later rest from our labors and receive our **crown?** Has any king ever been sad as he contemplated his coronation day drawing near? There will not be anything to be jealous or envious over. Every believer will be a king. Each person will wear a crown. Everyone will rejoice in other people's glory, and everyone will glory in the Lord Jesus Christ, who on that day will be all in all.

Verse 5

Young men, in the same way be submissive to those who are older. All of you, clothe yourselves with humility toward one another, because "God opposes the proud but gives grace to the humble."

Sin has upset everything. All the approaches people make to God are warped, as are their relationships to each other, until a new Spirit comes in to rectify this. This is exactly what this particular grace of **humility** does, which the apostle here recommends.

This grace controls the behavior:

1. Of the **young men . . . to those who are older.**
2. Of all men **toward one another.**
3. Of everyone toward God.

1. **Young men, in the same way be submissive to those who are older.** This I take to refer to an age difference, although it can be applied to a certain extent to those who are being governed by elders or presbyters, *presbuteroi,* who although they may not always be elderly should always give an exemplary and wise example. This is not a question of seniority but of ministry. Yet there is a sacred authority in it when it is rightly carried out that rightly commands the respect and obedience of those who carry out the government of the house of God.

The Spirit of Christ in his ministers is the thing that makes them truly elders who are "worthy of double honor" (see 1 Timothy 5:17). Without this, people may seek respect from other sources and, if they receive it, discover that they have only grasped a shadow.

From this, my brethren, learn that obedience is due to the discipline of God's house. This is all we plead for at this point. You must realize that if you refuse this and despise God's ordinance, he will feel you have been opposing him. If only everyone who has charge of God's house would look after God's interest completely! No matter what else seeks to take the place of God, nothing is lost by single-minded devotion to and love for our Lord's glory. "'Those who honor me I will honor, but those who despise me will be disdained'" (1 Samuel 2:30).

Submissive. Youth with their presumption and unbridled actions need to note this rule. It is an undeniable law, even written in nature, that younger people are to be **submissive** to elderly people. "Gray hair is a crown of splendor; it is attained by a righteous life" (Proverbs 16:31). It shines and has a kind of royalty over youth. But a graceless old age is a most despicable and lamentable sight. What advantages do unholy elderly men and women have just because they are old? Their white hairs merely indicate they are ready for wrath. "The righteous will flourish like a palm tree, they will grow like a cedar of Lebanon; planted in the house of the LORD, they will flourish in the courts of our God" (Psalm 92:12-13). The advantage of old age is that you can have great experience in the ways of God, disdain the world, greatly desire the love of God, and maintain a heavenly frame of mind and way of life.

It is a sad reflection to look back and think, "What have I done for God?" only to discover that you have done nothing except commit a world of sin against him!

2. All of you, clothe yourselves with humility toward one another. This explains the duty further. It is one that is universal and mutual— **toward one another.** This reverses the vain rivalry between people that arises out of self-love. Even the presence of Christ himself in all his humility did not prevent the disciples from asking the empty question, Who will be the greatest? "A dispute arose among them as to which of them was considered to be greatest. Jesus said to them, 'The kings of the Gentiles lord it over them; and those who exercise authority over them call themselves Benefactors. But you are not to be like that'" (Luke 22:24-26). The rule the apostle Peter gives is that each should work hard to be the lowest, **with humility toward one another.** The apostle Paul gives this same precept: "Honor one another above yourselves" (Romans 12:10). To insure that this is no empty ritual the apostle Peter tells Christians to **clothe** themselves with the grace of **humility.** Their **humility** must be as clear as the clothes they wear. But it must not be a mere show of humility, but heart lowliness, **humility** of mind.

As it is the bent of **humility** to in a sense hide other graces, so far as piety to God and our brethren will permit, so it would also willingly hide itself. It loves only to appear when it is necessary. It must be seen, and it is seen more often than many other graces, but it seeks not to appear. It is seen in the way a man or woman dresses with modesty. They do not dress in order to be noticed. Similarly, a truly humble person does not seek to be seen as being humble. Indeed, if it were not for running the risk of upsetting his brethren, he would rather disguise not only other things by **humility** but **humility** itself.

Therefore, the main point about **humility** is that its center is in the heart. Although **humility** will be observed in behavior, it should be seen as little as possible. It will say as little as possible about itself. Otherwise, humble speech and behavior only give a façade on the outside and do not represent the interior. This may be very refined and subtle, but it is the most dangerous kind of pride.

Remember how little we are acquainted with the real frame of Christianity. Some people commend this grace to other people but do not seek to **clothe** themselves in it. They love to be seen to be somebody and do not abase themselves. They find that the clothes of **humility** are too drab for them to wear. But when you view **humility** in the light of the Word, you will see its hidden richness. Do not only give it your approval, but put it on yourself. As is the case with all graces, so it is especially true of humility that though it makes the least, most unselfish show, when you come close to it you find it to be rich and comely. While it hides other graces, yet when they do appear under it, as sometimes they will, just a glance at them makes them much more esteemed.

Again, as with all graces, **humility** is especially prone to being counterfeited. To be low in your own eyes and willing to be so in the eyes of others—this is the very nature of heart humility. First, do not be deluded with a false conceit of advantages that you do not have. Second, do not be puffed up with vain conceit over the graces that you really possess. Third, do not be affected by the opinion of other people over what grace they may imagine you possess or over what they perceive you do actually possess. Is not the day coming when people will be taken off the false heights on which they stand and set on their own feet? "What a man is in God's sight, that is he and no more" (Francis of Assisi).

These are the ways in which you are to be humble in your life. First, look into yourself earnestly. Make a true evaluation of yourself. People select the good things in themselves but overlook their own defects. Every man is naturally his own flatterer; otherwise flatteries and false cries from other people would make little impression. They succeed because they are met with the same conceit. But let any man see his ignorance and set what he does not know against what he does know. He should place his secret follies and sins alongside his outward appearance of a blameless life. Then it will be impossible for him not to abase and abhor himself.

Second, look on the good in others and the evil in yourself. Make that comparison, and you will walk humbly. Most people do just the opposite, and that foolish and unjust comparison puffs them up.

Third, you are not required to be ignorant about the good that you genuinely possess. But beware of imagining that you possess what you do not have.

Fourth, pray much for a spirit of **humility**, which comes only through the Spirit of Christ. Otherwise, all your vileness will not humble you. When people hear about this grace or that grace, they soon think they possess it themselves and do not consider the natural enmity and rebellion of their own hearts and the necessity of receiving these graces from heaven. Therefore, in using all means of grace, be most dependent on the Divine Influence, and draw that grace to yourself through prayer.

Of all the evils of our corrupt nature, there is none more universal than pride, the greatest wickedness, exalting self in our own and other people's opinions. While I will not contest what was the first step in that complicated first sin, yet certainly the sin of pride was one, and a main ingredient in it. St. Augustine says truly, "That which first overcame man is the last thing he overcomes." We need to be continually watching and praying and fighting against our pride.

Above all, it is necessary that we watch ourselves in our best things, so self does not intrude, or so when it does break in, it is found and cast out again. This must happen if we are to have the kingdom of God established within us, if we are to do everything for God and for his glory. We need to be cut off from self and united to God, in order to have self-love turned into the love of God. And this is God's work. Nobody else can accomplish this. Therefore, the main weapon to use against pride, and in its conquest and in gaining **humility**, is certainly prayer. God bestows himself most on those who are most abundant in prayer. And those to whom he shows himself most are certainly the most humble.

"God opposes the proud." God **opposes**, that is, singles them out as his enemies and sets himself in battle array against them. That is the meaning of this word. Pride not only breaks rank but sets up a rebellion against God and does its best to dethrone him and usurp his place. Therefore, God orders his forces against it. Pride will not escape God's army and its own ruin. God will break it down and bring it low, for he is set on that course, and he will not be diverted.

"But gives grace to the humble." God's sweet dews and showers of grace slide off the mountains of pride, fall on the low valleys of humble hearts, and make them pleasant and fertile. The blown-up heart, puffed up with a fancy of fullness, has no room for grace. It is lifted up and is not fit to receive the graces that descend from above. "For the Lord bestows his blessings there, where he finds the vessels empty" (*The Imitation of Christ*).

Again, as the humble heart is most capable of receiving much, since it has been emptied and made holy and can hold the most, so it is the most thankful and acknowledges everything as having been received, while the proud cry out that everything is their own. The return of glory that is due from grace comes most freely and plentifully from a humble heart. God delights to enrich it with grace, and it delights in return to honor him with everything. The more it does this, the more readily God bestows still more upon it. This is the sweet communion between God and the humble soul. This is the noble ambition of **humility**, in respect of which all the aspirations of pride are brought low and abased. When all is reckoned, the lowliest mind is truly the highest.

Oh, my brethren, lack of this is the great reason behind everything else we lack. Why should our God bestow on us what we would bestow on our idol, self? Or if you do not idolize yourself, to idolize the thing, the gift that grace bestowed, is to put it in the place of God. Seek, therefore, to have your heart set on seeking grace, and do not rest in any gift or ignore God who gives all gifts. If we had this fixed in our hearts, our prayers would not be unanswered so often. "We are to rest in God above all things, and above all God's gifts" (*The Imitation of Christ*).

This is the only way to grow rich quickly. Come to God in your poverty and desire his riches, not for your own sake, but for his. In everything that you seek to possess, have your eye fixed on God's glory. What you have, use; and what you want, vow that you will use to God's glory. Only concern yourself with God's glory in everything that you seek to possess. Then you will be like Hannah in her prayer for her son: "The LORD has granted me what I asked of him. So now I give him [her son Samuel] to the LORD" (1 Samuel 1:27-28).

It is undoubtedly the secret pride and selfishness of our hearts that hinders much of the bounty of God's hand in the measure of our graces. The more we let go of ourselves, the more we will receive from God. How foolish we are if we refuse so blessed an exchange!

These verses in 1 Peter take account of our inner thoughts about ourselves and our behavior toward others and links them to another **humility**, in relation to God. They are inseparably connected to each other.

Verse 6

Humble yourselves, therefore, under God's mighty hand, that he may lift you up in due time.

This is pressed home by the words **God's mighty hand.** He is sovereign Lord of all, and all things bow to him. Therefore, it is right that you, his people, who profess loyalty and obedience to him, are most submissive and humble in your subjection to him in all things. Note the necessity of this action: **God's mighty hand.** It is a vain thing to flinch and struggle, for God does what he wishes. And his hand is so mighty that the greatest power of any creature is nothing in comparison to his. All is derived from God and therefore cannot stand against him. If you do not yield voluntarily, you will be forced into submission. If you will not be led, you will be pulled and drawn. Therefore, submission is your only option.

Another reason why this duty is driven home is that it contains certain advantages. Humble submission is the only way to achieve your goal. Do you want to be delivered and raised up from your affliction? You can only do this if you **humble yourselves . . . that he may lift you up in due time.**

This is the reason why God humbles you and weighs you down. When you are humbled, he lifts you up by his gracious hand. But it is not enough that he has humbled you by his hand, unless you also **humble yourselves** under his hand. Many people have endured great and numerous pressures, with one affliction following another, and have been humbled, and yet have not become humble. Their outward circumstances have humbled them, but they are not humble in their inner lives. Therefore, as soon as the pressure is off, they rise up again and grow as big as they were.

In due time. This is not the time that suits you, but God's wisely appointed time. You think, "I am sinking; if God does not help me now, it will be too late." But God sees it differently. He can let you sink still lower and bring you up again. He only acts at the most appropriate time. You cannot see this now, but you will see someday that God has chosen the best time. "Yet the LORD longs to be gracious to you; he rises to show you compassion. For the LORD is a God of justice. Blessed are all who wait for him" (Isaiah 30:18). Does God wait and you do not? What difficulty cannot firm belief in God's wisdom, power, and goodness surmount? So be humble under his hand. Submit not only your possessions, your health, your life, but your soul as well. Seek and wait for your pardon as a condemned rebel, with the rope around your neck. Lay yourself low before God, stoop at his feet, and ask permission to say, "Lord, I am justly under the sentence of death. If I fall under it, you are righteous, and I do now acknowledge this. But if it seems good to you to save the vilest, most wretched of sinners, and to show great mercy in pardoning such a great debt, the higher will be the glory of that mercy. However, I am resolved to wait until either you graciously receive me or absolutely reject me. If you do the latter, I do not have a word to say against it; but because you are gracious, I hope that you will yet have mercy on me." I dare say that the promise in the text belongs to such a soul, and **he may lift you up in due time.**

What if most or all of our life passes without feeling any spiritual comfort? Let us not overestimate this moment. Provided we can humbly wait for free grace and depend on the word of promise, we are safe. If the Lord will clearly shine on us and refresh us, this is much to be desired and prized. But what if he thinks it fit that we should be under a cloud of wrath all our days? It is but a moment. "For his anger lasts only a moment, but his favor lasts a lifetime; weeping may remain for a night, but rejoicing comes in the morning" (Psalm 30:5). What follows a lifetime of his favor is an endless lifetime. No evening follows the morning of eternity.

Verse 7

Cast all your anxiety on him because he cares for you.

Among other spiritual secrets this is a prime one—the combination of
lowliness and boldness, humble confidence. This is the true temperament of
a child of God toward his great and good Father. Nor can any have it but
those who are indeed God's children and have within them the spirit of
adoption that he sends into their hearts (see Galatians 4:6).

And these two the apostle here links: **Humble yourselves, therefore,
under God's mighty hand—Cast all your anxiety on him.** Upon that
same hand to which you should humble yourselves, you must cast all your
anxieties, all your care, for **he cares for you.**

Consider, first, the nature of this confidence—**Cast all your anxiety on
him**—and, second, its ground or basis—**because he cares for you.**

The Nature of This Confidence

Each of us has some desires and purposes that are predominant with us, in
addition to those that relate to our routine daily life. Our desires and cares
must be properly contained. What do we want? Do we think contentment
lies in so much and no less? When this is achieved, what we seek will appear
as far off as before. When children are at the foot of a high hill, they think it
reaches the heavens; and yet if they were at its summit, they would find
themselves as far off as before, or at least not close enough to make a difference. People think, "If only I had this, then I would be well." But when they
do achieve that, it is only a point from which they look higher and search
for something else.

We are indeed children when we think that the good of our estate lies in
its greatness and not how suitable it is for us. Here is a fool who wants to
possess certain clothes and thinks that the fancier and more expensive they
are, the happier he will be. Certainly as with dress, and with status and possessions and all other outward things, their benefit does not lie in their
greatness, but in how suitable they are for us. Our Saviour tells us specifically, "A man's life does not consist in the abundance of his possessions"
(Luke 12:15). Do you think great and rich people are more content than
people who have no riches? It is not the case. If they speak the truth, they
will tell you that this is not true. In place of need they have vain discontent-
ments such as a hawk that does not fly well or a dog that does not run well.
So then, I say, this is the first thing to be regulated. All childish, vain, need-
less cares are to be discharged and, as they are not worthy of casting upon
your God, are to be thrown out of your heart. Entertain no care at all except
those you wish to place in God's hands.

All necessary care God will receive. So then, rid yourself of all that you
cannot take to God. Seek a well-regulated, sober spirit. In the things of this
life, be content with food and clothing—not delicacies, but food; not orna-

ments, but clothes. This is the action our Saviour wants us to take: "So do not worry, saying, 'What shall we eat?' or 'What shall we drink?' or 'What shall we wear?'" (Matthew 6:31). First cut out superfluous care, then turn over to God the care of what is necessary. He will provide it. All that is required is for you to refer the matter to God's discretion entirely.

In your well-regulated affairs and desires, there is a diligent care and study of your necessary duty that God lays upon you. There is also a needed support in the work for its success, and this you ought to lay before God. In that way all the care is taken off you and transferred to God, even the duty that God lays on you. We offer our service, but the need for the skill and strength to carry it out we lay on God, and he allows us to do this. So for the success of the event we trust God completely. This is the way to walk contentedly and cheerfully homeward, leaning and resting all the way on him who is both our Guide and our Strength, who has us and all our good in his gracious hand. Much zeal for him and a desire for his glory, minding our duty in relation to that, is what he requires; and while we are bending our whole care to that, he undertakes the care of us and our condition. As St. Chrysostom said, "If you have a concern for the things that are God's, he will also be careful about you and yours."

The care of duty thus carried is sweet and light and does not clutter up the mind. It is united and gathered in God and rests there and walks in his hand all the way. He bears the weight of all our works and works them in us and for us. This is where our peace comes from. "LORD, you establish peace for us; all that we have accomplished you have done for us" (Isaiah 26:12). If you want to shake off the yoke of obedience, you will likewise be shaken off yourself. But if in humble diligence you walk in God's ways, trusting in his strength, there is nothing that concerns you and your work that God will not take care of. Are you troubled with fears, enemies, and snares? Untrouble yourself of that, for God is with you. "Teach me your way, O LORD; lead me in a straight path because of my oppressors" (Psalm 27:11). God will lead you. The Lord will forgive your sins. "You will again have compassion on us; you will tread our sins underfoot and hurl all our iniquities into the depths of the sea" (Micah 7:19). He will also rebuke your enemies. "Contend, O LORD, with those who contend with me; fight against those who fight against me" (Psalm 35:1). "No weapon forged against you will prevail, and you will refute every tongue that accuses you" (Isaiah 54:17). "When you pass through the waters, I will be with you; and when you pass through the rivers, they will not sweep over you. When you walk through the fire, you will not be burned; the flames will not set you ablaze" (Isaiah 43:2).

Do your own weaknesses discourage you? Has not God a way of helping in this? So pass this care on to him. Has not God said, "Then will the lame leap like a deer, and the tongue of the dumb shout for joy" (Isaiah

35:6)? Although there is nothing in you except unrighteousness and weakness, yet there is in God, for you, righteousness and strength. "They will say of me, 'In the LORD alone are righteousness and strength'" (Isaiah 45:24). When you are about to faint, a look to God will revive you. A believing look draws his strength into your soul and renews it. "He gives strength to the weary and increases the power of the weak" (Isaiah 40:29). Remember this: the more tender and weak you are, the more tender God is over you, and the stronger he will be in you. "He tends his flock like a shepherd: He gathers the lambs in his arms and carries them close to his heart; he gently leads those that have young" (Isaiah 40:11).

As for the success of your way of living, do not let that trouble you at all. That is in God's care. He wants you to unburden yourself of this completely and lay the burden on him. Do not worry yourself about how this or that will turn out. That is entirely up to God, and if you interfere with it, you immediately displease him and upset yourself. If you are struggling with what does not concern you and are agonizing over burdens that are not yours, it is no surprise if you are weighed down. Is it not right that if you bear the burdens your Lord calls you to pass on to him, you will be weighed down?

But how can my burden be removed? There is a faculty in this that not everyone has. A burden lies on them, and they are unable to cast it onto God. The way of relief is, doubtless, by praying and believing. These are the hands by which the soul can turn over to God what it itself cannot bear; all cares, the whole bundle, are most dexterously transferred in this way. "Do not be anxious about anything," says the apostle Paul (Philippians 4:6). A great word! But how can this happen? In this way, he says: "in everything, by prayer and petition, with thanksgiving, present your requests to God." Whatever is weighing you down, go and tell your Father. Put the matter into his hands, and so you will be freed from *merimna,* **anxiety**, that divisive care of which the world is full.

Do not be anxious anymore. When you are about to do anything or to suffer anything, go and tell God about it, and you will be done with worrying about it. Burden him with it, and you are no longer weighed down with anxiety. In this prayer faith acts; it is a believing request. "But when he asks, he must believe and not doubt" (James 1:6).

The Ground or Basis of This Confidence

Faith, in order to cast all anxiety on God, fixes on his promise. It cannot move but on firm ground, and the promises are that ground. For this purpose the apostle adds, **he cares for you.**

This must be certainly believed in the heart. First, there must be a firm belief in divine providence, that all things are managed and ruled by God with the highest power and wisdom. You must believe that God never sets aside his purposes and that no one can resist his power. "But the plans of the

LORD stand firm forever, the purposes of his heart through all generations" (Psalm 33:11).

Second, you must believe in his gracious providence to his own people, that God orders everything for their benefit. "And we know that in all things God works for the good of those who love him, who have been called according to his purpose" (Romans 8:28).

Third, you must have a particular confidence in God's goodwill toward you and his undertaking for you. Trust God, and that will be your condition. Cast your anxiety on him, and he takes it, for **he cares** about you. His royal Word is working on your behalf if you truly cast your care upon him. "Cast your cares on the LORD and he will sustain you; he will never let the righteous fall" (Psalm 55:22). Hand over your anxiety to him; heap it on him. He will bear it if you trust him.

The first inference to be drawn from this is that the children of God are the only people who have a sweet life. The world does not think this, and it regards them as poor, discontented people. But the world does not see what a carefree and secure life they are called to. While other people are struggling with all their individual projects and burdens and are eventually sunk by them, God's children are free of such pressure, for they have laid it all on God. If they make use of their advantage, they are not racked with worry about what may happen. They continue in God's strength, offering up their endeavors to him, and are certain about one thing—that all will be well. They lay their affairs and themselves on God and so are not oppressed by care. They have no care except for the care of love and how to please and honor their Lord. And for the skill and the strength they need, they also depend on God. From this springs unimaginable peace. "Do not be anxious about anything, but in everything, by prayer and petition, with thanksgiving, present your requests to God. And the peace of God, which transcends all understanding, will guard your hearts and your minds in Christ Jesus" (Philippians 4:6-7).

The second inference to be drawn from this is that the godly lack a great deal because they do not avail themselves of this privilege. They too often forget this sweet way and spend their days fretting, to no purpose. They wrestle with their burdens themselves and do not give their burdens completely to the Lord. They are overcome by anxiety, which God tells them to give to him, but which they refuse to do. They think they are sparing God, but in reality they are disobeying him and bringing dishonor to him, and so they grieve him. They find that this grief rebounds on them and still they do not learn to be wise.

Why do we deal with God in this way and bring grief on our souls at the same time? Oh, how unsuitable such a thing is to the child of God, for whom a life so much more excellent is provided! Has not God prepared a kingdom for you, and will he not provide all you need on the way to it? He knows that you need these things (see Matthew 6:32). Do not seek vain things, nor great things, for these likely are not fit for you. Rather, seek what is necessary in God's sight, and concentrate on that alone.

As for your spiritual state, hand that over to God's care as well. Do not be constantly concerned about thorny matters of doubt and arguments at every step you take. Rather, apply yourself simply to your duty. Slow as your progress may be, keep going, believe that God is gracious and pities you, and lay your cares on him. I am sure that many souls who have some grace in them stop making progress because they ask endless questions.

Learn to study resignation, for this is your great duty and will bring you great peace. Thus entrust everything into the Lord's hand, for what better hand is there? First, refer outward matters to God, heartily and fully. Then do not stay there, but go higher. If we have renounced the comforts of this world for God, let us renounce even spiritual comforts for God too. Put all in his will: "If I am in light, blessed are you; and if in darkness, even then you are also blessed." God may say, "Are not all comforts mine? I have them to bestow, and enough of them. Should not this allay your anxieties and strengthen your heart?" All mines of spiritual comfort and good are God's. So will he not furnish what is fit for you if you humbly wait for him and lay your worries upon his wisdom and love? This is the sure way to honor him with what we have and to obtain much of what we do not have. Certainly God deals best with those who refer everything to him.

Verses 8-9

Be self-controlled and alert. Your enemy the devil prowls around like a roaring lion looking for someone to devour. Resist him, standing firm in the faith, because you know that your brothers throughout the world are undergoing the same kind of sufferings.

The children of God, if they rightly take their Father's mind, are always free from perplexing anxiety, but they are never exempt from watching diligently. Thus we find here that they are allowed, in fact commanded, to **cast** all their care on their wise and loving Father and are assured of his care. Now, a worldly heart must not imagine that casting our care on God means we give up all watching. This is the ignorant and perverse mistake that the mind of the flesh makes. These two matters are linked to each other.

Cast all your anxiety on him . . . Be self-controlled and alert. This is the logic of Scripture. "For it is God who works in you to will and to act according to his good purpose" (Philippians 2:13). Thus you might possibly think you do not need to work at all, or if you do, it will be very easy. It is not so. "Therefore," says the apostle Paul, because "God . . . works in you to will and to act . . . continue to work out your salvation with fear and trembling" (Philippians 2:13, 12). We must work in humble obedience to God's command and in dependence on him who "works in you."

It is the same in this case. **Cast all your anxiety on him**, not so you may be free to pursue your own pleasure and slothful ease, but on the contrary so you may be more active and apt to watch. Now that you are free from the burden of troublesome anxiety, which would only weigh you down, you are more nimble, like a person who has had a load taken off his back, so you can walk and work and watch as a Christian should. That is why this burden is taken off you—so that you will be more able and disposed to carry out every duty that is placed upon you.

Observe how these two are linked, and then realize, first, that there is no right to believe without diligence and watchfulness. Realize that slothful reliance on blind thoughts of mercy will be a person's undoing. That kind of faith is a dead faith, and a deadly faith. Such people do not duly cast their care on God for their souls, for indeed they have no such care. Second, it is not right to be diligent without being believing.

There is in spiritual matters, as in other affairs, an anxious, perplexing care that disturbs the soul. It seems to have the heat of zeal and affection in it, but is not the natural heat that is healthy and prepares one for action. It is a diseased and feverish heat that makes one unfit for duty. It seems to make progress while it is in fact hindering progress. Instead of allowing people to make progress, it causes them to stumble and fall. Such is the distrustful care that many have about their spiritual life. They raise a hundred questions about the way they do everything. Indeed, we should endeavor to walk exactly and to examine our ways. We should do this especially in matters of holy things. We should do this in a diligent, calm, and composed way, for doubts retard progress and cause disorder in everything. But quietness of heart, firmly trusting in God for his strength and love in Christ, makes the work go well and is pleasing to God and refreshing to the soul.

Be self-controlled. The apostle has commanded this already in his letter. It is easy to attract people with a new idea, if our aim is to entertain people rather than edify them. There are only a few things that it is necessary for us to know and practice, and these are the ones that the apostle emphasizes.

This sobriety or seriousness of mind not only means temperance in eating and drinking, but in everything that concerns the flesh. Even diet, while not everything, is important. It is a most shameful idol to serve the stomach and to delight in feasts or to lose control of our appetites in our ordinary meals. "Eat to live, but live not to eat. There is no service so base as for a man to be a slave to his belly" (Bishop Bayly). But most people are guilty of this. We are to be weaned from this and raised above it in our minds. We are to "use the things of the world, as if not engrossed in them" (1 Corinthians 7:31).

We talk about this and listen to words about it, but we rarely apply it to ourselves. Every person has some trifle or earthly vanity, perhaps more than one, but especially a choice one that he will not allow to be taken away from him. We are like children who have a favorite toy. We have childish hearts, clinging to vanity. Some hanker after a particular position; others long for land or money. And we are drunk in our pursuit of these, so that though our hearts should be fixed on divine exercises, they cannot stand still, but go to and fro or fall down and go to sleep.

Therefore, these two matters are here linked to each other. **Be self-controlled and alert.** Overindulging ourselves with the delights or the desires and cares of earth makes us drowsy. The fumes that rise from them send us into a deep sleep. We lose interest both in God and in ourselves and our immortal souls.

The pleasures of sense are too gross for the divine soul. I call it divine, for by origin that is what it is. But we reduce it and make it flesh by gross earthly things, and so make it unfit to rise heavenward. Like drunkenness, intemperance in diet harms our natural spirits and makes them dull. In the same way love of inferior things makes the soul heavy, so that it cannot move freely in the spiritual realm. When some truth of grace is hindered by too much of the world, it is prevented from flowering.

If, then, you want to have free spirits for spiritual things, keep them under control in all temporal things. Do not give your hearts over to anything that belongs to this world. Learn to delight in God, and seek to taste his transcendent sweetness. That will curb all your inferior delights.

Be . . . alert. This watchfulness linked to self-control applies to every aspect of Christian living, since a Christian is surrounded with so many hazards and snares. "He who is contemptuous of his ways will die" (Proverbs 19:16). Most people travel nonchalantly through life. They attend public worship and have some form of private prayer but do not take care over how they live each day or what they say or to what or whom they give their hearts, though these things will most likely steal their hearts away from God.

Oh, my beloved, if only we knew our constant danger, it would shake us out of this miserable dead security that possesses us. We do not think about this, but there are traps set for us all along the way, in every path we tread and at every step we take, in our eating and drinking, in our work, at home and when we travel, even in God's house, and in our spiritual exercises both there and at home. If we were aware of this, or if we at least thought about it, we would take great care how we walked, and we would watch our words and our thoughts. "Above all else, guard your heart, for it is the wellspring of life. Put away perversity from your mouth; keep corrupt talk far from your lips. Let your eyes look straight ahead, fix your gaze directly before you. Make level paths for your feet and take only ways that are firm" (Proverbs 4:23-26).

Your enemy the devil. We are warned to **be alert**, and one reason given here is the devil's own alertness. There are usually two others listed with him as the main enemies of the soul—the world and our own flesh. But here **the devil** is specifically mentioned as the one who commands the war and uses the services of the other two against us.

We need to remember that Satan is against us and is hostile to us. If most people were asked, they would say they rarely think about this. They do not believe their spiritual life is in danger from him. As we keep a feeble guard against the allurements of the world and of our own corruption, so we do not keep a lookout for the devices of Satan but go on suspecting nothing, and so we become easy prey.

The least enemy who is despised and neglected often proves too great for us. The smallest appearances of evil, the least things that may prejudice our spiritual good, may do us great harm. Because we do not take any notice of them, they become very dangerous. They are under the command of a vigilant and skillful leader who knows how to take advantage whenever possible. Therefore, in things that we often regard as being of little account and not worth thinking about as possessing anything evil, we should learn to be suspicious and face this adversary. He usually hides himself and lies hidden until he attacks us when we are least expecting it. He is indeed **like a roaring lion.**

All his work is characterized by his aim to seek the destruction of our souls. The prey he hunts is souls, that they may be as miserable as himself. Therefore he is rightly called **your enemy.** He is the **enemy** of holiness and the **enemy** of our souls. The word *antidikos,* translated **enemy,** literally means an adversary or opponent in a lawsuit, an accuser in a court of law. The other common name for this evil spirit has a similar meaning; *diabolos* means to pierce through with darts and hence has come to mean to slander and to accuse. He studies our nature and attacks with suitable temptations. He knows our bias toward lust and worldly ways and pride. Sometimes he crouches down **like a . . . lion.** He waits for his opportunity and then pounces with a fierce assault.

The children of God are sometimes surprised by the strength of the devil's attacks. As the apostle says, he comes against us with "flaming arrows" (Ephesians 6:16). Though he is against humankind in general, he is especially enraged against God's children. He goes around and spots their weak points and then attacks them where they are least able to resist. He mounts special attacks against those who have made good progress in holiness and who are close to God. They were once under his power, and now that they have escaped from him, he pursues them, just as Pharaoh did with the Israelites. He roars after them as prey that was once in his den and under his paw but has now been rescued.

The similarity to a wild beast is in his strength, his diligence, and his cruelty. He has the strength of a **lion**; his diligence is shown in that he **prowls around**; and his cruelty is seen from his being a **roaring** lion, **looking for someone to devour.** In view of this, is it not most reasonable to **be alert**, to keep constant watch, and to see what comes in and what goes out? Should we not test everything the world offers and all the desires in our hearts? We should do this particularly after special new supplies of grace have been given, such as after the holy sacrament. At that point the devil will be most eager to catch rich booty. The pirates who allow the ships to go by empty keep them under close watch when they return heavily laden. So does this great pirate. Did he not assault our Saviour immediately after his baptism?

In order to stay **alert**, we must be **self-controlled.** This is a military metaphor. A drunken soldier is not fit to be on watch. We are exposed to the adversary when we indulge our various fancies and vanities. When we have made some progress in a conflict, or when the enemy appears to have retreated, we are most at risk and should stay **alert**. Beware when you think you are safest! That very thought makes you least safe. Always keep your spirits free from the lavish profusion of this world. Do not let your hearts become attached to anything in it. Be like Gideon's army, fit to follow God and victorious in him, not lying down to drink but just taking what is necessary. Remember our Saviour's own words: "Be careful, or your hearts will be weighed down with dissipation, drunkenness and the anxieties of life, and that day will close on you unexpectedly like a trap" (Luke 21:34).

Always pay more attention to your work and your warfare than to your pleasure and ease. Do not seek pleasure here. Your rest is not here. What a poor, short rest it would be if it were! Follow the Lord Jesus through conflicts and sufferings, and in a little while you will have victory, followed by everlasting triumph, rest, pleasure, and an unending feast, where there is no danger either of surfeiting or of wearying, but pure and perpetual delight. Convinced of this, you should be watchful. "Endure hardship with us like a good soldier of Christ Jesus. No one serving as a soldier gets involved in civilian affairs—he wants to please his commanding officer" (2 Timothy 2:3-4). Stand watching, and if you are attacked, resist.

Resist him, standing firm in the faith. Courage should be added to alertness. The person who watches and gives in seems to be like a person who is watching in order to welcome the enemy rather than to resist him. Bold resistance should continue even against countless assaults. For you have to deal with an enemy who will not easily give in but will try many different ways to defeat you. In all this, do not faint, but remain steadfast in your resistance.

This is easy to say, but how can it be achieved? This is how you will be able to do this.

Standing firm in the faith. Most people are in the grip of one of two evils—complacency or distrust. We easily fall from one into the other.

Therefore, the apostle exhorts us to stand firm against both these things. First, in the previous verse he warns us against assuming that everything is secure: **Be self-controlled and alert.** Here he warns us against distrust: **Resist him, standing firm in the faith.** He adds an encouraging consideration about the children of God in the world: **because you know that your brothers throughout the world are undergoing the same kind of sufferings.**

Standing firm, or solid, **in the faith.** This is absolutely necessary for resistance. We cannot fight on a quagmire. There is no hope of resistance unless you have some firm ground to stand on. Faith alone furnishes this. It lifts the soul up to the firm advanced ground of God's promises. There it cannot be moved, just as Mount Zion cannot be moved. The apostle Peter does not say you are to stand firm because of your own resolutions, but because you are **standing firm in the faith.** God's power, through faith, becomes ours, for it is contained in the word of promise. Faith takes hold of this and so finds almighty strength. "This is the victory that has overcome the world, even our faith" (1 John 5:4). Faith is our victory, and through it we overcome the prince of this world. Throughout the world all difficulties and all enemies are overcome by faith. Faith sets the stronger Lion of Judah against this **roaring lion** of the bottomless pit. And the delivering Lion opposes and defeats the devouring lion.

When the soul is surrounded on all sides so that it cannot escape, faith flies above it all and takes the soul up to Christ, where it is safe. That is the power of faith. It sets a soul in Christ, and there it looks down on all temptations like waves at the bottom of a rock, breaking themselves on the rock and becoming foam. When the floods of temptation rise and gather, and the soul is about to be swallowed up, then by faith it says, "Lord Jesus, you are my strength. I look to you for deliverance. Come now and rescue me!" In this way faith gains the victory. The guilt of sin is answered by Christ's blood, and the power of sin is conquered by his Spirit; and all afflictions that arise are nothing to these. Christ's love and presence make afflictions sweet and easy.

We make a mistake if we think of doing anything or being anything without Christ. We make a further mistake if we think anything is too hard for him to do. "Apart from me you can do nothing" (John 15:5). "I can do everything through him who gives me strength" (Philippians 4:13). "Everything." That is a big word, yet a true one. Humble confidence proves this is true when it is placed not in oneself, but in Christ. This kind of boasting is good. I am empowered by Christ. This frees the boast both from falsehood and from vanity. "My soul will boast in the LORD; let the afflicted hear and rejoice" (Psalm 34:2). Those who can truthfully say this can challenge the whole world and all its adverse powers, as the apostle Paul did in his own and in every believer's name:

Who shall separate us from the love of Christ? Shall trouble or hardship
or persecution or famine or nakedness or danger or sword? ... For I am
convinced that neither death nor life, neither angels nor demons, nei-
ther the present nor the future, nor any powers, neither height nor
depth, nor anything else in all creation, will be able to separate us from
the love of God that is in Christ Jesus our Lord.

—Romans 8:35-39

Because you know that your brothers throughout the world are
undergoing the same kind of sufferings. There is one thing that greatly
troubles the patience and weakens the faith of some Christians: they think
there is no one in the same condition that they are in. They do not believe
any other Christian has endured such temptations as they are facing. But the
apostle Paul bursts this deceit when he says, "No temptation has seized you
except what is common to man" (1 Corinthians 10:13). And here Peter
agrees: **Your brothers throughout the world are undergoing the same**
kind of sufferings.

We prefer to hear about ease and cannot, after all is said, bring our hearts
to accept that temptations and troubles are the saints' portion here and that
this is the royal way to the kingdom. But our King led the way in this
respect, and all his followers must go the same way.

Verse 10

And the God of all grace, who called you to his eternal glory in Christ,
after you have suffered a little while, will himself restore you and make
you strong, firm and steadfast.

The apostle closes his divine teaching and exhortations with a prayer, and
we follow this practice after the Word has been preached. St. Paul often did
the same, and even Christ did this, as is recorded in John 17, coming after
his sermon in the previous chapters. It would be good if both ministers and
people followed this way more often, in private, both for themselves and for
each other. Lack of this is the main thing that makes our preaching and hearing so barren and fruitless. The ministers of the Gospel should indeed be
like the angels of God, going between God and his people. In Luke 10 the
disciples are sent out to preach, and in Luke 11 they have the desire to pray:
"Lord, teach us to pray" (verse 1). Unless the seed sown by ministers is
secretly watered with their prayers and tears, little will germinate.

And the God of all grace, who called you to his eternal glory in
Christ. This prayer is similar to the apostle Paul's word to the Philippians:
"by prayer and petition, with thanksgiving, present your requests to God"
(Philippians 4:6).

In the prayer or petition consider, first, the matter and, second, the style.
The matter, or thing requested, is expressed in different brief words:

restore you and make you strong, firm and steadfast. While the two expressions in this verse mean roughly the same thing, they are not just repeated for the sake of repetition, for I believe the words are not entirely the same in their meaning. The first, **restore,** implies, more clearly than the rest, believers' advancement in victory over their remaining corruptions and infirmities and their progress toward perfection. The word **firm** has to do with both the inner inconstancy that is natural to us and the attacks of persecutions, temptations, and outward opposition. It implies the curing of the one and support against the other. **Make you strong** applies to the growth of their graces, especially gaining further graces in areas where they were weak. **Steadfast,** while it appears to be the same in substance as the word **firm,** nevertheless adds something that is well worth noting. It means to fix onto a sure foundation and so indeed may refer to him who is the foundation and strength of believers, on whom they build by faith— namely, Jesus Christ, in whom we have all, both victory over sin and an increase of grace, and also establishment of spirit and power so that we will persevere against all difficulties and assaults. Christ is that "precious cornerstone for a sure foundation" that is laid in Zion (Isaiah 28:16). That Rock supports the house founded on it, even in the midst of all winds and storms (Matthew 7:25).

And the God of all grace. Our Father is a spring of divine favor that cannot be drawn dry or diminished in any way.

The God of all grace is the God of imputed grace, of infused and increased grace, of furnished and assisting grace. The work of salvation is **all grace** from beginning to end. It is founded on free grace in the counsel of God, and it is brought about by his own hand. God's Son was sent in the flesh, and his Spirit, sent into the hearts of his chosen, applies Christ to the soul. **All grace** is in God, the living spring of grace. He is the God of pardoning grace who takes up all quarrels and makes one act serve for all reckonings between him and them. "I, even I, am he who blots out your transgressions, for my own sake, and remembers your sins no more" (Isaiah 43:25).

As he is the God of pardoning grace, so he is also the God of sanctifying grace, who refines and purifies all those he means to make into vessels of glory, and he has in his hand all the necessary means and ways of doing this. He purifies them through afflictions and outward trials, by the reproaches and hatreds of the world. The profane world knows little about how useful their enmity is to the graces and comforts of Christians when they dishonor and persecute them. In fact, Christians themselves hardly understand sometimes how great is the advantage of these things, until they come to wonder at their Father's wisdom and love.

But God's children are indeed most powerfully sanctified by the Spirit within them, without whom nothing else would be of any value to them.

The divine fire kindled within them is daily refining and sublimating them. The Spirit of Christ conquers sin and by the mighty flame of his love consumes the earth and dross that is in them. The Spirit of Christ makes their affections more spiritual and disengages them from all worldly delights. As they receive the beginning of grace freely, so they also receive all subsequent increases from the Spirit. Life from their Lord still flows and makes them grow, abates the power of sin, strengthens a fainting faith, quickens a languishing love, teaches the soul the ways of wounding, defeats strong corruptions, and fortifies its weak graces. God's grace in wonderful ways advances the good of his children by things not only harsh to them, such as afflictions and temptations, but through that which is directly opposite to their new nature, sin itself, for the grace of God raises them after they have fallen and strengthens them through their troubles. God's grace works humility and vigilance in them and sends them to Christ for strength, through the experience of their weaknesses and failings.

And as he is the God of pardoning grace and of sanctifying grace in the beginning and growth of it, so also he is the God of supporting grace. Without this controlling influence all the graces placed in us would lie dead and fail us in the time of our greatest need. This is the immediate assisting power that bears the soul through the hardest labors and sustains it in the sharpest conflicts, giving fresh strength. When we, with all the grace we have dwelling within us, are attacked, he steps in and pits his strength against the confident enemy who is at the point of triumph. When temptations have made an opening and have entered with great force, God's grace brings such help that they are driven back and beaten out. "For he [the Lord] will come like a pent-up flood that the breath of the LORD drives along" (Isaiah 59:19). Every siege can be broken by God's help, which comes from above.

From this a Christian learns that his strength is in God. For if God's received grace were always a sufficient safeguard and able to make itself good against all incursions, we might sometimes forget that we had received this grace and might look on it more as ours than as God's. We might have thought it was within us rather than flowing from God. But when all the forces we have are being overwhelmed, and yet we find the enemy being driven back, we are forced to acknowledge that it is God's hand at work. "God is our refuge and strength, an ever present help in trouble" (Psalm 46:1).

All of the apostle Paul's constant strength and grace in him could not stop that sharp, piercing point of temptation, whatever it was, from attacking him. "To keep me from becoming conceited because of these surpassingly great revelations, there was given me a thorn in my flesh, a messenger of Satan, to torment me" (2 Corinthians 12:7). He was driven to his knees, crying for help without which he could not hold out. "Three times I pleaded with the Lord to take it away from me" (verse 8). He was given an answer assuring him of help, a secret support that would strengthen him. "But he said to me, 'My grace is sufficient for you, for my power is made perfect in weakness'" (verse 9). God was telling the apostle Paul, "While your own grace, which I have already given you, is not enough, yet my grace—that is, the grace that is in me and that I will now give you for your help—will be enough."

This is our great advantage and comfort, that we have a Protector who is almighty and who is always at hand, who can and will hear us whenever we are surrounded and about to be defeated. Our King can and will hear us when we call and will send relief at the right time. We may be facing urgent hazards, but we will not be completely defeated. As we cry to him in our greatest needs, help appears. We may see the armies of the enemies first, but as we pray, we will see the chariots of fire and horsemen and will conclude that those with us are more than those who are with them (see 2 Kings 6:16-17).

The apostle Paul calls our God "the God who gives . . . encouragement" (Romans 15:5), and here he is said to be **the God of all grace**. In this we rejoice. In God's hand is everything that is good—our sanctification and consolation, assistance and assurance, **grace** and **glory**. His previous gifts did not discourage us from seeking more; indeed, they encourage us to go to him for our future needs. It is God's will that we have constant contact with him for all we need. He is so rich and so generous that he delights in our seeking and drawing much from him, and it is through believing and praying that we do so. If we did this more often, we would grow richer. But remember, all this grace that we can receive from **the God of all grace** must be from God **in Christ**. From him it flows to us, and to him we are directed. "For God was pleased to have all his fullness dwell in him" (Colossians 1:19). And this was for us, that we might know where to go to ask for help.

For the further opening up of God's riches expressed in this title **the God of all grace**, there is added one great act of grace—**who called you to his eternal glory**. This includes all the rest, for we have in it the beginning and the end of the work linked together—the first effect of grace on us in effectual calling, and the last accomplishment of it in **eternal glory**.

Who called you. I believe this calling does not simply mean the purpose of the Gospel in its general proclamation, in which the outward call lies, holding forth and setting before us **eternal glory** as the result of **grace**. Rather, it refers to the real bringing of a Christian to Christ, uniting him with Christ and so giving him a real and firm title to **glory**. This call powerfully works **grace** in the soul and secures **glory** to the soul. It gives it the right to that inheritance and fits it for it. And sometimes it gives it the evident and sweet assurance of it.

It is equally clear that the heirs of glory do not usually have this assurance within them, and hardly anyone has it all the time. Some travel on in a cloudy day and arrive home in this way, having sufficient light to find their way, but not seeing clearly the bright and full sunshine of assurance. Others have this assurance breaking forth at times but at other times are under a cloud, and some people have this assurance often. But since all meet in the end, so all agree in this in the beginning—that is, in the reality of the thing. They are made certain heirs of it in their effectual calling.

Through this the apostle advances his petition for their support and advancement in the way of **grace.** The way of our calling to so high and happy a position, if only we would consider it more often, would work on us and persuade us to have a better frame of mind and way of living. It would make our thoughts more noble and sublime, and our behavior would not be of this world.

All you who hear the Gospel are, in general, called to this **glory.** You have been told where and how you may lay hold of it. You have been told that if you will let go of your sins and embrace Jesus Christ, this **glory** will be yours. The way to obtain this gift is to receive Christ as Saviour, and at the same time as Lord and King. You are made his subjects, and so you are made kings.

The state to which Christians are called is not a poor and sad state, as the world believes. It is to no less than **eternal glory.** The world thinks it strange that believers do not indulge in the delights of sin. But they do not know about the infinite gain that Christians have, for they have exchanged the dross of this world for the pure gold of heaven. The world sees what the Christians leave, but they do not see what they are going toward, what their new purchase is in another place. They see what they suffer, but not what they look forward to and will attain at the end of those sufferings that will shortly cease. We may say, "How small is what I forsake, how great that which I pursue!"

What their future holds is glory, eternal glory, **his eternal glory,** true, real glory. Everything that goes under the name of glory here is but a shadow of this **glory.** People naturally desire glory and seek it. But they are naturally ignorant of its true nature and place. They seek it where it is not. As Solomon said, "Cast but a glance at riches, and they are gone, for they will surely sprout wings and fly off to the sky like an eagle" (Proverbs 23:5). Earthly glory has no substance or reality. But the **glory** above is true, real **glory.**

Eternal. This adds a great deal. People would have more reason to pursue the glory of the present world, such as it is, if it were lasting, if it stayed with them when they obtained it, and if they stayed with it to enjoy it. But how soon do they part! They pass away, and the glory passes away, both like smoke. Our life itself is like a vapor. And as for all the pomp and magnificence of those who have the greatest outward glory and make the fairest show, it is but a show, a pageant that goes through the street and is seen no more. But this **glory** has length of day with it—**eternal glory.** A single thought of that swallows up all the grandeur of the world and the noise of reckoning years and ages. Had one person continued, from creation to the end of the world, at the height of earthly dignity and glory, admired by all, yet at the end ending in everlasting oblivion, that would have been nothing when compared with this **eternal glory.** But alas, we cannot be made to believe and deeply take the impression of eternity, and this is our undoing.

In Christ. Your portion, while still outside Christ, was eternal shame and misery, but in him it is all **glory.** And this has in it likewise an evidence of the greatness of this **glory.** It can be no small estate that the blood of the Son of God has purchased.

His . . . glory. This **glory** is what God gives, and he gives it as his best gift to his chosen, his children. If there is anything that has delight or worth in the things he gives even to his enemies, if there is a variety of good things for those who hate him, oh, how excellent must those things be that he has reserved for his friends, for those he loves and causes to love him!

This **glory**, his gift, is in fact the beholding and enjoying of him. This we cannot now conceive, but one blessed day the soul will be full of God and will be satisfied and ravished with full vision! Should we not wonder that such a condition is provided for human beings, for wretched sinful people? "When I consider your heavens, the work of your fingers, the moon and the stars, which you have set in place, what is man that you are mindful of him, the son of man that you care for him?" (Psalm 8:3-4). And this is provided for me, who is as wretched as any who have fallen short of this **glory**, a base worm taken out of the mire and washed in the blood of Christ, then set to shine in glory without sin! Oh, the wonder of this! How it should excite us to praise God when we think of such a One who will bring us in this way to this crown! How this hope will sweeten the short sufferings of this life! And death itself, which is so deeply bitter in itself, is most of all sweetened by this, as being nearest it and setting us into it. It little matters that you are poor, diseased, and despised here! Consider what it will be like there. What can we either desire or fear if our heart is deeply fixed on **his . . . glory**? Who would refuse the interim—**after you have suffered a little while**? How soon this will all be over! Then we will know the beginning of this glory that never ends.

Verse 11

To him be the power for ever and ever. Amen.

People who do not pray a great deal do not realize their own needs and emptiness. Those who do not praise God a great deal know little about God's goodness and greatness. Humble Christians have hearts in some measure framed to both. They have within them the best Teacher, who tells them how to pray and how to praise and makes them delight in both.

So the apostle, having added prayer to his teaching, here adds praise to his prayer: **To him be the power for ever and ever. Amen.** The living praises of God spring from holy affection, and that affection springs from a divine light in the understanding. So the psalmist says, "sing ye praises with understanding" (Psalm 47:7, KJV). This is a spiritual knowledge by which God sets the soul in tune for his praises, and therefore most people cannot join in this song. They cannot sing it because they are ignorant of God and are not acquainted with him. Praise is unseemly in the mouth of fools. They spoil it and sing out of tune. Observe, first, what is ascribed and, second, its term or endurance. The former is expressed in two words: **Glory** (verse 10) and **power. Glory** is the shining forth of God's dignity and the knowledge and acknowledgment of it by his creatures. His excellency is confessed and praised, and his name is exalted, so that service and homage are paid to him. Nobody can add anything to him, for how could that be? But as it is the duty of such creatures as he has fitted for it to give him praise, it is also their happiness. All created things do indeed declare and speak of **his . . . glory.** The heavens declare his glory, and the earth and the sea echo his praises. But God has especially made his rational creatures so that they take notice of his glory in everything else he has made.

In this lower world it is human beings alone that are made capable of observing the glory of God and of offering him praises. George Herbert expressed it well in saying that man is "the world's High Priest":

> Man is the world's High Priest: he doth present
> The sacrifice for all; while they below
> Unto the service mutter an assent,
> Such as springs use that fall, and winds that blow.
> He that to praise and laud Thee doth refrain,
> Doth not refrain unto himself alone,
> But robs a thousand who would praise Thee fain;
> And doth commit a world of sin in one.

All the creatures bring their oblations of praise to him, to offer up for them and for himself, for whose use and comfort they are made. The light and motion of the heavens and all the variety of creatures below them say to man: "He who made us and you, and made us for you, is great and wise and worthy to be praised. And you are better able to say this than we; therefore praise him on our behalf and on your own. Oh, he is great and mighty; he is the Lord our Maker.

Power here means not only ability but authority and royal sovereignty. As God can do all things, so he rules and governs all things and is King of all the world and Lord paramount. All hold their crowns before him. "The nobles of the nations assemble as the people of the God of Abraham, for the kings of the earth belong to God; he is greatly exalted" (Psalm 47:9). He disposes states and kingdoms at his pleasure, establishes or changes, turns and overturns, all as seems good to him. He not only has the power to do this but the right to do this. "The Most High is sovereign over the kingdoms of men and gives them to anyone he wishes" (Daniel 4:32). He pours contempt on princes when they condemn his power.

The length of his glory is **for ever and ever.** Even in the short life of human beings, people who are raised very high in position and in popular esteem may, and often do, outlive their own glory. But the glory of God lasts as long as God himself, for he is unchangeable. His throne is **for ever and ever.** His wrath is **for ever and ever.** His mercy is **for ever and ever.** And therefore his **glory** is **for ever and ever.**

Should it not be lamented that God is so little glorified and praised? Should it not be lamented that the earth, being so full of his goodness, is so empty of his praise from those who enjoy and live on it?

How far are the majority of Christians from making it their great work to exalt God and ascribe power and glory to his name! They are so far from this that often all their ways dishonor him. They seek to advance themselves, to serve their own lusts and pleasures, but they do not think about God's glory at all. In fact, the apostle Paul's complaint holds good against us all: "Everyone looks out for his own interests, not those of Jesus Christ" (Philippians 2:21). It is true there are some exceptions, but they are so few that they are, as it were, drowned and smothered in the crowd of self-seekers, so that they are not seen. After all the judgments of God upon us, how often luxury and excess, uncleanness, and all kinds of profanity still defy the very light of the Gospel and the rule of holiness shining in it! Scarcely anything is a matter of common shame and scorn, but the power of godliness turns our true glory into shame, and we glory in that which is indeed our shame. Holiness is not only our truest glory but that in which the ever-glorious God especially glories. God has made himself particularly known by the name "The Holy God." And the express style of his glorious praises uttered by seraphim is, "Holy, holy, holy is the LORD Almighty; the whole earth is full of his glory" (Isaiah 6:3).

Instead of sanctifying and glorifying this holy name, how the language of hell—oaths and curses—abounds in our streets and houses! How frequently that blessed name, which angels are blessing and praising, is abused by base worms! Notwithstanding all the mercies multiplied upon us, where are our praises, our songs of deliverance, our ascribing glory and power to our God who has gone before us with loving-kindness and tender mercies? He has removed the strokes of his hand and made cities and villages populated again that were left desolate of inhabitants. [This was most probably written in 1653. The years 1652 and 1653 were remarkable for fine weather and plentiful harvests; and under Cromwell the country was enjoying a security and peace it had never known before and was already beginning to recover from the desolating influences of sword, pestilence, and famine.— Editor's note.]

Why do we not stir up our hearts, and one another, to extol the name of our God and say, "Give unto the Lord glory and strength; give unto the Lord the glory due to his name"? Have we not seen the pride and glory of all flesh stained and abased? Were there ever times that more revealed people's folly and weakness and God's wisdom and power? Oh, that our hearts were set to magnify God, according to that word so often repeated: "Let them give thanks to the LORD for his unfailing love and his wonderful deeds for men" (Psalm 107:8).

Reflect, second, on this: What wonder is it that the Lord loses the reverence of his praises at the hands of the common ungodly world when even his own people fall as far behind as they usually do? The dead cannot praise him, but those God has brought alive by his Spirit should not be taken with deadness and dullness when it comes to exalting God. For help in understanding this, take the following three directions.

The first direction is that we should seek a fit temper and must labor to have our hearts brought to a proper disposition for his praises. We should ensure that these are spiritual. All spiritual services require that, but this service most, as being indeed the most spiritual of all. Affection for the things of this earth draws the soul so low that it cannot rise to the height of a song of praise. If we thus observed ourselves, we would find that when we let our hearts entangle themselves in inferior desires and delights, they are unfitted generally for holy things, and especially for the praises of our holy God. Creature loves debase the soul and turn it to earth, and praise is altogether heavenly.

You should also seek a heart that is purified from self-love and is possessed with God's love. The heart that is ruled by its own interest is scarcely ever content, and is ever subject to new disquiet. If God's love dominated us, we would love his actions and bless his name in everything. We would be content to follow God's will, whatever it was. Thus we would say to everyone, "This is the will and the hand of my Father, who does everything well and wisely. Blessed be his name."

The soul that has this attitude would praise God even in the depths of troubles. This includes not just outward afflictions but the saddest inner condition, in which God would still be extolled. Such a person would say, "No matter how God deals with me, he is worthy to be loved and praised. He is great and holy; he is good and gracious. Whatever his way and thoughts toward me are, I wish him glory. If he decides to give me light and refreshment, I will bless him; and if he decides to give me darkness, I will bless him. Glory to his name!" This is the way pure love would view God and give him praise.

Work for a fixed heart. If it is refined from creature love and self-love, spirituality and love of God will fix it. Then it will be fit to praise, which an unstable, uncomposed heart can never be, any more than an instrument can be harmonious and fit to play if it has loose strings. Shall we not say with David, "My heart is steadfast, O God, my heart is steadfast; I will sing and make music" (Psalm 57:7)? Oh, that we would pray much that God would fix our hearts on him; and then, once he has done that, we would praise him much.

The second direction is that if any due disposition is once attained for praise, then the heart must study the matter of praise.

Study the infinite excellency of God in himself. While we know little about this, yet we know and should consider that his excellency is far beyond what all the creatures and all his works are able to testify about him. He transcends all we can speak or hear or know of him.

Look on him in his works. Can we behold the vast heavens above or the firm earth beneath us or all the variety of his works in both without being stirred to holy wonder that leads us on to sing his praises? Oh, his greatness and might and wisdom shining in all these! "How many are your works, O LORD! In wisdom you made them all; the earth is full of your creatures" (Psalm 104:24). But above all is that marvel of his works, the sending of his Son. This is the mystery that the apostles magnify in their writings, which is also so much magnified in this letter and which forms the chief incentive to the ascription of praise with which it closes.

This praise especially looks back to the style in the prayer in verse 10: **The God of all grace, who called you to his eternal glory in Christ.** This praise looks through the work of saving the redeemed by the blood of his Son and how he maintained his own work in them, then brought his chosen safe to glory. That perfecting and establishment is spoken about in the previous verses. It is this that so affected the apostle in the very beginning of this letter that he had to break out into praise: "Praise be to the God and Father of our Lord Jesus Christ! In his great mercy he has given us new birth into a living hope through the resurrection of Jesus Christ from the dead" (1:3). He begins there in praise, and here he ends in praise, and so encloses everything within that divine circle.

As we consider these things in general, we should also reflect on God's particular dealing with us, his good providence both in spiritual and temporal matters. If only we would look, we would find countless mercies. And if we knew the holy Scriptures better, and if we took more delight in them, they would make us more aware of these things and give us light to see them and warm our hearts and excite them to praising God for all his mercies to us.

The third direction concerns the heart that is partly disposed to praise. It should study this matter and give itself to praising God. Aim at praising God in everything. This is continual praise. See his glory in everything, and most of all desire, as your great end, that his name may be exalted. This is the excellent way indeed. We should start the song of praise here and long to be in heaven where it will never end. **To him be the power for ever and ever. Amen.**

Verses 12-14

With the help of Silas, whom I regard as a faithful brother, I have written to you briefly, encouraging you and testifying that this is the true grace of God. Stand fast in it. She who is in Babylon, chosen together with you, sends you her greetings, and so does my son Mark. Greet one another with a kiss of love. Peace to all of you who are in Christ.

This is a kind of postscript and contains a testimony of the bearer and the apostolic form of greeting. The apostle speaks of the length of his writing: **I have written to you briefly.** And he states his purpose in writing: **testifying that this is the true grace of God.** This is also the purpose of our preaching, and we should each seek to accomplish this by the Word and by mutual exhortations. Sometimes a few words can greatly help to establish us in the faith. We are not only to believe—we must also remember that there is truth in our hopes, and they do not deceive us. They are not imaginary, as the world thinks, but they are **the true grace of God.** When everything else vanishes, this truth will appear in its fullness.

An increase in Christian love, a growing respect and affection for one another, is not merely an empty compliment but is the very stamp and badge of Jesus Christ upon his followers. It is, therefore, to be observed most carefully that those who in any way willingly break away from this will be unhappy. Oh, let us beware of ever doing this. We must follow **peace,** even when it seems to fly away from us!

This **peace,** which belongs to those who are in Christ, is indeed within them and with God. But through him, it is also with **one another,** and in that respect it is to be desired jointly with the other.

Those who are in Christ are the only children and heirs of true **peace.** Others may dream of it and have false peace for a time, and wicked people may wish they possessed it. But that is a most vain hope and will come to nothing. But to want it for those who are in Christ is right, for all solid peace is founded on him and flows from him. "And the peace of God, which transcends all understanding, will guard your hearts and your minds in Christ Jesus" (Philippians 4:7).

2 Peter

By Griffith Thomas

Introduction

Before proceeding to the detailed study of the letter, it is useful to consider it as a whole. It should be read through at one sitting, to gain a general idea of its substance; then it might be read again, with special reference to the following points.

The Writer

1. Notice his claim for himself (1:1). He at once speaks of his personal relation to Christ and the spiritual experience arising out of that relationship.

2. He is an old man (1:13-14). Evidently the end of life is at hand. He speaks of his death as imminent.

3. He remembers early days. The reference to his approaching death (1:14) is clearly a reminiscence of the conversation between our Lord and himself recorded in John 21:18. He also refers in vivid detail to the Transfiguration (1:16-18). It is noteworthy that his companion on that occasion, John, also remembers and records his experience of the Transfiguration (John 1:14).

4. He alludes to his first letter (3:1).

5. He refers to St. Paul (3:15-16). This is striking testimony to the importance of St. Paul's writings in the church at that early date. It is also a beautiful and significant indication of the relationship between the two great apostles.

The Readers

1. They are generally referred to as Christians (1:1, 4).

2. They are not recent converts (1:12).

3. They evidently know the Old Testament (1:20; 2:4-8, 15). Whether they are Jewish or Gentile Christians, it is impossible to say.

4. They were in danger from false teachers (3:2, 17). The special peril was antinomianism, from men who professed godliness but were in reality reprobate (cf. Titus 1:16; 2 Timothy 3:5, 8).

The Purpose

A careful study of the letter will elicit the following points as included in the apostle's writing.

1. To remind them of pressing needs (3:1-2, 8, 17). Notice the special emphasis on the word *remembrance* (KJV).

2. To exhort them to holy diligence (1:5, 10; 3:14). Another keynote to the letter is found in the word *diligence* (KJV).

3. To warn them against deadly error (2:1; 3:3, 17). The danger felt was from those who in words pretended to be Christian teachers but whose deeds disgraced their profession.

4. To encourage them to experience spiritual progress (1:8, 11; 3:14, 18). The stress laid on "knowledge" and growth is another prominent feature of the letter.

This alternation of reminder and warning with exhortation and encouragement runs through the letter and shows the double purpose and aim. We see it summed up in 3:17-18 in the negative and positive aspects.

Analysis

Like the first letter, there is no clear and logical outline of the thought, but the general idea seems to be expressed in three main sections, each introduced by a personal reference to the writer himself, and each containing a special exhortation based on a special reason.

1. 1:1-11. Divine gifts (verses 1-4) and human response (verses 5-11). Exhortation to earnestness (verses 5, 10).

2. 1:12—2:22. Divine prophecy (1:16-21) and human travesty (2:1-22). Exhortation to watchfulness (1:19).

3. 3:1-18. Divine words (verse 2) and human mockery (verses 3-10). Exhortation to holiness (verses 11, 14, 18).

General Notes

1. The relation of 2 Peter to the first letter.
   a. The keynote of 1 Peter is "hope" in view of the present sufferings. The keynote of 2 Peter is "knowledge" in view of present dangers (1:2-3, 5, 8, 12, 20; 2:20-21; 3:3, 5, 8, 18).
   b. Second Peter is thus a sequel (3:1) written on account of different circumstances in the life of the church.

c. Several points of contact between the two letters should be noted.

(1) The end in view (1 Peter 1:5; 4:7; 2 Peter 3:10, 12).

(2) Prophecy and its definite source (1 Peter 1:10-11; 2 Peter 1:20-21).

(3) The small number of those saved from the Flood (1 Peter 3:20; 2 Peter 2:5; 3:6).

(4) A use of "goodness" ("virtue," KJV) that is unique in the New Testament (1 Peter 2:9; 2 Peter 1:3).

d. Several points of contrast are also evident.

(1) In 1 Peter Christ's death and resurrection are emphasized, in 2 Peter Christ's present exaltation.

(2) First Peter is full of Old Testament quotations and allusions; 2 Peter has no quotations, only allusions to historic facts.

2. The relationship between 2 Peter and Jude.

a. There is an evident use of one writing by the author of the other (compare 2 Peter 2:1-16 and Jude 4, 11).

b. Authorities differ as to which is earlier; some arguing for the priority of Jude (Alford, Salmon), others for the priority of 2 Peter (Lumby, Bigg).

3. The language and style. This is very picturesque and poetical, with quite a number of unusual words. Both letters are alike in these respects. Differences between them in regard to language and style are doubtless due to differences of topics and, it may be, of amanuenses.

A Special Note

Those who desire to study the questions connected with the genuineness of this letter are referred to Alford, Lumby (*Speakers' Commentary*), Caffin (*Pulpit Commentary*), and especially to Bigg's very able discussion (*International Critical Commentary*). There do not seem to be any other alternatives than genuineness and forgery. Either it is the work of the apostle Peter, or else his name is used to give it a show of authority. The latter alternative is surely no real instance of "an obvious literary device" (*Hastings' Bible Dictionary*) but rather would be a case of "religious fraud." The writer's claims to the name and position of apostle and to personal knowledge and experience of the Transfiguration are too definite and solemn to be questioned. The church of God has hardly been deceived all through the ages.

2 Peter
Chapter 1

Verses 1-4

Simon Peter, a servant and apostle of Jesus Christ, To those who through the righteousness of our God and Savior Jesus Christ have received a faith as precious as ours: Grace and peace be yours in abundance through the knowledge of God and of Jesus our Lord. His divine power has given us everything we need for life and godliness through our knowledge of him who called us by his own glory and goodness. Through these he has given us his very great and precious promises, so that through them you may participate in the divine nature and escape the corruption in the world caused by evil desires.

The opening words (verses 1-2) are marked by characteristic thoughts that run through the entire letter—for example, **faith, righteousness, Savior, knowledge.** Then a foundation is at once laid (verses 3-4) in a statement of the divine gifts by which alone the Christian life becomes possible.

Personal Greetings

1-2. Simon Peter, a servant and apostle of Jesus Christ, To those who through the righteousness of our God and Savior Jesus Christ have received a faith as precious as ours: Grace and peace be yours in abundance through the knowledge of God and of Jesus our Lord.

 1. The writer of the letter.

  a. His name: **Simon Peter.** The double name recalls the twofold aspect of his life—before and after discipleship to Christ. This combination of names is not found in St. Mark or Acts. The recurrence to the old name of the early days is an illustration of an old man's reminiscences. The Greek is "Simeon," as in Acts 15:14.

  b. His title: **servant and apostle** (compare Romans 1:1; Titus 1:1). Here we see the two sides of the Christian life—his general relationship as a servant, and his special position as an apostle. The order of the two is worth noting.

2. The recipients of the letter.

    a. Their spiritual position: **To those who . . . have received a faith as precious as ours.** In 1 Peter the Christians are first of all described by their geographical position. Here they are only described by their spiritual experience. **Precious** is a word characteristic of Peter's two letters (see 1 Peter 1:7, 19; 2:6-7). How is faith **precious**? Because it links us to God; it keeps us safe in God and is the channel of spiritual purification (Acts 15:9; Galatians 2:20; Hebrews 11:6; 1 Peter 1:5). In speaking of their faith as being **as precious as ours,** the apostle shows his tact and courtesy in putting himself on the same level of spiritual privilege. **Received** implies divine lot or gift. (The same word is used in Luke 1:9 and John 19:24.)

    b. Their spiritual foundation. **Through the righteousness** is literally "in the righteousness" and probably refers to God's righteousness as the object of our faith (see Romans 1:17; 3:26). Some think, however, that the reference here is not to the righteousness that makes atonement but to the justice of God that gives equally to all.

Note the use of the phrase **God and Savior,** probably referring to our Lord since there is no article with the second substantive (see 1:11; 2:20; 3:2, 18; Titus 2:13).

3. The greeting of the letter.

    a. The substance of the prayer: **Grace and peace.**

    b. The measure of the request: **in abundance.**

    c. The source of the supply: **through the knowledge of God and of Jesus our Lord.** See similar greetings in 1 Peter and Jude, and note the spiritual order of grace and peace as cause and effect. The reference to **knowledge** as the source of **grace and peace** at once brings into prominence the keyword of the letter. The Greek is *epignosis,* full or mature knowledge. It is found fifteen times in St. Paul, once in Hebrews, four times in 2 Peter, and nowhere else. All spiritual grace comes from our personal knowledge and experience of God (see verse 3). Those who "know their God" will be strong (Daniel 11:32; see also Job 22:21 and John 17:3).

The Divine Provision

3-4. His divine power has given us everything we need for life and godliness through our knowledge of him who called us by his own glory and goodness. Through these he has given us his very great and precious promises, so that through them you may participate in the divine nature and escape the corruption in the world caused by evil desires.

1. Its character: **life and godliness** (verse 3). Note these two elements of Christian experience: the possession of **life** and its expression in **godliness**. The latter word is found here and in 3:11 and is specially characteristic of the Pastoral letters. The order of the two is also to be noted.

2. Its spirit: **given us** (verses 3 and 4). Notice the emphasis in this representation of the thought of God's free and full gift. Not human merit but divine love characterizes this provision.

3. Its extent: **everything** (verse 3). That is, **everything** for the commencement, continuance, and completion of the Christian life is thus provided. The certainty and encouragement of this assurance is evident.

4. Its guarantee: **His divine power** (verse 3). This is the adequate and permanent assurance to the believer of the provision for his life.

5. Its secret: **through our knowledge of him who called us by his own glory and goodness** (verse 3). This divine provision only becomes available in union and communion with God. Note again the reference to **knowledge**, and let it be remembered that this word always implies much more than intellectual perception, for it includes spiritual experience. Note the Revised Version translation of the last clause: "by his own glory and virtue." The Greek word translated "virtue" (see also 1 Peter 2:9; Philippians 4:8) is used by the Septuagint to translate "glory." Here it evidently refers to the divine nature and perhaps is best rendered "energy." The thought is that God calls us by his character of glory and power. The King James Version is clearly inaccurate here.

6. Its channel: **his very great and precious promises** (verse 4). These are God's means of bringing us into the knowledge of him and thereby providing us with all things needed **for life and godliness.** The promises of the Gospel include all, whether of the old or new covenants (see 2 Corinthians 1:20; 7:1; Galatians 3:14, 22; Ephesians 1:13; Hebrews 9:15; 10:36; 11:9, 11, 13, 39).

7. Its purpose: **so that through them you may participate in the divine nature** (verse 4). This promise introduces us to fellowship with God, through which we are made partakers of his divine life. For **participate** see 2 Corinthians 13:1-4; Philippians 2:1; Hebrews 12:10. This is the culmination of redemption—union and communion with God (1 John 1:3).

8. Its prerequisite: **escape the corruption in the world caused by evil desires** (verse 4). Here the apostle indicates their former experience and at the same time their full deliverance from it. Like Lot, they have escaped (2:18, 20). It is only after having escaped that God's purpose of fellowship becomes possible.

Topics for study

1. The revelation of God to man.
   a. His righteousness (verse 1).
   b. His knowledge (verse 2).

c. His power (verse 3).
2. The gifts of God to men.
   a. Faith (verse 1).
   b. Graces (verses 2-3).
   c. Promises (verse 4).
3. The purposes of God for man.
   a. Life (verse 3).
   b. Godliness (verse 3).
   c. Union (verse 4).

Verses 5-11

For this very reason, make every effort to add to your faith goodness; and to goodness, knowledge; and to knowledge, self-control; and to self-control, perseverance; and to perseverance, godliness; and to godliness, brotherly kindness; and to brotherly kindness, love. For if you possess these qualities in increasing measure, they will keep you from being ineffective and unproductive in your knowledge of our Lord Jesus Christ. But if anyone does not have them, he is nearsighted and blind, and has forgotten that he has been cleansed from his past sins. Therefore, my brothers, be all the more eager to make your calling and election sure. For if you do these things, you will never fall, and you will receive a rich welcome into the eternal kingdom of our Lord and Savior Jesus Christ.

The apostle has laid the foundation in the divine gifts (verses 1-4) provided in sufficiency and bounty for life and godliness. Now comes the complementary truth of the need of human response to divine provision. The keynote of the passage is **make every effort** (verse 5) and **be all the more eager** (verse 10).

The Earnest Call to Diligence

5. For this very reason, make every effort to add to your faith.

1. The divine foundation: **For this very reason.** This phrase refers back to the divine gifts already mentioned. These constitute the foundation of diligence and the adequate incentive to earnest effort.

2. The human condition: **your faith.** This is the one prerequisite of all progress in the Christian life. There must be **faith** at the root of all else. Note the emphasis laid on faith as the basis of Christianity all through the New Testament.

3. The special responsibility: **add to your faith.** The word in the original points to a very personal relation and response to the divine gift. God multiplies **grace and peace** (verse 2); then the believer adds diligence (verse 5). Note the phrase **make every effort.** The words mean "haste," eagerness based on earnestness.

The Clear Marks of Diligence

5-7. Add to your faith goodness; and to goodness, knowledge; and to knowledge, self-control; and to self-control, perseverance; and to perseverance, godliness; and to godliness, brotherly kindness; and to brotherly kindness, love.

1. Their elements. Seven elements of diligence are mentioned, showing the completeness of God's gift (verse 3). The seven elements are **goodness, knowledge, self-control, perseverance, godliness, brotherly kindness,** and **love.**

Goodness ("virtue," KJV)—manly energy or courage (see verse 3; 1 Peter 2:9; Philippians 4:8). These are the only instances of the word in the New Testament. In the Septuagint it is used to express the Hebrew for "glory and praise." Hence the King James Version translation of 1 Peter 2:9.

Knowledge. Another emphasis on this great requirement (see verses 2-3).

Self-control ("temperance," KJV).

Perseverance ("patience," KJV). Note the relationship between the two words **self-control** and **perseverance**—power over that which is within (**self-control**) and power over that which is outside (**perseverance**).

Godliness, or reverence, is a prominent word here and throughout the Pastoral letters.

Brotherly kindness. This is another link with the first letter (1 Peter 1:22; 2:17; 3:8: 4:8; 5:9)—the special love of Christians to each other.

Love. The general attitude of all people.

2. Their order. Note that **faith** is the foundation and **love** the culmination. Every grace in between springs out of **faith** and is intended to be expressed ultimately in **love.** For faith as foundation see Romans 14:2-3. For love as crown, see 1 Timothy 1:5. Each element is the foundation or soil of the other.

3. Their completeness. They cover all our relationships and attitudes. The first two are active graces, the second two are passive, the next refers to God, the sixth to the church, and the last to all people. As there is this necessary connection between each one, we should note that each and all are expected to be in every Christian, not some in some Christians and others in others (see Galatians 5:22). "Fruit of the Spirit," not "fruits." The nine elements constitute one cluster to be exemplified in every Christian life. So is it here with these seven marks of diligence.

The Blessed Results of Diligence

8. For if you possess these qualities in increasing measure, they will keep you from being ineffective and unproductive in your knowledge of our Lord Jesus Christ.

1. Permanence of character: **if you possess these qualities.** The word implies "yours permanently." It is stronger than the ordinary verb "to be"

and indicates an abiding possession. The importance of character as the result of persistent action cannot be overrated.

2. Depth of character: **in increasing measure**. This addition shows the extent to which the apostle would lead his readers. The terms indicating "abundance" and "fullness" are also very frequent in St. Paul with reference to the depth and extent of Christian experience and life (see Romans 15:13-14).

3. Reality of character: **they will keep you from being ineffective and unproductive in your knowledge of our Lord Jesus Christ.** Reality of character is seen in this description—not **ineffective and unproductive**. The purpose of this is indicated in the words **in your knowledge of our Lord Jesus Christ.**

The Sad Absence of Diligence

9. But if anyone does not have them, he is nearsighted and blind, and has been cleansed from his past sins.

The apostle now turns the thoughts of the readers in an entirely opposite direction and shows the deplorable effects of a lack of diligence.

1. Lack of spiritual power: **But if anyone does not have them.** Literally, "he in whom these things are not present." Note the sad picture suggested by these words, the entire absence of all the elements that go to make up a real, strong Christian life.

2. Lack of spiritual perception: **he is nearsighted and blind.** Nearsighted Christians are a sad and sorry fact in the Christian church. This weakness of spiritual sight, insight, and foresight is always due to unfaithfulness in Christian living. Some translate this phrase "seeing only what is near," as though it were a transitive verb—"closing the eyes" or "blinking," suggesting deliberate and willful action as the outcome of previous unfaithfulness.

3. Loss of spiritual privilege: **has forgotten that he has been cleansed from his past sins.** The possibility here indicated is almost too terrible to contemplate. To think that a person should actually forget the early experiences of conversion and the joy of salvation! Yet all this is clearly regarded as possible and as resulting from an unwillingness to "add diligently" after receiving God's gifts.

A Renewed Exhortation to Diligence

10. Therefore, my brothers, be all the more eager to make your calling and election sure. For if you do these things, you will never fall.

1. Its strong incentives: **Therefore.** That is, because of the solemn alternatives just mentioned. The possibilities of failure in the Christian life are intended to act as powerful motives to continued and increasing earnestness.

2. Its personal appeal: **my brothers.** Note the writer's tenderness as he

brings these naturally unpalatable truths before the readers. This affectionate appeal is characteristic of the apostle in his two letters.

3. Its definite object: **to make your calling and election sure.** Are these two words **calling** and **election** synonymous, or are they two stages of the divine process? (See Matthew 22:14.) Note how in 1 Peter 1:2-3, the divine side is mainly emphasized; here it is the human, **your calling.** The thought of making our election **sure** suggests the human response of the believer to the divine revelation. The certainty concerns the believer's own conscious experience of what God's calling and election means.

The Permanent Outcome of Diligence

10-11. Therefore, my brothers, be all the more eager to make your calling and election sure. For if you do these things, you will never fall, and you will receive a rich welcome into the eternal kingdom of our Lord and Savior Jesus Christ.

1. Present steadfastness: **if you do these things, you will never fall** (verse 10). Note the strength, the assurance, and the completeness of this promise (see Jude 24).

2. Future glory. The apostle looks forward as well as around and encourages his readers with the thought of what diligence will be theirs hereafter.

    a. The nature of the glory: **welcome into the eternal kingdom.**

    b. The measure of the glory: **a rich welcome.** Not a bare entrance, but "sweeping through the gates." Compare verses 5 and verse 11. We supply, and then God will supply. The phrase here has been aptly translated, "God will spare no expense" concerning your entrance into the everlasting kingdom.

Thoughts on the Christian life

1. The divine provisions (verses 1-4).
2. The needed earnestness (verses 5-10).
3. The perfect symmetry (verses 5-7).
4. The spiritual power (verse 8).
5. The sad possibilities (verse 9).
6. The glorious prospects (verses 10-11).

Verses 12-21

So I will always remind you of these things, even though you know them and are firmly established in the truth you now have. I think it is right to refresh your memory as long as I live in the tent of this body, because I know that I will soon put it aside, as our Lord Jesus Christ has made clear to me. And I will make every effort to see that after my

departure you will always be able to remember these things. We did not follow cleverly invented stories when we told you about the power and coming of our Lord Jesus Christ, but we were eyewitnesses of his majesty. For he received honor and glory from God the Father when the voice came to him from the Majestic Glory, saying, "This is my Son, whom I love; with him I am well pleased." We ourselves heard this voice that came from heaven when we were with him on the sacred mountain. And we have the word of the prophets made more certain, and you will do well to pay attention to it, as to a light shining in a dark place, until the day dawns and the morning star rises in your hearts. Above all, you must understand that no prophecy of Scripture came about by the prophet's own interpretation. For prophecy never had its origin in the will of man, but men spoke from God as they were carried along by the Holy Spirit.

Christian Certainties

The exhortations of verses 5-11 are now confirmed by a personal appeal and by a consideration of the certainties of Christianity as shown by, first, the apostolic witness to Christ and, second, the prophetic revelation of the Old Testament.

Personal Solicitude

12-15. So I will always remind you of these things, even though you know them and are firmly established in the truth you now have. I think it is right to refresh your memory as long as I live in the tent of this body, because I know that I will soon put it aside, as our Lord Jesus Christ has made clear to me. And I will make every effort to see that after my departure you will always be able to remember these things.

This second section of the letter, like the first, commences with a personal reference to the apostle's relationship to his readers.

1. His personal determination: **So I will always remind you of these things** (verse 12). He shows the importance of the truth he is teaching and the great dangers faced by those to whom he is writing.

2. His definite purpose: **even though you know them** (verse 12). We see in these words his conviction about the importance of truth and his consciousness of their constant need of it.

3. His gentle reminder: **and are firmly established in the truth you now have** (verse 12). What a characteristic touch this is. He fears to give any impression of complaint or distrust, and so he reminds them that he is doing what might seem to be more than is needed. Notice this reference to **established in the truth.** The Greek here is literally "strengthened" (see 3:16-17; 1 Peter 5:10; Luke 22:32). Peter is thus doing the very work his Master commanded.

4. His brief opportunity (verses 13-14). Evidently he regards his depar-

ture, his physical death, as imminent. For **tent** (tabernacle) see 2 Corinthians 5:1-4. The allusion to our Lord's prediction (John 21:18) is clear. Peter never forgot that memorable conversation (1 Peter 5:1).

5. His wise foresight: **After my departure . . . remember these things** (verse 15). For **departure** see Luke 9:31, a record of the Transfiguration, where the Greek is literally "exodus." What did Peter mean by making provision for them to **remember these things after his death?** Did he intend to write something more? Or is this a reference to the Gospel of Mark, written under his influence? Probably the latter. It is generally thought that the voluminous apocryphal literature of the second century that was issued in the name of Peter was prompted by this verse.

Personal Testimony

16-18. We did not follow cleverly invented stories when we told you about the power and coming of our Lord Jesus Christ, but we were eyewitnesses of his majesty. For he received honor and glory from God the Father when the voice came to him from the Majestic Glory, saying, "This is my Son, whom I love; with him I am well pleased." We ourselves heard this voice that came from heaven when we were with him on the sacred mountain.

The apostle now strengthens his position by a reference to his own personal witness of the realities of Christ's revelation. He takes the Transfiguration as the special point of his testimony.

1. The substance of the message: **the power and coming of our Lord Jesus Christ.** Notice the two aspects of the apostle's thought. Some authorities think they constitute one phrase—the coming power or powerful coming. Perhaps, however, it is possible to distinguish them and to regard **the power** as referring to the first coming of Christ (Romans 1:4), and **coming** (literally, "presence") to the second coming of the Lord. It would seem as though the latter word does indeed refer to the second coming of Christ (compare James 5:7-8), though Dr. Chase (*Hastings' Bible Dictionary*) thinks the first coming is meant, since the context is historical, not prophetical.

2. The reality of the message: **We did not follow cleverly invented stories.** The word translated **stories** means myths or allegorical teachings, a favorite word in the Pastoral letters (1 Timothy 1:4; 4:7; 2 Timothy 4:4; Titus 1:14). The apostle Peter implies in the words he uses that he had not wasted his time in carefully tracing out a lot of sophisticated myths when he declared to them the Gospel.

3. The proof of the message: **we were eyewitnesses of his majesty** (verse 16); see Luke 9:32-33. The transfiguration of our Lord is here seen as an anticipation of the Second Coming when the Son of man will come in his glory. In many respects the Transfiguration was a microcosm of the

eternal future. There we see the heavenly glory, the Old Testament saints, the New Testament disciples, the kingly Son, and the divine Father.

4. The corroboration of the message: **For he received honor and glory from God** (verse 17). The apostle thus shows that the Father's testimony to his Son was the crowning proof of the power and authority of the gospel message. Peter's allusion to **the Majestic Glory** is doubtless a reminiscence of the Shekinah glory of the Transfiguration (Matthew 17:5).

5. The confirmation of the message (verse 18). Once again the apostle introduces his own testimony. Not only did he see the glory of the Son, but he heard the voice. (Note St. John's reminiscence of the same event in John 1:14: "We have seen his glory.")

Prophetic Revelation

19-21. And we have the word of the prophets made more certain, and you will do well to pay attention to it, as to a light shining in a dark place, until the day dawns and the morning star rises in your hearts. Above all, you must understand that no prophecy of Scripture came about by the prophet's own interpretation. For prophecy never had its origin in the will of man, but men spoke from God as they were carried along by the Holy Spirit.

We now pass from apostolic to prophetic testimony to the power and coming of our Lord, just as in 1 Peter 1:10-12 the apostle bears his witness to the divine authority of the Scriptures of the old covenant.

1. The divine assurance is granted: **And we have the word of the prophets made more certain** (verse 19). The probable force of this phrase is that Old Testament prophecy had become more sure by being confirmed by the Transfiguration. The coming of Christ was thus the fulfillment of prophetic testimony. The King James Version can hardly stand here, as it seems to imply that prophecy is "more sure" than the divine voice at the Transfiguration.

2. The earnest attention required: **you will do well to pay attention to it** (verse 19). He thus urges them to make a careful study of the Old Testament revelation.

3. The deep necessity stated: **as to a light shining in a dark place** (verse 19). This allusion to **a dark place** shows the need of the divine light about which he is speaking. The word translated **dark** is literally "dry" or "squalid" and gives the idea of a light revealing the dirt and filth of sin. This is the actual state of the world (see Isaiah 50:11; John 8:12). We see also what Peter thought of **prophecy**—a light in the middle of squalor. This is always the character and power of Scripture.

4. The glorious expectation described: **until the day dawns and the morning star rises in your hearts** (verse 19). This seems to be a reference to the second coming of our Lord. **The day dawns,** and then the glorious appearing follows. On this view the words **in your hearts** must be sepa-

rated from the phrase **until the day dawns**, and it would seem best, though it is somewhat awkward, to link **in your hearts** with **do well**, the intervening words being parenthetical. If **in your hearts** is taken with **the day dawns** it is implied that the Christians were at that time in darkness, which gives an entirely erroneous idea to the whole meaning of the apostle.

5. The definite explanation given (verses 20-21). The Old Testament Scriptures were a light in a dark place because, the apostle tells us, they came from God and not from man, and on this account they shed light over earth's squalid and desert places. The word translated **interpretation** (verse 20) is found only here in the New Testament, though its corresponding verb is found in Mark 4:34, Acts 19:39, and the Septuagint of Genesis 41:12. It means "unloosing," "unfolding," "disclosing." The word **own** ("private") is never translated "private" in any other passage, though it occurs 113 times. The meaning, therefore, is: no prophecy comes from the prophets' own unfolding, for prophecy did not come by the will of man, but by the Holy Spirit.

The point of these verses is, in fact, not the interpretation of Scripture but the origin of Scripture; not what Scripture means but what Scripture is. Any use of the context to oppose "private opinion" is therefore entirely wide of the mark. If, however, it is urged that verse 20 must mean "interpretation," then we must understand an ellipsis in verse 21: "neither can it be interpreted by the will of man." But there can be little doubt that the former is the true meaning of the passage.

Further Notes

1. The elements of true ministry.
    a. Pastoral earnestness (verses 12, 13, 15).
    b. Prominence given to the truth of God (verses 12, 13, 15, 16, 19-21).
    c. Personal testimony based on personal experience (verses 16, 18).
Consider how these elements were exemplified in the ministry of Peter, and note the absolute necessity of them in every form of Christian testimony.
2. The foundations of spiritual assurance.
The apostle frequently lays stress on "knowledge" as the great safeguard of power and true, steadfast Christian living. In the passage before us he states the grounds or foundations of this personal knowledge or assurance.
    a. Prophetic revelation (verses 19-21).
    b. Apostolic confirmation (verses 16-18).
    c. Personal attestation (verses 12, 19).
It will thus be seen that we have here in perfect combination and order the divine word of truth verified by individual experience. In this combination will be found the absolute guarantee of religious and moral certitude.

2 Peter
Chapter 2

Verses 1-9

But there were also false prophets among the people, just as there will be false teachers among you. They will secretly introduce destructive heresies, even denying the sovereign Lord who bought them—bringing swift destruction on themselves. Many will follow their shameful ways and will bring the way of truth into disrepute. In their greed these teachers will exploit you with stories they have made up. Their condemnation has long been hanging over them, and their destruction has not been sleeping. For if God did not spare angels when they sinned, but sent them to hell, putting them into gloomy dungeons to be held for judgment; if he did not spare the ancient world when he brought the flood on its ungodly people, but protected Noah, a preacher of righteousness, and seven others; if he condemned the cities of Sodom and Gomorrah by burning them to ashes, and made them an example of what is going to happen to the ungodly; and if he rescued Lot, a righteous man, who was distressed by the filthy lives of lawless men (for that righteous man, living among them day after day, was tormented in his righteous soul by the lawless deeds he saw and heard)—if this is so, then the Lord knows how to rescue godly men from trials and to hold the unrighteous for the day of judgment, while continuing their punishment.

False Teachers

The contrast between 1:19-21 and this chapter is sudden and striking. The thesis here is false teachers, and we see the "burning lava of the apostle's indignation" (Farrar). The whole chapter is virtually one long paragraph, but there are certain stages that mark the course of the thought. We notice

273

three aspects of false teachers and their work. First, their character (verse 1); second, their influence (verses 2-3a); third, their doom (verses 3b-9).

Their Character

1. But there were also false prophets among the people, just as there will be false teachers among you. They will secretly introduce destructive heresies, even denying the sovereign Lord who bought them— bringing swift destruction on themselves.

1. Illustrated in the Old Testament: **But there were also false prophets among the people.** The force of **also** is to be noted, implying "false" as well as "true" prophets. For Old Testament examples see Deuteronomy 13:1-5; 1 Kings 22; Jeremiah 23; Ezekiel 13.

2. Foretold in the New Testament: **just as there will be false teachers among you** (compare Matthew 7:15; 24:11-12). These predictions of his Master the apostle now confirms (see also Jude 4).

3. Described by the apostle. Three marks of these false teachers are now emphasized.

    a. **They will secretly introduce destructive heresies** (verse 1)—that is, heresies causing destruction (see Philippians 3:19). Note carefully that heresy in the New Testament implies false conduct and not erroneous opinion only. The root idea is that of choice, indicating deliberate and willful severance from right thought and righteous paths.

    b. They will deny Christ: **even denying the sovereign Lord who bought them.** Note these three characteristic phrases: **deny, sovereign Lord, bought.** How striking and significant for Peter to speak of another denial. What memories the word must have called up (see Matthew 10:33). The word for **sovereign Lord** is the root of our English word *despot,* implying absolute lordship and dominion. Concerning **who bought them,** see 1 Corinthians 6:20; 7:23; 1 Peter 1:18-19. How solemn is the thought that these men were fighting against the divine purchase of redemption. In the New Testament sense of the word, heresy is always a denial of Christ, for it is the determination to go our own way and to set at nought his personal work and authority.

    c. They will involve themselves in destruction: **bringing swift destruction on themselves** (see Philippians 3:19).

Their Influence

2-3a. Many will follow their shameful ways and will bring the way of truth into disrepute. In their greed these teachers will exploit you with stories they have made up.

The following points, describing the effects of the false teachers and their work, bear sad and solemn testimony to the deep-rooted and awful nature of their influence.

1. It was widespread: **Many will follow** (verse 2).

2. It was immoral: **their shameful ways** (verse 2). See 1 Peter 4:3.

3. It was blasphemous: **will bring the way of truth into disrepute** (verse 2). Christianity is characterized as "the Way" in the book of Acts (9:2; 16:17; 18:25; 19:9; 22:4; 24:14). The phrase **bring . . . into disrepute** is literally, "will be blasphemed." It is evident that the sin is tantamount to our modern idea of blasphemy.

4. It was treacherous: **in their greed these teachers will exploit you with stories they have made up** (verse 3). These false teachers would use counterfeit or fabricated words in order to deceive their dupes, though all the while their main object was greedy gain and a covetous trafficking in holy things.

Their Doom

3b-9. Their condemnation has long been hanging over them, and their destruction has not been sleeping. For if God did not spare angels when they sinned, but sent them to hell, putting them into gloomy dungeons to be held for judgment; if he did not spare the ancient world when he brought the flood on its ungodly people, but protected Noah, a preacher of righteousness, and seven others; if he condemned the cities of Sodom and Gomorrah by burning them to ashes, and made them an example of what is going to happen to the ungodly; and if he rescued Lot, a righteous man, who was distressed by the filthy lives of lawless men (for that righteous man, living among them day after day, was tormented in his righteous soul by the lawless deeds he saw and heard)—if this is so, then the Lord knows how to rescue godly men from trials and to hold the unrighteous for the day of judgment, while continuing their punishment.

1. Its certainty stated: **Their condemnation has long been hanging over them, and their destruction has not been sleeping** (verse 3). The judgment is thus seen as one that was threatened long ago but not yet inflicted, though absolutely certain. The phrase **has been hanging over them** is literally, "is not idle." The second statement, **has not been sleeping**, literally "does not blink," is a picturesque assertion of the unerring certainty of punishment.

2. Its certainty illustrated (verses 4-8): **For if God did not spare angels when they sinned, but sent them to hell, putting them into gloomy dungeons to be held for judgment; if he did not spare the ancient world when he brought the flood on its ungodly people, but protected Noah, a preacher of righteousness, and seven others; if he condemned the cities of Sodom and Gomorrah by burning them to ashes, and made them an example of what is going to happen to the ungodly; and if he**

275

rescued Lot, a righteous man, who was distressed by the filthy lives of lawless men (for that righteous man, living among them day after day, was tormented in his righteous soul by the lawless deeds he saw and heard)...

Notice here the three examples from the Old Testament given to illustrate and confirm the certainty of judgment.

a. The fall of the angels (verse 4); see Jude 6 and Genesis 6:2. The Greek describes the place of punishment as Tartarus, that is, the deepest abyss of the lower world. The word is only found here.

b. The Flood (verse 5). **Noah ... and seven others.** Note the allusion to the fewness of those saved at the Flood (also made in 1 Peter 3:20).

c. The cities of the plain (verses 6-8). Note the description of Lot as **righteous** (verses 7-8). This is a suggestive and striking comment on and an addition to the Old Testament narrative (Genesis 19). What a picture of personal righteousness in judicial standing with God, combined with sad weakness in spiritual state and condition.

Note: The **For if** (verse 4) has no main clause, though it may be implied in the beginning of verse 9.

3. Its certainty assured (verse 9): **if this is so, then the Lord knows how to rescue godly men from trials and to hold the unrighteous for the day of judgment, while continuing their punishment.**

a. By divine knowledge: **the Lord knows how.**

b. By divine protection of the godly: **to rescue godly men from trials.**

c. By divine reservation of the ungodly: **and to hold the unrighteous for the day of judgment.**

Suggestions on Several Points Arising from This Narrative

Special attention may be concentrated on the following.

1. The awful possibilities of evil.

a. Imitating the good.

b. Making a travesty of the good.

c. Destroying the good.

2. The unerring judgment of sin.

a. **Swift** (verse 1).

b. Sure (verse 3).

c. Complete (verse 9).

3. The urgent need of watchfulness.

a. Because error counterfeits good.

b. Because evil lures the good.

c. Because of the intimate connection between error in teaching and evil in practice.

4. The glorious certainties of the godly.

a. A divine Redeemer (verse 1).

b. A **way of truth** (verse 2).

c. A sure protection (verse 9).

Note: As the Greek in this section and in the whole chapter contains a number of unusual words and phrases, it has been thought best to give a general idea of the main thought without entering upon a detailed comment of words and phrases. For a due consideration of these, one of the leading Greek commentaries, such as that by Alford and Bigg, is essential.

Verses 10-16

This is especially true of those who follow the corrupt desire of the sinful nature and despise authority. Bold and arrogant, these men are not afraid to slander celestial beings; yet even angels, although they are stronger and more powerful, do not bring slanderous accusations against such beings in the presence of the Lord. But these men blaspheme in matters they do not understand. They are like brute beasts, creatures of instinct, born only to be caught and destroyed, and like beasts they too will perish. They will be paid back with harm for the harm they have done. Their idea of pleasure is to carouse in broad daylight. They are blots and blemishes, reveling in their pleasures while they feast with you. With eyes full of adultery, they never stop sinning; they seduce the unstable; they are experts in greed—an accursed brood! They have left the straight way and wandered off to follow the way of Balaam son of Beor, who loved the wages of wickedness. But he was rebuked for his wrongdoing by a donkey—a beast without speech—who spoke with a man's voice and restrained the prophet's madness.

False Teachers

Here is a further and fuller description of false teachers, especially those of the worst sort (verse 10). This passage is difficult to follow in full detail. St. Jude should be read closely side by side with it. Note that the evil is regarded as existing among those who had made a profession of Christianity. The treatment seems to follow the same general line as in verses 1-9, dealing with character, influence, and judgment.

Character Described

1. Corrupt desire: **This is especially true of those who follow the corrupt desire of the sinful nature** (verse 10). Note again the reference to uncleanness as a mark of these false teachers.

2. Willfulness: **. . . despise authority . . . slander celestial beings** (verse 10). Whom do these false teachers **slander**? Some think angels, although it

is difficult to see how this can happen. Probably it refers to willful contempt of all authority, especially our Lord's.

Verse 11 is obscure and difficult. Perhaps the best interpretation is to say it refers to good angels. When withstanding evil, these angels do not abuse their opponents; so how much more should evil men avoid doing so. Concerning **such beings in the presence of the Lord** (verse 11), see Jude 9.

3. Brutishness: **They are like brute beasts, creatures of instinct** (verse 12). Here is another reference to self-indulgence.

4. Recklessness: **these men blaspheme in matters they do not understand** (verse 12).

5. Sensuality: **Their idea of pleasure is to carouse in broad daylight** (verse 13). Riotousness in the daytime was thought of as the height of self-indulgence and sin (Acts 2:15; Romans 13:13; 1 Thessalonians 5:7).

6. Hypocrisy: **They are blots and blemishes** (verse 13). The idea seems to be that these false and evil teachers associated themselves with the Christian love feasts and yet all the while were living in sin.

7. Infamy: **they never stop sinning; they seduce the unstable** (verse 14). Here we see the depth of their sin. Not only do they themselves indulge in awful iniquity, but they actually entice weak and young Christians in the same direction. Note the reference to Balaam, and see Numbers 31:8, 16 for its appropriateness.

Influence Depicted

17-19. These men are springs without water and mists driven by a storm. Blackest darkness is reserved for them. For they mouth empty, boastful words and, by appealing to the lustful desires of sinful human nature, they entice people who are just escaping from those who live in error. They promise them freedom, while they themselves are slaves of depravity—for a man is a slave to whatever has mastered him.

1. Emptiness: **springs without water** (verse 17). They have no real vitality.

2. Instability: **mists driven by a storm** (verse 17). This describes a situation of no settled principles or position.

3. Boastfulness: **boastful words** (verse 18). Here is an example of bluster in order to dupe.

4. Seductiveness: **appealing to the lustful desires of sinful human nature** (verse 18). Here is another reference to the awful character of their life.

5. Heartlessness: **they entice people who are just escaping** (verse 18). Note this appeal to passion when dealing with unsettled souls recently converted (Matthew 18:6).

6. Deception: **they promise them freedom, while they themselves are slaves of depravity** (verse 19). **Freedom**—a striking temptation to the newly converted.

7. Powerlessness: **they themselves are slaves of depravity** (verse 19). Here is a description of the real character of these people.

Doom Declared

20-22. If they have escaped the corruption of the world by knowing our Lord and Savior Jesus Christ and are again entangled in it and over-come, they are worse off at the end than they were at the beginning. It would have been better for them not to have known the way of right-eousness, than to have known it and then to turn their backs on the sacred commandment that was passed on to them. Of them the proverbs are true: "A dog returns to its vomit," and, "A sow that is washed goes back to her wallowing in the mud."

We now have brought before us in vivid and solemn detail the outcome of this false teaching—terrible judgment on those who practiced it.

1. Sinful entanglement: **entangled in it** (verse 20). This is the first stage. They are in the meshes of the net that, however, is not yet closed upon them.

2. Moral disaster: **and overcome** (verse 20). This follows as the result of the entanglement to those who are unwilling to break through the net.

3. Spiritual degeneration: **They are worse off at the end than they were at the beginning** (verse 20). See Matthew 12:43-45. Peter is making a clear allusion to the Master's teaching.

4. Utter apostasy: **turn their backs . . . wallowing** (verses 21-22). The apostle says it would have been better if they had not known the way of righteousness, because the Gospel had been treated unfairly, and the fault and sin of the failure was theirs (see Hebrews 6:4-6; 10:26). Note the terse description of Christianity here as **the sacred commandment** (verse 21); see 1 Timothy 6:14. Christianity is thus summed up in a word implying holiness and obedience, character and behavior. Mark the expression **passed on** (verse 21); see Jude 3. Concerning verse 22, see Proverbs 26:11. Contrast the pig returning to the mire and the sheep returning to the Shepherd (1 Peter 2:25). The merely reformed character often returns to sin, but the saved sinner who backslides returns to the Shepherd of souls.

2 Peter
Chapter 3

Verses 1-10

Dear friends, this is now my second letter to you. I have written both of them as reminders to stimulate you to wholesome thinking. I want you to recall the words spoken in the past by the holy prophets and the command given by our Lord and Savior through your apostles. First of all, you must understand that in the last days scoffers will come, scoffing and following their own evil desires. They will say, "Where is this 'coming' he promised? Ever since our fathers died, everything goes on as it has since the beginning of creation." But they deliberately forget that long ago by God's word the heavens existed and the earth was formed out of water and by water. By these waters also the world of that time was deluged and destroyed. By the same word the present heavens and earth are reserved for fire, being kept for the day of judgment and destruction of ungodly men. But do not forget this one thing, dear friends: With the Lord a day is like a thousand years, and a thousand years are like a day. The Lord is not slow in keeping his promise, as some understand slowness. He is patient with you, not wanting anyone to perish, but everyone to come to repentance. But the day of the Lord will come like a thief. The heavens will disappear with a roar; the elements will be destroyed by fire, and the earth and everything in it will be laid bare.

This Letter's Safeguards

1. Its affectionate tone: **Dear friends** (verse 1). Four times in the chapter this Greek word occurs, showing clearly the apostle's tender and humble tone, which contrasts with the apostolic authority he could have used.

2. Its practical purpose: **as reminders to stimulate you** (verse 1). Thus he reiterates the thought of 1:12-13, wishing to arouse them to godly life

even though he had written to them so recently. He bears hearty testimony to the reality of their spiritual life by speaking of their **wholesome thinking** or **pure minds** (KJV) (see also 1 Corinthians 5:8; 2 Corinthians 1:12; 2:17; Philippians 1:10). This is in marked contrast with the darkened minds of the false teachers of chapter 2. Also see Ephesians 4:18.

3. Its special appeal: **recall the words . . . and the command** (verse 2). As in 1:16-21, the apostle brings together a reference here from Old Testament prophecy and from apostolic teaching and wants to focus their attention on this teaching with all its special application to the dangers surrounding them. Note the singular number of the **command** as summing up apostolic teaching (see also 2:21).

The Urgent Motive

3-4. First of all, you must understand that in the last days scoffers will come, scoffing and following their own evil desires. They will say, "Where is this 'coming' he promised? Ever since our fathers died, everything goes on as it has since the beginning of creation."

The apostle now explains why he makes this earnest appeal. It is because of the dangers ahead, which may be described in three ways.

1. Scoffing: **scoffers will come** (verse 3). Note the phrase, **first of all**, and see also 1:20, "above all," which calls for special attention. **The last days** seem to refer to the close of the Messianic dispensation (see Isaiah 2:2; Acts 2:17; Hebrews 1:2; James 5:3; 1 Peter 1:20). Scoffing has not been limited to any one age of the church. See Psalm 1:1.

2. Sinfulness: **following their own evil desires** (verse 3). The link between scoffing and evil living is worth noting. The latter is almost invariably an accompaniment of the former.

3. Skepticism: **"Where is this 'coming' he promised?"** (verse 4), that is, the fulfillment of the promise (see Isaiah 5:19). This is the doctrinal error that underlaid the sinful life of the false teachers. **Fathers** seems to refer to Old Testament times (see Romans 9:5 and Hebrews 1:1).

The Thorough Exposure

5-7. But they deliberately forget that long ago by God's word the heavens existed and the earth was formed out of water and by water. By these waters also the world of that time was deluged and destroyed. By the same word the present heavens and earth are reserved for fire, being kept for the day of judgment and destruction of ungodly men.

The apostle proceeds to show the unreality and deliberate sin of the attitude just described.

1. Willfulness revealed: **they deliberately forget** (verse 5). We can thus see the true meaning of their scoffing and sin. It is due solely and entirely to deliberate willfulness. "Evil is wrought for lack of will to do good."

2. Willfulness corrected: **the world ... was ... destroyed** (verse 6). The apostle shows that the assumption of immutability made by the scoffers is unwarranted and untrue. The world had not always been unchanged, for the Flood had taken place; water was always there, ready to do God's will. See also Genesis 1:6-10.

3. Willfulness warned against (verse 7). The scoffers are told that as formerly water was God's instrument, so now fire is available, and it is only waiting for God's time. Note the emphasis on **reserved** (RV, "stored up"; see 2:4, 9; in contrast, see 1 Peter 1:4).

Note: It has been suggested that we have in this chapter a reference to three distinct heavens. First, **the heavens** that were of old (verse 5); second, **the ... heavens** that are now (verse 7); and, third, the **new** heavens (verse 13). According to this interpretation, verse 6 refers to some catastrophe that happened between the events recorded in Genesis 1:1 and Genesis 1:2, thus producing the chaos mentioned in Genesis 1:2—"formless and empty"; but it seems best to interpret verse 6 as describing the Flood. The scoffers are thus solemnly warned that though God may delay, his judgments are certain and his instrument ready at hand.

The Complete Explanation

8-10. But do not forget this one thing, dear friends: With the Lord a day is like a thousand years, and a thousand years are like a day. The Lord is not slow in keeping his promise, as some understand slowness. He is patient with you, not wanting anyone to perish, but everyone to come to repentance. But the day of the Lord will come like a thief. The heavens will disappear with a roar; the elements will be destroyed by fire, and the earth and everything in it will be laid bare.

Now, for the sake of Christians who may possibly be themselves perplexed by the delay, a clear statement is given about the facts of the case. The explanation is found in the character and purpose of God.

1. The perfect wisdom of God: **With the Lord a day is like a thousand years** (verse 8). See Psalm 90:4. The difference between the divine and human computation of time is here clearly shown as one part of the explanation of apparent delay.

2. The long-suffering mercy of God: **not wanting anyone to perish** (verse 9). See Ezekiel 18:23; 33:11. Thus the scoffers were actually rejecting God's mercy and showing contempt for his perseverance, which extended even to them if they would only see it.

3. The absolute righteousness of God: **But the day of the Lord will come** (verse 10). Thus divine patience is balanced by justice, and we are told:

    a. The certainty of the coming: **will come.**

    b. The character of the coming: **like a thief** (see Matthew 24:42; Luke 12:39-40; 1 Thessalonians 5:2; Revelation 3:3; 16:15).

c. The consequences of the coming: **The heavens will disappear with a roar.** It will then be clearly seen that nature is far from immutable. Note other references to physical convulsions as accompanying the day of God (Isaiah 34:4; 51:6; Mark 13:24-25). **The elements** seem to be the heavenly bodies in this verse.

Suggestions

1. Some elements of unbelief.
   a. Doctrinal error (verse 5).
   b. Contemptuous opinion (verse 4).
   c. Impure conduct (verse 3).

Note the order of these three elements and how the outward expression is stated first by the apostle (verse 3) and the trouble then traced to its source.

2. Some encouragements to faith.
   a. The Word of God remembered (verse 2).
   b. The wisdom of God trusted (verse 8).
   c. The warning of God heeded (verses 9-10).

Verses 11-18

Since everything will be destroyed in this way, what kind of people ought you to be? You ought to live holy and godly lives as you look forward to the day of God and speed its coming. That day will bring about the destruction of the heavens by fire, and the elements will melt in the heat. But in keeping with his promise we are looking forward to a new heaven and a new earth, the home of righteousness. So then, dear friends, since you are looking forward to this, make every effort to be found spotless, blameless and at peace with him. Bear in mind that our Lord's patience means salvation, just as our dear brother Paul also wrote you with the wisdom that God gave him. He writes the same way in all his letters, speaking in them of these matters. His letters contain some things that are hard to understand, which ignorant and unstable people distort, as they do the other Scriptures, to their own destruction. Therefore, dear friends, since you already know this, be on your guard so that you may not be carried away by the error of lawless men and fall from your secure position. But grow in the grace and knowledge of our Lord and Savior Jesus Christ. To him be glory both now and forever! Amen.

Last Words

This letter draws to a close with some personal and practical exhortations based on the previous warnings and instructions.

The Believer's Hope

1. Its substance.
    a. **The day of the Lord** (verse 10).
    b. **The day of God** (verse 12).

Is it possible that these two expressions mark two stages of the future? **The day of the Lord** will **come like a thief** (verse 10) and will be linked with physical catastrophes. **The day of God** is spoken about as that time on account of which (according to the literal Greek) these physical convulsions are to take place and as the ushering in of **a new heaven and a new earth.** The day of the Lord, from its first mention in Isaiah 2:12, is always associated with terror and judgment. Possibly we may distinguish the two and say that the day of the Lord represents our Lord's coming to judgment before the Millennium (Revelation 20), while the day of God is the ushering in of eternity, when God will be "all in all" (1 Corinthians 15:28). In any case the Christian's hope is set on the crowing day that is coming.

2. Its accompaniments.
    a. The dissolution of the present order (verse 12).
    b. The introduction of a new order (verse 13).

Thus the same thing will take place in the future through fire as took place in the past through water (Genesis 9:11; see also Isaiah 45:17; Revelation 21:1).

3. Its character (verse 13).
    a. It is to be righteous: **righteousness.**
    b. It is to be permanent: **home of . . .** That is, where **righteousness** has its fixed abode. This will be a remarkable contrast to the present state of things, where so much unrighteousness seems to live.

4. Its warrant (verse 13): **In keeping with his promise** (see verses 4-5). The foundation of Christian hope is the sure Word of God (1:19; Acts 3:21).

The Believer's Attitude

The apostle now enlarges very fully on the various and varied aspects of the Christian life and conduct in view of the glories and solemnities of the future.

1. Expectation (verses 11-14). **Since everything will be destroyed in this way, what kind of people ought you to be? You ought to live holy and godly lives as you look forward to the day of God and speed its coming. That day will bring about the destruction of the heavens by fire, and the elements will melt in the heat. But in keeping with his promise we are looking forward to a new heaven and a new earth, the home of righteousness. So then, dear friends, since you are looking for-**

ward to this, make every effort to be found spotless, blameless and at peace with him.

Note the emphasis on watching (**look**, verse 12), literally "expecting."

2. Earnestness.

    a. In service: **as you look forward** (verse 12). The King James Version "hasting unto" is inaccurate. The text must mean either "earnestly longing for" or "hastening." It implies eagerness for the coming, an eagerness shown in prayer ("your kingdom come"), and effort. Who knows whether the coming has not been delayed because of the unfaithfulness of Christians?

    b. In character: **make every effort** (verse 14). Not only in relation to others, but in relation to our own life the apostle urges earnestness.

3. Holiness.

    a. Of behavior: **You ought to live holy and godly lives** (verse 11). This verse is very strong. "What sort of people you need to continue to be in all kinds of holy behavior." Concerning behavior— **to live**, see 1 Peter 1:15. It is a favorite word of the apostle.

    b. In character: **spotless, blameless and at peace** (verse 14). Compare this with the **blots and blemishes** of the false teachers (2:13). In these two words, **spotless** and **blameless**, we see the kind of character God wants us to have.

4. Reverence: **godly lives** (verse 11). This is another example of a word almost entirely associated with Peter and Paul, implying the attitude of godly fear.

5. Assurance: **at peace with him** (verse 14). This describes the attitude of the believer as he meets his Lord without shame (see 1 John 2:28; 4:17).

6. Patience: **Bear in mind that our Lord's patience means salvation** (verse 15); it gives men time to be saved. This thought is intended to stimulate the readers to endure present problems and opposition (see Romans 2:4; 9:22).

7. Watchfulness: **be on your guard so that you are not carried away** (verse 17). To be forewarned is to be forearmed, as the apostle clearly shows.

8. Growth: **but grow** (verse 18). See 1:2, 8. Thus **grace** opens and closes this letter. It is clearly implied that they are already in **grace**, and they are to grow and make progress in it.

9. Praise: **To him be glory** (verse 18). In spite of perplexities, defections, and oppositions, Christians are exhorted to praise God **both now and forever!**

The Believer's Secret

The Christian's attitude in view of the hope that is set before him is only made possible by a careful consideration and personal realization of the secrets and conditions of holiness and progress laid down in the Word of God. Of these conditions four are named or suggested in this passage.

1. Divine teaching (verses 15-16). **Bear in mind that our Lord's patience means salvation, just as our dear brother Paul also wrote you with the wisdom that God gave him. He writes the same way in all his letters, speaking in them of these matters. His letters contain some things that are hard to understand, which ignorant and unstable people distort, as they do the other Scriptures, to their own destruction.** The allusions in these verses to the Scriptures, both the Old and New Testament, clearly indicate the necessity and value of God's revelation for growth in the Christian life and for the maintenance of the believer's true attitude, whether in opposition to the dangers around or in reference to the glories of the future.

Note: The reference to Paul is given as a confirmation of this call to patience. It tells its own story of, first, the true and brotherly relationship between Peter and Paul and, second, the estimate already given to the letters of Paul, which are thus associated with the Old Testament Scriptures as the Word of God. **Ignorant** and unsteadfast souls were already twisting Paul's writings. Probably the reference is a general one, or it may be specifically to Paul's letters to the Galatians, Ephesians, and Colossians, included in the churches of Asia Minor, to which Peter was writing (1 Peter 1:1). It is thought with great probability that it was St. Paul's doctrine of justification that was particularly causing **their own destruction** (verse 16). Concerning **unstable** (verse 16), see 1:12; 2:14; 1 Peter 5:10. It is significant and important to notice that though difficulties and misconceptions in regard to Scripture are mentioned, the Scriptures themselves were not on this account withheld from the people.

2. Divine warning: **be on your guard** (verse 17). The Christians are here clearly reminded in affectionate terms, **dear friends,** of the dangers around them and of the possibility of their own failure in facing them. The apostle is anxious in case they should "fall once for all" (see Greek text).

3. Divine grace: **grow in the grace** (verse 18). Their position as surrounded by grace is here brought to their notice. Grace surrounds and upholds, grace is the atmosphere of their life, and as they abide in it they are to "keep on growing" (Greek). It is only by continuous growth that the possibility of the terrible fall is effectually prevented.

4. Divine fellowship: **knowledge of our Lord and Savior Jesus Christ** (verse 18). This is also part of the atmosphere of their spiritual existence. Knowledge of God here, as elsewhere, implies personal experience and conscious fellowship, and this is one of the prime secrets of Christian steadfastness and progress. Thus the letter ends as it began, with its keynote of **knowledge.**